Luise Mühlbach

Henry VIII. and His Court

Or, Catharine Parr. An historical novel

Luise Mühlbach

Henry VIII. and His Court
Or, Catharine Parr. An historical novel

ISBN/EAN: 9783337149529

Printed in Europe, USA, Canada, Australia, Japan

Cover: Foto ©ninafisch / pixelio.de

More available books at **www.hansebooks.com**

HENRY VIII
AND HIS COURT
OR, CATHERINE PARR

An Historical Novel

BY

L. MÜHLBACH

Author of Frederick the Great and His Court, Joseph II and His Court, Merchant of Berlin, Etc.

TRANSLATED FROM THE GERMAN BY

Rev. H. N. PIERCE, D.D.

NEW YORK

THOMAS NELSON & SONS

381 FOURTH AVENUE

CONTENTS.

CHAPTER	PAGE
I.—Choosing a Confessor	1
II.—The Queen and her Friend	10
III.—King Henry the Eighth	20
IV.—King by the Wrath of God	29
V.—The Rivals	41
VI.—The Intercession	51
VII.—Henry the Eighth and his Wives	55
VIII.—Father and Daughter	73
IX.—Lendemain	86
X.—The King's Fool	91
XI.—The Ride	102
XII.—The Declaration	109
XIII.—"Le Roi S'ennuit"	120
XIV.—The Queen's Friend	130
XV.—John Heywood	141
XVI.—The Confidant	148
XVII.—Gammer Gurton's Needle	159
XVIII.—Lady Jane	170
XIX.—Loyola's General	178
XX.—The Prisoner	185
XXI.—Princess Elizabeth	198
XXII.—Henry Howard, Earl of Surrey	213
XXIII.—Brother and Sister	219
XXIV.—The Queen's Toilet	230

CHAPTER	PAGE
XXV.—The Queen's Rosette	250
XXVI.—Revenge	273
XXVII.—The Acknowledgment	282
XXXIII.—Intrigues	294
XXIX.—The Accusation	302
XXX.—The Feast of Death	316
XXXI.—The Queen	323
XXXII.—Undeceived	347
XXXIII.—New Intrigues	365
XXXIV.—The King and the Priest	373
XXXV.—Chess-Play	387
XXXVI.—The Catastrophe	407
XXXVII.—" Le Roi est Mort—Vive la Reine!"	420

HENRY VIII. AND HIS COURT.

CHAPTER I.

CHOOSING A CONFESSOR.

IT was in the year 1543. King Henry the Eighth of England that day once more pronounced himself the happiest and most enviable man in his kingdom, for to-day he was once more a bridegroom, and Catharine Parr, the youthful widow of Baron Latimer, had the perilous happiness of being selected as the king's sixth consort.

Merrily chimed the bells of all the steeples of London, announcing to the people the commencement of that holy ceremony which sacredly bound Catharine Parr to the king as his sixth wife. The people, ever fond of novelty and show, crowded through the streets toward the royal palace to catch a sight of Catharine, when she appeared at her husband's side upon the balcony, to show herself to the English people as their queen, and to receive their homage in return.

Surely it was a proud and lofty success for the widow of a petty baron to become the lawful wife of the King of England, and to wear upon her brow a royal crown! But yet Catharine Parr's heart was moved with a strange fear, her cheeks were pale and cold, and before the altar her closely compressed lips scarcely had the power to part, and pronounce the binding "*I will.*"

At last the sacred ceremony was completed. The two spiritual dignitaries, Gardiner, bishop of Winchester, and

Cranmer, archbishop of Canterbury, then, in accordance with court etiquette, led the young bride into her apartments, in order to bless them, and once more to pray with her, before the worldly festivities should begin.

Catharine, however, pale and agitated, had yet sustained her part in the various ceremonies of the day with a true queenly bearing and dignity; and, as now with head proudly erect and firm step, she walked with a bishop at either side through the splendid apartments, no one suspected how heavy a burden weighed upon her heart, and what baleful voices were whispering in her breast.

Followed by her new court, she had traversed with her companions the state apartments, and now reached the inner rooms. Here, according to the etiquette of the time, she must dismiss her court, and only the two bishops and her ladies of honor were permitted to accompany the queen into the drawing-room. But farther than this chamber even the bishops themselves might not follow her. The king himself had written down the order for the day, and he who swerved from this order in the most insignificant point would have been proclaimed guilty of high treason, and perhaps have been led out to death.

Catharine, therefore, turned with a languid smile to the two high ecclesiastics, and requested them to await here her summons. Then beckoning to her ladies of honor, she withdrew into her boudoir.

The two bishops remained by themselves in the drawing-room. The circumstance of their being alone seemed to impress them both alike and unpleasantly; for a dark scowl gathered on the brows of both, and they withdrew, as if at a concerted signal, to the opposite sides of the spacious apartment.

A long pause ensued. Nothing was heard save the regular ticking of a large clock of rare workmanship which stood over the fireplace, and from the street afar off, the rejoicing of the people, who surged toward the palace like a roaring sea.

Gardiner had stepped to the window, and was looking up with his peculiar dark smile at the clouds which, driven by the tempest, were sweeping across the heavens.

Cranmer stood by the wall on the opposite side, and sunk in sad thoughts, was contemplating a large portrait of Henry the Eighth, the masterly production of Holbein. As he gazed on that countenance, indicative at once of so much dignity and so much ferocity; as he contemplated those eyes which shone with such gloomy severity, those lips on which was a smile at once voluptuous and fierce, there came over him a feeling of deep sympathy with the young woman whom he had that day devoted to such splendid misery. He reflected that he had, in like manner, already conducted two wives of the king to the marriage altar, and had blessed their union. But he reflected, too, that he had also, afterward, attended both these queens when they ascended the scaffold.

How easily might this pitiable young wife of the king fall a victim to the same dark fate! How easily might Catharine Parr, like Anne Boleyn and Catharine Howard, purchase her short-lived glory with an ignominious death! At any time an inconsiderate word, a look, a smile, might be her ruin. For the king's choler and jealousy were incalculable, and, to his cruelty, no punishment seemed too severe for those by whom he fancied himself injured.

Such were the thoughts which occupied Bishop Cranmer. They softened him, and caused the dark wrinkles to disappear from his brow.

He now smiled to himself at the ill-humor which he had felt shortly before, and upbraided himself for having been so little mindful of his holy calling, and for having exhibited so little readiness to meet his enemy in a conciliating spirit.

For Gardiner was his enemy: *that* Cranmer very well knew. Gardiner had often enough showed him this by his deeds, as he had also taken pains by his words to assure him of his friendship.

But even if Gardiner hated him, it did not therefore follow that Cranmer was obliged to return that hatred; that he should denominate him his enemy, whom he, in virtue of their mutual high calling, was bound to honor and love as his brother.

The noble Cranmer was, therefore, ashamed of his momentary ill-humor. A gentle smile lighted up his peaceful countenance. With an air at once dignified and friendly, he crossed the room and approached the Bishop of Winchester.

Lord Gardiner turned toward him with morose looks, and, without advancing from the embrasure of the window in which he was standing, waited for Cranmer to advance to him. As he looked into that noble, smiling countenance, he had a feeling as if he must raise his fist and dash it into the face of this man, who had the boldness to wish to be his equal, and to contend with him for fame and honor.

But he reflected in good time that Cranmer was still the king's favorite, and therefore he must proceed to work against him with great caution.

So he forced these fierce thoughts back into his heart, and let his face again assume its wonted grave and impenetrable expression.

Cranmer now stood close before him, and his bright, beaming eye was fixed upon Gardiner's sullen countenance.

"I come to your highness," said Cranmer, in his gentle, pleasant voice, "to say to you that I wish with my whole heart the queen may choose you for her confessor and spiritual director, and to assure you that, should this be the case, there will not be in my soul, on that account, the least rancor, or the slightest dissatisfaction. I shall fully comprehend it, if her majesty chooses the distinguished and eminent Bishop of Winchester as her confessor, and the esteem and admiration which I entertain for you can only be enhanced thereby. In confirmation of this, permit me to offer you my hand."

He presented his hand to Gardiner, who, however, took it reluctantly and but for a moment.

"Your highness is very noble, and at the same time a very subtle diplomatist, for you only wish in an adroit and ingenious way to give me to understand how I am to act should the queen choose you for her spiritual director. But that she will do so, you know as well as I. It is, therefore, for me only a humiliation which etiquette imposes when she compels me to stand here and wait to see whether I shall be chosen, or contemptuously thrust aside."

"Why will you look at matters in so unfriendly a light?" said Cranmer, gently. "Wherefore will you consider it a mark of contempt, if you are not chosen to an office to which, indeed, neither merit nor worthiness can call us, but only the personal confidence of a young woman?"

"Oh! you admit that I shall not be chosen?" cried Gardiner, with a malicious smile.

"I have already told you that I am wholly uninformed as to the queen's wish, and I think it is known that the Bishop of Canterbury is wont to speak the truth."

"Certainly that is known, but it is known also that Catharine Parr was a warm admirer of the Bishop of Canterbury; and now that she has gained her end and become queen, she will make it her duty to show her gratitude to him."

"You would by that insinuate that I have made her queen. But I assure your highness, that here also, as in so many other matters which relate to myself, you are falsely informed."

"Possibly!" said Gardiner, coldly. "At any rate, it is certain that the young queen is an ardent advocate of the abominable new doctrine which, like the plague, has spread itself from Germany over all Europe, and scattered mischief and ruin through all Christendom. Yes, Catharine Parr, the present queen, leans to that heretic against whom the Holy Father at Rome has hurled his crushing anathema. She is an adherent of the Reformation."

"You forget," said Cranmer, with an arch smile, "that this anathema was hurled against the head of our king also, and that it has shown itself equally ineffectual against Henry the Eighth as against Luther. Besides, I might remind you that we no longer call the Pope of Rome, 'Holy Father,' and that you yourself have recognized the king as the head of our church."

Gardiner turned away his face in order to conceal the vexation and rage which distorted his features. He felt that he had gone too far, that he had betrayed too much of the secret thoughts of his soul. But he could not always control his violent and passionate nature; and however much a man of the world and diplomatist he might be, still there were moments when the fanatical priest got the better of the man of the world, and the diplomat was forced to give way to the minister of the church.

Cranmer pitied Gardiner's confusion, and, following the native goodness of his heart, he said pleasantly: "Let us not strive here about dogmas, nor attempt to determine whether Luther or the pope is most in the wrong. We stand here in the chamber of the young queen. Let us, therefore, occupy ourselves a little with the destiny of this young woman whom God has chosen for so brilliant a lot."

"Brilliant?" said Gardiner, shrugging his shoulders. "Let us first wait for the termination of her career, and then decide whether it has been brilliant. Many a queen before this has fancied that she was resting on a couch of myrtles and roses, and has suddenly become conscious that she was lying on a red-hot gridiron, which consumed her."

"It is true," murmured Cranmer, with a slight shudder, "it is a dangerous lot to be the king's consort. But just on that account let us not make the perils of her position still greater, by adding to them our own enmity and hate. Just on that account I beg you (and on my part I pledge you my word for it) that, let the choice of the queen be as it may, there may be no feeling of anger, and no desire for revenge in consequence. My God, the poor women are such odd beings, so unaccountable in their wishes and in their inclinations!"

"Ah! it seems you know the women very intimately," cried Gardiner, with a malicious laugh. "Verily, were you not Archbishop of Canterbury, and had not the king prohibited the marriage of ecclesiastics as a very grave crime, one might suppose that you had a wife yourself, and had gained from her a thorough knowledge of female character."

Cranmer, somewhat embarrassed, turned away, and seemed to evade Gardiner's piercing look. "We are not speaking of myself," said he at length, "but of the young queen, and I entreat for her your good wishes. I have seen her to-day almost for the first time, and have never spoken with her, but her countenance has touchingly impressed me, and it appeared to me, her looks besought us to remain at her side, ready to help her on this difficult pathway, which five wives have already trod before her, and in which they found only misery and tears, disgrace, and blood."

"Let Catharine beware then that she does not forsake the right way, as her five predecessors have done!" exclaimed Gardiner. "May she be prudent and cautious, and may she be enlightened by God, that she may hold the true faith, and have true wisdom, and not allow herself to be seduced into the crooked path of the godless and heretical, but remain faithful and steadfast with those of the true faith!"

"Who can say who are of the true faith?" murmured Cranmer, sadly. "There are so many paths leading to heaven, who knows which is the right one?"

"That which *we* tread!" cried Gardiner, with all the overweening pride of a minister of the church. "Woe to the queen should she take any other road! Woe to her if she lends her ear to the false doctrines which come ringing over here from Germany and Switzerland, and in the worldly prudence of her heart imagines that she can rest secure! I will be her most faithful and zealous servant, if she is with me; I will be her most implacable enemy if she is against me."

"And will you call it *being against you*, if the queen does not choose you for her confessor?"

"Will you ask me to call it, being for me?"

"Now God grant that she may choose you!" exclaimed Cranmer, fervently, as he clasped his hands and raised his eyes to heaven. "Poor, unfortunate queen! The first proof of thy husband's love may be thy first misfortune! Why gave he thee the liberty of choosing thine own spiritual director? Why did he not choose for thee?"

And Cranmer dropped his head upon his breast, and sighed deeply.

At this instant the door of the royal chamber opened, and Lady Jane, daughter of Earl Douglas, and first maid of honor to the queen, made her appearance on the threshold.

Both bishops regarded her in breathless silence. It was a serious, a solemn moment, the deep importance of which was very well comprehended by all three.

"Her majesty the queen," said Lady Jane, in an agitated voice, "her majesty requests the presence of Lord Cranmer, archbishop of Canterbury, in her cabinet, in order that she may perform her devotions with him."

"Poor queen!" murmured Cranmer, as he crossed the room to go to Catharine—"poor queen! she has just made an implacable enemy."

Lady Jane waited till Cranmer had disappeared through the door, then hastened with eager steps to the bishop of Winchester, and dropping on her knee, humbly said, "Grace, your highness, grace! My words were in vain, and were not able to shake her resolution."

Gardiner raised up the kneeling maiden, and forced a smile. "It is well," said he, "I doubt not of your zeal. You are a true handmaid of the church, and she will love and reward you for it as a mother! It is then decided. The queen is——"

"Is a heretic," whispered Lady Jane. "Woe to her!"

"And will you be true, and will you faithfully adhere to us?"

"True, in every thought of my being, and every drop of my heart's blood."

"So shall we overcome Catharine Parr, as we overcame Catharine Howard. To the block with the heretic! We found means of bringing Catharine Howard to the scaffold; you, Lady Jane, must find the means of leading Catharine Parr the same way."

"I will find them," said Lady Jane, quietly. "She loves and trusts me. I will betray her friendship in order to remain true to my religion."

"Catharine Parr then is lost," said Gardiner, aloud.

"Yes, she is lost," responded Earl Douglas, who had just entered, and caught the last words of the bishop. "Yes, she is lost, for we are her inexorable and ever-vigilant enemies. But I deem it not altogether prudent to utter words like these in the queen's drawing-room. Let us therefore choose a more favorable hour. Besides, your highness, you must betake yourself to the grand reception-hall, where the whole court is already assembled, and now only awaits the king to go in formal procession for the young queen, and conduct her to the balcony. Let us go, then."

Gardiner nodded in silence, and betook himself to the reception-hall.

Earl Douglas with his daughter followed him. "Catharine Parr is lost," whispered he in Lady Jane's ear. "Catharine Parr is lost, and you shall be the king's seventh wife."

Whilst this was passing in the drawing-room, the young queen was on her knees before Cranmer, and with him sending up to God fervent prayers for prosperity and peace. Tears filled her eyes, and her heart trembled as if before some approaching calamity.

CHAPTER II.

THE QUEEN AND HER FRIEND.

At last this long day of ceremonies and festivities drew near its close, and Catharine might soon hope to be, for the time, relieved from this endless presenting and smiling, from this ever-renewed homage.

At her husband's side she had shown herself on the balcony to receive the greetings of the people, and to bow her thanks. Then in the spacious audience-chamber her newly appointed court had passed before her in formal procession, and she had exchanged a few meaningless, friendly words with each of these lords and ladies. Afterward she had, at her husband's side, given audience to the deputations from the city and from Parliament. But it was only with a secret shudder that she had received from their lips the same congratulations and praises with which the authorities had already greeted five other wives of the king.

Still she had been able to smile and seem happy, for she well knew that the king's eye was never off of her, and that all these lords and ladies who now met her with such deference, and with homage apparently so sincere, were yet, in truth, all her bitter enemies. For by her marriage she had destroyed so many hopes, she had pushed aside so many who believed themselves better fitted to assume the lofty position of queen! She knew that these victims of disappointment would never forgive her this; that she, who was but yesterday their equal, had to-day soared above them as queen and mistress; she knew that all these were watching with spying eyes her every word and action, in order, it might be, to forge therefrom an accusation or a death-warrant.

But nevertheless she smiled! She smiled, though she felt that the choler of the king, so easily kindled and so cruelly vindictive, ever swung over her head like the sword of Damocles.

She smiled, so that this sword might not fall upon her.

At length all these presentations, this homage and rejoicing were well over, and they came to the more agreeable and satisfactory part of the feast.

They went to dinner. That was Catharine's first moment of respite, of rest. For when Henry the Eighth seated himself at table, he was no longer the haughty monarch and the jealous husband, but merely the proficient *artiste* and the impassioned gourmand; and whether the pastry was well seasoned, and the pheasant of good flavor, was for him then a far more important question than any concerning the weal of his people, and the prosperity of his kingdom.

But after dinner came another respite, a new enjoyment, and this time a more real one, which indeed for a while banished all gloomy forebodings and melancholy fears from Catharine's heart, and suffused her countenance with the rosy radiance of cheerfulness and happy smiles. For King Henry had prepared for his young wife a peculiar and altogether novel surprise. He had caused to be erected in the palace of Whitehall a stage, whereon was represented, by the nobles of the court, a comedy from Plautus. Heretofore there had been no other theatrical exhibitions than those which the people performed on the high festivals of the church, the morality and the mystery plays. King Henry the Eighth was the first who had a stage erected for worldly amusement likewise, and caused to be represented on it subjects other than mere dramatized church history. As he freed the church from its spiritual head, the pope, so he wished to free the stage from the church, and to behold upon it other more lively spectacles than the roasting of saints and the massacre of inspired nuns.

And why, too, represent such mock tragedies on the stage, when the king was daily performing them in reality? The burning of Christian martyrs and inspired virgins was, under the reign of the Christian king Henry, such a usual and every-day occurrence, that it could afford a piquant entertainment neither to the court nor to himself.

But the representation of a Roman comedy, that, however, was a new and piquant pleasure, a surprise for the young queen. He had the "Curculio" played before his wife, and if Catharine indeed could listen to the licentious and shameless jests of the popular Roman poet only with bashful blushes, Henry was so much the more delighted by it, and accompanied the obscenest allusions and the most indecent jests with his uproarious laughter and loud shouts of applause.

At length this festivity was also over with, and Catharine was now permitted to retire with her attendants to her private apartments.

With a pleasant smile, she dismissed her cavaliers, and bade her women and her second maid of honor, Anna Askew, go into her boudoir and await her call. Then she gave her arm to her friend Lady Jane Douglas, and with her entered her cabinet.

At last she was alone, at last unwatched. The smile disappeared from her face, and an expression of deep sadness was stamped upon her features.

"Jane," said she, "pray thee shut the doors and draw the window curtains, so that nobody can see me, nobody hear me, no one except yourself, my friend, the companion of my happy childhood. Oh, my God, my God, why was I so foolish as to leave my father's quiet, lonely castle and go out into the world, which is so full of terror and horror?"

She sighed and groaned deeply; and burying her face in her hands, she sank upon the ottoman, weeping and trembling.

Lady Jane observed her with a peculiar smile of malicious satisfaction.

"She is queen and she weeps," said she to herself. "My God, how can a woman possibly feel unhappy, and she a queen?"

She approached Catharine, and, seating herself on the tabouret at her feet, she impressed a fervent kiss on the queen's drooping hand.

"Your majesty weeping!" said she, in her most insinuating tone. "My God, you are then unhappy; and I received with a loud cry of joy the news of my friend's unexpected good fortune. I thought to meet a queen, proud, happy, and radiant with joy; and I was anxious and fearful lest the queen might have ceased to be my friend. Wherefore I urged my father, as soon as your command reached us, to leave Dublin and hasten with me hither. Oh, my God! I wished to see you in your happiness and in your greatness."

Catharine removed her hands from her face, and looked down at her friend with a sorrowful smile. "Well," said she, "are you not satisfied with what you have seen? Have I not the whole day displayed to you the smiling queen, worn a dress embroidered with gold? did not my neck glitter with diamonds? did not the royal diadem shine in my hair? and sat not the king by my side? Let that, then, be sufficient for the present. You have seen the queen all day long. Allow me now for one brief, happy moment to be again the feeling, sensitive woman, who can pour into the bosom of her friend all her complaint and her wretchedness. Ah, Jane, if you knew how I have longed for this hour, how I have sighed after you as the only balm for my poor smitten heart, smitten even to death, how I have implored Heaven for this day, for this one thing—'Give me back my Jane, so that she can weep with me, so that I may have one being at my side who understands me, and does not allow herself to be imposed upon by the wretched splendor of this outward display!'"

"Poor Catharine!" whispered Lady Jane, "poor queen!"

Catharine started and laid her hand, sparkling with brilliants, on Jane's lips. "Call me not thus!" said she. "Queen! My God, is not all the fearful past heard again in that word? Queen! Is it not as much as to say, condemned to the scaffold and a public criminal trial? Ah, Jane! a deadly tremor runs through my members. I am Henry the Eighth's sixth queen; I shall also be executed, or, loaded with disgrace, be repudiated."

Again she hid her face in her hands, and her whole frame shook; so she saw not the smile of malicious satisfaction with which Lady Jane again observed her. She suspected not with what secret delight her friend heard her lamentations and sighs.

"Oh! I am at least revenged!" thought Jane, while she lovingly stroked the queen's hair. "Yes, I am revenged! She has robbed me of a crown, but she is wretched; and in the golden goblet which she presses to her lips she will find nothing but wormwood! Now, if this sixth queen dies not on the scaffold, still we may perhaps so work it that she dies of anxiety, or deems it a pleasure to be able to lay down again her royal crown at Henry's feet."

Then said she aloud: "But why these fears, Catharine? The king loves you; the whole court has seen with what tender and ardent looks he has regarded you to-day, and with what delight he has listened to your every word. Certainly the king loves you."

Catharine seized her hand impulsively. "The king loves me," whispered she, "and I, I tremble before him. Yes, more than that, his love fills me with horror! His hands are dipped in blood; and as I saw him to-day in his crimson robes I shuddered, and I thought, How soon, and my blood, too, will dye this crimson!"

Jane smiled. "You are sick, Catharine," said she. "This good fortune has taken you by surprise, and your overstrained nerves now depict before you all sorts of frightful forms. That is all."

"No, no, Jane; these thoughts have ever been with me. They have attended me ever since the king selected me for his wife."

"And why, then, did you not refuse him?" asked Lady Jane. "Why did you not say 'no' to the king's suit?"

"Why did I not do it, ask you? Ah, Jane, are you such a stranger at this court as not to know, then, that one must either fulfil the king's behests or die? My God, they envy me! They call me the greatest and most potent woman of England. They know not that I am poorer and more powerless than the beggar of the street, who at least has the power to refuse whom she will. I could not refuse. I must either die or accept the royal hand which was extended to me; and I would not die yet, I have still so many claims on life, and it has hitherto made good so few of them! Ah, my poor, hapless existence! what has it been, but an endless chain of renunciations and deprivations, of leafless flowers and dissolving views? It is true, I have never learned to know what is usually called misfortune. But is there a greater misfortune than not to be happy; than to sigh through a life without wish or hope; to wear away the endless, weary days of an existence without delight, yet surrounded with luxury and splendor?"

"You were not unfortunate, and yet you are an orphan, fatherless and motherless?"

"I lost my mother so early that I scarcely knew her. And when my father died I could hardly consider it other than a blessing, for he had never shown himself a father, but always only as a harsh, tyrannical master to me."

"But you were married?"

"Married!" said Catharine, with a melancholy smile. "That is to say, my father sold me to a gouty old man, on whose couch I spent a few comfortless, awfully wearisome years, till Lord Neville made me a rich widow. But what did my independence avail me, when I had bound myself in new fetters? Hitherto I had been the slave of my father, of my husband; now I was the slave of my wealth. I ceased to be a sick-nurse to become steward of my estate. Ah! this was the most tedious period of my life. And yet I owe to it my only real happiness, for at that period I became acquainted with you, my Jane, and my heart, which had never yet learned to know a tenderer feeling, flew to you with all the impetuosity of a first passion. Believe me, my Jane, when this long-missing nephew of my husband came and snatched away from me his hereditary estate, and, as the lord, took possession of it, then the thought that I must leave you and your father, the neighboring proprietor, was my only grief. Men commiserated me on account of my lost property. I thanked God that He had relieved me of this load, and I started for London, that I might at last live and feel, that I might learn to know real happiness or real misery."

" And what did you find? "

" Misery, Jane, for I am queen."

" Is that your sole unhappiness? "

" My only one, but it is great enough, for it condemns me to eternal anxiety, to eternal dissimulation. It condemns me to feign a love which I do not feel, to endure caresses which make me shudder, because they are an inheritance from five unfortunate women. Jane, Jane, do you comprehend what it is to be obliged to embrace a man who has murdered three wives and put away two? to be obliged to kiss this king whose lips open just as readily to utter vows of love as sentences of death? Ah, Jane, I speak, I live, and still I suffer all the agonies of death! They call me a queen, and yet I tremble for my life every hour, and conceal my anxiety and fear beneath the appearance of happiness! My God, I am five-and-twenty, and my heart is still the heart of a child; it does not yet know itself, and now it is doomed never to learn to know itself; for I am Henry's wife, and to love another is, in other words, to wish to mount the scaffold. The scaffold! Look, Jane. When the king approached me and confessed his love and offered me his hand, suddenly there rose before me a fearful picture. It was no more the king whom I saw before me, but the hangman; and it seemed

to me that I saw three corpses lying at his feet, and with
a loud scream I sank senseless before him. When I revived, the king was holding me in his arms. The shock
of this unexpected good fortune, he thought, had made me
faint. He kissed me and called me his bride; he thought
not for a moment that I could refuse him. And I—despise
me, Jane—I was such a dastard, that I could not summon
up courage for a downright refusal. Yes, I was so craven
also, as to be unwilling to die. Ah, my God, it appeared to
me that life at that moment beckoned to me with thousands of joys, thousands of charms, which I had never
known, and for which my soul thirsted as for the manna
in the wilderness. I would live, live at any cost. I would
gain myself a respite, so that I might once more share happiness, love, and enjoyment. Look, Jane, men call me ambitious. They say I have given my hand to Henry because he is king. Ah, they know not how I shuddered at
this royal crown. They know not that in anguish of heart
I besought the king not to bestow his hand upon me, and
thereby rouse all the ladies of his kingdom as foes against
me. They know not that I confessed that I loved him,
merely that I might be able to add that I was ready, out of
love to him, to sacrifice my own happiness to his, and so
conjured him to choose a consort worthy of himself, from
the hereditary princesses of Europe.* But Henry rejected
my sacrifice. He wished to make a queen, in order to possess a wife, who may be his own property—whose blood, as
her lord and master, he can shed. So I am queen. I have
accepted my lot, and henceforth my existence will be a
ceaseless struggle and wrestling with death. I will at least
sell my life as dearly as possible; and the maxim which
Cranmer has given me shall hereafter be my guide on
the thorny path of life."

"And how runs this maxim?" asked Jane.

"Be wise as serpents and harmless as doves," replied

* "La vie d'Élizabeth, Reine d'Angleterre, traduite de l'Italien de
Monsieur Grégoire Leti," vol. ii. Amsterdam, 1694.

Catharine, with a languid smile, as she dropped her head upon her breast and surrendered herself to her painful and foreboding reflections.

Lady Jane stood opposite to her, and gazed with cruel composure upon the painfully convulsed countenance and at times violently trembling form of the young queen for whom all England that day kept festival, and who yet was sitting before her so wretched and full of sorrow.

Suddenly Catharine raised her head. Her countenance had now assumed an entirely different expression. It was now firm, resolute, and dauntless. With a slight inclination of the head she extended her hand to Lady Jane, and drew her friend more closely to her.

"I thank you, Jane," said she, as she imprinted a kiss upon her forehead—"I thank you! You have done my heart good and relieved it of its oppressive load of secret anguish. He who can give his grief utterance, is already half cured of it. I thank you, then, Jane! Henceforth, you will find me calm and cheerful. The woman has wept before you, but the queen is aware that she has a task to accomplish as difficult as it is noble, and I give you my word for it, she will accomplish it. The new light which has risen on the world shall no more be dimmed by blood and tears, and no more in this unhappy land shall men of sense and piety be condemned as insurgents and traitors! This is the task which God has set me, and I swear that I will accomplish it! Will you help me in this, too, Jane?"

Lady Jane responded faintly in a few words, which Catharine did not understand, and as she looked up to her, she noticed, with astonishment, the corpse-like pallor which had suddenly overspread the countenance of her maid of honor.

Catharine gave a start, and fixed on her face a surprised and searching look.

Lady Jane cast down her eyes before that searching and flashing glance. Her fanaticism had for the moment got the better of her, and much as she was wont at other times to hide her thoughts and feelings, it had, at that moment, carried her away and betrayed her to the keen eye of her friend.

"It is now a long while since we saw each other," said Catharine, sadly. "Three years! It is a long time for a young girl's heart! And you were those three years with your father in Dublin, at that rigidly popish court. I did not consider that! But however much your opinions may have changed, your heart, I know, still remains the same, and you will ever be the proud, high-minded Jane of former days, who could never stoop to tell a lie—no, not even if this lie would procure her profit and glory. I ask you then, Jane, what is your religion? Do you believe in the Pope of Rome, and the Church of Rome as the only channel of salvation? or do you follow the new teaching which Luther and Calvin have promulgated?"

Lady Jane smiled. "Would I have risked appearing before you, if I still reckoned myself of the Roman Catholic Church? Catharine Parr is hailed by the Protestants of England as the new patroness of the persecuted doctrine, and already the Romish priests hurl their anathemas against you, and execrate you and your dangerous presence here. And you ask me, whether I am an adherent of that church which maligns and damns you? You ask me whether I believe in the pope, who has laid the king under an interdict—the king, who is not only my lord and master, but also the husband of my precious and noble Catharine? Oh, queen, you love me not when you can address such a question to me."

And as if overcome by painful emotion, Lady Jane sank down at Catharine's feet, and hid her head in the folds of the queen's robe.

Catharine bent down to raise her and take her to her heart. Suddenly she started, and a deathly paleness overspread her face. "The king," whispered she, "the king is coming!"

CHAPTER III.

KING HENRY THE EIGHTH.

CATHARINE was not deceived. The doors were opened, and on the threshold appeared the lord marshal, with his golden mace.

"His majesty the king!" whispered he, in his grave, solemn manner, which filled Catharine with secret dread, as though he were pronouncing the sentence of death over her.

But she forced a smile and advanced to the door to receive the king. Now was heard a thunder-like rumble, and over the smoothly carpeted floor of the anteroom came rolling on the king's house equipage. This house equipage consisted of a large chair, resting on castors, which was moved by men in the place of horses, and to which they had, with artful flattery, given the form of a triumphal car of the old victorious Roman Cæsars, in order to afford the king, as he rolled through the halls, the pleasant illusion that he was holding a triumphal procession, and that it was not the burden of his heavy limbs which fastened him to his imperial car. King Henry gave ready credence to the flattery of his truckle-chair and his courtiers, and as he rolled along in it through the saloons glittering with gold, and through halls adorned with Venetian mirrors, which reflected his form a thousandfold, he liked to lull himself into the dream of being a triumphing hero, and wholly forgot that it was not his deeds, but his fat, that had helped him to his triumphal car.

For that monstrous mass which filled up the colossal chair, that mountain of purple-clad flesh, that clumsy, almost shapeless mass, that was Henry the Eighth, king of merry England. But that mass had a head—a head full of dark and wrathful thoughts, a heart full of bloodthirsty and cruel lusts. The colossal body was indeed, by its physical weight, fastened to the chair. Yet his mind never rested, but he hovered, with the talons and flashing eye of the bird of prey, over his people, ever ready to pounce upon some innocent dove, to drink her blood, and tear out her heart, that he might lay it, all palpitating, as an offering on the altar of his sanguinary god.

The king's sedan now stopped, and Catharine hastened forward with smiling face, to assist her royal husband in alighting.

Henry greeted her with a gracious nod, and rejected the proffered aid of the attendant pages.

"Away," said he, "away! My Catharine alone shall extend me her hand, and give me a welcome to the bridal chamber. Go, we feel to-day as young and strong as in our best and happiest days, and the young queen shall see that it is no decrepit graybeard, tottering with age, who woos her, but a strong man rejuvenated by love. Think not, Kate, that I use my car because of weakness. No, it was only my longing for you which made me wish to be with you the sooner."

He kissed her with a smile, and, lightly leaning on her arm, alighted from his car.

"Away with the equipage, and with all of you!" said he. "We wish to be alone with this beautiful young wife, whom the lord bishops have to-day made our own."

At a signal from his hand, the brilliant *cortège* withdrew, and Catharine was alone with the king.

Her heart beat so wildly that it made her lips tremble, and her bosom swell high.

Henry saw it, and smiled; but it was a cold, cruel smile, and Catharine grew pale before it.

"He has only the smile of a tyrant," said she to herself. "With this same smile, by which he would now give expression to his love, he yesterday, perhaps, signed a death-warrant, or will, to-morrow, witness an execution."

"Do you love me, Kate?" suddenly said the king, who had till now observed her in silence and thoughtfulness. "Say, Kate, do you love me?"

He looked steadily into her eyes, as though he would read her soul to the very bottom.

Catharine sustained his look, and did not drop her eyes. She felt that this was the decisive moment which determined her whole future; and this conviction restored to her all her self-possession and energy.

She was now no longer the shy, timid girl, but the resolute, proud woman, who was ready to wrestle with fate for greatness and glory.

"Do you love me, Kate?" repeated the king; and his brow already began to darken.

"I know not," said Catharine, with a smile, which enchanted the king, for there was quite as much graceful coquetry as bashfulness on her charming face.

"You know not?" replied Henry, astonished. "Now, by the Mother of God, it is the first time in my life that a woman has ever been bold enough to return me such an answer! You are a bold woman, Kate, to hazard it, and I praise you for it. I love bravery, because it is something I so rarely see. They all tremble before me, Kate—all! They know that I am not intimidated by blood, and in the might of my royalty I subscribe a death-warrant with the same calmness of soul as a love-letter."

"Oh, you are a great king," murmured Catharine.

Henry did not notice her. He was wholly buried in one of those self-contemplations to which he so willingly surrendered himself, and which generally had for their subject his own greatness and sovereignty.

"Yes," continued he, and his eyes, which, in spite of his corpulency and his extremely fleshy face, were yet large and wide open, shone more brightly. "Yes, they all tremble before me, for they know that I am a righteous and powerful king, who spares not his own blood, if it is necessary to punish and expiate crime, and with inexorable hand punishes the sinner, though he were the nearest to the throne. Take heed to yourself, therefore, Kate, take heed to yourself. You behold in me the avenger of God, and the judge of men. The king wears the crimson, not because it is beautiful and glossy, but because it is red like blood, and because it is the king's highest prerogative to shed the blood of his delinquent subjects, and thereby expiate human crime. Thus only do I conceive of royalty, and thus only will I carry it out till the end of my days. Not the right to pardon, but the right to punish, is that whereby the ruler manifests himself before the lower classes of mankind. God's thunder should be on his lips, and the king's wrath should descend like lightning on the head of the guilty."

"But God is not only wrathful, but also merciful and forgiving," said Catharine, as she lightly and shyly leaned her head on the king's shoulder.

"Just that is the prerogative of God above kings; that He can, as it pleases Him, show mercy and grace, where we can only condemn and punish. There must be something in which God is superior to kings, and greater than they. But how, Kate, you tremble, and the lovely smile has vanished from your countenance! Be not afraid of me, Kate! Be always frank with me, and without deceit; then I shall always love you, and iniquity will then have no power over you. And now, Kate, tell me, and explain to me. You do not know that you love me?"

"No, I do not know, your majesty. And how should I be able to recognize, and know, and designate by name what is strange to me, and what I have never before felt?"

"How, you have never loved, Kate?" asked the king, with a joyful expression.

"Never. My father maltreated me, so that I could feel for him nothing but dread and terror."

"And your husband, child? That man who was my predecessor in the possession of you. Did you not love your husband either?"

"My husband?" asked she, abstractedly. "It is true, my father sold me to Lord Neville, and as the priest had joined our hands, men called him my husband. But he very well knew that I did not love him, nor did he require my love. He needed a nurse, not a wife. He had given me his name as a father gives his to a daughter; and I was his daughter, a true, faithful, and obedient daughter, who joyfully fulfilled her duty and tended him till his death."

"And after his death, child? Years have elapsed since then, Kate. Tell me, and I conjure you, tell me the truth, the simple, plain truth! After the death of your husband, then even, did you never love?"

He gazed with visible anxiety, with breathless expectation, deep into her eyes; but she did not drop them.

"Sire," said she, with a charming smile, "till a few weeks past, I have often mourned over myself; and it seemed to me that I must, in the desperation of my singular and cold nature, lay open my breast, in order to search there for the heart, which, senseless and cold, had never betrayed its existence by its stronger beating. Oh, sire, I was full of trouble about myself; and in my foolish rashness, I accused Heaven of having robbed me of the noblest feeling and the fairest privilege of any woman—the capacity of loving."

"Till the past few weeks, did you say, Kate?" asked the king, breathless with emotion.

"Yes, sire, until the day on which you, for the first time, graciously afforded me the happiness of speaking with me."

The king uttered a low cry, and drew Catharine, with impetuous vehemence, into his arms.

"And since, tell me now, you dear little dove, since then, does your heart throb?"

"Yes, sire, it throbs, oh, it often throbs to bursting! When I hear your voice, when I behold your countenance, it is as if a cold tremor rilled through my whole being, and drove all my blood to the heart. It is as though my heart anticipated your approach before my eyes discern you. For even before you draw near me, I feel a peculiar trembling of the heart, and the breath is stifled in my bosom; then I always know that you are coming, and that your presence will relieve this peculiar tension of my being. When you are not by me I think of you, and when I sleep I dream of you. Tell me, sire, you who know every thing, tell me, know you now whether I love you?"

"Yes, yes, you love me," cried Henry, to whom this strange and joyous surprise had imparted youthful vivacity and warmth. "Yes, Kate, you love me; and if I may trust your dear confession, I am your first love. Repeat it yet again; you were nothing but a daughter to Lord Neville?"

"Nothing more, sire!"

"And after him have you had no love?"

"None, sire!"

"And can it be that so happy a marvel has come to pass? and that I have made, not a widow, but a young maiden, my queen?"

As he now gazed at her with warm, passionate, tender looks, Catharine cast down her eyes, and a deep blush covered her sweet face.

"Ah, a woman's bashful blushes, what an exquisite sight!" cried the king, and while he wildly pressed Catharine to his bosom, he continued: "Oh, are we not foolish and short-sighted men, all of us, yes, even we kings? In order that I might not be, perhaps, forced to send my sixth wife also to the scaffold, I chose, in trembling dread of the deceitfulness of your sex, a widow for my queen, and this widow with a blessed confession, mocks at the new law of the wise Parliament, and makes good to me what she never promised." *

* After Catharine Howard's infidelity and incontinency had been proved, and she had atoned for them by her death, Parliament enacted a law "that if the king or his successors should intend to marry any woman whom they took to be a clean and pure maid—if she, not being so, did not declare the same to the king, it should be high treason; and all who knew it, and did not reveal it, were guilty of misprision of treason."—"Burnet's History of the Reformation of the Church of England." London, 1681 (vol. i, p. 313).

"Come, Kate, give me a kiss. You have opened before me to-day a happy, blissful future, and prepared for me a great and unexpected pleasure. I thank you for it, Kate, and the Mother of God be my witness, I will never forget it."

And drawing a rich diamond ring from his own finger, and putting it upon Catharine's, he continued: "Be this ring a remembrancer of this hour, and when you hereafter present it to me, with a request, I will grant that request, Kate!"

He kissed her forehead, and was about to press her more closely in his arms, when suddenly from without was heard the dull roll of drums, and the ringing of bells.

The king started a moment and released Catharine from his arms. He listened; the roll of drums continued, and now and then was heard in the distance, that peculiar thundering and yet sullen sound, which so much resembles the roar and rush of the sea, and which can be produced only by a large and excited mob.

The king, with a fierce curse, pushed open the glass door leading to the balcony, and walked out.

Catharine gazed after him with a strange, half-timid, half-scornful look. "I have not at least told him that I love him," muttered she. "He has construed my words as it suited his vanity. No matter. I *will* not die on the scaffold!"

With a resolute step, and firm, energetic air, she followed the king to the balcony. The roll of drums was kept up, and from all the steeples the bells were pealing. The night was dark and calm. All London seemed to slumber, and the dark houses around about stood up out of the universal darkness like huge coffins.

Suddenly the horizon began to grow bright, and on the sky appeared a streak of fiery red, which, blazing up higher and higher, soon illuminated the entire horizon with a crimson glow, and even shed its glaring fiery beams over the balcony on which stood the royal pair.

Still the bells clanged and clamored; and blended with their peals was heard now and then, in the distance, a piercing shriek and a clamor as of thousands and thousands of confusedly mingled voices.

Suddenly the king turned to Catharine, and his countenance, which was just then overspread by the fire-light as with a blood-red veil, had now assumed an expression of savage, demoniacal delight.

"Ah," said he, "I know what it is. You had wholly bewildered me, and stolen away my attention, you little enchantress. I had for a moment ceased to be a king, because I wished to be entirely your lover. But now I bethink me again of my avenging sovereignty! It is the fagot-piles about the stake which flame so merrily yonder. And that yelling and clamor indicate that my merry people are enjoying with all their soul the comedy which I have had played before them to-day, for the honor of God, and my unimpeachable royal dignity."

"The stake!" cried Catharine, trembling. "Your majesty does not mean thereby to say that right yonder, men are to die a cruel, painful death—that the same hour in which their king pronounces himself happy and content, some of his subjects are to be condemned to dreadful torture, to a horrible destruction! Oh, no! my king will not overcloud his queen's wedding-day with so dark a veil of death. He will not wish to dim my happiness so cruelly."

The king laughed. "No, I will not darken it, but light it up with bright flames," said he; and as, with outstretched arm, he pointed over to the glaring heavens, he continued: "There are our wedding-torches, my Kate, and the most sacred and beautiful which I could find, for they burn to the honor of God and of the king.* And the heavenward flaring flames which carries up the souls of the heretics will give to my God joyous intelligence of His most faithful and

* "Life of King Henry the Eighth, founded on Authentic and Original Documents." By Patrick Fraser Tytler. (Edinburgh, 1837, p. 440.)

obedient son, who, even on the day of his happiness, forgets not his kingly duty, but ever remains the avenging and destroying minister of his God."

He looked frightful as he thus spoke. His countenance, lit up by the fire, had a fierce, threatening expression; his eyes blazed; and a cold, cruel smile played about his thin, firmly-pressed lips.

"Oh, he knows no pity!" murmured Catharine to herself, as in a paroxysm of anguish she stared at the king, who, in fanatical enthusiasm, was looking over toward the fire, into which, at his command, they were perhaps hurling to a cruel, torturing death, some poor wretch, to the honor of God and the king. "No, he knows no pity and no mercy."

Now Henry turned to her, and laying his extended hand softly on the back of her slender neck, he spanned it with his fingers, and whispered in her ear tender words and vows of love.

Catharine trembled. This caress of the king, however harmless in itself, had in it for her something dismal and dreadful. It was the involuntary, instinctive touch of the headsman, who examines the neck of his victim, and searches on it for the place where he will make the stroke. Thus had Anne Boleyn once put her tender white hands about her slender neck, and said to the headsman, brought over from Calais specially for her execution: "I pray you strike me well and surely! I have, indeed, but a slim little neck." * Thus had the king clutched his hand about the neck of Catharine Howard, his fifth wife, when, certain of her infidelity, he had thrust her from himself with fierce execrations, when she would have clung to him. The dark marks of that grip were still visible upon her neck when she laid it on the block.†

And this dreadful twining of his fingers Catharine must now endure as a caress; at which she must smile, which she must receive with all the appearance of delight.

While he spanned her neck, he whispered in her

* Tytler, p. 382. † Leti, vol. i, p. 193.

ear words of tenderness, and bent his face close to her cheeks.

But Catharine heeded not his passionate whispers. She saw nothing save the blood-red handwriting of fire upon the sky. She heard nothing save the shrieks of the wretched victims.

"Mercy, mercy!" faltered she. "Oh, let this day be a day of festivity for all your subjects! Be merciful, and if you would have me really believe that you love me, grant this first request which I make of you. Grant me the lives of these wretched ones. Mercy, sire, mercy!"

And as if the queen's supplication had found an echo, suddenly was heard from the chamber a wailing, despairing voice, repeating loudly and in tones of anguish: "Mercy, your majesty, mercy!" The king turned round impetuously, and his face assumed a dark, wrathful expression. He fastened his searching eyes on Catharine, as though he would read in her looks whether she knew who had dared to interrupt their conversation.

But Catharine's countenance expressed unconcealed astonishment. "Mercy, mercy!" repeated the voice from the interior of the chamber.

The king uttered an angry exclamation, and hastily withdrew from the balcony.

CHAPTER IV.

KING BY THE WRATH OF GOD.

"WHO dares interrupt us?" cried the king, as with headlong step he returned to the chamber—"who dares speak of mercy?"

"I dare!" said a young lady, who, pale, with distorted features, in frightful agitation, now hastened to the king and prostrated herself before him.

"Anne Askew!" cried Catharine, amazed. "Anne, what want you here?"

"I want mercy, mercy for those wretched ones, who are suffering yonder," cried the young maiden, pointing with an expression of horror to the reddened sky. "I want mercy for the king himself, who is so cruel as to send the noblest and the best of his subjects to the slaughter like miserable brutes!"

"Oh, sire, have compassion on this poor child!" besought Catharine, turning to Henry, "compassion on her impassioned excitement and her youthful ardor! She is as yet unaccustomed to these frightful scenes—she knows not yet that it is the sad duty of kings to be constrained to punish, where they might prefer to pardon!"

Henry smiled; but the look which he cast on the kneeling girl made Catharine tremble. There was a death-warrant in that look!

"Anne Askew, if I mistake not, is your second maid of honor?" asked the king; "and it was at your express wish that she received that place?"

"Yes sire."

"You knew her, then?"

"No, sire! I saw her a few days ago for the first time. But she had already won my heart at our first meeting, and I feel that I shall love her. Exercise forbearance, then, your majesty!"

But the king was still thoughtful, and Catharine's answers did not yet satisfy him.

"Why, then, do you interest yourself for this young lady, if you did not know her?"

"She has been so warmly recommended to me."

"By whom?"

Catharine hesitated a moment; she felt that she had, perhaps, in her zeal, gone too far, and that it was imprudent to tell the king the truth. But the king's keen, penetrating look was resting on her, and she recollected that he had, the first thing that evening, so urgently and solemnly conjured her to always tell him the truth. Besides, it was no secret at court who the protector of this young maiden was, and who had been the means of her obtaining the place of maid of honor to the queen, a place which so many wealthy and distinguished families had solicited for their daughters.

"Who recommended this lady to you?" repeated the king, and already his ill-humor began to redden his face, and make his voice tremble.

"Archbishop Cranmer did so, sire," said Catharine as she raised her eyes to the king, and looked at him with a smile surpassingly charming.

At that moment was heard without, more loudly, the roll of drums, which nevertheless was partially drowned by piercing shrieks and horrible cries of distress. The blaze of the fire shot up higher, and now was seen the bright flame, which with murderous rage licked the sky above.

Anne Askew, who had kept respectful silence during the conversation of the royal pair, now felt herself completely overcome by this horrible sight, and bereft of the last remnant of self-possession.

"My God, my God!" said she, quivering from the internal tremor, and stretching her hands beseechingly toward the king, "do you not hear that frightful wail of the wretched? Sire, by the thought of your own dying hour, I conjure you have compassion on these miserable beings! Let them not, at least, be thrown alive into the flames. Spare them this last frightful torture."

King Henry cast a wrathful look on the kneeling girl; then strode past her to the door, which led into the adjoining hall, in which the courtiers were waiting for their king.

He beckoned to the two bishops, Cranmer and Gardiner, to come nearer, and ordered the servants to throw the hall doors wide open.

The scene now afforded an animated and singular spectacle, and this chamber, just before so quiet, was suddenly changed to the theatre of a great drama, which was perhaps to end tragically. In the queen's bedchamber, a small room, but furnished with the utmost luxury and splendor, the principal characters of this scene were congregated. In the middle of the space stood the king in his robes, embroidered with gold and sparkling with jewels, which were irradiated by the bright light of the chandelier. Near him was seen the young queen, whose beautiful and lovely face was turned in anxious expectation toward the king, in whose stern and rigid features she sought to read the development of this scene.

Not far from her still knelt the young maiden, hiding in her hands her face drenched in tears; while farther away, in the background, were the two bishops observing with grave, cool tranquillity the group before them. Through the open hall doors were descried the expectant and curious countenances of the courtiers standing with their heads crowded close together in the space before the doors; and opposite to them, through the open door leading to the balcony, was seen the fiery, blazing sky, and heard the clanging of the bells and the rolling of the drums, the piercing shrieks and the yells of the people.

A deep silence ensued, and when the king spoke, the tone of his voice was so hard and cold, that an involuntary shudder ran through all present.

"My Lord Bishops of Winchester and Canterbury," said the king, "we have called you that you may, by the might of your prayers and the wisdom of your words, rid this young girl here from the devil, who, without doubt, has the mastery over her, since she dares charge her king and master with cruelty and injustice."

The two bishops drew nearer to the kneeling girl; each laid a hand upon her shoulder, and bent over her, but the one with an expression of countenance wholly different from that of the other.

Cranmer's look was gentle and serious, and at the same

time a compassionate and encouraging smile played about his thin lips.

Gardiner's features on the contrary bore the expression of cruel, cold-hearted irony; and the smile which rested on his thick, protruding lips was the joyful and merciless smile of a priest ready to sacrifice a victim to his idol.

"Courage, my daughter, courage and prudence!" whispered Cranmer.

"God, who blesses the righteous and punishes and destroys sinners, be with thee and with us all!" said Gardiner.

But Anne Askew recoiled with a shudder from the touch of his hand, and with an impetuous movement pushed it away from her shoulder.

"Touch me not; you are the hangman of those poor people whom they are putting to death down yonder," said she impetuously; and as she turned to the king and extended her hands imploringly toward him, she cried: "Mercy, King Henry, mercy!"

"Mercy!" repeated the king, "mercy, and for whom? Who are they that they are putting to death down there? Tell me, forsooth, my lord bishops, who are they that are led to the stake to-day? Who are the condemned?"

"They are heretics, who devote themselves to this new false doctrine which has come over to us from Germany, and who dare refuse to recognize the spiritual supremacy of our lord and king," said Bishop Gardiner.

"They are Roman Catholics, who regard the Pope of Rome as the chief shepherd of the Church of Christ, and will regard nobody but him as their lord," said Bishop Cranmer.

"Ah, behold this young maiden accuses us of injustice," cried the king; "and yet, you say that not heretics alone are executed down there, but also Romanists. It appears to me then that we have justly and impartially, as always, punished only criminals and given over the guilty to justice."

"Oh, had you seen what I have seen," said Anne Askew, shuddering, "then would you collect all your vital energies for a single cry, for a single word—mercy! and that word would you shout out loud enough to reach yon frightful place of torture and horror."

"What saw you, then?" asked the king, smiling.

Anne Askew had stood up, and her tall, slender form now lifted itself, like a lily, between the sombre forms of the bishops. Her eye was fixed and glaring; her noble and delicate features bore the expression of horror and dread.

"I saw," said she, "a woman whom they were leading to execution. Not a criminal, but a noble lady, whose proud and lofty heart never harbored a thought of treason or disloyalty, but who, true to her faith and her convictions, would not forswear the God whom she served. As she passed through the crowd, it seemed as if a halo encompassed her head, and covered her white hair with silvery rays; all bowed before her, and the hardest natures wept over the unfortunate woman who had lived more than seventy years, and yet was not allowed to die in her bed, but was to be slaughtered to the glory of God and of the king. But she smiled, and graciously saluting the weeping and sobbing multitude, she advanced to the scaffold as if she were ascending a throne to receive the homage of her people. Two years of imprisonment had blanched her cheek, but had not been able to destroy the fire of her eye, or the strength of her mind, and seventy years had not bowed her neck or broken her spirit. Proud and firm, she mounted the steps of the scaffold, and once more saluted the people and cried aloud, 'I will pray to God for you.' But as the headsman approached and demanded that she should allow her hands to be bound, and that she should kneel in order to lay her head upon the block, she refused, and angrily pushed him away. 'Only traitors and criminals lay their head on the block!' exclaimed she, with a loud, thundering voice. 'There is no occasion for me to do so, and I will not submit to your bloody laws as long as there is a breath in me. Take, then, my life, if you can.'

"And now began a scene which filled the hearts of the lookers-on with fear and horror. The countess flew like a hunted beast round and round the scaffold. Her white hair streamed in the wind; her black grave-clothes rustled around her like a dark cloud, and behind her, with uplifted axe, came the headsman, in his fiery red dress; he, ever endeavoring to strike her with the falling axe, but she, ever trying, by moving her head to and fro, to evade the descending stroke. But at length her resistance became weaker; the blows of the axe reached her, and stained her white hair, hanging loose about her shoulders, with crimson streaks. With a heart-rending cry, she fell fainting. Near her, exhausted also, sank down the headsman, bathed in sweat. This horrible wild chase had lamed his arm and broken his strength. Panting and breathless, he was not able to drag this fainting, bleeding woman to the block, or to lift up the axe to separate her noble head from the body.* The crowd shrieked with distress and horror, imploring and begging for mercy, and even the lord chief justice could not refrain from tears, and he ordered the cruel work to be suspended until the countess and the headsman should have regained strength; for a living, not a dying person was to be executed: thus said the law. They made a pallet for the countess on the scaffold and endeavored to restore her; invigorating wine was supplied to the headsman, to renew his strength for the work of death; and the crowd turned to the stakes which were prepared on both sides of the scaffold, and at which four other martyrs were to be burnt. But I flew here like a hunted doe, and now, king, I lie at your feet. There is still time. Pardon, king, pardon for the Countess of Somerset, the last of the Plantagenets."

"Pardon, sire, pardon!" repeated Catharine Parr, weeping and trembling, as she clung to her husband's side.

* Tytler, p. 430.

"Pardon!" repeated Archbishop Cranmer; and a few of the courtiers re-echoed it in a timid and anxious whisper.

The king's large, brilliant eyes glanced around the whole assembly, with a quick, penetrating look. "And you, my Lord Bishop Gardiner," asked he, in a cold, sarcastic tone, "will you also ask for mercy, like all these weak-hearted souls here?"

"The Lord our God is a jealous God," said Gardiner, solemnly, "and it is written that God will punish the sinner unto the third and fourth generation."

"And what is written shall stand true!" exclaimed the king, in a voice of thunder. "No mercy for evil-doers, no pity for criminals. The axe must fall upon the head of the guilty, the flames shall consume the bodies of criminals."

"Sire, think of your high vocation!" exclaimed Anne Askew, in a tone of enthusiasm. "Reflect what a glorious name you have assumed to yourself in this land. You call yourself the head of the Church, and you want to rule and govern upon earth in God's stead. Exercise mercy, then, for you entitle yourself king by the grace of God."

"No, I do not call myself king by God's grace; I call myself king by God's wrath!" exclaimed Henry, as he raised his arm menacingly. "It is my duty to send sinners to God; may He have mercy on them there above, if He will! I am the punishing judge, and I judge mercilessly, according to the law, without compassion. Let those whom I have condemned appeal to God, and may He have mercy upon them. I cannot do it, nor will I. Kings are here to punish, and they are like to God, not in His love, but in His avenging wrath."

"Woe, then, woe to you and to all of us!" exclaimed Anne Askew. Woe to you, King Henry, if what you now say is the truth! Then are they right, those men who are bound to yonder stakes, when they brand you with the name of tyrant; then is the Bishop of Rome right when he upbraids you as an apostate and degenerate son, and hurls his anathemas against you! Then you know not God, who is love and mercy; then you are no disciple of the Saviour, who has said, 'Love your enemies, bless them that curse you.' Woe to you, King Henry, if matters are really so bad with you; if——"

"Silence, unhappy woman, silence!" exclaimed Catharine; and as she vehemently pushed away the furious girl she grasped the king's hand, and pressed it to her lips. "Sire," whispered she, with intense earnestness, "sire, you told me just now that you loved me. Prove it by pardoning this maiden, and having consideration for her impassioned excitement. Prove it by allowing me to lead Anne Askew to her room and enjoin silence upon her."

But at this moment the king was wholly inaccessible to any other feelings than those of anger and delight in blood.

He indignantly repelled Catharine, and without moving his sharp, penetrating look from the young maiden, he said in a quick, hollow tone: "Let her alone; let her speak; let no one dare to interrupt her!"

Catharine, trembling with anxiety and inwardly hurt at the harsh manner of the king, retired with a sigh to the embrasure of one of the windows.

Anne Askew had not noticed what was going on about her. She remained in that state of exaltation which cares for no consequences and which trembles before no danger. She would at this moment have gone to the stake with cheerful alacrity, and she almost longed for this blessed martyrdom.

"Speak, Anne Askew, speak!" commanded the king. "Tell me, do you know what the countess, for whose pardon you are beseeching me, has done? Know you why those four men were sent to the stake?"

"I do know, King Henry, by the wrath of God," said the maiden, with burning passionateness. "I know why you have sent the noble countess to the slaughter-house, and why you will exercise no mercy toward her. She is of noble, of royal blood, and Cardinal Pole is her son. You would punish the son through the mother, and because you cannot throttle the cardinal, you murder his mother."

"Oh, you are a very knowing child!" cried the king, with an inhuman, ironical laugh. "You know my most secret thoughts and my most hidden feelings. Without doubt you are a good papist, since the death of the popish countess fills you with such heart-rending grief. Then you must confess, at the least, that it is right to burn the four heretics!"

"Heretics!" exclaimed Anne, enthusiastically, "call you heretics those noble men who go gladly and boldly to death for their convictions and their faith? King Henry! King Henry! Woe to you if these men are condemned as heretics! They alone are the faithful, they are the true servants of God. They have freed themselves from human supremacy, and as you would not recognize the pope, so they will not recognize you as head of the Church! God alone, they say, is Lord of the Church and Master of their consciences, and who can be presumptuous enough to call them criminals?"

"I!" exclaimed Henry the Eighth, in a powerful tone. "I dare do it. I say that they are heretics, and that I will destroy them, will tread them all beneath my feet, all of them, all who think as they do! I say that I will shed the blood of these criminals, and prepare for them torments at which human nature will shudder and quake. God will manifest Himself by me in fire and blood! He has put the sword into my hand, and I will wield it for His glory. Like St. George, I will tread the dragon of heresy beneath my feet!"

And haughtily raising his crimsoned face and rolling his great bloodshot eyes wildly around the circle, he continued: "Hear this all of you who are here assembled; no mercy for heretics, no pardon for papists. It is I, I alone, whom the Lord our God has chosen and blessed as His hangman and executioner! I am the high-priest of His Church, and he who dares deny me, denies God; and he who is so presumptuous as to do reverence to any other head of the Church, is a priest of Baal and kneels to an idolatrous image. Kneel down all of you before me, and reverence in me God, whose earthly representative I am, and who reveals Himself through me in His fearful and exalted majesty. Kneel down, for I am sole head of the Church and high-priest of our God!"

And as if at one blow all knees bent; all those haughty cavaliers, those ladies sparkling with jewels and gold, even the two bishops and the queen fell upon the ground.

The king gazed for a moment on this sight, and, with radiant looks and a smile of triumph, his eyes ran over this assembly, consisting of the noblest of his kingdom, humbled before him.

Suddenly they were fastened on Anne Askew.

She alone had not bent her knee, but stood in the midst of the kneelers, proud and upright as the king himself.

A dark cloud passed over the king's countenance.

"You obey not my command?" asked he.

She shook her curly head and fixed on him a steady, piercing look. "No," said she, "like those over yonder whose last death-groan we even now hear, like them, I say: To God alone is honor due, and He alone is Lord of His Church! If you wish me to bend my knee before you as my king, I will do it, but I bow not to you as the head of the holy Church!"

A murmur of surprise flew through the assembly, and every eye was turned with fear and amazement on this bold young girl, who confronted the king with a countenance smiling and glowing with enthusiasm.

At a sign from Henry the kneelers arose and awaited in breathless silence the terrible scene that was coming.

A pause ensued. King Henry himself was struggling for breath, and needed a moment to collect himself.

Not as though wrath and passion had deprived him of speech. He was neither wrathful nor passionate, and it was only *joy* that obstructed his breathing—the joy of having again found a victim with which he might satisfy his desire for blood, on whose agony he might feast his eyes, whose dying sigh he might greedily inhale.

The king was never more cheerful than when he had signed a death-warrant. For then he was in full enjoyment of his greatness as lord over the lives and deaths of millions of other men, and this feeling made him proud and happy, and fully conscious of his exalted position.

Hence, as he now turned to Anne Askew, his countenance was calm and serene, and his voice friendly, almost tender.

"Anne Askew," said he, "do you know that the words you have now spoken make you guilty of high treason?"

"I know it, sire."

"And you know what punishment awaits traitors?"

"Death, I know it."

"Death by fire!" said the king with perfect calmness and composure.

A hollow murmur ran through the assembly. Only one voice dared give utterance to the word mercy.

It was Catharine, the king's consort, who spoke this one word. She stepped forward, and was about to rush to the king and once more implore his mercy and pity. But she felt herself gently held back. Archbishop Cranmer stood near her, regarding her with a serious and beseeching look.

"Compose yourself, compose yourself," murmured he. "You cannot save her; she is lost. Think of yourself, and of the pure and holy religion whose protectress you are. Preserve yourself for your Church and your companions in the faith!"

"And must she die?" asked Catharine, whose eyes filled with tears as she looked toward the poor young child, who was confronting the king with such a beautiful and innocent smile.

"Perhaps we may still save her, but this is not the moment for it. Any opposition now would only irritate the king the more, and he might cause the girl to be instantly thrown into the flames of the fires still burning yonder! So let us be silent."

"Yes, silence," murmured Catharine, with a shudder, as she withdrew again to the embrasure of the window.

"Death by fire awaits you, Anne Askew!" repeated the king. "No mercy for the traitress who vilifies and scoffs at her king!"

CHAPTER V.

THE RIVALS.

AT the very moment when the king was pronouncing, in a voice almost exultant, Anne Askew's sentence of death, one of the king's cavaliers appeared on the threshold of the royal chamber and advanced toward the king.

He was a young man of noble and imposing appearance, whose lofty bearing contrasted strangely with the humble and submissive attitude of the rest of the courtiers. His tall, slim form was clad in a coat of mail glittering with gold; over his shoulders hung a velvet mantle decorated with a princely crown; and his head, covered with dark ringlets, was adorned with a cap embroidered with gold, from which a long white ostrich-feather drooped to his shoulder. His oval face presented the full type of aristocratic beauty; his cheeks were of a clear, transparent paleness; about his slightly pouting mouth played a smile, half contemptuous and half languid; the high, arched brow and delicately chiselled aquiline nose gave to his face an expression at once bold and thoughtful. The eyes alone were not in harmony with his face; they were neither languid like the mouth, nor pensive like the brow. All the fire and all the bold and wanton passion of youth shot from those dark, flashing eyes. When he looked down, he might have been taken for a completely worn-out, misanthropic aristocrat; but when he raised those ever-flashing and sparkling eyes, then was seen the young man full of dashing courage and ambitious desires, of passionate warmth and measureless pride.

He approached the king, as already stated, and as he bent his knee before him, he said in a full, pleasant voice: "Mercy, sire, mercy!"

The king stepped back in astonishment, and turned upon the bold speaker a look almost of amazement.

"Thomas Seymour!" said he. "Thomas, you have returned, then, and your first act is again an indiscretion and a piece of foolhardy rashness?"

The young man smiled. "I have returned," said he, "that is to say, I have had a sea-fight with the Scots and taken from them four men-of-war. With these I hastened hither to present them to you, my king and lord, as a wedding-gift, and just as I entered the anteroom I heard your voice pronouncing a sentence of death. Was it not natural, then, that I, who bring you tidings of a victory, should have the heart to utter a prayer for mercy, for which, as it seems, none of these noble and proud cavaliers could summon up courage?"

"Ah!" said the king, evidently relieved and fetching a deep breath, "then you knew not at all for whom and for what you were imploring pardon?"

"Yet!" said the young man, and his bold glance ran with an expression of contempt over the whole assembly—"yet, I saw at once who the condemned must be, for I saw this young maiden forsaken by all as if stricken by the plague, standing alone in the midst of this exalted and brave company. And you well know, my noble king, that at court one recognizes the condemned and those fallen into disgrace by this, that every one flies from them, and nobody has the courage to touch such a leper even with the tip of his finger!"

King Henry smiled. "Thomas Seymour, Earl of Sudley, you are now, as ever, imprudent and hasty," said he.

"You beg for mercy without once knowing whether she for whom you beg it is worthy of mercy."

"But I see that she is a woman," said the intrepid young earl. "And a woman is always worthy of mercy, and it becomes every knight to come forward as her defender, were it but to pay homage to her sex, so fair and so frail, and yet so noble and mighty. Therefore I beg mercy for this young maiden!"

Catharine had listened to the young earl with throbbing heart and flushed cheeks. It was the first time that she had seen him, and yet she felt for him a warm sympathy, an almost tender anxiety.

"He will plunge himself into ruin," murmured she; "he will not save Anne, but will make himself unhappy. My God, my God, have a little compassion and pity on my anguish!"

She now fixed her anxious gaze on the king, firmly resolved to rush to the help of the earl, who had so nobly and magnanimously interested himself in an innocent woman, should the wrath of her husband threaten him also. But, to her surprise, Henry's face was perfectly serene and contented.

Like the wild beast, that, following its instinct, seeks its bloody prey only so long as it is hungry, so King Henry felt satiated for the day. Yonder glared the fires about the stake, at which four heretics were burned; there stood the scaffold on which the Countess of Somerset had just been executed; and now, within this hour, he had already found another new victim for death. Moreover, Thomas Seymour had always been his favorite. His audacity, his liveliness, his energy, had always inspired the king with respect; and then, again, he so much resembled his sister, the beautiful Jane Seymour, Henry's third wife.

"I cannot grant you this favor, Thomas," said the king. "Justice must not be hindered in her course, and where she has passed sentence, mercy must not give her the lie; and it was the justice of your king which pronounced sentence at that moment. You were guilty, therefore, of a double wrong, for you not only besought mercy, but you also brought an accusation against my cavaliers. Do you really believe that, were this maiden's cause a just one, no knight would have been found for her?"

"Yes, I really believe it," cried the earl, with a laugh. "The sun of your favor had turned away from this poor girl, and in such a case your courtiers no longer see the figure wrapped in darkness."

"You are mistaken, my lord; I have seen it," suddenly said another voice, and a second cavalier advanced from the anteroom into the chamber. He approached the king, and, as he bent his knee before him, he said, in a loud, steady voice: "Sire, I also beg mercy for Anne Askew!"

At this moment was heard from that side of the room where the ladies stood, a low cry, and the pale, affrighted face of Lady Jane Douglas was for a moment raised above the heads of the other ladies. No one noticed it. All eyes were directed toward the group in the middle of the room; all looked with eager attention upon the king and these two young men, who dared protect one whom he had sentenced.

"Henry Howard, Earl of Surrey!" exclaimed the king; and now an expression of wrath passed over his countenance. "How! you, too, dare intercede for this girl? You, then, grudge Thomas Seymour the pre-eminence of being the most discreet man at my court?"

"I will not allow him, sire, to think that he is the bravest," replied the young man, as he fixed on Thomas Seymour a look of haughty defiance, which the other answered by a cold, disdainful smile.

"Oh," said he, with a shrug of his shoulders, "I willingly allow you, my dear Earl of Surrey, to tread behind me, at your convenience, the path, the safety of which I first tested at the peril of my life. You saw that I had not, as yet, lost either my head or my life in this reckless undertaking, and that has given you courage to follow my example. That is a new proof of your *prudent* valor, my Honorable Earl of Surrey, and I must praise you for it."

A hot flush suffused the noble face of the earl, his eyes shot lightning, and, trembling with rage, he laid his hand on his sword. "Praise from Thomas Seymour is——"

"Silence!" interposed the king, imperatively. "It must not be said that two of the noblest cavaliers of my court have turned the day, which should be one of festivity to all of you, into a day of contention. I command you, therefore, to be reconciled. Shake hands, my lords, and let your reconciliation be sincere. I, the king command it!"

The young men gazed at each other with looks of hatred and smothered rage, and their eyes spoke the insulting and defiant words which their lips durst no longer utter. The king had ordered, and, however great and powerful they might be, the king was to be obeyed. They, therefore, extended their hands to each other, and muttered a few low, unintelligible words, which might be, perhaps, a mutual apology, but which neither of them understood.

"And now, sire," said the Earl of Surrey, "now I venture to reiterate my prayer. Mercy, your majesty, mercy for Anne Askew!"

"And you, Thomas Seymour, do you also renew your petition?"

"No, I withdraw it. Earl Surrey protects her; I, therefore, retire, for without doubt she is a criminal; your majesty says so, and, therefore, it is so. It would ill become a Seymour to protect a person who has sinned against the king."

This new indirect attack on Earl Surrey seemed to make on all present a deep but very varied impression. Here, faces were seen to turn pale, and there, to light up with a malicious smile; here, compressed lips muttered words of threatening, there, a mouth opened to express approbation and agreement.

The king's brow was clouded and troubled; the arrow which Earl Sudley had shot with so skilful a hand had hit. The king, ever suspicious and distrustful, felt so much the more disquieted as he saw that the greater part of his cavaliers evidently reckoned themselves friends of Henry Howard, and that the number of Seymour's adherents was but trifling.

"These Howards are dangerous, and I will watch them carefully," said the king to himself; and for the first time his eye rested with a dark and hostile look on Henry Howard's noble countenance.

But Thomas Seymour, who wished only to make a thrust at his old enemy, had at the same time decided the fate of poor Anne Askew. It was now almost an impossibility to speak in her behalf, and to implore pardon for her was to become a partaker of her crime. Thomas Seymour had abandoned her, because, as traitress to her king, she had rendered herself unworthy of his protection. Who now would be so presumptuous as to still protect the traitress?

Henry Howard did it; he reiterated his supplication for Anne Askew's pardon. But the king's countenance grew darker and darker, and the courtiers watched with dread the coming of the moment when his wrath would dash in pieces the poor Earl of Surrey.

In the row of ladies also, here and there, a pale face was visible, and many a beautiful and beaming eye was dimmed with tears at the sight of this gallant and handsome cavalier, who was hazarding even his life for a woman.

"He is lost!" murmured Lady Jane Douglas; and, completely crushed and lifeless, she leaned for a moment against the wall. But she soon recovered herself, and her eye beamed with bold resolution. "I will try and save him!" she said to herself; and, with firm step, she advanced from the ladies' ranks, and approached the king.

A murmur of applause ran through the company, and all faces brightened and all eyes were bent approvingly on Lady Jane. They knew that she was the queen's friend, and an adherent of the new doctrine; it was, therefore, very marked and significant when she supported the Earl of Surrey in his magnanimous effort.

Lady Jane bowed her beautiful and haughty head before the king, and said, in her clear, silvery voice: " Sire, in the name of all the women, I also beseech you to pardon Anne Askew, because she is a woman. Lord Surrey has done so because a true knight can never be false to himself and his ever high and sacred obligation: to be the protector of those who are helpless and in peril is enough for him. A real gentleman asks not whether a woman is worthy of his protection; he grants it to her, simply because she is a woman, and needs his help. And while I, therefore, in the name of all the women, thank the Earl of Surrey for the assistance that he has been desirous to render to a woman, I unite my prayer with his, because it shall not be said that we women are always cowardly and timid, and never venture to hasten to the help of the distressed. I, therefore, ask mercy, sire, mercy for Anne Askew!"

"And I," said the queen, as she again approached the king, " I add my prayers to hers, sire. To-day is the feast of love, *my* festival, sire! To-day, then, let love and mercy prevail."

She looked at the king with so charming a smile, her eyes had an expression so radiant and happy, that the king could not withstand her.

He was, therefore, in the depths of his heart, ready to let the royal clemency prevail for this time; but he wanted a pretext for this, some way of bringing it about. He had solemnly vowed to pardon no heretic, and he might not break his word merely because the queen prayed for mercy.

"Well, then," said he, after a pause, " I will comply with your request. I will pardon Anne Askew, provided she will retract, and solemnly abjure all that she has said. Are you satisfied with that, Catharine?"

" I am satisfied," said she; sadly.

"And you, Lady Jane Douglas, and Henry Howard, Earl of Surrey?"

"We are satisfied."

All eyes were now turned again upon Anne Askew, who, although every one was occupied by her concerns, had been entirely overlooked and left unnoticed.

Nor had she taken any more notice of the company than they of her. She had scarcely observed what was going on about her. She stood leaning against the open door leading to the balcony, and gazed at the flaming horizon. Her soul was with those pious martyrs, for whom she was sending up her heart-felt prayers to God, and whom she, in her feverish exaltation, envied their death of torture. Entirely borne away from the present, she had heard neither the petitions of those who protected her, nor the king's reply.

A hand laid upon her shoulder roused her from her reverie.

It was Catharine, the young queen, who stood near her.

"Anne Askew," said she, in a hurried whisper, "if your life is dear to you, comply with the king's demand."

She seized the young girl's hand, and led her to the king.

"Sire," said she, in a full voice, "forgive the exalted and impassioned agony of a poor girl, who has now, for the first time, been witness of an execution, and whose mind has been so much impressed by it that she is scarcely conscious of the mad and criminal words that she has uttered before you! Pardon her, then, your majesty, for she is prepared cheerfully to retract."

A cry of amazement burst from Anne's lips, and her eyes flashed with anger, as she dashed the queen's hand away from her.

"I retract!" exclaimed she, with a contemptuous smile. "Never, my lady, never! No! as sure as I hope for God to be gracious to me in my last hour, I retract not! It is true, it was agony and horror that made me speak; but what I have spoken is yet, nevertheless, the truth. Horror caused me to speak, and forced me to show my soul undisguised. No, I retract not! I tell you, they who have been executed over yonder are holy martyrs, who have ascended to God, there to enter an accusation against their royal hangman. Ay, they are holy, for eternal truth had illumined their souls, and it beamed about their faces bright as the flames of the fagots into which the murderous hand of an unrighteous judge had cast them. Ah, I must retract! I, forsooth, am to do as did Shaxton, the miserable and unfaithful servant of his God, who, from fear of earthly death, denied the eternal truth, and in blaspheming pusillanimity perjured himself concerning the holy doctrine.* King Henry, I say unto you, beware of dissemblers and perjurers; beware of your own haughty and arrogant thoughts. The blood of martyrs cries to Heaven against you, and the time will come when God will be as merciless to you as you have been to the noblest of your subjects! You deliver them over to the murderous flames, because they will not believe what the priests of Baal preach; because they will not believe in the real transubstantiation of the chalice; because they deny that the natural body of Christ is, after the sacrament, contained in the sacrament, no matter whether the priest be a good or a bad man.† You give them over to the executioner, because they serve the truth, and are faithful followers of the Lord their God!"

"And you share the views of these people whom you call martyrs?" asked the king, as Anne Askew now paused for a moment and struggled for breath.

"Yes, I share them!"

"You deny, then, the truth of the six articles?"

"I deny them!"

"You do not see in me the head of the Church?"

"God only is Head and Lord of the Church!"

A pause followed—a fearful, awful pause.

Every one felt that for this poor young girl there was no hope, no possible escape; that her doom was irrevocably sealed.

There was a smile on the king's countenance.

* Burnet, vol. i, p. 341.   † Ibid.

The courtiers knew that smile, and feared it yet more than the king's raging wrath.

When the king thus smiled, he had taken his resolve. Then there was with him no possible vacillation or hesitation, but the sentence of death was resolved on, and his bloodthirsty soul rejoiced over a new victim.

"My Lord Bishop of Winchester," said the king, at length, " come hither."

Gardiner drew near and placed himself by Anne Askew, who gazed at him with angry, contemptuous looks.

"In the name of the law I command you to arrest this heretic, and hand her over to the spiritual court," continued the king. "She is damned and lost. She shall be punished as she deserves!"

Gardiner laid his hand on Anne Askew's shoulder. "In the name of the law of God, I arrest you!" said he, solemnly.

Not a word more was spoken. The lord chief justice had silently followed a sign from Gardiner, and touching Anne Askew with his staff, ordered the soldiers to conduct her thence.

With a smile, Anne Askew offered them her hand, and surrounded by the soldiers and followed by the Bishop of Winchester and the lord chief justice, walked erect and proudly out of the room.

The courtiers had divided and opened a passage for Anne and her attendants. Now their ranks closed again, as the sea closes and flows calmly on when it has just received a corpse. To them all Anne Askew was already a corpse, as one buried. The waves had swept over her and all was again serene and bright.

The king extended his hand to his young wife, and, bending down, whispered in her ear a few words, which nobody understood, but which made the young queen tremble and blush.

The king, who observed this, laughed and impressed a kiss on her forehead. Then he turned to his court:

"Now, good-night, my lords and gentlemen," said he, with a gracious inclination of the head. "The feast is at an end, and we need rest."

"Forget not the Princess Elizabeth," whispered Archbishop Cranmer, as he took leave of Catharine, and pressed to his lips her proffered hand.

"I will not forget her," murmured Catharine, and, with throbbing heart and trembling with inward dread, she saw them all retire, and leave her alone with the king.

CHAPTER VI.

THE INTERCESSION.

"AND now, Kate," said the king, when all had withdrawn, and he was again alone with her, "now let us forget everything, save that we love each other."

He embraced her and with ardor pressed her to his breast. Wearied to death, she bowed her head on his shoulder and lay there like a shattered rose, completely broken, completely passive.

"You give me no kiss, Kate?" said Henry, with a smile. "Are you then yet angry with me that I did not comply with your first request? But what would you have me do, child? How, indeed, shall I keep the crimson of my royal mantle always fresh and bright, unless I continually dye it anew in the blood of criminals? Only he who punishes and destroys is truly a king, and trembling mankind will acknowledge him as such. The tenderhearted and gracious king it despises, and his pitiful weakness it laughs to scorn. Bah! Humanity is such a wretched, miserable thing, that it only respects and acknowledges him who makes it tremble. And people are such contemptible, foolish children, that they have respect only for him who makes them feel the lash daily, and every now and then whips a few of them to death. Look at me, Kate: where is there a king who has reigned longer and more happily than I? whom the people love more and obey better than me? This arises from the fact that I have already signed more than two hundred death-warrants,* and because every one believes that, if he does not obey me, I will without delay send his head after the others!"

"Oh, you say you love me," murmured Catharine, "and you speak only of blood and death while you are with me."

The king laughed. "You are right, Kate," said he, "and yet, believe me, there are other thoughts slumbering in the depths of my heart, and could you look down into it, you would not accuse me of coldness and unkindness. I love you truly, my dear, virgin bride, and, to prove it, you shall now ask a favor of me. Yes, Kate, make me a request, and, whatever it may be, I pledge you my royal word, it shall be granted you. Now, Kate, think, what will please you? Will you have brilliants, or a castle by the sea, or, perhaps, a yacht? Would you like fine horses, or it may be some one has offended you, and you would like his head? If so, tell me, Kate, and you shall have his head; a wink from me, and it drops at your feet. For I am almighty and all-powerful, and no one is so innocent and pure, that my will cannot find in him a crime which will cost him his life. Speak, then, Kate; what would you have? What will gladden your heart?"

Catharine smiled in spite of her secret fear and horror.

"Sire," said she, "you have given me so many brilliants, that I can shine and glitter with them, as night does with her stars. If you give me a castle by the sea, that is, at the same time, banishing me from Whitehall and your presence; I wish, therefore, for no castle of

* Tytler, p. 428. Leti, vol. i, p. 187.

my own. I wish only to dwell with you in your castles, and my king's abode shall be my only residence."

"Beautifully and wisely spoken," said the king; "I will remember these words if ever your enemies endeavor to send you to a dwelling and a castle other than that which your king occupies. The Tower is also a castle, Kate, but I give you my royal word you shall never occupy that castle. You want no treasures and no castles? It is, then, somebody's head that you demand of me?"

"Yes, sire, it is the head of some one!"

"Ah, I guessed it, then," said the king with a laugh. "Now speak, my little bloodthirsty queen, whose head will you have? Who shall be brought to the block?"

"Sire, it is true I ask you for the head of a person," said Catharine, in a tender, earnest tone, "but I wish not that head to fall, but to be lifted up. I beg you for a human life—not to destroy it, but, on the contrary, to adorn it with happiness and joy. I wish to drag no one to prison, but to restore to one, dearly beloved, the freedom, happiness, and splendid position which belong to her. Sire, you have permitted me to ask a favor. Now, then, I beg you to call the Princess Elizabeth to court. Let her reside with us at Whitehall. Allow her to be ever near me, and share my happiness and glory. Sire, only yesterday the Princess Elizabeth was far above me in rank and position, but since your all-powerful might and grace have to-day elevated me above all other women, I may now love the Princess Elizabeth as my sister and dearest friend. Grant me this, my king! Let Elizabeth come to us at Whitehall, and enjoy at our court the honor which is her due." *

The king did not reply immediately; but in his quiet and smiling air one could read that his young consort's request had not angered him. Something like an emotion flitted across his face, and his eyes were for a moment dimmed with tears.

* Leti, vol. i, p. 147. Tytler, p. 410.

Perhaps just then a pale, soul-harrowing phantom passed before his mind, and a glance at the past showed him the beautiful and unfortunate mother * of Elizabeth, whom he had sentenced to a cruel death at the hands of the public executioner, and whose last word nevertheless was a blessing and a message of love for him.

He passionately seized Catharine's hand and pressed it to his lips. "I thank you! You are unselfish and generous. That is a very rare quality, and I shall always highly esteem you for it. But you are also brave and courageous, for you have dared what nobody before you has dared; you have twice on the same evening interceded for one condemned and one fallen into disgrace. The fortunate, and those favored by me, have always had many friends, but I have never yet seen that the unfortunate and the exiled have also found friends. You are different from these miserable, cringing courtiers; different from this deceitful and trembling crowd, that with chattering teeth fall down and worship me as their god and lord; different from these pitiful, good-for-nothing mortals, who call themselves my people, and who allow me to yoke them up, because they are like the ox, which is obedient and serviceable, only because he is so stupid as not to know his own might and strength. Ah, believe me, Kate, I would be a milder and more merciful king, if the people were not such an utterly stupid and contemptible thing; a dog, which is so much the more submissive and gentle the more you maltreat him. You, Kate, you are different, and I am glad of it. You know, I have forever banished Elizabeth from my court and from my heart, and still you intercede for her. That is noble of you, and I love you for it, and grant you your request. And that you may see how I love and trust you, I will now reveal to you a secret: I have long since wished to have Elizabeth with me, but I was ashamed, even to myself, of this weakness. I have long yearned once again

* Anne Boleyn.

to look into my daughter's large deep eyes, to be a kind
and tender father to her, and make some amends to her
for the wrong I perhaps may have done to her mother.
For sometimes, in sleepless nights, Anne's beautiful face
comes up before me and gazes at me with mournful, mild
look, and my whole heart shudders before it. But I could
not confess this to anybody, for then they might say that I
repented what I had done. A king must be infallible, like
God himself, and never, through regret or desire to compensate, confess that he is a weak, erring mortal, like
others. You see why I repressed my longing and parental
tenderness, which was suspected by no one, and appeared
to be a heartless father, because nobody would help me
and make it easy for me to be a tender father. Ah, these
courtiers! They are so stupid, that they can understand
only just what is echoed in our words; but what our heart
says, and longs for, of that they know nothing. But you
know, Kate; you are an acute woman, and a high-minded
one besides. Come, Kate, a thankful father gives you
this kiss, and this, ay, this, your husband gives you, my
beautiful, charming queen."

CHAPTER VII.

HENRY THE EIGHTH AND HIS WIVES.

THE calm of night had now succeeded to the tempest
of the day, and after so much bustle, festivity, and rejoicing, deep quiet now reigned in the palace of Whitehall,
and throughout London. The happy subjects of King
Henry might, without danger, remain for a few hours at
least in their houses, and behind closed shutters and bolted doors, either slumber and dream, or give themselves
to their devotional exercises, on account of which they had

that day, perhaps, been denounced as malefactors. They might, for a few hours, resign themselves to the sweet, blissful dream of being freemen untrammelled in belief and thought. For King Henry slept, and likewise Gardiner and the lord chancellor had closed their watchful, prying, devout, murderous eyes, and reposed awhile from the Christian employment of ferreting out heretics.

And like the king, the entire households of both their majesties were also asleep and resting from the festivities of the royal wedding-day, which, in pomp and splendor, by far surpassed the five preceding marriages.

It appeared, however, as though not all the court officials were taking rest, and following the example of the king. For in a chamber, not far from that of the royal pair, one could perceive, from the bright beams streaming from the windows, in spite of the heavy damask curtains which veiled them, that the lights were not yet extinguished; and he who looked more closely would have observed that now and then a human shadow was portrayed upon the curtain.

So the occupant of this chamber had not yet gone to rest, and harassing must have been the thoughts which cause him to move so restlessly to and fro.

This chamber was occupied by Lady Jane Douglas, first maid of honor to the queen. The powerful influence of Gardiner, Bishop of Winchester, had seconded Catharine's wish to have near her the dear friend of her youth, and, without suspecting it, the queen had given a helping hand to bring nearer to their accomplishment the schemes which the hypocritical Gardiner was directing against her.

For Catharine knew not what changes had taken place in the character of her friend in the four years in which she had not seen her. She did not suspect how fatal her sojourn in the strongly Romish city of Dublin had been to the easily impressible mind of her early playmate, and how much it had transformed her whole being.

Lady Jane, once so sprightly and gay, had become a bigoted Romanist, who, with fanatical zeal, believed that she was serving God when she served the Church, and paid unreserved obedience to her priests.

Lady Jane Douglas had therefore—thanks to her fanaticism and the teachings of the priests—become a complete dissembler. She could smile, while in her heart she secretly brooded over hatred and revenge. She could kiss the lips of those whose destruction she had perhaps just sworn. She could preserve a harmless, innocent air, while she observed everything, and took notice of every breath, every smile, every movement of the eyelashes.

Hence it was very important for Gardiner, Bishop of Winchester, to bring his "friend" of the queen to court, and make of this disciple of Loyola an ally and friend.

Lady Jane Douglas was alone; and, pacing up and down her room, she thought over the events of the day.

Now, that no one was observing her, she had laid aside that gentle, serious mien, which one was wont to see about her at other times; her countenance betrayed in rapid changes all the various sad and cheerful, tempestuous and tender feelings which agitated her.

She who had hitherto had only *one* aim before her eyes, to serve the Church, and to consecrate her whole life to this service; she whose heart had been hitherto open only to ambition and devotion, she felt to-day wholly new and never-susupected feelings springing up within her. A new thought had entered into her life, the woman was awakened in her, and beat violently at that heart which devotion had overlaid with a hard coating.

She had tried to collect herself in prayer, and to fill her soul so entirely with the idea of God and her Church, that no earthly thought or desire could find place therein. But ever and again arose before her mind's eye the noble countenance of Henry Howard, ever and again she fancied that she heard his earnest, melodious voice, which made her heart shake and tremble like a magical incantation.

She had at first struggled against these sweet fancies, which forced upon her such strange and undreamed-of thoughts; but at length the woman in her got the better of the fanatical Romanist, and, dropping into a seat, she surrendered herself to her dreams and fancies.

"Has he recognized me?" asked she of herself. "Does he still remember that a year ago we saw each other daily at the king's court in Dublin?"

"But no," added she mournfully, "he knows nothing of it. He had then eyes and sense only for his young wife. Ah, and she was beautiful and lovely as one of the Graces. But I, am not I also beautiful? and have not the noblest cavaliers paid me homage, and sighed for me in unavailing love? How comes it, then, that where I would please, there I am always overlooked? How comes it, that the only two men, for whose notice I ever cared, have never shown any preference for me? I felt that I loved Henry Howard, but this love was a sin, for the Earl of Surrey was married. I therefore tore my heart from him by violence, and gave it to God, because the only man whom I could love did not return my affection. But even God and devotion are not able to entirely fill a woman's heart. In my breast there was still room for ambition; and since I could not be a happy wife, I would at least be a powerful queen. Oh, everything was so well devised, so nicely arranged! Gardiner had already spoken of me to the king, and inclined him to his plan; and while I was hastening at his call from Dublin hither, this little Catharine Parr comes between and snatches him from me, and overturns all our schemes. I will never forgive her. I will find a way to revenge myself. I will force her to leave this place, which belongs to me, and if there is no other way for it, she must go the way of the scaffold, as did Catharine Howard. I will be Queen of England, I will——"

She suddenly interrupted her soliloquy, and listened. She thought she heard a slight knock at the door.

She was not mistaken; this knock was now repeated, and indeed with a peculiar, significant stroke.

"It is my father!" said Lady Jane, and, as she resumed again her grave and quiet air, she proceeded to open the door.

"Ah, you expected me, then?" said Lord Archibald Douglas, kissing his daughter's forehead.

"Yes, I expected you, my father," replied Lady Jane with a smile. "I knew that you would come to communicate to me your experiences and observations during the day, and to give me directions for the future."

The earl seated himself on the ottoman, and drew his daughter down by him.

"No one can overhear us, can they?"

"Nobody, my father! My women are sleeping in the fourth chamber from here, and I have myself fastened the intervening doors. The anteroom through which you came is, as you know, entirely empty, and nobody can conceal himself there. It remains, then, only to fasten the door leading thence into the corridor, in order to be secure from interruption."

She hastened into the anteroom to fasten the door.

"Now, my father, we are secure from listeners," said she, as she returned and resumed her place on the ottoman.

"And the walls, my child? know you whether or no the walls are safe?· You look at me with an expression of doubt and surprise! My God, what a harmless and innocent little maiden you still are! Have I not constantly reiterated the great and wise lesson, ' Doubt everything and mistrust everything, even what you see.' He who will make his fortune at court, must first of all mistrust everybody, and consider everybody his enemy, whom he is to flatter, because he can do him harm, and whom he is to hug and kiss, until in some happy embrace he can either plunge a dagger into his breast wholly unobserved, or pour poison into his mouth. Trust neither men nor walls,

Jane, for I tell you, however smooth and innocent both may appear, still there may be found an ambuscade behind the smooth exterior. But I will for the present believe that these walls are innocent, and conceal no listeners. I will believe it, because I know this room. Those were fine and charming days in which I became acquainted with it. Then I was yet young and handsome, and King Henry's sister was not yet married to the King of Scotland, and we loved each other so dearly. Ah, I could relate to you wonderful stories of those happy days. I could——"

"But, my dear father," interrupted Lady Jane, secretly trembling at the terrible prospect of being forced to listen yet again to the story of his youthful love, which she had already heard times without number, "but, my dear father, doubtless you have not come hither so late at night in order to relate to me what I—forgive me, my lord—what I long since knew. You will rather communicate to me what your keen and unerring glance has discovered here."

"It is true," said Lord Douglas, sadly. "I now sometimes become loquacious—a sure sign that I am growing old. I have, by no means, come here to speak of the past, but of the present. Let us, then, speak of it. Ah, I have to-day perceived much, seen much, observed much, and the result of my observations is, you will be King Henry's seventh wife."

"Impossible, my lord!" exclaimed Lady Jane, whose countenance, in spite of her will, assumed an expression of delight.

Her father remarked it. "My child," said he, "I observe that you have not yet your features entirely under your control. You aimed just now, for example, to play the coy and humble, and yet your face had the expression of proud satisfaction. But this by the way! The principal thing is, you will be King Henry's seventh wife! But in order to become so, there is need for great heedfulness, a complete knowledge of present relations, constant observation of all persons, impenetrable dissimulation, and lastly, above all things, a very intimate and profound knowledge of the king, of the history of his reign, and of his character. Do you possess this knowledge? Know you what it is to wish to become King Henry's seventh wife, and how you must begin in order to attain this? Have you studied Henry's character?"

"A little, perhaps, but certainly not sufficiently. For, as you know, my lord, worldly matters have lain upon my heart less than the holy Church, to whose service I have consecrated myself, and to which I would have presented my whole being, my whole soul, my whole heart, as a sacrifice, had not you yourself determined otherwise concerning me. Ah, my father, had I been allowed to follow my inclination, I would have retired into a convent in Scotland in order to spend my life in quiet contemplation and pious penances, and close my soul and ear to every profane sound. But my wishes have not been regarded; and, by the mouth of His venerable and holy priests, God has commanded me to remain in the world, and take upon myself the yoke of greatness and regal splendor. If I then struggle and strive to become queen, this is done, not because the vain pomp and glory allure me, but solely because through me the Church, out of which is no salvation, may find a fulcrum to operate on this weak and fickle king, and because I am to bring him back again to the only true faith."

"Very well played!" cried her father, who had stared her steadily in the face while she was speaking. "On my word, very well played. Everything was in perfect harmony, the gesticulation, the play of the eyes, and the voice. My daughter, I withdraw my censure. You have perfect control over yourself. But let us speak of King Henry. We will now subject him to a thorough analysis, and no fibre of his heart, no atom of his brain shall remain unnoticed by us. We will observe him in his domestic, his political, and his religious life, and get a perfectly clear view of every peculiarity of his character, in order that we may deal with him accordingly. Let us, then, speak first of his wives. Their lives and deaths afford you excellent finger-posts; for I do not deny that it is an extremely difficult and dangerous undertaking to be Henry's consort. There is needed for it much personal courage and very great self-control. Know you which, of all his wives, possessed these in the highest degree? It was his first consort, *Catharine of Aragon!* By Heaven, she was a sensible woman, and born a queen! Henry, avaricious as he was, would gladly have given the best jewel in his crown, if he could have detected but a shadow, the slightest trace of unfaithfulness in her. But there was absolutely no means of sending this woman to the scaffold, and at that time he was as yet too cowardly and too virtuous to put her out of the way by poison. He, therefore, endured her long, until she was an old woman with gray hairs, and disagreeable for his eyes to look upon. So after he had been married to her seventeen years, the good, pious king was all at once seized with a conscientious scruple, and because he had read in the Bible, ' Thou shalt not marry thy sister,' dreadful pangs of conscience came upon the noble and crafty monarch. He fell upon his knees and beat his breast, and cried: ' I have committed a great sin; for I have married my brother's wife, and consequently my sister. But I will make amends for it. I will dissolve this adulterous marriage!'—Do you know, child, why he would dissolve it?"

"Because he loved Anne Boleyn!" said Jane, with a smile.

"Perfectly correct! Catharine had grown old, and Henry was still a young man, and his blood shot through his veins like streams of fire. But he was yet somewhat virtuous and timid, and the main peculiarity of his character was as yet undeveloped. *He was not yet bloodthirsty,* that is to say, he had not yet licked blood. But you will see how with each new queen his desire for blood increased, till at length it has now become a wasting disease. Had he then had the system of lies that he now has, he would somehow have bribed a slanderer, who would have declared that he was Catharine's lover. But he was yet so innocent; he wanted yet to gratify his darling lusts in a perfectly legal way. So Anne Boleyn must become his queen, that he might love her. And in order to attain this, he threw down the glove to the whole world, became an enemy to the pope, and set himself in open opposition to the holy head of the Church. Because the Holy Father would not dissolve his marriage, King Henry became an apostate and atheist. He constituted himself head of his Church, and, by virtue of his authority as such, he declared his marriage with Catharine of Aragon null and void. He said that he had not in his heart given his consent to this marriage, and that it had not consequently been properly consummated.* It is true, Catharine had in the Princess Mary a living witness of the consummation of her marriage, but what did the enamored and selfish king care about that? Princess Mary was declared a bastard, and the queen was now to be nothing more than the widow of the Prince of Wales. It was strictly forbidden to longer give the title and to show the honor due to a queen, to the woman who for seventeen years had been Queen of England, and had been treated and honored as such. No one was permitted to call her anything but the Princess of Wales; and that nothing might disturb the good people or the noble queen herself in this illusion, Catharine was banished from the court and exiled to a castle, which she had once occupied as consort of Arthur, Prince of Wales. And Henry likewise allowed her only the attendance and pension which the law appoints to the widow of the Prince of Wales.†

"I have ever held this to be one of the most prudent and subtle acts of our exalted king, and in the whole history of this divorce the king conducted himself with admirable consistency and resolution. But this is to say, he

* Burnet, vol. i, p. 37. † Burnet, vol. i, p. 120.

was excited by opposition. Mark this, then, my child, for this is the reason why I have spoken to you of these things so much at length. Mark this, then: King Henry is every way entirely unable to bear contradiction, or to be subjected to restraint. If you wish to win him to any purpose, you must try to draw him from it; you must surround it with difficulties and hinderances. Therefore show yourself coy and indifferent; that will excite him. Do not court his looks; then will he seek to encounter yours. And when finally he loves you, dwell so long on your virtue and your conscience, that at length Henry, in order to quiet your conscience, will send this troublesome Catharine Parr to the block, or do as he did with Catharine of Aragon, and declare that he did not mentally give his consent to this marriage, and therefore Catharine is no queen, but only Lord Neville's widow. Ah, since he made himself high-priest of his Church, there is no impediment for him in matters of this kind, for only God is mightier than he.

"The beautiful Anne Boleyn, Henry's second wife, proved this. I have seen her often, and I tell you, Jane, she was of wondrous beauty. Whoever looked upon her, could not but love her, and he whom she smiled upon felt himself fascinated and glorified. When she had borne to the king the Princess Elizabeth, I heard him say, that he had attained the summit of his happiness, the goal of his wishes, for the queen had borne him a daughter, and so there was a regular and legitimate successor to his throne. But this happiness lasted only a brief time.

"The king conceived one day that Anne Boleyn was not, as he had hitherto believed, the most beautiful woman in the world; but that there were women still more beautiful at his court, who therefore had a stronger vocation to become Queen of England. He had seen Jane Seymour, and she without doubt was handsomer than Anne Boleyn, for she was not as yet the king's consort, and there was an obstacle to his possession of her—the Queen Anne Boleyn. This obstacle must be go out of the way.

"Henry, by virtue of his plentitude of power, might again have been divorced from his wife, but he did not like to repeat himself, he wished to be always original; and no one was to be allowed to say that his divorces were only the cloak of his capricious lewdness.

"He had divorced Catharine of Aragon on account of conscientious scruples; therefore, some other means must be devised for Anne Boleyn.

"The shortest way to be rid of her was the scaffold. Why should not Anne travel that road, since so many had gone it before her? for a new force had entered into the king's life: *the tiger had licked blood!* His instinct was aroused, and he recoiled no more from those crimson rills which flowed in the veins of his subjects.

"He had given Lady Anne Boleyn the crimson mantle of royalty, why then should she not give him her crimson blood? For this there was wanted only a pretext, and this was soon found. Lady Rochfort was Jane Seymour's aunt, and she found some men, of whom she asserted that they had been lovers of the fair Anne Boleyn. She, as the queen's first lady of the bed-chamber, could of course give the most minute particulars concerning the matter, and the king believed her. He believed her, though these four pretended lovers of the queen, who were executed for their crime, all, with the exception of a single one, asseverated that Anne Boleyn was innocent, and that they had never been in her presence. The only one who accused the queen of illicit intercourse with him was James Smeaton, a musician.* But he had been promised his life for this confession. However, it was not thought advisable to keep this promise, for fear that, when confronted with the queen, he might not have the strength to sustain his assertion. But not to be altogether unthankful to him for so useful a confession, they showed him the favor of

* Tytler.

not executing him with the axe, but the more agreeable and easier death of hanging was vouchsafed to him.*

"So the fair and lovely Anne Boleyn must lay her head upon the block. The day on which this took place, the king had ordered a great hunt, and early that morning we rode out to Epping Forest. The king was at first unusually cheerful and humorous, and he commanded me to ride near him, and tell him something from the *chronique scandaleuse* of our court. He laughed at my spiteful remarks, and the worse I calumniated, the merrier was the king. Finally, we halted; the king had talked and laughed so much that he had at last become hungry. So he encamped under an oak, and, in the midst of his suite and his dogs, he took a breakfast, which pleased him very much, although he had now become a little quieter and more silent, and sometimes turned his face toward the direction of London with visible restlessness and anxiety. But suddenly was heard from that direction the dull sound of a cannon. We all knew that this was the signal which was to make known to the king that Anne Boleyn's head had fallen. We knew it, and a shudder ran through our whole frames. The king alone smiled, and as he arose and took his weapon from my hand, he said, with cheerful face, 'It is done, the business is finished. Unleash the dogs, and let us follow the boar.' †

"That," said Lord Douglas, sadly, "that was King Henry's funeral discourse over his charming and innocent wife."

"Do you regret her, my father?" asked Lady Jane, with surprise. "But Anne Boleyn was, it seems to me, an enemy of our Church, and an adherent of the accursed new doctrine."

Her father shrugged his shoulders almost contemptu-

* Burnet, vol. i, p. 205.
† The king's very words. Tytler, p. 383. The oak under which this took place is still pointed out in Epping Forest, and in fact is not less remarkable as the oak of Charles II.

ously. "That did not prevent Lady Anne from being one of the fairest and loveliest women of Old England. And, besides, much as she inclined to the new doctrine, she did us essential good service, for she it was who bore the blame of *Thomas More's death*. Since he had not approved her marriage with the king, she hated him, as the king hated him because he would not take the oath of supremacy. Henry, however, would have spared him, for, at that time, he still possessed some respect for learning and virtue, and Thomas More was so renowned a scholar that the king held him in reverence. But Anne Boleyn demanded his death, and so Thomas More must be executed. Oh, believe me, Jane, that was an important and sad hour for all England, the hour when Thomas More laid his head upon the block. We only, we gay people in the palace of Whitehall, we were cheerful and merry. We were dancing a new kind of dance, the music of which was written by the king himself, for you know the king is not merely an author, but also a composer, and as he now writes pious books, so he then composed dances.* That evening, after we had danced till we were tired, we played cards. Just as I had won a few guineas from the king, the lieutenant of the Tower came with the tidings that the execution was over, and gave us a description of the last moments of the great scholar. The king threw down his cards, and, turning an angry look on Anne Boleyn, said, in an agitated voice, 'You are to blame for the death of this man!' Then he arose and withdrew to his apartments, whither no one was permitted to follow him, not even the queen.† You see, then, that Anne Boleyn had a claim on our gratitude, for the death of Thomas More delivered Old England from another great peril. Melanchthon and Bucer, and with them several of the greatest pulpit orators of Germany, had set out to come to London, and, as delegates of the Germanic Protestant princes, to nominate the king as

* Granger's "Biographical History of England," vol. i, p. 137.
† Tytler, p. 354.

head of their alliance. But the terrible news of the execution of their friend frightened them back, and caused them to return when half-way here.*

"Peace, then, to the ashes of unhappy Anne Boleyn! However, she was avenged too, avenged on her successor and rival, for whose sake she was made to mount the scaffold—avenged on Jane Seymour."

"But she was the king's beloved wife," said Jane, "and when she died the king mourned for her two years."

"He mourned!" exclaimed Lord Douglas, contemptuously. "He has mourned for all his wives. Even for Anne Boleyn he put on mourning, and in his white mourning apparel, the day after Anne's execution, he led Jane Seymour to the marriage altar.† This outward mourning, what does it signify? Anne Boleyn also mourned for Catharine of Aragon, whom she had pushed from the throne. For eight weeks she was seen in yellow mourning on account of Henry's first wife; but Anne Boleyn was a shrewd woman, and she knew very well that the yellow mourning dress was exceedingly becoming to her." ‡

"But the king's mourning was not merely external," said Lady Jane. "He mourned really, for it was two years before he resolved on a new marriage."

Earl Douglas laughed. "But he cheered himself during these two years of widowhood with a very beautiful mistress, the French Marchioness de Montreuil, and he would have married her had not the prudent beauty preferred returning to France, because she found it altogether too dangerous to become Henry's consort. For it is not to be denied, a baleful star hovers over Henry's queens, and none of them has descended from the throne in a natural way."

"Yet, father, Jane Seymour did so in a very natural way; she died in childbed."

"Well, yes, in childbed. And yet by no natural death,

---

* Tytler, p. 357.   Leti, vol. i, p. 180.
† Granger, vol. i, p.119.   ‡ Ibid.

for she could have been saved. But Henry did not wish to save her. His love had already grown cool, and when the physicians asked him whether they should save the mother or the child, he replied, 'Save the child, and let the mother die. I can get wives enough.'* Ah, my daughter, I hope you may not die such a natural death as Jane Seymour did, for whom, as you say, the king mourned two years. But after that period, something new, something altogether extraordinary happened to the king. He fell in love with a picture, and because, in his proud self-conceit, he was convinced that the fine picture which Holbein had made of *him*, was not at all flattered, but entirely true to nature, it did not occur to him that Holbein's likeness of the Princess Anne of Cleves might be somewhat flattered, and not altogether faithful. So the king fell in love with a picture, and sent ambassadors to Germany to bring the original of the portrait to England as his bride. He himself went to meet her at Rochester, where she was to land. Ah, my child, I have witnessed many queer and droll things in my eventful life, but the scene at Rochester, however, is among my most spicy recollections. The king was as enthusiastic as a poet, and deep in love as a youth of twenty, and so began our romantic wedding-trip, on which Henry disguised himself and took part in it, assuming the name of my cousin. As the king's master of horse, I was honored with the commission of carrying to the young queen the greeting of her ardent husband, and begging her to receive the knight, who would deliver to her a present from the king. She granted my request with a grin which made visible a frightful row of yellow teeth. I opened the door, and invited the king to enter. Ah, you ought to have witnessed that scene! It is the only farcial passage in the bloody tragedy of Henry's married life. You should have seen with what hasty impatience the king rushed in, then suddenly, at the sight of her, staggered back and stared at

* Burnet.

the princess. Slowly retiring, he silently thrust into my hand the rich present that he had brought, while at the same time he threw a look of flaming wrath on Lord Cromwell, who had brought him the portrait of the princess and won him to this marriage. The romantic, ardent lover vanished with this look at his beloved. He approached the princess again—this time not as a cavalier, but, with harsh and hasty words, he told her he was the king himself. He bade her welcome in a few words, and gave her a cold, formal embrace. He then hastily took my hand and drew me out of the room, beckoning the rest to follow him. And when at length we were out of the atmosphere of this poor ugly princess, and far enough away from her, the king, with angry countenance, said to Cromwell: 'Call you that a beauty? She is a Flanders mare, but no princess.' *
Anne's ugliness was surely given her of God, that by it, the Church, in which alone is salvation, might be delivered from the great danger which threatened it. For had Anne of Cleves, the sister, niece, granddaughter and aunt of all the Protestant princes of Germany, been beautiful, incalculable danger would have threatened our church. The king could not overcome his repugnance, and again his conscience, which always appeared to be most tender and scrupulous, when it was farthest from it and most regardless, must come to his aid.

"The king declared that he had been only in appearance, not in his innermost conscience, disposed to this marriage, from which he now shrank back, because it would be, properly speaking, nothing more than perfidy, perjury, and bigamy. For Anne's father had once betrothed her to the son of the Duke of Lorraine, and had solemnly pledged him his word to give her as a wife to the young duke as soon as she was of age; rings had been exchanged and the marriage contract already drawn up. Anne of Cleves, therefore, was virtually already married, and Henry, with his tender conscience, could not make one already married

* Burnet, p. 174. Tytler, p. 417.

his wife.* He made her, therefore, his sister, and gave her the palace at Richmond for a residence, in case she wished to remain in England. She accepted it; her blood, which crept coldly and quietly through her veins, did not rise at the thought of being despised and repudiated. She accepted it, and remained in England.

"She was rejected because she was ugly; and now the king selected Catharine Howard for his fifth consort, because she was pretty. Of this marriage I know but little to tell you, for, at that time, I had already gone to Dublin as minister, whither you soon followed me. Catharine was very beautiful, and the king's heart, now growing old, once more flamed high with youthful love. He loved her more warmly than any other of his wives. He was so happy in her that, kneeling down publicly in the church, with a loud voice he thanked God for the happiness which his beautiful young queen afforded him. But this did not last long. Even while the king was extolling it, his happiness had reached its highest point, and the next day he was dashed down into the abyss. I speak without poetical exaggeration, my child. The day before, he thanked God for his happiness, and the next morning Catharine Howard was already imprisoned and accused, as an unfaithful wife, a shameless strumpet.† More than seven lovers had preceded her royal spouse, and some of them had accompanied her even on the progress through Yorkshire, which she made with the king her husband. This time it was no pretence, for he had not yet had time to fall in love with another woman, and Catharine well knew how to enchain him and ever' to kindle new flames within him. But just because he loved her, he could not forgive her for having deceived him. In love there is so much cruelty and hatred; and Henry, who but yesterday lay at her feet, burned to-day with rage and jealousy, as yesterday with love and rapture. In his rage, however, he still loved her, and when he held in his hand indubitable proof of her

* Burnet. † Tytler, p. 432.

guilt, he wept like a child. But since he could no longer be her lover, he would be her hangman; since she had spotted the crimson of his royal mantle, he would dye it afresh with her own crimson blood. And he did so. Catharine Howard was forced to lay her beautiful head upon the block, as Anne Boleyn had done before her; and Anne's death was now once more avenged. Lady Rochfort had been Anne Boleyn's accuser, and her testimony had brought that queen to the scaffold; but now she was convicted of being Catharine Howard's assistant and confidante in her love adventures, and with Catharine, Lady Rochfort also ascended the scaffold.

"Ah, the king needed a long time to recover from this blow. He searched two years for a pure, uncontaminated virgin, who might become his queen without danger of the scaffold. But he found none; so he took then Lord Neville's widow, Catharine Parr. But you know, my child, that Catharine is an unlucky name for Henry's queens. The first Catharine he repudiated, the second he beheaded. What will he do with the third?"

Lady Jane smiled. "Catharine does not love him," said she, "and I believe she would willingly consent, like Anne of Cleves, to become his sister, instead of his wife."

"Catharine does not love the king?" inquired Lord Douglas, in breathless suspense. "She loves another, then!"

"No, my father! Her heart is yet like a sheet of white paper: no single name is yet inscribed there."

"Then we must write a name there, and this name must drive her to the scaffold, or into banishment," said her father impetuously. "It is your business, my child, to take a steel graver, and in some way write a name in Catharine's heart so deep and indelibly, that the king may some day read it there."

CHAPTER VIII.

FATHER AND DAUGHTER.

BOTH now kept silent for a long time. Lord Douglas had leaned back on the ottoman, and, respiring heavily, seemed to breathe a little from the exertion of his long discourse. But while he rested, his large, piercing eyes were constantly turned to Jane, who, leaning back on the cushion, was staring thoughtfully into the empty air, and seemed to be entirely forgetful of her father's presence.

A cunning smile played for a moment over the countenance of the earl as he observed her, but it quickly disappeared, and now deep folds of care gathered on his brow.

As he saw that Lady Jane was plunging deeper and deeper into reverie, he at length laid his hand on her shoulder and hastily asked, "What are you thinking of, Jane?"

She gave a sudden start, and looked at the earl with an embarrassed air.

"I am thinking of all that you have been saying to me, my father," replied she, calmly. "I am considering what benefit to our object I can draw from it."

Lord Douglas shook his head, and smiled incredulously. At length he said solemnly: "Take care, Jane, take care that your heart does not deceive your head. If we would reach our aim here, you must, above all things, maintain a cool heart and a cool head. Do you still possess both, Jane?"

In confusion she cast down her eyes before his penetrating look. Lord Douglas noticed it, and a passionate word was already on his lips. But he kept it back. As a prudent diplomat, he knew that it is often more politic to destroy a thing by ignoring it, than to enter into an open contest with it. The feelings are like the dragons' teeth of Theseus. If you contend with them, they always grow again anew, and with renewed energy, out of the soil.

Lord Douglas, therefore, was very careful not to notice his daughter's confusion. "Pardon me, my daughter, if, in my zeal and my tender care for you, I go too far. I know that your dear and beautiful head is cool enough to wear a crown. I know that in your heart dwell only ambition and religion. Let us, then, further consider what we have to do in order to attain our end.

"We have spoken of Henry as a husband, of Henry as a man; and I hope you have drawn some useful lessons from the fate of his wives. You have learned that it is necessary to possess all the good and all the bad qualities of woman in order to control this stiff-necked and tyrannical, this lustful and bigoted, this vain and sensual man, whom the wrath of God has made King of England. You must, before all things, be perfect master of the difficult art of coquetry. You must become a female Proteus—to-day a Messalina, to-morrow a nun; to-day one of the *literati*, to-morrow a playful child; you must ever seek to surprise the king, to keep him on the stretch, to enliven him. You must never give way to the dangerous feeling of security, for in fact King Henry's wife is never safe. The axe always hangs over her head, and you must ever consider your husband as only a fickle lover, whom you must every day captivate anew."

"You speak as though I were already queen," said Lady Jane, smiling; "and yet I cannot but think that, in order to come to that, many difficulties are to be overcome, which may indeed perhaps be insuperable."

"Insuperable!" exclaimed her father with a shrug of the shoulders. "With the aid of the holy Church, no hinderance is insuperable. Only, we must be perfectly acquainted with our end and our means. Do not despise, then, to sound the character of this king ever and again, and be certain you will always find in him some new hidden recess, some surprising peculiarity. We have spoken of him as a husband and the father of a family, but of his religious and political standing I have as yet told you nothing. And yet that, my child, is the principal point in his whole character.

"In the first place, then, Jane, I will tell you a secret. The king, who has constituted himself high-priest of his Church—whom the pope once called 'the Knight of the Truth and the Faith'—the king has at the bottom of his heart no religion. He is a wavering reed, which the wind turns this way to-day, and that way to-morrow. He knows not his own will, and, coquetting with both parties, to-day he is a heretic, in order to exhibit himself as a strong, unprejudiced, enlightened man; to-morrow a Catholic, in order to show himself an obedient and humble servant of God, who seeks and finds his happiness only in love and piety. But for both confessions of faith he possesses at heart a profound indifference; and had the pope at that time placed no difficulties in his way, had he consented to his divorce from Catharine, Henry would have always remained a very good and active servant of the Catholic Church. But they were imprudent enough to irritate him by contradiction; they stimulated his vanity and pride to resistance; and so Henry became a church reformer, not from conviction, but out of pure love of opposition. And that, my child, you must never forget, for, by means of this lever, you may very well convert him again to a devout, dutiful, and obedient servant of our holy Church. He has renounced the pope, and usurped the supremacy of the Church, but he cannot summon up courage to carry out his work and throw himself wholly into the arms of the Reformation. However much he has opposed the person of the pope, still he has always remained devoted to the Church, although perhaps he does not know it himself. He is no Catholic, and he hears mass; he has broken up the monasteries, and yet forbids priests to marry; he has the Lord's supper administered under both kinds, and believes in the real transubstantiation of the wine into the Redeemer's holy blood. He destroys the convents, and yet commands that vows of chastity, spoken by man or woman, must be faithfully kept; and lastly, auricular confession is still a necessary constituent of his Church. And these he calls his six articles,* and the foundation of his English Church. Poor, short-sighted and vain man! He knows not that he has done all this, only because he wanted to be the pope himself, and he is nothing more than an anti-pope of the Holy Father at Rome, whom he, in his blasphemous pride, dares call 'the Bishop of Rome.'"

"But, for this audacity," said Jane, with looks of burning rage, "the anathema has struck him and laid a curse upon his head, and given him up to the hatred, contempt, and scorn of his own subjects. Therefore, the Holy Father has justly named him 'the apostate and lost son, the blaspheming usurper of the holy Church.' Therefore, the pope has declared his crown forfeited, and promised it to him who will vanquish him by force of arms. Therefore, the pope has forbidden any of his subjects to obey him, and respect and recognize him as king." †

"And yet he remains King of England, and his subjects still obey him in slavish submission," exclaimed Earl Douglas, shrugging his shoulders. "It is very unwise to go so far in threats, for one should never threaten with punishment which he is not likewise able to really execute. This Romish interdict has rather been an advantage to the king, than done him harm, for it has forced the king into haughtier opposition, and proved to his subjects that a man may really be under an interdict, and yet in prosperity and the full enjoyment of life."

"The pope's excommunication has not hurt the king at all; his throne has not felt the slightest jar from it, but the apostasy of the king has deprived the Holy See at Rome of a very perceptible support; therefore we must bring the faithless king back to the holy Church, for she needs him. And this, my daughter, is the work that God and the will of His holy representative have placed in your

---

* Burnet, vol. i, p. 259. Tytler, p. 402. † Leti, vol. i, p. 134.

hands. A noble, glorious, and at the same time profitable work, for it makes you a queen! But I repeat, be cautious, never irritate the king by contradiction. Without their knowing it, we must lead the wavering where salvation awaits them. For, as we have said, he is a waverer; and in the haughty pride of his royalty, he has the presumption to wish to stand above all parties, and to be himself able to found a new Church, a Church which is neither Catholic nor Protestant, but *his* Church; to which, in the six articles, the so-called 'Bloody Statute,' he has given its laws.

"He will not be Protestant nor Catholic, and, in order to show his impartiality, he is an equally terrible persecutor of both parties. So that it has come to pass that we must say, ' In England, Catholics are hanged, and those not such are burned.' * It gives the king pleasure to hold with steady and cruel hand the balance between the two parties, and on the same day that he has a papist incarcerated, because he has disputed the king's supremacy, he has one of the reformed put upon the rack, because he has denied the real transubstantiation of the wine, or perhaps has disputed concerning the necessity of auricular confession. Indeed, during the last session of Parliament, five men were hanged because they disputed the supremacy, and five others burned because they professed the reformed views! And this evening, Jane—this, the king's wedding-night—by the special order of the king, who wanted to show his impartiality as head of the Church, Catholics and Protestants have been coupled together like dogs, and hurried to the stake, the Catholics being condemned as traitors, and the others as heretics!" †

" Oh," said Jane, shuddering and turning pale, " I will not be Queen of England. I have a horror of this cruel, savage king, whose heart is wholly without compassion or pity!"

Her father laughed. " Do you not then know, child,

* Leti, vol. i, p. 142. † Tytler, p. 28.

how you can make the hyena gentle, and the tiger tame? You throw them again and again a fresh prey, which they may devour, and since they love blood so dearly, you constantly give them blood to drink, so that they may never thirst for it. The king's only steady and unchanging peculiarity is his cruelty and delight in blood; one then must always have some food ready for these, then he will ever be a very affectionate and gracious king and husband.

"And there is no lack of objects for this bloodthirstiness. There are so many men and women at his court, and when he is precisely in a bloodthirsty humor, it is all the same to Henry whose blood he drinks. He has shed the blood of his wives and relatives; he has executed those whom he called his most confidential friends; he has sent the noblest men of his kingdom to the scaffold.

"Thomas More knew him very well, and in a few striking words he summed up the whole of the king's character. Ah, it seems to me that I see now the quiet and gentle face of this wise man, as I saw him standing in yonder bay-window, and near him the king, his arms around the neck of High-Chancellor More, and listening to his discourse with a kind of reverential devotion. And when the king had gone, I walked up to Thomas More and congratulated him on the high and world-renowned favor in which he stood with the king. 'The king really loves you,' said I. 'Yes,' replied he, with his quiet, sad smile, 'yes, the king truly loves me. But that would not for one moment hinder him from giving my head for a valuable diamond, a beautiful woman, or a hand's breadth of land in France.' *
He was right, and for a beautiful woman, the head of this sage had to fall, of whom the most Christian emperor and king, Charles V., said: 'Had I been the master of such a servant, of whose ability and greatness we have had so much experience for many years; had I possessed an ad-

* Leti, vol. i, p. 194.

viser so wise and earnest as Thomas More was, I would rather have lost the best city of my realm, than so worthy a servant and counsellor.' *

"No, Jane, be that your first and most sacred rule, never to trust the king, and never reckon on the duration of his affection and the manifestations of his favor. For, in the perfidy of his heart, it often pleases him to load with tokens of his favor those whose destruction he has already resolved upon, to adorn and decorate with orders and jewels to-day those whom to-morrow he is going to put to death. It flatters his self-complacency, like the lion, to play a little with the puppy he is about to devour. Thus did he with Cromwell, for many years his counsellor and friend, who had committed no other crime than that of having first exhibited to the king the portrait of the ugly Anne of Cleves, whom Holbein had turned into a beauty. But the king took good care not to be angry with Cromwell, or to reproach him for it. Much more —in recognition of his great services, he raised him to the earldom of Essex, decorated him with the Order of the Garter and appointed him lord chamberlain; and then, when Cromwell felt perfectly secure and proudly basked in the sunshine of royal favor, then all at once the king had him arrested and dragged to the tower, in order to accuse him of high treason.† And so Cromwell was executed, because Anne of Cleves did not please the king, and because Hans Holbein had flattered her picture.

"But now we have had enough of the past, Jane. Now let us speak of the present and of the future, my daughter. Let us now first of all devise the means to overthrow this woman who stands in our way. When she is once overthrown, it will not be very difficult for us to put you in her place. For you are now here, near the king. The great mistake in our earlier efforts was, that we were not present and could work only through go-

* Tytler, p. 354. † Ibid, p. 423.

betweens and confidants. The king did not see you, and since the unlucky affair with Anne of Cleves he mistrusts likenesses; I very well knew that, for I, my child, confide in no one, not even in the most faithful and noblest friends. I rely upon nobody but ourselves. Had we been here, you would now be Queen of England instead of Catharine Parr. But, to our misfortune, I was still the favorite of the Regent of Scotland, and as such, I could not venture to approach Henry. It was necessary that I should fall into disgrace there, in order to be again sure of the king's favor here.

"So I fell into disgrace and fled with you hither. Now, then, here we are, and let the fight begin. And you have to-day already taken an important step toward our end. You have attracted the notice of the king, and established yourself still more securely in the favor of Catharine. I confess, Jane, I am charmed with your prudent conduct. You have this day won the hearts of all parties, and it was wonderfully shrewd in you to come to the aid of the Earl of Surrey, as you at the same time won to you the heretical party, to which Anne Askew belongs. Oh, it was indeed, Jane, a stroke of policy that you made. For the Howard family is the most powerful and greatest at court, and Henry, Earl of Surrey, is one of its noblest representatives. Therefore we have now already a powerful party at court, which has in view only the high and holy aim of securing a victory for the holy Church, and which quietly and silently works only for this —to again reconcile the king to the pope. Henry Howard, Earl of Surrey, like his father, the Duke of Norfolk, is a good Catholic, as his niece Catharine Howard was; only she, besides God and the Church, was a little too fond of the images of God—fine-looking men. It was this that gave the victory to the other party, and forced the Catholic to succumb to the heretical party at court. Yes, for the moment, Cranmer with Catharine has got the better of us, but soon Gardiner with Jane Douglas will overcome the heretics, and send them to the scaffold. That is our plan, and, God permitting, we will carry it out."

"But it will be a difficult undertaking," said Lady Jane, with a sigh. "The queen is a pure, transparent soul; she has a shrewd head and a clear glance. She is, moreover, guileless in her thoughts, and recoils with true maidenly timidity from every sin."

"We must cure her of this timidity, and that is your task, Jane. You must despoil her of these strict notions about virtue. With flattering voice you must ensnare her heart, and entice it to sin."

"Oh, that is an infernal plot!" said Lady Jane, turning pale. "That, my father, would be a crime, for that would be not only destroying her earthly happiness, but also imperilling her soul. I must entice her to a crime; that is your dishonorable demand! But I will not obey you! It is true, I hate her, for she stands in the way of my ambition. It is true I will destroy her, for she wears the crown which I wish to possess; but never will I be so base as to pour into her very heart the poison by which she shall fall. Let her seek the poison for herself; I will not hold back her hand; I will not warn her. Let her seek the ways of sin herself: I will not tell her that she has erred; but I will, from afar, dog her, and watch each step, and listen for every word and sigh, and when she has committed a crime, then I will betray her, and deliver her up to her judges. That is what I can and will do. I will be the demon to drive her from paradise in God's name, but not the serpent to entice her in the devil's name to sin."

She paused, and, panting for breath, sunk back upon the cushion; but her father's hand was laid upon her shoulder with a convulsive grip, and pale with rage and with eyes flashing with anger, he stared at her.

A cry of terror burst from Lady Jane. She, who never had seen her father but smiling and full of kindness, scarcely recognized that countenance, distorted with rage. She could scarcely convince herself that this man, with eyes darting fire, scowling eyebrows and lips quivering with rage, was really her father.

"You will not?" exclaimed he, with a hollow, threatening voice. "You dare rebel against the holy commands of the Church? Have you, then, forgotten what you promised to the Holy Fathers, whose pupil you are? Have you forgotten that the brothers and sisters of the Holy League are permitted to have no other will than that of their masters! Have you forgotten the sublime vow which you made to our master, Ignatius Loyola? Answer me, unfaithful and disobedient daughter of the Church! Repeat to me the oath which you took when he received you into the holy Society of the Disciples of Jesus! Repeat your oath, I say!"

As if constrained by an invisible power, Jane had arisen, and now stood, her hands folded across her breast, submissive and trembling before her father, whose erect, proud, and wrathful form towered above her.

"I have sworn," said she, "to subject my own thought, and will, my life, and endeavors, obediently to the will of the Holy Father. I have sworn to be a blind tool in the hands of my masters, and to do only what they command and enjoin. I have vowed to serve the holy Church, in which alone is salvation, in every way and with all the means at my command; and I will despise none of these means, consider none trifling, disdain none, provided it leads to the end. For the end sanctifies the means, and nothing is a sin which is done for the honor of God and the Church!"

"*Ad majorem Dei gloriam!*" said her father, devoutly folding his hands. "And you know what awaits you, if you violate your oath?"

"Earthly disgrace and eternal destruction await me. The curse of all my brethren and sisters awaits me—eternal damnation and punishment. With thousands of torments and tortures of the rack, will the Holy Fathers put me to death; and as they kill my body and throw it as food to the beasts of prey, they will curse my soul and deliver it over to purgatory."

"And what awaits you if you remain faithful to your oath, and obey the commands given you?"

"Honor and glory on earth, besides eternal blessedness in heaven."

"Then you will be a queen on earth and a queen in heaven. You know, then, the sacred laws of the society, and you remember your oath?"

"I remember it."

"And you know that the holy Loyola, before he left us, gave the Society of Jesus, in England, a master and general, whom all the brethren and sisters must serve and submit to, to whom they owe blind obedience and service without questioning?"

"I know it."

"And you know, likewise, by what sign the associates may recognize the general?"

"By Loyola's ring, which he wears on the forefinger of his right hand."

"Behold here this ring!" said the earl, drawing his hand out of his doublet.

Lady Jane uttered a cry, and sank almost senseless at his feet.

Lord Douglas, smiling graciously, raised her in his arms. "You see, Jane, I am not merely your father, but your master also. And you will obey me, will you not?"

"I will obey!" said she, almost inaudibly, as she kissed the hand with the fatal ring.

"You will be to Catharine Parr, as you have expressed it, the serpent, that seduces her to sin?"

"I will."

"You will beguile her into sin, and entice her to indulge a love which must lead her to destruction?"

"I will do it, my father."

"I will now tell you whom she is to love, and who is to be the instrument of destruction. You will so manage the queen that she will love Henry Howard, Earl of Surrey."

Jane uttered a scream, and clung to the back of a chair to keep from falling.

Her father observed her with penetrating, angry looks. "What means this outcry? Why does this choice surprise you?" asked he.

Lady Jane had already gained her self-possession. "It surprised me," said she, "because the earl is betrothed."

A singular smile played about the earl's lips. "It is not the first time," said he, "that even a man already married has become dangerous to a woman's heart, and often the very impossibility of possession adds fuel to the flames of love. Woman's heart is ever so full of selfishness and contradiction."

Lady Jane cast down her eyes, and made no reply. She felt that the piercing and penetrating look of her father was resting on her face. She knew that, just then, he was reading her soul, although she did not look at him.

"Then you no longer refuse?" asked he, at length. "You will inspire the young queen with love for the Earl of Surrey?"

"I will endeavor to do it, my father."

"If you try, with a real and energetic determination to succeed, you will prevail. For, as you said, the queen's heart is still free; it is, then, like a fruitful soil, which is only waiting for some one to sow the seed in it, to bring forth flowers and fruit. Catharine Parr does not love the king; you will, then, teach her to love Henry Howard."

"Yet, my father," said Lady Jane, with a sarcastic smile, "to bring about this result, one must, before all things, be acquainted with a magic spell, through the might of which the earl will first glow with love for Catharine. For the queen has a proud soul, and she will never so forget her dignity as to love a man who is not inflamed with an ardent passion for her. But the earl has not only a bride, but, as it is said, a mistress also."

"Ah! you consider it, then, perfectly unworthy of a woman to love a man who does not adore her?" asked the earl, in a significant tone. "I am rejoiced to hear this from my daughter, and thus to be certain that she will not fall in love with the Earl of Surrey, who is everywhere else called 'the lady-killer.' And if you have informed yourself in so surprising a manner as to the earl's private relations, you have done so, without doubt, only because your sagacious and subtle head has already guessed what commission I would give you with respect to the earl. Besides, my daughter, you are in error: and if a certain high, but not on that account the less very unfortunate lady, should happen to really love the Earl of Surrey, her lot will, perhaps, be the common one—to practise resignation."

An expression of joyful surprise passed over the countenance of Lady Jane, while her father thus spoke; but it was forced to instantly give way to a deathly paleness, as the earl added: "Henry Howard is destined for Catharine Parr, and you are to help her to love so hotly this proud, handsome earl, who is a faithful servant of the Church, wherein alone is salvation, that she will forget all considerations and all dangers."

Lady Jane ventured one more objection. She caught eagerly at her father's words, to seek still for some way of escape.

"You call the earl a faithful servant of our Church," said she, "and yet you would implicate him also in your dangerous plot? You have not, then, my father, considered that it is just as pernicious to love the queen as to be loved by her? And, without doubt, if love for the Earl of Surrey bring the queen to the scaffold, the head of the earl will fall at the same time, no matter whether he return her love or not."

The earl shrugged his shoulders.

"When the question is about the weal of the Church and our holy religion, the danger which, thereby, it may be, threatens one of our number, must not frighten us back. Holy sacrifices must be always offered to a holy cause. Well and good, then, let the earl's head fall, provided the only saving Church gains new vigor from this blood of martyrs. But see, Jane, the morning already begins to dawn, and I must hasten to leave you, lest these courtiers, ever given to slandering, may in some way or other take the father for a lover, and cast suspicion on the immaculate virtue of my Jane. Farewell, then, my daughter! We both, now, know our *rôles*, and will take care to play them with success. You are the friend and confidante of the queen, and I the harmless courtier, who tries, now and then, to gain a smile from the king by some kind and merry jest. That is all. Good-morning, then, Jane, and good-night. For you must sleep, my child, so that your cheeks may remain fresh and your eyes bright. The king hates pining pale-faces. Sleep, then, future Queen of England!"

He gently kissed her forehead, and left the room with lingering step.

Lady Jane stood and listened to the sound of his footsteps gradually dying away, when she sank on her knees, wholly crushed, utterly stunned.

"My God, my God!" murmured she, while streams of tears flooded her face, " and I am to inspire the queen with love for the Earl of Surrey, and I—I love him!"

CHAPTER IX.

LENDEMAIN.

THE great levée was over. Sitting beside the king on the throne, Catharine had received the congratulations of her court; and the king's smiling look, and the tender words which, in undertone, he now and then addressed to the queen, had manifested to the prudent and expert courtiers that the king was to-day just as much enamored of his young consort as he had been yesterday of his bride. Therefore, every one exerted himself to please the queen, and to catch every look, every smile, which she let fall, like sunbeams, here and there, in order to see for whom they were intended, so that they might, perchance, by this means, divine who were to be the future favorites of the queen, and be the first to become intimate with them.

But the young queen directed her looks to no one in particular. She was friendly and smiling, yet one felt that this friendliness was constrained, this smile full of sadness. The king alone did not notice it. He was cheerful and happy, and it seemed to him, therefore, that nobody at his court could dare sigh when he, the king, was satisfied.

After the grand presentation, at which all the great and noble of the realm had passed in formal procession before the royal pair, the king had, according to the court etiquette of the time, given his hand to his consort, led her down from the throne and conducted her to the middle of the hall, in order to present to her the personages in waiting at her court.

But this walk from the throne to the centre of the hall had greatly fatigued the king; this promenade of thirty steps was for him a very unusual and troublesome performance, and the king longed to change to something else more agreeable. So he beckoned to the chief master of ceremonies, and bade him open the door leading into the dining-room. Then he ordered his "house equipage" to be brought up, and, seating himself in it with the utmost stateliness, he had the sedan kept at the queen's side, waiting impatiently till the presentation should at last conclude, and Catharine accompany him to lunch.

The announcements of the maids of honor and female

attendants had been already made, and now came the gentlemen's turn.

The chief master of ceremonies read from his list the names of those cavaliers who were, henceforth, to be in waiting near the queen, and which names the king had written down with his own hand. And at each new appointment a slight expression of pleased astonishment flitted across the faces of the assembled courtiers, for it was always one of the youngest, handsomest, and most amiable lords whom the master of ceremonies had to name.

Perhaps the king proposed to play a cruel game at hazard, in surrounding his consort with the young men of his court; he wished to plunge her into the midst of danger, either to let her perish there, or, by her avoiding danger, to be able to place the unimpeachable virtue of his young wife in the clearest light.

The list had begun with the less important offices, and, ever ascending higher, they now came to positions the highest and of greatest consequence.

Still the queen's master of horse and the chamberlain had not been named, and these were without doubt the most important charges at the queen's court. For one or the other of these officers was always very near the queen. When she was in the palace, the lord of the chamber had to remain in the anteroom, and no one could approach the queen but through his mediation. To him the queen had to give her orders with regard to the schemes and pleasures of the day. He was to contrive new diversions and amusements. He had the right of joining the queen's narrow evening circle, and to stand behind the queen's chair when the royal pair, at times, desired to sup without ceremony.

This place of chief chamberlain was, therefore, a very important one; for since it confined him a large part of the day in the queen's presence, it was scarcely avoidable that the lord chamberlain should become either the confidential and attentive friend, or the malevolent and lurking enemy of the queen!

But the place of master of horse was of no less consequence. For as soon as the queen left the palace, whether on foot or in a carriage, whether to ride in the forest or to glide down the Thames in her gilded yacht, the master of horse must be ever at her side, must ever attend her. Indeed, this service was still more exclusive, still more important. For, though the queen's apartments were open to the lord chamberlain, yet, however, he was never alone with her. The attending maids of honor were always present and prevented there being any *têtes-à-têtes* or intimacy between the queen and her chamberlain.

But with the master of horse it was different—since many opportunities presented themselves, when he could approach the queen unnoticed, or at least speak to her without being overheard. He had to offer her his hand to assist her in entering her carriage; he could ride near the door of her coach; he accompanied her on water excursions and pleasure rides, and these last were so much the more important because they afforded him, to a certain extent, opportunity for a *tête-à-tête* with the queen. For only the master of horse was permitted to ride at her side; he even had precedence of the ladies of the suite, so as to be able to give the queen immediate assistance in case of any accident, or the stumbling of her horse. Therefore, no one of the suite could perceive what the queen said to the master of horse when he rode at her side.

It was understood, therefore, how influential this place might be. Besides, when the queen was at Whitehall, the king was almost always near her; while, thanks to his daily increasing corpulency, he was not exactly in a condition to leave the palace otherwise than in a carriage.

It was therefore very natural that the whole company at court awaited with eager attention and bated breath the moment when the master of ceremonies would name these two important personages, whose names had been kept so secret that nobody had yet learned them. That morning, just before he handed the list to the master of ceremonies, the king had written down these two names with his own hand.

Not the court only, but also the king himself, was watching for these two names. For he wished to see the effect of them, and, by the different expression of faces, estimate the number of the friends of these two nominees. The young queen alone exhibited the same unconcerned affability; her heart only beat with uniform calmness, for she did not once suspect the importance of the moment.

Even the voice of the master of ceremonies trembled slightly, as he now read, " To the place of high chamberlain to the queen, his majesty appoints my Lord Henry Howard, Earl of Surrey."

An approving murmur was heard, and almost all faces manifested glad surprise.

" He has a great many friends," muttered the king. "He is dangerous, then! " An angry look darted from his eyes upon the young earl, who was now approaching the queen, to bend his knee before her and to press to his lips the proffered hand.

Behind the queen stood Lady Jane, and as she beheld thus close before her the young man, so handsome, so long yearned for, and so secretly adored; and as she thought of her oath, she felt a violent pang, raging jealousy, killing hatred toward the young queen, who had, it is true, without suspecting it, robbed her of the loved one, and condemned her to the terrible torture of pandering to her.

The chief master of ceremonies now read in a loud solemn voice, " To the place of master of horse, his majesty appoints my Lord Thomas Seymour, Earl of Sudley."

It was very well that the king had at that moment directed his whole attention to his courtiers, and sought to read in their appearance the impression made by this nomination.

Had he observed his consort, he would have seen that an expression of delighted surprise flitted across Catharine's countenance, and a charming smile played round her lips.

But the king, as we have said, thought only of his court; he saw only that the number of those who rejoiced at Seymour's appointment did not come up to that of those who received Surrey's nomination with so much applause.

Henry frowned and muttered to himself, " These Howards are too powerful. I will keep a watchful eye upon them."

Thomas Seymour approached the queen, and, bending his knee before her, kissed her hand. Catharine received him with a gracious smile. " My lord," said she, " you will at once enter on service with me, and indeed, as I hope, in such manner as will be acceptable to the whole court. My lord, take the fleetest of your coursers, and hasten to Castle Holt, where the Princess Elizabeth is staying. Carry her this letter from her royal father, and she will follow you hither. Tell her that I long to embrace in her a friend and sister, and that I pray her to pardon me if I cannot give up to her exclusively the heart of her king and father, but that I also must still keep a place in the same for myself. Hasten to Castle Holt, my lord, and bring us Princess Elizabeth."

CHAPTER X.

THE KING'S FOOL.

Two years had passed away since the king's marriage, and still Catharine Parr had always kept in favor with her husband; still her enemies were foiled in their attempts to ruin her, and raise the seventh queen to the throne.

Catharine had ever been cautious, ever discreet. She had always preserved a cold heart and a cool head. Each morning she had said to herself that this day might be her last; that some incautious word, some inconsiderate act, might deprive her of her crown and her life. For Henry's savage and cruel disposition seemed, like his corpulency, to increase daily, and it needed only a trifle to inflame him to the highest pitch of rage—rage which, each time, fell with fatal stroke on him who aroused it.

A knowledge and consciousness of this had made the queen cautious. She did not wish to die yet. She still loved life so much. She loved it because it had as yet afforded her so little delight. She loved it because she had so much happiness, so much rapture and enjoyment yet to hope from it. She did not wish to die yet, for she was ever waiting for that life of which she had a foretaste only in her dreams, and which her palpitating and swelling heart told her was ready to awake in her, and, with its sunny, brilliant eyes, arouse her from the winter sleep of her existence.

It was a bright and beautiful spring day. Catharine wanted to avail herself of it, to take a ride and forget for one brief hour that she was a queen. She wanted to enjoy the woods, the sweet May breeze, the song of birds, the green meadows, and to inhale in full draughts the pure air.

She wanted to ride. Nobody suspected how much secret delight and hidden rapture lay in these words. No one suspected that for months she had been looking forward with pleasure to this ride, and scarcely dared to wish for it, just because it would be the fulfilment of her ardent wishes.

She was already dressed in her riding-habit, and the little red velvet hat, with its long, drooping white feather, adorned her beautiful head. Walking up and down the room, she was waiting only for the return of the lord chamberlain, whom she had sent to the king to inquire whether he wished to speak with her before her ride.

Suddenly the door opened, and a strange apparition showed itself on the threshold. It was a small, compact masculine figure, clad in vesture of crimson silk, which was trimmed in a style showy and motley enough, with puffs and bows of all colors, and which, just on account of its motley appearance, contrasted strangely enough with the man's white hair, and earnest and sombre face.

"Ah, the king's fool," said Catharine, with a merry laugh. "Well, John, what is it that brings you here? Do you bring me a message from the king, or have you made a bold hit, and wish me to take you again under my protection?"

"No, queen," said John Heywood, seriously, "I have made no bold hit, nor do I bring a message from the king. I bring nothing but myself. Ah, queen, I see you want to laugh, but I pray you forget for a moment that John Heywood is the king's fool, and that it does not become him to wear a serious face and indulge sad thoughts like other men."

"Oh, I know that you are not merely the king's fool, but a poet also," said Catharine, with a gracious smile.

"Yes," said he, "I am a poet, and therefore it is altogether proper for me to wear this fool's cap, for poets are all fools, and it were better for them to be hung on the nearest tree instead of being permitted to run about in their crazy enthusiasm, and babble things on account of which people of sense despise and ridicule them. I am a poet, and therefore, queen, I have put on this fool's dress, which places me under the king's protection, and allows me to say to him all sorts of things which nobody else has the courage to speak out. But to-day, queen, I come to you neither as a fool nor as a poet, but I come to you because I wish to cling to your knees and kiss your feet. I come because I wish to tell you that you have made John Heywood forever your slave. He will from this time forth lie like a dog before your threshold and guard you from every enemy and every evil which may press upon you.

Night and day he will be ready for your service, and know neither repose nor rest, if it is necessary to fulfil your command or your wish."

As he thus spoke, with trembling voice and eyes dimmed with tears, he knelt down and bowed his head at Catharine's feet.

"But what have I done to inspire you with such a feeling of thankfulness?" asked Catharine with astonishment. "How have I deserved that you, the powerful and universally dreaded favorite of the king, should dedicate yourself to my service?"

"What have you done?" said he. "My lady, you have saved my son from the stake! They had condemned him—that handsome noble youth—condemned him, because he had spoken respectfully of Thomas More; because he said this great and noble man did right to die, rather than be false to his convictions. Ah, nowadays, it requires such a trifle to condemn a man to death! a couple of thoughtless words are sufficient! And this miserable, lickspittle Parliament, in its dastardliness and worthlessness, always condemns and sentences, because it knows that the king is always thirsty for blood, and always wants the fires of the stake to keep him warm. So they had condemned my son likewise, and they would have executed him, but for you. But you, whom God has sent as an angel of reconciliation on this regal throne reeking with blood; you who daily risk your life and your crown to save the life of some one of those unfortunates whom fanaticism and thirst for blood have sentenced, and to procure their pardon, you have save my son also."

"How! that young man who was to be burned yesterday, was your son?"

"Yes, he was my son."

"And you did not tell the king so? and you did not intercede for him?"

"Had I done so, he would have been irretrievably lost! For you well know the king is so proud of his impartiality and his virtue! Oh, had he known that Thomas is my son he would have condemned him to death, to show the people that Henry the Eighth everywhere strikes the guilty and punishes the sinner, whatever name he may bear, and whoever may intercede for him. Ah, even your supplication would not have softened him, for the high-priest of the English Church could never have pardoned this young man for not being the legitimate son of his father, for not having the right to bear his name, because his mother was the spouse of another man whom Thomas must call father."

"Poor Heywood! Yes, now I understand. The king would, indeed, never have forgiven this; and had he known it, your son would have inevitably been condemned to the stake."

"You saved him, queen! Do you not believe now that I shall be forever thankful to you?"

"I do believe it," said the queen, with a pleasant smile, as she extended her hand for him to kiss. "I believe you, and I accept your service."

"And you will need it, queen, for a tempest is gathering over your head, and soon the lightning will flash and the thunders roll."

"Oh, I fear not! I have strong nerves!" said Catharine, smiling. "When a storm comes, it is but a refreshing of nature, and I have always seen that after a storm the sun shines again."

"You are a brave soul!" said John Heywood, sadly.

"That is, I am conscious of no guilt!"

"But your enemies will invent a crime to charge you with. Ah, as soon as it is the aim to calumniate a neighbor and plunge him in misery, men are all poets!"

"But you just now said that poets are crack-brained, and should be hung to the first tree. We will, therefore, treat these slanderers as poets, that is all."

"No, that is not all!" said John Heywood, energetically. "For slanderers are like earth-worms. You cut them in pieces, but instead of thereby killing them, you multiply each one and give it several heads."

"But what is it, then, that I am accused of?" exclaimed Catharine, impatiently. "Does not my life lie open and clear before you all? Do I ever take pains to have any secrets? Is not my heart like a glass house, into which you can all look, to convince yourselves that it is a soil wholly unfruitful, and that not a single poor little flower grows there?"

"Though this be so, your enemies will sow weeds and make the king believe that it is burning love which has grown up in your heart."

"How! They will accuse me of having a love-affair?" asked Catharine, and her lips slightly trembled.

"I do not know their plans yet; but I will find them out. There is a conspiracy at work. Therefore, queen, be on your guard! Trust nobody, for foes are ever wont to conceal themselves under hypocritical faces and deceiving words."

"If you know my enemies, name them to me!" said Catharine, impatiently. "Name them to me, that I may beware of them."

"I have not come to accuse anybody, but to warn you. I shall, therefore, take good care not to point out your enemies to you; but I will name your friends to you."

"Ah, then, I have friends, too!" whispered Catharine, with a happy smile.

"Yes, you have friends; and, indeed, such as are ready to give their blood and life for you."

"Oh, name them, name them to me!" exclaimed Catharine, all of a tremble with joyful expectation.

"I name first, Cranmer, archbishop of Canterbury. He is your true and staunch friend, on whom you can build. He loves you as queen, and he prizes you as the associate whom God has sent him to bring to completion, here at the court of this most Christian and bloody king, the holy work of the Reformation, and to cause the light of knowledge to illuminate this night of superstition and priestly domination. Build strongly on Cranmer, for he is your surest and most invariable supporter, and should he sink, your fall would inevitably follow. Therefore, not only rely on him, but also protect him, and look upon him as your brother; for what you do for him, you do for yourself."

"Yes, you are right," said Catharine, thoughtfully. "Cranmer is a noble and staunch friend; and often enough already he has protected me, in the king's presence, against those little pin-prickings of my enemies, which do not indeed kill, but which make the whole body sore and faint."

"Protect him, and thus protect yourself."

"Well, and the other friends?"

"I have given Cranmer the precedence; but now, queen, I name myself as the second of your friends. If Cranmer is your staff, I will be your dog; and, believe me, so long as you have such a staff and so faithful a dog, you are safe. Cranmer will warn you of every stone that lies in your way, and I will bite and drive off the enemies, who, hidden behind the thicket, lurk in the way to fall upon you from behind."

"I thank you! Really, I thank you!" said Catharine, heartily. "Well, and what more?"

"More?" inquired Heywood with a sad smile.

"Mention a few more of my friends."

"Queen, it is a great deal, if one in a lifetime has found two friends upon whom he can rely, and whose fidelity is not guided by selfishness. You are perhaps the only crowned head that can boast of such friends."

"I am a woman," said Catharine, thoughtfully, "and many women surround me and daily swear to me unchanging faithfulness and attachment. How! are all these unworthy the title of friends? Is even Lady Jane Douglas unworthy; she, whom I have called my friend these many long years, and whom I trust as a sister? Tell me, John

Heywood, you who, as it is said, know everything, and search out everything that takes place at court, tell me, is not Lady Jane Douglas my friend?"

John Heywood suddenly became serious and gloomy, and looked on the ground, absorbed in reflection. Then he swept his large, bright eyes all around the room, in a scrutinizing manner, as if he wished to convince himself that no listener was really concealed there, and stepping close up to the queen, he whispered: "Trust her not; she is a papist, and Gardiner is her friend."

"Ah, I suspected it," whispered Catharine, sadly.

"But listen, queen; give no expression to this suspicion by look, or words, or by the slightest indication. Lull this viper into the belief that you are harmless; lull her to sleep, queen. She is a venomous and dangerous serpent, which must not be roused, lest, before you suspect it, it bite you on the heel. Be always gracious, always confidential, always friendly toward her. Only, queen, do not tell her what you would not confide to Gardiner and Earl Douglas likewise. Oh, believe me, she is like the lion in the doge's palace at Venice. The secrets that you confide to her will become accusations against you before the tribunal of blood."

Catharine shook her head with a smile. "You are too severe, John Heywood. It is possible that the religion which she secretly professes has estranged her heart from me, but she would never be capable of betraying me, or of leaguing herself with my foes. No, John, you are mistaken. It would be a crime to believe thus. My God, what a wicked and wretched world it must be in which we could not trust even our most faithful and dearest friends!"

"The world is indeed wicked and wretched, and one must despair of it, or consider it a merry jest, with which the devil tickles our noses. For me, it is such a jest, and therefore, queen, I have become the king's fool, which at least gives me the right of spurting out upon the crawling brood all the venom of the contempt I feel for mankind, and of speaking the truth to those who have only lies, by dripping honey, ever on their lips. The sages and poets are the real fools of our day, and since I did not feel a vocation to be a king, or a priest, a hangman, or a lamb for sacrifice, I became a fool."

"Yes, a fool, that is to say, an epigrammatist, whose biting tongue makes the whole court tremble."

"Since I cannot, like my royal master, have these criminals executed, I give them a few sword-cuts with my tongue. Ah, I tell you, you will much need this ally. Be on your guard, queen: I heard this morning the first growl of the thunder, and in Lady Jane's eyes I observed the stealthy lightning. Trust her not. Trust no one here but your friends Cranmer and John Heywood."

"And you say, that in all this court, among all these brilliant women, these brave cavaliers, the poor queen has not a single friend, not a soul, whom she may trust, on whom she may lean? Oh, John Heywood, think again, have pity on the poverty of a queen. Think again. Say, *only* you two? No friend but you?"

And the queen's eyes filled with tears, which she tried in vain to repress.

John Heywood saw it and sighed deeply. Better than the queen herself perhaps, he had read the depths of her heart, and knew its deep wound. But he also had sympathy with her pain, and wished to mitigate it a little.

"I recollect," said he, gently and mournfully—"yes, I recollect, you have yet a third friend at this court."

"Ah, a third friend!" exclaimed Catharine, and again her voice sounded cheery and joyous. "Name him to me, name him! For you see clearly I am burning with impatience to hear his name."

John Heywood looked into Catharine's glowing countenance with a strange expression, at once searching and mournful, and for a moment dropped his head upon his breast and sighed.

"Now, John, give me the name of this third friend."

"Do you not know him, queen?" asked Heywood, as he again stared steadily in her face. Do you not know him? It is Thomas Seymour, Earl of Sudley."

There passed as it were a sunbeam over Catharine's face, and she uttered a low cry.

John Heywood said, sadly: "Queen, the sun strikes directly in your face. Take care that it does not blind your bright eyes. Stand in the shade, your majesty, for, hark! there comes one who might report the sunshine in your face for a conflagration."

Just then the door opened, and Lady Jane appeared on the threshold. She threw a quick, searching glance around the room, and an imperceptible smile passed over her beautiful pale face.

"Your majesty," said she solemnly, "everything is ready. You can begin your ride when it pleases you. The Princess Elizabeth awaits you in the anteroom, and your master of horse already holds the stirrup of your steed."

"And the lord chamberlain?" asked Catharine, blushing, "has he no message from the king to bring me?"

"Ay!" said the Earl of Surrey as he entered. "His majesty bids me tell the queen that she may extend her ride as far as she wishes. The glorious weather is well worth that the Queen of England should enjoy it, and enter into a contest with the sun."

"Oh, the king is the most gallant of cavaliers," said Catharine, with a happy smile. "Now come, Jane, let us ride."

"Pardon me, your majesty," said Lady Jane, stepping back. "I cannot to-day enjoy the privilege of accompanying your majesty. Lady Anne Ettersville is to-day in attendance."

"Another time, then, Jane! And you, Earl Douglas, you ride with us?"

"The king, your majesty, has ordered me to his cabinet."

"Behold now a queen abandoned by all her friends!" said Catharine cheerily, as with light, elastic step she passed through the hall to the courtyard.

"Here is something going on which I must fathom!" muttered John Heywood, who had left the hall with the rest. "A mousetrap is set, for the cats remain at home, and are hungry for their prey."

Lady Jane had remained behind in the hall with her father. Both had stepped to the window, and were silently looking down into the yard, where the brilliant cavalcade of the queen and her suite was moving about in motley confusion.

Catharine had just mounted her palfrey; the noble animal, recognizing his mistress, neighed loudly, and, giving a snort, reared up with his noble burden.

Princess Elizabeth, who was close to the queen, uttered a cry of alarm. "You will fall, queen," said she, "you ride such a wild animal."

"Oh, no, indeed," said Catharine, smiling; "Hector is not wild. It is with him as with me. This charming May air has made us both mettlesome and happy. Away, then, my ladies and lords! our horses must be to-day swift as birds. We ride to Epping Forest."

And through the open gateway dashed the cavalcade. The queen in front; at her right, the Princess Elizabeth; at her left, the master of horse, Thomas Seymour, Earl of Sudley.

When the train had disappeared, father and daughter stepped back from the window, and looked at each other with strange, dark, and disdainful looks.

"Well, Jane?" said Earl Douglas, at length. "She is still queen, and the king becomes daily more unwieldy and ailing. It is time to give him a seventh queen."

"Soon, my father, soon."

"Loves the queen Henry Howard at last?"

"Yes, he loves her!" said Jane, and her pale face was now colorless as a winding-sheet.

"I ask, whether *she* loves *him?*"

"She will love him!" murmured Jane, and then suddenly mastering herself, she continued: "but it is not enough to make the queen in love; doubtless it would be still more efficient if some one could instill a new love into the king. Did you see, father, with what ardent looks his majesty yesterday watched me and the Duchess of Richmond?"

"Did I see it? The whole court talked about it."

"Well, now, my father, manage it so that the king may be heartily bored to-day, and then bring him to me. He will find the Duchess of Richmond with me."

"Ah, a glorious thought! You will surely be Henry's seventh queen."

"I will ruin Catharine Parr, for she is my rival, and I hate her!" said Jane, with glowing cheeks and flashing eyes. "She has been queen long enough, and I have bowed myself before her. Now she shall fall in the dust before me, and I will set my foot upon her head."

CHAPTER XI.

THE RIDE.

It was a wondrous morning. The dew still lay on the grass of the meadows, over which they had just ridden to reach the thicket of the forest, in whose trees resounded the melodious voices of blithe birds. Then they rode along the banks of a babbling forest stream, and spied the deer that came forth into the glade on the other side, as if they wanted, like the queen and her train, to listen to the song of the birds and the murmuring of the fountains.

Catharine felt a nameless, blissful pleasure swell her bosom. She was to-day no more the queen, surrounded by perils and foes; no more the wife of an unloved, tyrannical husband; not the queen trammelled with the shackles of etiquette. She was a free, happy woman, who, in presageful, blissful trepidation, smiled at the future, and said to each minute, "Stay, stay, for thou art so beautiful!"

It was a sweet, dreamy happiness, the happiness of that hour. With glad heart, Catharine would have given her crown for it, could she have prolonged this hour to an eternity.

He was at her side—he of whom John Heywood had said, that he was among her most trustful and trusty friends. He was there; and even if she did not dare to look at him often, often to speak to him, yet she felt his presence, she perceived the glowing beams of his eyes, which rested on her with consuming fire. Nobody could observe them. For the court rode behind them, and before them and around them was naught but Nature breathing and smiling with joy, naught but heaven and God.

She had forgotten however that she was not quite alone, and that while Thomas Seymour rode on her left, on her right was Princess Elizabeth—that young girl of fourteen years—that child, who, however, under the fire of suffering and the storms of adversity, was early forced to precocious bloom, and whose heart, by the tears and experience of her unhappy childhood, had acquired an early ripeness. Elizabeth, a child in years, had already all the strength and warmth of a woman's feelings. Elizabeth, the disowned and disinherited princess, had inherited her father's pride and ambition; and when she looked on the queen, and perceived that little crown wrought on her velvet cap in diamond embroidery, she felt in her bosom a sharp pang, and remembered, with feelings of bitter grief, that this crown was destined never to adorn her head, since the king, by solemn act of Parliament, had excluded her from the succession to the throne.*

But for a few weeks this pain had been more gentle, and less burning. Another feeling had silenced it. Elizabeth who was never to be queen or sovereign—Elizabeth might be a wife at least. Since she was denied a crown, they should at least allow her instead a wife's happiness; they should not grudge her the privilege of twining in her hair a crown of myrtle.

She had been early taught to ever have a clear consciousness of all her feelings; nor had she now shrunk from reading the depths of her heart with steady and sure eye.

She knew that she loved, and that Thomas Seymour was the man whom she loved.

But the earl? Did he love her in return? Did he understand the child's heart? Had he, beneath the childish face, already recognized the passionate, proud woman? Had he guessed the secrets of this soul, at once so maidenly and chaste, and yet so passionate and energetic?

Thomas Seymour never betrayed a secret, and what he had, it may be, read in the eyes of the princess, and what he had, perhaps, spoken to her in the quiet shady walks of Hampton Court, or in the long, dark corridors of Whitehall, was known to no one save those two. For Elizabeth had a strong, masculine soul; she needed no confidant to share her secrets; and Thomas Seymour had feared even, like the immortal hair-dresser of King Midas, to dig a hole and utter his secret therein; for he knew very well that, if the reed grew up and repeated his words, he might, for these words, lay his head on the block.

Poor Elizabeth! She did not even suspect the earl's secret and her own were not, however, the same; she did not suspect that Thomas Seymour, if he guessed her secret, might, perhaps, avail himself of it to make thereof a brilliant foil for his own secret.

He had, like her, ever before his eyes the diamond

* Tytler, p. 340.

crown on the head of the young queen, and he had noticed well how old and feeble the king had become of late.

As he now rode by the side of the two princesses, he felt his heart swell with a proud joy, and bold and ambitious schemes alone occupied his soul.

The two women understood nothing of this. They were both too much occupied with their own thoughts; and while Catharine's eyes swept with beaming look the landscape far and wide, the brow of the princess was slightly clouded, and her sharp eye rested with a fixed and watchful gaze on Thomas Seymour.

She had noticed the impassioned look which he had now and then fastened on the queen. The slight, scarcely perceptible tremor of his voice, when he spoke, had not escaped her.

Princess Elizabeth was jealous; she felt the first torturing motions of that horrible disease which she had inherited from her father, and in the feverish paroxysms of which the king had sent two of his wives to the scaffold.

She was jealous, but not of the queen; much more, she dreamed not that the queen might share and return Seymour's love. It never came into her mind to accuse the queen of an understanding with the earl. She was jealous only of the looks which he directed toward the queen; and because she was watching those looks, she could not at the same time read the eyes of her young stepmother also; she could not see the gentle flames which, kindled by the fire of his looks, glowed in hers.

Thomas Seymour had seen them, and had he now been alone with Catharine, he would have thrown himself at her feet and confided to her all the deep and dangerous secrets that he had so long harbored in his breast; he would have left to her the choice of bringing him to the block, or of accepting the love which he consecrated to her.

But there, behind them, were the spying, all-observing, all-surmising courtiers; there was the Princess Elizabeth, who, had he ventured to speak to the queen, would have conjectured from his manner the words which she could not understand; for love sees so clearly, and jealousy has such keen ears!

Catharine suspected nothing of the thoughts of her companions. She alone was happy; she alone gave herself up with full soul to the enjoyment of the moment. She drew in with intense delight the pure air; she drank in the odor of the meadow blossoms; she listened with thirsty ear to the murmuring song which the wind wafted to her from the boughs of the trees. Her wishes extended not beyond the hour; she rested in the full enjoyment of the presence of her beloved. He was there—what needed she more to make her happy?

Her wishes extended not beyond this hour. She was only conscious how delightful it was thus to be at her beloved's side, to breathe the same air, to see the same sun, the same flowers on which his eyes rested, and on which their glances at least might meet in *kisses* which were denied to their lips.

But as they thus rode along, silent and meditative, each occupied with his own thoughts, there came the assistance for which Thomas Seymour had prayed, fluttering along in the shape of a fly.

At first this fly sported and buzzed about the nose of the fiery, proud beast which the queen rode; and as no one noticed it, it was not disturbed by Hector's tossing of his mane, but crept securely and quietly to the top of the noble courser's head, pausing a little here and there, and sinking his sting into the horse's flesh, so that he reared and began loudly to neigh.

But Catharine was a bold and dexterous rider, and the proud spirit of her horse only afforded her delight, and gave the master of horse an opportunity to praise her skill and coolness.

Catharine received with a sweet smile the encomiums of her beloved. But the fly kept creeping on, and, impelled by a diabolic delight, now penetrated the horse's ear.

The poor, tormented animal made a spring forward. This spring, instead of freeing him from his enemy, made him penetrate the ear still farther, and sink his sting still deeper into the soft fleshy part of the same.

Stung by the maddening pain, the horse cast off all control, and, heedless of bridle and scorning the bit, dashed forward in a furious run—forward over the meadow swift as an arrow, resistless as the lightning.

"On, on, to the queen's rescue!" thundered the master of horse, and with mad haste, away flew he also over the meadow.

"To the help of the queen!" repeated Princess Elizabeth, and she likewise spurred her horse and hurried forward, accompanied by the whole suite.

But what is the speed of a horse ever so swift, but yet in his senses, compared with the raving madness of a crazy courser, that, despising all subjection, and mocking at the bridle, dashes ahead, foaming with the sense of freedom and unrestraint, uncontrollable as the surge lashed by the storm!

Already far behind them lay the meadows, far behind them the avenues leading through the woods, and over brooks and ditches, over meadows and wastes, Hector was dashing on.

The queen still sat firmly in the saddle; her cheeks were colorless; her lips trembled; but her eye was still bright and clear. She had not yet lost her presence of mind; she was perfectly conscious of her danger. The din of screaming, screeching voices, which she heard at first, had long since died away in silence behind her. An immense solitude, the deep silence of the grave, was around her. Naught was heard save the panting and snorting of the horse; naught but the crash and clatter of his hoofs.

Suddenly, however, this sound seemed to find an echo. It was repeated over yonder. There was the same snorting and panting; there was the same resounding trampling of hoofs.

And now, oh, now, struck on Catharine's ear the sound of a voice only too well loved, and made her scream aloud with delight and desire.

But this cry frightened anew the enraged animal. For a moment, exhausted and panting, he had slackened in his mad race; now he sprang forward with renewed energy; now he flew on as if impelled by the wings of the wind.

But ever nearer and nearer sounded the loved voice, ever nearer the tramp of his horse.

They were now upon a large plain, shut in on all sides by woods. While the queen's horse circled the plain in a wide circuit, Seymour's, obedient to the rein, sped directly across it, and was close behind the queen.

"Only a moment more! Only hold your arms firmly around the animal's neck, that the shock may not hurl you off, when I lay hold of the rein!" shouted Seymour, and he set his spurs into his horse's flanks, so that he sprang forward with a wild cry.

This cry roused Hector to new fury. Panting for breath, he shot forward with fearful leaps, now straight into the thicket of the woods.

"I hear his voice no more," murmured Catharine. And at length overcome with anxiety and the dizzy race, and worn out with her exertions, she closed her eyes; her senses appeared to be about leaving her.

But at this moment, a firm hand seized with iron grasp the rein of her horse, so that he bowed his head, shaking, trembling, and almost ashamed, as though he felt he had found his lord and master.

"Saved! I am saved!" faltered Catharine, and breathless, scarcely in her senses, she leaned her head on Seymour's shoulder.

He lifted her gently from the saddle, and placed her on the soft moss beneath an ancient oak. Then he tied the horses to a bough, and Catharine, trembling and faint, sank on her knees to rest after such violent exertion.

CHAPTER XII.

THE DECLARATION.

THOMAS SEYMOUR returned to Catharine. She still lay there with closed eyes, pale and motionless.

He gazed on her long and steadily; his eyes drank in, in long draughts, the sight of this beautiful and noble woman, and he forgot at that moment that she was a queen.

He was at length alone with her. At last, after two years of torture, of resignation, of dissimulation, God had granted him this hour, for which he had so long yearned, which he had so long considered unattainable. Now it was there, now it was his.

And had the whole court, had King Henry himself, come right then, Thomas Seymour would not have heeded it; it would not have affrighted him. The blood had mounted to his head and overcome his reason. His heart, still agitated and beating violently from his furious ride and his anxiety for Catharine, allowed him to hear no other voice than that of passion.

He knelt by the queen and seized her hand.

Perhaps it was this touch which roused her from her unconsciousness. She raised her eyes and gazed around with a perplexed look.

"Where am I?" breathed she in a low tone.

Thomas Seymour pressed her hand to his lips. "You are with the most faithful and devoted of your servants, queen!"

"Queen!" This word roused her from her stupor, and caused her to raise herself half up.

"But where is my court? Where is the Princess Elizabeth? Where are all the eyes that heretofore watched me? Where are all the listeners and spies who accompany the queen?"

"They are far away from here," said Seymour in a tone

which betrayed his secret delight. "They are far away from here, and need at least an hour's time to come up with us. An hour, queen! are you aware what that is to me? An hour of freedom, after two years of imprisonment! An hour of happiness, after two years of daily torture, daily endurance of the torments of hell!"

Catharine, who had at first smiled, had now become grave and sad.

Her eye rested on the cap which had fallen from her head and lay near her on the grass.

She pointed with trembling finger to the crown, and said softly, "Recognize you that sign, my lord?"

"I recognize it, my lady; but in this hour, I no longer shrink back at it. There are moments in which life is at its crowning point, and when one heeds not the abyss that threatens close beneath. Such an hour is the present. I am aware that this hour makes me guilty of high treason and may send me to the block; but nevertheless I will not be silent. The fire which burns in my breast consumes me. I must at length give it vent. My heart, that for years has burned upon a funeral pyre, and which is so strong that in the midst of its agonies it has still ever felt a sensation of its blessedness—my heart must at length find death or favor. You shall hear me, queen!"

"No, no," said she, almost in anguish, "I will not, I cannot hear you! Remember that I am Henry the Eighth's wife, and that it is dangerous to speak to her. Silence, then, earl, silence, and let us ride on."

She would have arisen, but her own exhaustion and Lord Seymour's hand caused her to sink back again.

"No, I will not be silent," said he. "I will not be silent until I have told you all that rages and glows within me. The Queen of England may either condemn me or pardon me, but she shall know that to me she is not Henry the Eighth's wife, but only the most charming and graceful, the noblest and loveliest woman in England. I will tell her that I never recollect she is my queen, or, if I do so, it is only to curse the king, who was presumptuous enough to set this brightly sparkling jewel in his bloody crown."

Catharine, almost horrified, laid her hand on Seymour's lips. "Silence, unhappy man, silence! Know you that it is your sentence of death which you are now uttering? Your sentence of death, if any soul hears you?"

"But no one hears me. No one save the queen, and God, who, however, is perhaps more compassionate and merciful than the queen. Accuse me then, queen; go and tell your king that Thomas Seymour is a traitor; that he dares love the queen. The king will send me to the scaffold, but I shall nevertheless deem myself happy, for I shall at least die by your instrumentality. Queen, if I cannot live for you, then beautiful it is to die for you!"

Catharine listened to him wholly stupefied, wholly intoxicated. This was, for her, language wholly new and never heard before, at which her heart trembled in blissful awe, which rushed around her in enchanting melodies and lulled her into a sweet stupefaction. Now she herself even forgot that she was queen, that she was the wife of Henry, the bloodthirsty and the jealous. She was conscious only of this, that the man whom she had so long loved, was now kneeling at her side. With rapture she drank in his words, which struck upon her ear like exquisite music.

Thomas Seymour continued. He told her all he had suffered. He told her he had often resolved to die, in order to put an end to these tortures, but that then a glance of her eye, a word from her lips, had given him strength to live, and still longer endure these tortures, which were at the same time so full of rapture.

"But now, queen, now my strength is exhausted, and it is for you to give me life or death. To-morrow I will ascend the scaffold, or you shall permit me to live, to live for you."

Catharine trembled and looked at him wellnigh astounded. He seemed so proud and imperative, she almost felt a fear for him, but it was the happy fear of a loving, meek woman before a strong, commanding man.

"Know you," said she, with a charming smile, "that you almost have the appearance of wishing to command me to love you?"

"No, queen," said he, proudly, "I cannot command you to love me, but I bid you tell me the truth. I bid you do this, for I am a man who has the right to demand the truth of a woman face to face. And I have told you, you are not the queen to me. You are but a beloved, an adored woman. This love has nothing to do with your royalty, and while I confess it to you, I do not think that you abase yourself when you receive it. For the true love of a man is ever the holiest gift that he can present to a woman, and if a beggar dedicates it to a queen, she must feel herself honored by it. Oh, queen, I am a beggar. I lie at your feet and raise my hands beseechingly to you; but I want not charity, I want not your compassion and pity, which may, perhaps, grant me an alms to lessen my misery. No, I want you yourself. I require all or nothing. It will not satisfy me that you forgive my boldness, and draw the veil of silence over my mad attempt. No, I wish you to speak, to pronounce my condemnation or a benediction on me. Oh, I know you are generous and compassionate, and even if you despise my love and will not return it, yet, it may be, you will not betray me. You will spare me, and be silent. But I repeat it, queen, I do not accept this offer of your magnanimity. You are to make me either a criminal or a god; for I am a criminal if you condemn my love, a god if you return it."

"And do you know, earl," whispered Catharine, "that you are very cruel? You want me to be either an accuser or an accomplice. You leave me no choice but that of being either your murderess or a perjured and adulterous woman—a wife who forgets her plighted faith and her sacred duty, and defiles the crown which my husband has placed upon my head with stains, which Henry will wash out with my own blood and with yours also."

"Let it be so, then," cried the earl, almost joyfully. "Let my head fall, no matter how or when, if you but love me; for then I shall still be immortal; for a moment in your arms is an eternity of bliss."

"But I have already told you that not only your head, but mine also, is concerned in this matter. You know the king's harsh and cruel disposition. The mere suspicion is enough to condemn me. Ah, if he knew what we have just now spoken here, he would condemn me, as he condemned Catharine Howard, though I am not guilty as she was. Ah, I shudder at the thought of the block; and you, Earl Seymour, you would bring me to the scaffold, and yet you say you love me!"

Seymour sunk his head mournfully upon his breast and sighed deeply. "You have pronounced my sentence, queen, and though you are too noble to tell me the truth, yet I have guessed it. No, you do not love me, for you see with keen eyes the danger that threatens you, and you fear for yourself. No, you love me not, else you would think of nothing save love alone. The dangers would animate you, and the sword which hangs over your head you would not see, or you would with rapture grasp its edge and say, 'What is death to me, since I am happy! What care I for dying, since I have felt immortal happiness!' Ah, Catharine, you have a cold heart and a cool head. May God preserve them both to you; then will you pass through life quietly and safely; but you will yet be a poor, wretched woman, and when you come to die, they will place a royal crown upon your coffin, but love will not weep for you. Farewell, Catharine, Queen of England, and since you cannot love him, give Thomas Seymour, the traitor, your sympathy at least."

He bowed low and kissed her feet, then he arose and walked with firm step to the tree where he had tied the horses. But now Catharine arose, now she flew to him, and grasping his hand, asked, trembling and breathless, "What are you about to do? whither are you going?"

"To the king, my lady."

"And what will you do there?"

"I will show him a traitor who has dared love the queen. You have just killed my heart; he will kill only my body. That is less painful, and I will thank him for it."

Catharine uttered a cry, and with passionate vehemence drew him back to the place where she had been resting.

"If you do what you say, you will kill me," said she, with trembling lips. "Hear me, hear! The moment you mount your horse to go to the king, I mount mine too; but not to follow you, not to return to London, but to plunge with my horse down yonder precipice. Oh, fear nothing; they will not accuse you of my murder. They will say that I plunged down there with my horse, and that the raging animal caused my death."

"Queen, take good heed, consider well what you say!" exclaimed Thomas Seymour, his countenance clearing up and his face flaming with delight. "Bear in mind that your words must be either a condemnation or an avowal. I wish death, or your love! Not the love of a queen, who thinks to be gracious to her subject, when for the moment she elevates him to herself; but the love of a woman who bows her head in meekness and receives her lover as at the same time her lord. Oh, Catharine, be well on your guard! If you come to me with the pride of a queen, if there be even one thought in you which tells you that you are bestowing a favor on a subject as you take him to your heart, then be silent and let me go hence. I am proud, and as nobly born as yourself, and however love throws me conquered at your feet, yet it shall not bow my head in the dust! But if you say that you love me, Catharine, for that I will consecrate my whole life to you. I will be your lord, but your slave also. There shall be in me no thought, no feeling, no wish that is not devoted and subservient to you. And when I say that I will be your lord, I mean not thereby that I will not lie forever at your feet and bow my head in the dust, and say to you: Tread on it, if it seem good to you, for I am your slave!"

And speaking thus, he dropped on his knees and pressed to her feet his face, whose glowing and noble expression ravished Catharine's heart.

She bent down to him, and gently lifting his head, looked with an indescribable expression of happiness and love deep into his beaming eyes.

"Do you love me?" asked Seymour, as he put his arm softly around her slender waist, and arose from his kneeling attitude.

"I love you!" said she, with a firm voice and a happy smile. "I love you, not as a queen, but as a woman; and if perchance this love bring us both to the scaffold, well then we shall at least die together, to meet again there above!"

"No, think not now of dying, Catharine, think of living—of the beautiful, enchanting future which is beckoning to us. Think of the days which will soon come, and in which our love will no longer require secresy or a veil, but when we will manifest it to the whole world, and can proclaim our happiness from a full glad breast! Oh, Catharine, let us hope that compassionate and merciful death will loose at last the unnatural bonds that bind you to that old man Then, when Henry is no more, then will you be mine, mine with your entire being, with your whole life; and instead of a proud regal crown, a crown of myrtle shall adorn your head! Swear that to me, Catharine; swear that you will become my wife, as soon as death has set you free."

The queen shuddered and her cheeks grew pale. "Oh," said she with a sigh, "death then is our hope and perhaps the scaffold our end!"

"No, Catharine, love is our hope, and happiness our

end. Think of life, of our future! God grant my request. Swear to me here in the face of God, and of sacred and calm nature around us, swear to me, that from the day when death frees you from your husband you will be mine, my wife, my consort! Swear to me, that you, regardless of etiquette and unmindful of tyrannical custom, will be Lord Seymour's wife, before the knell for Henry's death has died away. We will find a priest, who may bless our love and sanctify the covenant that we have this day concluded for eternity! Swear to me, that, till that wished-for day, you will keep for me your truth and love, and never forget that my honor is yours also, that your happiness is also mine!"

"I swear it!" said Catharine, solemnly. "You may depend upon me at all times and at all hours. Never will I be untrue to you; never will I have a thought that is not yours. I will love you as Thomas Seymour deserves to be loved, that is with a devoted and faithful heart. It will be my pride to subject myself to you, and with glad soul will I serve and follow you, as your true and obedient wife."

"I accept your oath!" said Seymour, solemnly. "But in return I swear that I will honor and esteem you as my queen and mistress. I swear to you that you shall never find a more obedient subject, a more unselfish counsellor, a more faithful husband, a braver champion, than I will be. 'My life for my queen, my entire heart for my beloved'; this henceforth shall be my motto, and may I be disowned and despised by God and by you, if ever I violate this oath."

"Amen!" said Catharine, with a bewitching smile.

Then both were silent. It was that silence which only love and happiness knows—that silence which is so rich in thoughts and feelings, and therefore so poor in words!

The wind rustled whisperingly in the trees, among whose dark branches here and there a bird's warbling or flute-like notes resounded. The sun threw his emerald light over the soft velvety carpet of the ground, which, rising and falling in gentle, undulating lines, formed lovely little hollows and hillocks, on which now and then was seen here and there the slender and stately figure of a hart, or a roe, that, looking around searchingly with his bright eyes, started back frightened into the thicket on observing these two human figures and the group of horses encamped there.

Suddenly this quiet was interrupted by the loud sound of the hunter's horn, and in the distance were heard confused cries and shouts, which were echoed by the dense forest and repeated in a thousand tones.

With a sigh the queen raised her head from the earl's shoulder.

The dream was at an end; the angel came with flaming sword to drive her from paradise.

For she was no longer worthy of paradise. The fatal word had been spoken, and while it brought her love, it had perjured her.

Henry's wife, his by her vow taken before the altar, had betrothed herself to another, and given him the love that she owed her husband.

"It is passed," said he, mournfully. "These sounds call me back to my slavery. We must both resume our *rôles.* I must become queen again."

"But first swear to me that you will never forget this hour; that you will ever think upon the oaths which we have mutually sworn."

She looked at him almost astounded. "My God! can truth and love be forgotten?"

"You will remain ever true, Catharine?"

She smiled. "See, now, my jealous lord, do I address such questions to you?"

"Oh, queen, you well know that you possess the charm that binds forever."

"Who knows?" said she dreamily, as she raised her

enthusiastic look to heaven, and seemed to follow the bright silvery clouds which were sailing slowly across the blue ether.

Then her eyes fell on her beloved, and laying her hand softly upon his shoulder, she said: "Love is like God—eternal, primeval, and ever present! But you must believe in it to feel its presence; you must trust it to be worthy of its blessing!"

But the hallooing and the clangor of the horns came nearer and nearer. Even now was heard the barking of the dogs and the tramp of horses.

The earl had untied the horses, and led Hector, who was now quiet and gentle as a lamb, to his mistress.

"Queen," said Thomas Seymour, "two delinquents now approach you! Hector is my accomplice, and had it not been that the fly I now see on his swollen ear had made him raving, I should be the most pitiable and unhappy man in your kingdom, while now I am the happiest and most enviable."

The queen made no answer, but she put both her arms around the animal's neck and kissed him.

"Henceforth," said she, "then I will ride only Hector, and when he is old and unfit for service——"

"He shall be tended and cared for in the stud of Countess Catharine Seymour!" interrupted Thomas Seymour, as he held the queen's stirrup and assisted her into the saddle.

The two rode in silence toward the sound of the voices and horns, both too much occupied by their own thoughts to interrupt them by trifling words.

"He loves me!" thought Catharine. "I am a happy, enviable woman, for Thomas Seymour loves me."

"She loves me!" thought he, with a proud, triumphant smile. "I shall, therefore, one day become Regent of England."

Just then they came out on the large level meadow, through which they had previously ridden, and over which now came, scattered here and there in motley confusion, the entire royal suite, Princess Elizabeth at the head.

"One thing more!" whispered Catharine. "If you ever need a messenger to me, apply to John Heywood. He is a friend whom we can trust."

And she sprang forward to meet the princess, to recount to her all the particulars of her adventure, and her happy rescue by the master of horse.

Elizabeth, however, listened to her with glowing looks and thoughts distracted, and as the queen then turned to the rest of her suite, and, surrounded by her ladies and lords, received their congratulations, a slight sign from the princess called Thomas Seymour to her side.

She allowed her horse to curvet some paces forward, by which she and the earl found themselves separated a little from the rest, and were sure of being overheard by no one.

"My lord," said she, in a vehement, almost threatening voice, "you have often and in vain besought me to grant you an interview. I have denied you. You intimated that you had many things to say to me, for which we must be alone, and which must reach no listener's ear. Well, now, to-day I grant you an interview, and I am at last inclined to listen to you."

She paused and waited for a reply. But the earl remained silent. He only made a deep and respectful bow, bending to the very neck of his horse. "Well and good; I will go to this rendezvous were it but to blind Elizabeth's eyes, that she may not see what she never ought to see. That was all."

The young princess cast on him an angry look, and a dark scowl gathered on her brow. "You understand well how to control your joy," said she; "and any one to see you just now would think——"

"That Thomas Seymour is discreet enough not to let even his rapture be read in his countenance at this dangerous court," interrupted the earl in a low murmur. "When, princess, may I see you and where?"

"Wait for the message that John Heywood will bring you to-day," whispered Elizabeth, as she sprang forward and again drew near the queen.

"John Heywood, again!" muttered the earl. "The confidant of both, and so my hangman, if he wishes to be!"

CHAPTER XIII.

"LE ROI S'ENNUIT."

KING HENRY was alone in his study. He had spent a few hours in writing on a devout and edifying book, which he was preparing for his subjects, and which, in virtue of his dignity as supreme lord of the Church, he designed to commend to their reading instead of the Bible.

He now laid down his pen, and, with infinite complacency, looked over the written sheets, which were to be to his people a new proof of his paternal love and care, and so convince them that Henry the Eighth was not only the noblest and most virtuous of kings, but also the wisest.

But this reflection failed to make the king more cheerful to-day; perhaps because he had already indulged in it too frequently. To be alone, annoyed and disturbed him —there were in his breast so many secret and hidden voices, whose whispers he dreaded, and which, therefore, he sought to drown—there were so many recollections of blood, which ever and again rose before him, however often he tried to wash them out in fresh blood, and which the king was afraid of, though he assumed the appearance of never repenting, never feeling disquietude.

With hasty hand he touched the gold bell standing by him, and his face brightened as he saw the door open immediately, and Earl Douglas make his appearance on the threshold.

"Oh, at length!" said the lord, who had very well understood the expression of Henry's features; "at length, the king condescends to be gracious to his people."

"I gracious?" asked the king, utterly astonished. "Well, how am I so?"

"By your majesty's resting at length from his exertions, and giving a little thought to his valuable and needful health. When you remember, sire, that England's weal depends solely and alone on the weal of her king, and that you must be and remain healthy, that your people likewise may be healthy."

The king smiled with satisfaction. It never came into his head to doubt the earl's words. It seemed to him perfectly natural that the weal of his people depended on his person; but yet it was always a lofty and beautiful song, and he loved to have his courtiers repeat it.

The king, as we have said, smiled, but there was something unusual in that smile, which did not escape the earl.

"He is in the condition of a hungry anaconda," said Earl Douglas to himself. "He is on the watch for prey, and he will be bright and lively again just as soon as he has tasted a little human flesh and blood. Ah, luckily we are well supplied in that way. Therefore, we will render unto the king what is the king's. But we must be cautious and go to work warily."

He approached the king and imprinted a kiss on his hand.

"I kiss this hand," said he, "which has been to-day the fountain through which the wisdom of the head has been poured forth on this blessed paper. I kiss this paper, which will announce and explain to happy England God's pure and unadulterated word; but yet I say let this suffice for the present, my king; take rest; remember awhile that you are not only a sage, but also a man."

"Yes and truly a weak and decrepit one!" sighed the

king, as with difficulty he essayed to rise, and in so doing leaned so heavily and the earl's arm that he almost broke down under the monstrous load.

"Decrepit!" said Earl Douglas, reproachfully. "Your majesty moves to-day with as much ease and freedom as a youth, and my arm was by no means needed to help you up."

"Nevertheless, we are growing old!" said the king, who, from his weariness, was unusually sentimental and low-spirited to-day.

"Old!" repeated Earl Douglas. "Old, with those eyes darting fire, and that lofty brow, and that face, in every feature so noble! No, your majesty, kings have this in common with the gods—they never grow old."

"And therein they resemble parrots to a hair!" said John Heywood, who just then entered the room. "I own a parrot which my great-grandfather inherited from his great-grandfather, who was hair-dresser to Henry the Fourth, and which to-day still sings with the same volubility as he did a hundred years ago: 'Long live the king! long live this paragon of virtue, sweetness, beauty, and mercy! Long live the king!' He has cried this for hundreds of years, and he has repeated it for Henry the Fifth and Henry the Sixth, for Henry the Seventh and Henry the Eighth! And wonderful, the kings have changed, but the song of praise has always been appropriate, and has ever been only the simple truth! Just like yours, my Lord Douglas! Your majesty may depend upon it, he speaks the truth, for he is near akin to my parrot, which always calls him 'My cousin,' and has taught him his immortal song of praise to kings."

The king laughed, while Earl Douglas cast at John Heywood a sharp, spiteful look.

"He is an impudent imp, is he not, Douglas?" said the king.

"He is a fool!" replied he, with a shrug.

"Exactly, and therefore I just now told you the truth.

For you know children and fools speak the truth. And I became a fool just on this account, that the king, whom you all deceive by your lies, may have about him some creature, besides his looking-glass, to tell him the truth."

"Well, and what truth will you serve up for me to-day?"

"It is already served, your majesty. So lay aside for a little your regal crown and your high priesthood, and conclude to be for awhile a carnivorous beast. It is very easy to become a king. For that, nothing more is necessary than to be born of a queen under a canopy. But it is very difficult to be a man who has a good digestion. It requires a healthy stomach and a light conscience. Come, King Henry, and let us see whether you are not merely a king, but also a man that has a good stomach." And with a merry laugh he took the king's other arm and led him with the earl into the dining-room.

The king, who was an extraordinary eater, silently beckoned his suite to take their places at the table, after he had seated himself in his gilded chair. With grave and solemn air he then received from the hands of the master of ceremonies the ivory tablet on which was the bill of fare for the day. The king's dinner was a solemn and important affair. A multitude of post-wagons and couriers were ever on the way to bring from the remotest ends of the earth dainties for the royal table. The bill of fare, therefore, to-day, as ever, exhibited the choicest and rarest dishes; and always when the king found one of his favorite ones written down he made an assenting and approving motion of the head, which always lighted up the face of the master of ceremonies like a sunbeam. There were birds' nests brought from the East Indies by a fast-sailing vessel, built specially for the purpose. There were hens from Calcutta and truffles from Languedoc, which the poet-king, Francis the First of France, had the day before sent to his royal brother as a special token of affection. There was the sparkling wine of Champagne, and the fiery wine of the Island of Cyprus, which the Republic of Venice had sent to the king as a mark of respect. There were the heavy wines of the Rhine, which looked like liquid gold, and diffused the fragrance of a whole bouquet of flowers, and with which the Protestant princes of Northern Germany hoped to fuddle the king, whom they would have gladly placed at the head of their league. There, too, were the monstrous, gigantic partridge pastries, which the Duke of Burgundy had sent, and the glorious fruits of the south, from the Spanish coast, with which the Emperor Charles the Fifth supplied the King of England's table. For it was well known that, in order to make the King of England propitious, it was necessary first to satiate him; that his palate must first be tickled, in order to gain his head or his heart.

But to-day all these things seemed insufficient to give the king the blissful pleasure which, at other times, was wont to be with him when he sat at table. He heard John Heywood's jests and biting epigrams with a melancholy smile, and a cloud was on his brow.

To be in cheerful humor, the king absolutely needed the presence of ladies. He needed them as the hunter needs the roe to enjoy the pleasure of the chase—that pleasure which consists in killing the defenceless and in declaring war against the innocent and peaceful.

The crafty courtier, Earl Douglas, readily divined Henry's dissatisfaction, and understood the secret meaning of his frowns and sighs. He hoped much from them, and was firmly resolved to draw some advantage therefrom, to the benefit of his daughter, and the harm of the queen.

"Your majesty," said he, "I am just on the point of turning traitor, and accusing my king of an injustice."

The king turned his flashing eyes upon him, and put his hand, sparkling with jewelled rings, to the golden goblet filled with Rhenish wine.

"Of an injustice—me—your king?" asked he, with stammering tongue.

"Yes, of an injustice, inasmuch as you are for me God's visible representative on earth. I would blame God if He withdrew from us for a day the brightness of the sun, the gorgeousness and perfume of His flowers, for since we children of men are accustomed to enjoy these glories, we have in a certain measure gained a right to them. So I accuse you because you have withdrawn from us the embodied flowers and the incarnate suns; because you have been so cruel, sire, as to send the queen to Epping Forest."

"Not so; the queen wanted to ride," said Henry, peevishly. "The spring weather attracted her, and since I, alas! do not possess God's exalted attribute of ubiquity, I was, no doubt, obliged to come to the resolution of being deprived of her presence. There is no horse capable of carrying the King of England."

"There is Pegasus, however, and in masterly manner you know how to manage him. But how, your majesty! the queen wanted to ride, though she was deprived of your presence thereby? She wanted to ride, though this pleasure-ride was at the same time a separation from you? Oh how cold and selfish are women's hearts! Were I a woman, I would never depart from your side, I would covert no greater happiness than to be near you, and to listen to that high and exalted wisdom which pours from your inspired lips. Were I a woman——"

"Earl, I opine that your wish is perfectly fulfilled," said John Heywood seriously. "You make in all respects the impression of an old woman!"

All laughed. But the king did not laugh; he remained serious and looked gloomily before him.

"It is true," muttered he, "she seemed excited with joy about this excursion, and in her eyes shone a fire I have seldom seen there. There must be some peculiar circumstance connected with this ride. Who accompanied the queen?"

"Princess Elizabeth," said John Heywood, who had heard everything, and saw clearly the arrow that the earl had shot at the queen. "Princess Elizabeth, her true and dear friend, who never leaves her side. Besides, her maids of honor, who, like the dragon in the fable, keep watch over the beautiful princess."

"Who else is in the queen's company?" inquired Henry, sullenly.

"The master of horse, Earl of Sudley," said Douglas, "and——"

"That is an observation in the highest degree superfluous," interrupted John Heywood; "it is perfectly well understood by itself that the master of horse accompanies the queen. That is just as much his office as it is yours to sing the song of your cousin, my parrot."

"He is right," said the king quickly. "Thomas Seymour must accompany her, and it is my will also. Thomas Seymour is a faithful servant, and this he has inherited from his sister Jane, my much loved queen, now at rest with God, that he is devoted to his king in steadfast affection."

"The time has not yet come when one may assail the Seymours," thought the earl. "The king is yet attached to them; so he will feel hostile toward the foes of the Seymours. Let us then begin our attack on Henry Howard—that is to say, on the queen."

"Who accompanied the queen besides?" inquired Henry the Eighth, emptying the golden beaker at a draught, as though he would thereby cool the fire which already began to blaze within him. But the fiery Rhenish wine instead of cooling only heated him yet more; it drove, like a tempest, the fire kindled in his jealous heart in bright flames to his head, and made his brain glow like his heart.

"Who else accompanied her beside these?" asked Earl Douglas carelessly. "Well, I think, the lord chamberlain, Earl of Surrey."

A dark scown gathered on the king's brow. The lion had scented his prey.

"The lord chamberlain is not in the queen's train!" said John Heywood earnestly.

"No," exclaimed Earl Douglas. "The poor earl. That will make him very sad."

"And why think you that will make him sad?" asked the king in a voice very like the roll of distant thunder.

"Because the Earl of Surrey is accustomed to live in the sunshine of royal favor, sire; because he resembles that flower which always turns its head to the sun, and receives from it vigor, color, and brilliancy."

"Let him take care that the sun does not scorch him," muttered the king.

"Earl," said John Heywood, "you must put on your spectacles so that you can see better. This time you have confounded the sun with one of its satellites. Earl Surrey is far too prudent a man to be so foolish as to gaze at the sun, and thereby blind his eyes and parch his brain. And so he is satisfied to worship one of the planets that circle round the sun."

"What does the fool intend to say by that?" asked the earl contemptuously.

"The wise will thereby give you to understand that you have this time mistaken your daughter for the queen," said John Heywood, emphasizing sharply every word, "and that it has happened to you, as to many a great astrologer, you have taken a planet for a sun."

Earl Douglas cast a dark, spiteful look at John Heywood, who answered it with one equally piercing and furious.

Their eyes were firmly fixed on each other's, and in those eyes they both read all the hatred and all the bitterness which were working in the depths of their souls. Both knew that they had from that hour sworn to each other an enmity burning and full of danger.

The king had noticed nothing of this dumb but significant scene. He was looking down, brooding over his gloomy thoughts, and the storm-clouds rolling around his brow gathered darker and darker.

With an impetuous movement he arose from his seat, and this time he needed no helping hand to stand up. Wrath was the mighty lever that threw him up.

The courtiers arose from their seats in silence, and nobody besides John Heywood observed the look of understanding which Earl Douglas exchanged with Gardiner, bishop of Winchester, and Wriothesley, the lord chancellor.

"Ah, why is not Cranmer here?" said John Heywood to himself. "I see the three tiger-cats prowling, so there must be prey to devour somewhere. Well, I will at any rate keep my ears open wide enough to hear their roaring."

"The dinner is over, gentlemen!" said the king hastily; and the courtiers and gentlemen in waiting silently withdrew to the anteroom.

Only Earl Douglas, Gardiner, and Wriothesley, remained in the hall, while John Heywood crept softly into the king's cabinet and concealed himself behind the hanging of gold brocade which covered the door leading from the king's study to the outer anteroom.

"My lords," said the king, "follow me into my cabinet. As we are dull, the most advisable thing for us to do is to divert ourselves while we occupy ourselves with the weal of our beloved subjects, and consult concerning their happiness and what is conducive to their welfare. Follow me then, and we will hold a general consultation."

"Earl Douglas, your arm!" and as the king leaned on it and walked slowly toward the cabinet, at the entrance of which the lord chancellor and the Bishop of Winchester were waiting for him, he asked in a low voice: "You say that Henry Howard dares ever intrude himself into the queen's presence?"

"Sire, I did not say that; I meant only that he is constantly to be seen in the queen's presence."

"Oh, you mean that she perhaps authorizes him to do so," said the king, grinding his teeth.

"Sire, I hold the queen to be a noble and dutiful wife."

"I should be quite inclined to lay your head at your feet if you did not!" said the king, in whose face the first lightning of the bursting cloud of wrath began to flash.

"My head belongs to the king!" said Earl Douglas respectfully. "Let him do with it as he pleases."

"But Howard—you mean, then, that Howard loves the queen?"

"Yes, sire, I dare affirm that."

"Now, by the Mother of God, I will tread the serpent under my feet, as I did his sister!" exclaimed Henry, fiercely. "The Howards are an ambitious, dangerous, and hypocritical race."

"A race that never forgets that a daughter of their house has sat on your throne."

"But they shall forget it," cried the king, "and I must wash these proud and haughty thoughts out of their brain with their own blood. They have not then learned, from the example of their sister, how I punish disloyalty. This insolent race needs another fresh example. Well, they shall have it. Only put the means in my hand, Douglas, only a little hook that I can strike into the flesh of these Howards, and I tell you, with that little hook I will drag them to the scaffold. Give me proof of the earl's criminal love, and I promise you that for this I will grant you what you ask."

"Sire, I will give you this proof."

"When?"

"In four days, sire! At the great contest of the poets, which you have ordered to take place on the queen's birthday."

"I thank you, Douglas, I thank you," said the king with an expression almost of joy. In four days you will have rid me of the troublesome race of Howards."

"But, sire, if I cannot give the proof you demand without accusing one other person?"

The king, who was just about to pass the door of his cabinet, stood still, and looked steadily into the earl's eyes. "Then," said he, in a tone peculiarly awful, "you mean the queen? Well, if she is guilty, I will punish her. God has placed the sword in my hand that I may bear it to His honor and to the terror of mankind. If the queen has sinned, she will be punished. Furnish me the proof of Howard's guilt, and do not trouble yourself if we thereby discover the guilt of others. We shall not timidly shrink back, but let justice take its course."

CHAPTER XIV.

THE QUEEN'S FRIEND.

EARL DOUGLAS, Gardiner, and Wriothesley, had accompanied the king into his cabinet.

At last the great blow was to be struck, and the plan of the three enemies of the queen, so long matured and well-considered, was to be at length put in execution. Therefore, as they followed the king, who with unwonted activity preceded them, they exchanged with each other one more look of mutual understanding.

By that look Earl Douglas said, "The hour has come. Be ready!"

And the looks of his friends responded, "We are ready!"

John Heywood, who, hidden behind the hangings, saw and observed everything, could not forbear a slight shudder at the sight of these four men, whose dark and hard features seemed incapable of being touched by any ray of pity or mercy.

There was first the king, that man with the Protean countenance, across which storm and sunshine, God and the devil traced each minute new lines; who could be now an inspired enthusiast, and now a bloodthirsty tyrant; now a sentimental wit, and anon a wanton reveler; the king, on whose constancy nobody, not even himself, could rely; ever ready, as it suited his caprice or his interest, to betray his most faithful friend, and to send to the scaffold to-day those whom but yesterday he had caressed and assured of his unchanging affection; the king, who considered himself privileged to indulge with impunity his low appetites, his revengeful impulses, his bloodthirsty inclinations; who was devout from vanity, because devotion afforded him an opportunity of identifying himself with God, and of regarding himself in some sort the patron of Deity.

There was Earl Douglas, the crafty courtier with ever-smiling face, who seemed to love everybody, while in fact he hated all; who assumed the appearance of perfect harmlessness, and seemed to be indifferent to everything but pleasure, while nevertheless secretly he held in his hand all the strings of that great net which encompassed alike court and king—Earl Douglas, whom the king loved for this alone, because he generally gave him the title of grand and wise high-priest of the Church, and who was, notwithstanding this, Loyola's vicegerent, and a true and faithful adherent of that pope who had damned the king as a degenerate son and given him over to the wrath of God.

Lastly, there were the two men with dark, malignant looks, with inflexible, stony faces, which were never lighted up by a smile, or a gleam of joy; who always condemned, always punished, and whose countenances never brightened save when the dying shriek of the condemned, or the groans of some poor wretch upon the rack, fell upon their ears; who were the tormentors of humanity, while they called themselves the ministers and servants of God.

"Sire," said Gardiner, when the king had slowly taken his seat upon the ottoman—"sire, let us first ask the blessing of the Lord our God on this hour of conference. May God, who is love, but who is wrath also, may He enlighten and bless us!"

The king devoutly folded his hands, but it was only a prayer of wrath that animated his soul.

"Grant, O God, that I may punish Thine enemies, and everywhere dash in pieces the guilty!"

"Amen!" said Gardiner, as he repeated with solemn earnestness the king's words.

"Send us the thunderbolt of Thy wrath," prayed Wriothesley, "that we may teach the world to recognize Thy power and glory!"

Earl Douglas took care not to pray aloud. What *he* had to request of God was not allowed to reach the ear of the king.

"Grant, O God," prayed he in his heart, "grant that my work may prosper, and that this dangerous queen may ascend the scaffold, to make room for my daughter, who is destined to bring back into the arms of our holy mother, the Church, this guilty and faithless king."

"And now, my lords," said the king, fetching a long breath, "now tell me how stand matters in my kingdom, and at my court?"

"Badly," said Gardiner. "Unbelief again lifts up its head. It is a hydra. If you strike off one of its heads, two others immediately spring up in its place. This cursed sect of reformists and atheists multiplies day by day, and our prisons are no longer sufficient to contain them; and when we drag them to the stake, their joyful and courageous death always makes fresh proselytes and fresh apostates."

"Yes, matters are bad," said the Lord Chancellor Wriothesley; "in vain have we promised pardon and forgiveness to all those who would return penitent and contrite; they laugh to scorn our offers of pardon, and prefer a death of torture to the royal clemency. What avails it that we have burnt to death Miles Coverdale, who had the hardihood to translate the Bible? His death appears to have been only the tocsin that aroused other fanatics, and, without our being able to divine or suspect where all these books come from, they have overflowed and deluged the whole land; and we now already have more than four translations of the Bible. The people read them with eagerness; and the corrupt seek of mental illumination and free-thinking waxes daily more powerful and more pernicious."

"And now you, Earl Douglas?" asked the king, when the lord chancellor ceased. "These noble lords have told me how matters stand in my kingdom. You will advise me what is the aspect of things at my court."

"Sire," said Earl Douglas, slowly and solemnly—for he wished each word to sink into the king's breast like a poisoned arrow—"sire, the people but follow the example which the court sets them. How can you require faith of the people, when under their own eyes the court turns faith to ridicule, and when infidels find at court aid and protection?"

"You accuse, but give no names," said the king, impatiently. "Who dares at my court be a protector of heretics?"

"Cranmer, Archbishop of Canterbury!" said the three men, as with one mouth. The signal-word was spoken, the standard of a bloody struggle set up.

"Cranmer?" repeated the king thoughtfully. "He has, however, always been a faithful servant and an attentive friend to me. It was he who delivered me from the unholy bond with Catharine of Aragon: it was he too who warned me of Catharine Howard, and furnished me with proofs of her guilt. Of what misdemeanor do you accuse him?"

"He denies the six articles," said Gardiner, whose malicious face now glowed with bitter hatred. "He reprobates auricular confession, and believes not that the voluntarily taken vows of celibacy are binding."

"If he does that, then he is a traitor!" cried the king, who was fond of always throwing a reverence for chastity and modesty, as a kind of holy mantle, over his own profligate and lewd life; and whom nothing more embittered than to encounter another on that path of vice which he himself, by virtue of his royal prerogative, and his crown by the grace of God, could travel in perfect safety.

"If he does that, then he is a traitor! My arm of vengeance will smite him!" repeated the king again. "It was I who gave my people the six articles, as a sacred and authoritative declaration of faith; and I will not suffer this only true and right doctrine to be assailed and obscured. But you are mistaken, my lords. I am acquainted with Cranmer, and I know that he is loyal and faithful."

"And yet it is he," said Gardiner, "who confirms these heretics in their obduracy and stiff-neckedness. He is the cause why these lost wretches do not, from the fear of divine wrath at least, return to you, their sovereign and high-priest. For he preaches to them that God is love and mercy; he teaches them that Christ came into the world in order to bring to the world love and the forgiveness of sins, and that they alone are Christ's true disciples and servants who emulate His love. Do you not see then, sire, that this is a covert and indirect accusation against yourself, and that while he praises pardoning love, he at the same time condemns and accuses your righteous and punitory wrath?"

The king did not answer immediately, but sat with his eyes fixed, grave and pondering. The fanatical priest had gone too far; and, without being aware of it, it was he himself who was that very instant accusing the king.

Earl Douglas felt this. He read in the king's face that he was just then in one of those moments of contrition which sometimes came over him when his soul held involuntary intercourse with itself. It was necessary to arouse the sleeping tiger and point out to him some prey, so as to make him again bloodthirsty.

"It would be proper if Cranmer preached only Christian love," said he. "Then would he be only a faithful servant of his Lord, and a follower of his king. But he gives to the world an abominable example of a disobedient and perfidious servant; he denies the truth of the six articles, not in words, but in deeds. You have ordered that the priests of the Church remain single. Now, then, the Archbishop of Canterbury is married!"

"Married!" cried the king, his visage glowing with rage. "Ah, I will chastise him, this transgressor of my holy laws! A minister of the Church, a priest, whose whole life should be naught but an exhibition of holiness, an endless communion with God, and whose high calling it is to renounce fleshly lusts and earthly desires! And he is married! I will make him feel the whole weight of my royal anger! He shall learn from his own experience that the king's justice is inexorable, and that in every case he smites the head of the sinner, be he who he may!"

"Your majesty is the embodiment of wisdom and justice," said Douglas, "and your faithful servants well know, if the royal justice is sometimes tardy in smiting guilty offenders, this happens not through your will, but through your servants who venture to stay the arm of justice."

"When and where has this happened?" asked Henry; and his face flushed with rage and excitement. "Where is the offender whom I have not punished? Where in my realm lives a being who has sinned against God or his king, and whom I have not dashed to atoms?"

"Sire," said Gardiner solemnly, "Anne Askew is yet alive."

"She lives to mock at your wisdom and to scoff at your holy creed!" cried Wriothesley.

"She lives, because Bishop Cranmer wills that she should not die," said Douglas, shrugging his shoulders.

The king broke out into a short, dry laugh. "Ah, Cranmer wills not that Anne Askew die!" said he, sneering. "He wills not that this girl, who has so fearfully offended against her king, and against God, should be punished!"

"Yes, she has offended fearfully, and yet two years have passed away since her offence," cried Gardiner—"two years which she has spent in deriding God and mocking the king!"

"Ah," said the king, "we have still hoped to turn this young, misguided creature from the ways of sin and error to the path of wisdom and repentance. We wished for once to give our people a shining example of our willingness to forgive those who repent and renounce their heresy, and to restore them to a participation of our royal favor. Therefore it was that we commissioned you, my lord bishop, by virtue of your prayers and your forcible and convincing words, to pluck this poor child from the claws of the devil, who has charmed her ear."

"But she is unbending," said Gardiner, grinding his teeth. "In vain have I depicted to her the pains of hell, which await her if she return not to the faith; in vain have I subjected her to every variety of torture and penance; in vain have I sent to her in prison other converts, and had them pray with her night and day incessantly; she remains unyielding, hard as stone, and neither the fear of punishment nor the prospect of freedom and happiness has the power to soften that marble heart."

"There is one means yet untried," said Wriothesley— "a means, moreover, which is a more effective preacher of repentance than the most enthusiastic orators and the most fervent prayers, and which I have to thank for bringing back to God and the faith many of the most hardened heretics."

"And this means is——"

"The rack, your majesty."

"Ah, the rack!" replied the king, with an involuntary shudder.

"All means are good that lead to the holy end!" said Gardiner, devoutly folding his hands.

"The soul must be saved, though the body be pierced with wounds!" cried Wriothesley.

"The people must be convinced," said Douglas, "that the lofty spirit of the king spares not even those who are under the protection of influential and might personages. The people murmur that this time justice is not permitted to prevail, because Archbishop Cranmer protects Anne Askew, and the queen is her friend."

"The queen is never the friend of a criminal!" said Henry, vehemently.

"Perchance she does not consider Anne Askew a criminal," responded Earl Douglas, with a slight smile. "It is known, indeed, that the queen is a great friend of the Reformation; and the people, who dare not call her a heretic—the people call her 'the Protestant.'"

"Is it, then, really believed that it is Catharine who protects Anne Askew, and keeps her from the stake?" inquired the king, thoughtfully.

"It is so thought, your majesty."

"They shall soon see that they are mistaken, and that Henry the Eighth well deserves to be called the Defender of the Faith and the Head of his Church!" cried the king, with burning rage. "For when have I shown myself so long-suffering and weak in punishing, that people believe me inclined to pardon and deal gently? Have I not sent to the scaffold even Thomas More and Cromwell, two renowned and in a certain respect noble and high-minded men, because they dared defy my supremacy and oppose the doctrine and ordinance which I commanded them to believe? Have I not sent to the block two of my queens—two beautiful young women, in whom my heart was well pleased, even when I punished them—because they had provoked my wrath? Who, after such brilliant examples of our annihilating justice, who dare accuse us of forbearance?"

"But at that time, sire," said Douglas, in his soft, insinuating voice, "but at that time no queen as yet stood at your side who called heretics true believers, and favored traitors with her friendship."

The king frowned, and his wrathful look encountered the friendly and submissive countenance of the earl. "You know I hate these covert attacks," said he. "If you can tax the queen with any crime, well now, do so. If you cannot, hold your peace!"

"The queen is a noble and virtuous lady," said the earl, "only she sometimes permits herself to be led away by her magnanimous spirit. Or how, your majesty, can it possibly be with your permission that my lady the queen maintains a correspondence with Anne Askew?"

"What say you? The queen in correspondence with Anne Askew?" cried the king in a voice of thunder. "That is a lie, a shameless lie, hatched up to ruin the queen; for it is very well known that the poor king, who has been so often deceived, so often imposed upon, believes himself to have at last found in this woman a being whom he can trust, and in whom he can put faith. And they grudge him that. They wish to strip him of this last hope also, that his heart may harden entirely to stone, and no emotion of pity evermore find access to him. Ah, Douglas, Douglas, beware of my wrath, if you cannot prove what you say!"

"Sire, I can prove it! For Lady Jane herself, no longer ago than yesterday, was made to give up a note from Anne Askew to the queen."

The king remained silent for a while, and gazed fixedly on the ground. His three confidants observed him with breathless, trembling expectation.

At length the king raised his head again, and turned his gaze, which was now grave and steady, upon the lord chancellor.

"My Lord Chancellor Wriothesley," said he, "I empower you to conduct Anne Askew to the torture-room, and try whether the torments which are prepared for the body are perchance able to bring this erring soul to an acknowledgment of her faults. My Lord Bishop Gardiner, I promise my word that I will give attention to your accusation against the Archbishop of Canterbury, and that, if it be well founded, he shall not escape punishment. My Lord Douglas, I will give my people and all the world proof that I am still God's righteous and avenging vicegerent on earth, and that no consideration can restrain my wrath, no after-thought stay my arm, whenever it is ready to fall and smite the head of the guilty. And now, my lords, let us declare this session at an end. Let us breathe a little from these exertions, and seek some recreation for one brief hour.

"My Lords Gardiner and Wriothesley, you are now at liberty. You, Douglas, will accompany me into the small reception-room. I want to see bright and laughing faces around me. Call John Heywood, and if you meet any ladies in the palace, of course I beg them to shed on us a little of that sunshine which you say is peculiarly woman's."

He laughed, and, leaning on the earl's arm, left the cabinet.

Gardiner and Wriothesley stood there in silence, watching the king, who slowly and heavily traversed the adjacent hall, and whose cheery and laughing voice came ringing back to them.

"He is a weathercock, turning every moment from side to side," said Gardiner, with a contemptuous shrug of the shoulders.

"He calls himself God's sword of vengeance, but he is nothing more than a weak tool, which we bend and use at our will," muttered Wriothesley, with a hoarse laugh. "Poor, pitiful fool, deeming himself so mighty and sturdy; imagining himself a free king, ruling by his sovereign will alone, and yet he is but our servant and drudge! Our great work is approaching its end, and we shall one day triumph. Anne Askew's death is the sign of a new covenant, which will deliver England and trample the heretics like dust beneath our feet. And when at length we shall have put down Cranmer, and brought Catharine Parr to the scaffold, then will we give King Henry a queen who will reconcile him with God and the Church, out of which is no salvation."

"Amen, so be it!" said Gardiner; and arm in arm they both left the cabinet.

Deep stillness now reigned in that little spot, and nobody saw John Heywood as he now came from behind the hanging, and, completely worn out and faint, slipped for a moment into a chair.

"Now I know, so far at least, the plan of these bloodthirsty tiger-cats," muttered he. "They wish to give Henry a popish queen; and so Cranmer must be overthrown, that, when they have deprived the queen of this powerful prop, they may destroy her also and tread her in the dust. But as God liveth, they shall not succeed in this! God is just, and He will at last punish these evildoers. And supposing there is no God, then will we try a little with the devil himself. No, they shall not destroy the noble Cranmer and this beautiful, high-minded queen. I forbid it—I, John Heywood, the king's fool. I will see everything, observe everything, hear everything. They shall find me everywhere on their path; and when they poison the king's ear with their diabolical whisperings, I will heal it again with my merry deviltries. The king's fool will be the guardian angel of the queen."

CHAPTER XV.

JOHN HEYWOOD.

AFTER so much care and excitement, the king needed an hour of recreation and amusement. Since the fair young queen was seeking these far away in the chase, and amid the beauties of Nature, Henry must, no doubt, be content to seek them for himself, and in a way different from the queen's. His unwieldiness and his load of flesh prevented him from pursuing the joys of life beyond his own halls; so the lords and ladies of his court had to bring them hither to him, and station the flitting goddess of Joy, with her wings fettered, in front of the king's trundle-chair.

The gout had that day again overcome that mighty king of earth; and a heavy, grotesque mass it was which sat there in the elbow-chair.

But the courtiers still called him a fine-looking and fascinating man; and the ladies still smiled on him and said, by their sighs and by their looks, that they loved him; that he was ever to them the same handsome and captivating man that he was twenty years before, when yet young, fine-looking, and slim. How they smile upon him, and ogle him! How Lady Jane, the maiden otherwise so haughty and so chaste, does wish to ensnare him with her bright eyes as with a net! How bewitchingly does the Duchess of Richmond, that fair and voluptuous woman, laugh at the king's merry jests and *double entendres!*

Poor king! whose corpulency forbids him to dance as he once had done with so much pleasure and so much dexterity! Poor king! whose age forbids him to sing as once he had done to the delight both of the court and himself!

But there are yet, however, pleasant, precious, joyous hours, when the man revives some little in the king; when even youth once more again awakes within him, and smiles in a few dear, blessed pleasures.

The king still has at least eyes to perceive beauty, and a heart to feel it.

How beautiful Lady Jane is, this white lily with the dark, star-like eyes! How beautiful Lady Richmond, this full-blown red rose with the pearl-white teeth!

And they both smile at him; and when the king swears he loves them, they bashfully cast down their eyes and sigh.

"Do you sigh, Jane, because you love me?"

"Oh, sire, you mock me. It would be a sin for me to love you, for Queen Catharine is living."

"Yes, she is living!" muttered the king; and his brow darkened; and for a moment the smile disappeared from his lips.

Lady Jane had committed a mistake. She had reminded the king of his wife when it was yet too soon to ask for her death.

John Heywood read this in the countenance of his royal master, and resolved to take advantage of it. He wished to divert the attention of the king, and to draw it away from the beautiful, captivating women who were juggling him with their bewitching charms.

"Yes, the queen lives!" said he, joyfully, "and God be praised for it! For how tedious and dull it would be at this court had we not our fair queen, who is as wise as Methuselah, and innocent and good as a new-born babe! Do you not, Lady Jane, say with me, God be praised that Queen Catharine is living?"

"I say so with you!" said Jane, with ill-concealed vexation.

"And you, King Henry, do you not say it too?"

"Of course, fool!"

"Ah, why am I not King Henry?" sighed John Heywood. "King, I envy you, not your crown, or your royal mantle; not your attendants or your money. I envy you only this, that you can say, 'God be praised that my wife is still alive!' while I never know but one phrase, 'God have pity, my wife is still alive!' Ah, it is very seldom, king, that I have heard a married man speak otherwise! You are in that too, as in all things else, an exception, King Henry; and your people have never loved you more warmly and purely than when you say, 'I thank God that my consort is alive!' Believe me, you are perhaps the only man at your court who speaks after this manner, however ready they may be to be your parrots, and re-echo what the lord high-priest says."

"The only man that loves his wife?" said Lady Richmond. "Behold now the rude babbler! Do you not believe, then, that we women deserve to be loved?"

"I am convinced that you do not."

"And for what do you take us, then?"

"For cats, which God, since He had no more cat-skin, stuck into a smooth hide!"

"Take care, John, that we do not show you our claws!" cried the duchess, laughing.

"Do it anyhow, my lady! I will then make a cross, and ye will disappear. For devils, you well know, cannot endure the sight of the holy cross, and ye are devils."

John Heywood, who was a remarkably fine singer, seized the mandolin, which lay near him, and began to sing.

It was a song, possible only in those days, and at Henry's voluptuous and at the same time canting court—a song full of the most wanton allusions, of the most cutting jests against both monks and women; a song which made Henry laugh, and the ladies blush; and in which John Heywood had poured forth in glowing dithyrambics all his secret indignation against Gardiner, the sneaking hypocrite of a priest, and against Lady Jane, the queen's false and treacherous friend.

But the ladies laughed not. They darted flashing glances at John Heywood; and Lady Richmond earnestly and resolutely demanded the punishment of the perfidious wretch who dared to defame women.

The king laughed still harder. The rage of the ladies was so exceedingly amusing.

"Sire," said the beautiful Richmond, "he has insulted not us, but the whole sex; and in the name of our sex, I demand revenge for the affront."

"Yes, revenge!" cried Lady Jane, hotly.

"Revenge!" repeated the rest of the ladies.

"See, now, what pious and gentle-hearted doves ye are!" cried John Heywood.

The king said, laughingly: "Well, now, you shall have your will—you shall chastise him."

"Yes, yes, scourge me with rods, as they once scourged the Messiah, because He told the Pharisees the truth. See here! I am already putting on the crown of thorns."

He took the king's velvet cap with solemn air, and put it on.

"Yes, whip him, whip him!" cried the king, laughing, as he pointed to the gigantic vases of Chinese porcelain, containing enormous bunches of roses, on whose long stems arose a real forest of formidable-looking thorns.

"Pull the large bouquets to pieces; take the roses in your hand, and whip him with the stems!" said the king, and his eyes glistened with inhuman delight, for the scene promised to be quite interesting. The rose-stems were long and hard, and the thorns on them pointed and sharp as daggers. How nicely they would pierce the flesh, and how he would yell and screw his face, the good-natured fool!

"Yes, yes, let him take off his coat, and we will whip him!" cried the Duchess of Richmond; and the women, all joining in the cry, rushed like furies upon John Heywood, and forced him to lay aside his silk upper garment. Then they hurried to the vases, snatched out the bouquets, and with busy hands picked out the longest and stoutest stems. And loud were their exclamations of satisfaction, if the thorns were right and sharp, such as would penetrate the flesh of the offender right deeply.

The king's laughter and shouts of approval animated them more and more, and made them more excited and furious. Their cheeks glowed, their eyes glared; they resembled Bacchantes circling the god of riotous joviality with their shouts of "Evoe! evoe!"

"Not yet! do not strike yet!" cried the king. "You must first strengthen yourselves for the exertion, and fire your arms for a powerful blow!"

He took the large golden beaker which stood before him and, tasting it, presented it to Lady Jane.

"Drink, my lady, drink, that your arm may be strong!"

And they all drank, and with animated smiles pressed their lips on the spot which the king's mouth had touched. And now their eyes had a brighter flame, and their cheeks a more fiery glow.

A strange and exciting sight it was, to see those beautiful women burning with malicious joy and thirst for vengeance, who for the moment had laid aside all their elegant attitudes, their lofty and haughty airs, to transform themselves into wanton Bacchantes, bent on chastising the offender, who had so often and so bitterly lashed them all with his tongue.

"Ah, I would a painter were here!" said the king. "He should paint us a picture of the chaste nymphs of Diana pursuing Actæon. You are Actæon, John!"

"But they are not the chaste nymphs, king; no, far from it," cried Heywood, laughing, "and between these fair women and Diana I find no resemblance, but only a difference."

"And in what consists the difference, John?"

"Herein, sire, that Diana carried her horn at her side; but these fair ladies make their husbands wear their horns on the forehead!"

A loud peal of laughter from the gentlemen, a yell of rage from the ladies, was the reply of this new epigram of John Heywood.

They arranged themselves in two rows, and thus formed a lane through which John Heywood had to pass.

"Come, John Heywood, come and receive your punishment"; and they raised their thorny rods threateningly, and flourished them with angry gestures high above their heads.

The scene was becoming to John in all respects very *piquant,* for these rods had very sharp thorns, and only a thin linen shirt covered his back.

With bold step, however, he approached the fatal passage through which he was to pass.

Already he beheld the rods drawn back; and it seemed to him as if the thorns were even now piercing his back.

He halted, and turned with a laugh to the king. "Sire, since you have condemned me to die by the hands of these nymphs, I claim the right of every condemned criminal—a last favor."

"The which we grant you, John."

"I demand that I may put on these fair women one condition—one condition on which they may whip me. Does your majesty grant me this?"

"I grant it!"

"And you solemnly pledge me the word of a king that this condition shall be faithfully kept and fulfilled?"

"My solemn, kingly word for it!"

"Now, then," said John Heywood, as he entered the passage, "now, then, my ladies, my condition is this: that one of you who has had the most lovers, and has oftenest decked her husband's head with horns, let her lay the first stroke on my back." *

A deep silence followed. The raised arms of the fair women sank. The roses fell from their hands and dropped to the ground. Just before so bloodthirsty and revengeful, they seemed now to have become the softest and gentlest of beings.

But could their looks have killed, their fire certainly

---

* Flogel's "Geschichte der Hofnarren," p. 899.

would have consumed poor John Heywood, who now gazed at them with an insolent sneer, and advanced into the very midst of their lines.

"Now, my ladies, you strike him not?" asked the king.

"No, your majesty, we despise him too much even to wish to chastise him," said the Duchess of Richmond.

"Shall your enemy who has injured you go thus unpunished?" asked the king. "No, no, my ladies; it shall not be said that there is a man in my kingdom whom I have let escape when so richly deserving punishment. We will, therefore, impose some other punishment on him. He calls himself a poet, and has often boasted that he could make his pen fly as fast as his tongue! Now, then, John, show us in this manner that you are no liar! I command you to write, for the great court festival which takes place in a few days, a new interlude; and one indeed, hear you, John, which is calculated to make the greatest growler merry, and over which these ladies will be forced to laugh so heartily, that they will forget all their ire!"

"Oh," said John dolefully, "what an equivocal and lewd poem it must be to please these ladies and make them laugh! My king, we must, then, to please these dear ladies, forget a little our chastity, modesty, and maiden bashfulness, and speak in the spirit of the ladies—that is to say, as lasciviously as possible."

"You are a wretch!" said Lady Jane; "a vulgar hypocritical fool."

"Earl Douglas, your daughter is speaking to you," said John Heywood, calmly. "She flatters you much, your tender daughter."

"Now then, John, you have heard my orders, and will you obey them? In four days will this festival begin; I give you two days more. In six days, then, you have to write a new interlude. And if he fails to do it, my ladies, you shall whip him until you bring the blood; and that without any condition."

Just then was heard without a flourish of trumpets and the clatter of horse-hoofs.

"The queen has returned," said John Heywood, with a countenance beaming with joy, as he fixed his smiling gaze full of mischievous satisfaction on Lady Jane. "Nothing further now remains for you to do, but dutifully to meet your mistress upon the great staircase, for, as you so wisely said before, *the queen still lives.*"

Without waiting for an answer, John Heywood ran out and rushed through the anteroom and down the steps to meet the queen. Lady Jane watched him with a dark, angry look; and as she turned slowly to the door to go and meet the queen, she muttered low between her closely-pressed lips: "The fool must die, for he is the queen's friend!"

CHAPTER XVI.

THE CONFIDANT.

THE queen was just ascending the steps of the great public staircase, and she greeted John Heywood with a friendly smile.

"My lady," said he aloud, "I have a few words in private to say to you, in the name of his majesty."

"Words in private!" repeated Catharine, as she stopped upon the terrace of the palace. "Well, then, fall back, my lords and ladies; we wish to receive his majesty's mysterious message."

The royal train silently and respectfully withdrew into the large anteroom of the palace, while the queen remained alone with John Heywood on the terrace.

"Now, speak, John."

"Queen, heed well my words, and grave them deep on your memory! A conspiracy is forged against you, and in a few days, at the great festival, it will be ripe for execution. Guard well, therefore, every word you utter, ay, even your very thoughts. Beware of every dangerous step, for you may be certain that a listener stands behind you! And if you need a confidant, confide in no one but me! I tell you, a great danger lies before you, and only by prudence and presence of mind will you be able to avoid it."

This time the queen did not laugh at her friend's warning voice. She was serious; she even trembled.

She had lost her proud sense of security and her serene confidence—she was no longer guiltless—she had a dangerous secret to keep, consequently she felt a dread of discovery; and she trembled not merely for herself, but also for him whom she loved.

"And in what consists this plot?" asked she, with agitation.

"I do not yet understand it; I only know that it exists. But I will search it out, and if your enemies lurk about you with watchful eyes, well, then, I will have spying eyes to observe them."

"And is it I alone that they threaten?"

"No, queen, your friend also."

Catharine trembled. "What friend, John?"

"Archbishop Cranmer."

"Ah, the archbishop!" replied she, drawing a deep breath.

"And is he all, John? Does their enmity pursue only me and him?"

"Only you two!" said John Heywood, sadly, for he had fully understood the queen's sigh of relief, and he knew that she had trembled for another. "But remember, queen, that Cranmer's destruction would be likewise your own; and that as you protect the archbishop, he also will protect you with the king—you, queen, and your *friends*."

Catharine gave a slight start, and the crimson on her cheek grew deeper.

"I shall always be mindful of that, and ever be a true and real friend to him and to you; for you two are my only friends: is it not so?"

"No, your majesty, I spoke to you of yet a third, of Thomas Seymour."

"Oh, he!" cried she with a sweet smile. Then she said suddenly, and in a low quick voice: "You say I must trust no one here but you. Now, then, I will give you a proof of my confidence. Await me in the green summer-house at twelve o'clock to-night. You must be my attendant on a dangerous excursion. Have you courage, John?"

"Courage to lay down my life for you, queen!"

"Come, then, but bring your weapon with you."

"At your command! and is that your only order for to-day?"

"That is all, John! only," added she, with hesitation and a slight blush, "only, if you perchance meet Earl Sudley, you may say to him that I charged you to greet him in my name."

"Oh!" sighed John Heywood, sadly.

"He has to-day saved my life, John," said she, as if excusing herself. "It becomes me well, then, to be grateful to him."

And giving him a friendly nod, she stepped into the porch of the castle.

"Now let anybody say again, that chance is not the most mischievous and spiteful of all devils!" muttered John Heywood. "This devil, chance, throws in the queen's way the very person she ought most to avoid; and she must be, as in duty bound, very grateful to a lover. Oh, oh, so he has saved her life? But who knows whether he may not be one day the cause of her losing it!"

He dropped his head gloomily upon his breast, when suddenly he heard behind him a low voice calling his name; and as he turned, he saw the young Princess Elizabeth hastening toward him with a hurried step.

She was at that moment very beautiful. Her eyes gleamed with the fire of passion; her cheeks glowed; and about her crimson lips there played a gentle, happy smile. She wore, according to the fashion of the time, a close-fitting high-necked dress, which showed off to perfection the delicate lines of her slender and youthful form, while the wide standing collar concealed the somewhat too great length of her neck, and made her ruddy, as yet almost childish face stand out as it were from a pedestal. On either side of her high, thoughtful brow, fell, in luxurious profusion, light flaxen curls; her head was covered with a black velvet cap, from which a white feather drooped to her shoulders.

She was altogether a charming and lovely apparition, full of nobleness and grace, full of fire and energy; and yet, in spite of her youthfulness, not wanting in a certain grandeur and dignity. Elizabeth, though still almost a child, and frequently bowed and humbled by misfortune, yet ever remained her father's own daughter. And though Henry had declared her a bastard and excluded her from the succession to the throne, yet she bore the stamp of her royal blood in her high, haughty brow; in her keen, flashing eye.

As she now stood before John Heywood, she was not, however, the haughty, imperious princess, but merely the shy, blushing maiden, who feared to trust her first girlish secret to another's ear, and ventured only with trembling hand to draw aside the veil which concealed her heart.

"John Heywood," said she, "you have often told me that you loved me; and I know that my poor unfortunate mother trusted you, and summoned you as a witness of her innocence. You could not at that time save the mother, but will you now serve Anne Boleyn's daughter, and be her faithful friend?"

"I will," said Heywood, solemnly, "and as true as there is a God above us, you shall never find me a traitor."

"I believe you, John; I know that I may trust you.

Listen then, I will now tell you my secret—a secret which no one but God knows, and the betrayal of which might bring me to the scaffold. Will you then swear to me, that you will never, under any pretext, and from any motive whatsoever, betray to anybody, so much as a single word of what I am now about to tell you? Will you swear to me, never to intrust this secret to any one, even on your death-bed, and not to betray it even in the confessional?"

"Now as regards that, princess," said John, with a laugh, "you are perfectly safe. I never go to confession, for confession is a highly-spiced dish of popery on which I long since spoilt my stomach; and as concerns my death-bed, one cannot, under the blessed and pious reign of Henry the Eighth, altogether know whether he will be really a participant of any kind, or whether he may not make a far more speedy and convenient trip into eternity by the aid of the hangman."

"Oh, be serious, John—do, I pray you! Let the fool's mask, under which you hide your sober and honest face, not hide it from me also. Be serious, John, and swear to me that you will keep my secret."

"Well, then, I swear, princess; I swear by your mother's spirit to betray not a word of what you are going to tell me."

"I thank you, John. Now lean this way nearer to me, lest the breeze may catch a single word of mine and bear it farther. John, I love!"

She saw the half-surprised, half-incredulous smile which played around John Heywood's lips. "Oh," continued she, passionately, "you believe me not. You consider my fourteen years, and you think the child knows nothing yet of a maiden's feelings. But remember, John, that those girls who live under a warm sun are early ripened by his glowing rays, and are already wives and mothers when they should still be dreaming children. Well, now, I too am the daughter of a torrid zone, only mine has not been the sun of prosperity, and it has been sorrow and misfortune which have matured my heart. Believe me, John, I love! A glowing, consuming fire rages within me; it is at once my delight and my misery, my happiness and my future.

"The king has robbed me of a brilliant and glorious future; let them not, then, grudge me a happy one, at least. Since I am never to be a queen, I will at least be a happy and beloved wife. If I am condemned to live in obscurity and lowliness, at the very least, I must not be prohibited from adorning this obscure and inglorious existence with flowers, which thrive not at the foot of the throne, and to illuminate it with stars more sparkling than the refulgence of the most radiant kingly crown."

"Oh, you are mistaken about your own self!" said John Heywood, sorrowfully. "You choose the one only because the other is denied. You would love only because you cannot rule; and since your heart, which thirsts for fame and honor, can find no other satisfaction, you would quench its thirst with some other draught, and would administer love as an opiate to lull to rest its burning pains. Believe me, princess, you do not yet know yourself! You were not born to be merely a loving wife, and your brow is much too high and haughty to wear only a crown of myrtle. Therefore, consider well what you do, princess! Be not carried away by your father's passionate blood, which boils in your veins also. Think well before you act. Your foot is yet on one of the steps to the throne. Draw it not back voluntarily. Maintain your position; then, the next step brings you again one stair higher up. Do not voluntarily renounce your just claim, but abide in patience the coming of the day of retribution and justice. Only do not yourself make it impossible, that there may then be a full and glorious reparation. *Princess* Elizabeth may yet one day be queen, provided she has not exchanged her name for one less glorious and noble."

"John Heywood," said she, with a bewitching smile, "I have told you I love him."

"Well, love him as much as you please, but do it in silence, and tell him not of it; but teach your love resignation."

"John, he knows it already."

"Ah, poor princess! you are still but a child, that sticks its hands in the fire with smiling bravery and scorches them, because it knows not that fire burns."

"Let it burn, John, burn! and let the flames curl over my head! Better be consumed in fire than perish slowly and horribly with a deadly chill! I love him, I tell you, and he already knows it!"

"Well, then, love him, but, at least, do not marry him!" cried John Heywood, surlily.

"Marry!" cried she, with astonishment. "Marry! I had never thought of it."

She dropped her head upon her breast, and stood there, silent and thoughtful.

"I am much afraid I made a blunder, then!" muttered John Heywood. "I have suggested a new thought to her. Ah, ah, King Henry has done well in appointing me his fool! Just when we deem ourselves the wisest, we are the greatest fools!"

"John," said Elizabeth, as she raised her head again and smiled to him in a glow of excitement, "John, you are entirely right; if we love, we must marry."

"But I said just the contrary, princess!"

"All right!" said she, resolutely. "All this belongs to the future; we will busy ourselves with the present. I have promised my lover an interview."

"An interview!" cried John Heywood, in amazement. "You will not be so foolhardy as to keep your promise?"

"John Heywood," said she, with an air of approaching solemnity, "King Henry's daughter will never make a promise without fulfilling it. For better or for worse, I will always keep my plighted word, even if the greatest misery and ruin were the result!"

John Heywood ventured to offer no further opposition.

There was at this moment something peculiarly lofty, proud, and truly royal in her air, which impressed him with awe, and before which he bowed.

"I have granted him an interview because he wished it," said Elizabeth; "and, John, I will confess it to you, my own heart longed for it. Seek not, then, to shake my resolution; it is as firm as a rock. But if you are not willing to stand by me, say so, and I will then look about me for another friend, who loves me enough to impose silence on his thoughts."

"But who, perhaps, will go and betray you. No, no, it has been once resolved upon, and unalterably; so no one but I must be your confidant. Tell me, then, what I am to do, and I will obey you."

"You know, John, that my apartments are situated in yonder wing, overlooking the garden. Well, in my dressing-room, behind one of the large wall pictures, I have discovered a door leading into a lonely, dark corridor. From this corridor there is a passage up into yonder tower. It is unoccupied and deserted. Nobody ever thinks of entering that part of the castle, and the quiet of the grave reigns throughout those apartments, which nevertheless are furnished with a magnificence truly regal. There will I receive him."

"But how shall he make his way thither?"

"Oh, do not be concerned; I have thought over that many days since; and while I was refusing my lover the interview for which he again and again implored me, I was quietly preparing everything so as to be able one day to grant it to him. To-day this object is attained, and to-day have I fulfilled his wish, voluntarily and unasked; for I saw he had no more courage to ask again. Listen, then. From the tower, a spiral staircase leads down to a small door, through which you gain entrance into the garden. I have a key to this door. Here it is. Once in possession of this key, he has nothing further to do but remain behind in the park this evening, instead of leaving the castle; and by means of this he will come to me, for I will wait for him in the tower, in the large room directly opposite the staircase landing. Here, take the key; give it to him, and repeat to him all that I have said."

"Well, princess, there remains for you now only to appoint the hour at which you will receive him there."

"The hour," said she, as she turned away her blushing face. "You understand, John, that it is not feasible to receive him there by day, because there is by day not a single moment in which I am not watched."

"You will then receive him by night!" said John Heywood, sadly. "At what hour?"

"At midnight! And now you know all; and I beg you, John, hasten and carry him my message; for, look, the sun is setting, and it will soon be night."

She nodded to him with a smile, and turned to go.

"Princess, you have forgotten the most important point. You have not yet told me his name."

"My God! and you do not guess it? John Heywood, who has such sharp eyes, sees not that there is at this court but a single one that deserves to be loved by a daughter of the king!"

"And the name of this single one is——"

"Thomas Seymour, Earl of Sudley!" whispered Elizabeth, as she turned away quickly and entered the castle.

"Oh, Thomas Seymour!" said John Heywood, utterly astounded. As if paralyzed with horror, he stood there motionless, staring up at the sky and repeating over and over, "Thomas Seymour! Thomas Seymour! So he is a sorcerer who administers a love-potion to all the women, and befools them with his handsome, saucy face. Thomas Seymour! The queen loves him; the princess loves him; and then there is this Duchess of Richmond, who will by all means be his wife! This much, however, is certain, he is a traitor who deceives both, because to both he has made the same confession of love. And there again is that imp, chance, which compels me to be the confidant of both these women. But I will be well on my guard against executing both my commissions to this sorcerer. Let him at any rate become the husband of the princess; perhaps this would be the surest means of freeing the queen from her unfortunate love."

He was silent, and still gazed up thoughtfully at the sky. "Yes," said he then, quite cheerfully, "thus shall it be. I will combat the one love with the other. For the queen to love him, is dangerous. I will therefore so conduct matters that she must hate him. I will remain her confidant. I will receive her letters and her commissions, but I will burn her letters and not execute her commissions. I am not at liberty to tell her that the faithless Thomas Seymour is false to her, for I have solemnly pledged my word to the princess never to breathe her secret to any one; and I will and must keep my word. Smile and love, then; dream on thy sweet dream of love, queen; I wake for thee; I will cause the dark cloud resting on thee to pass by. It may, perhaps, touch thine heart; but thy noble and beautiful head—*that* at least it shall not be allowed to crush; that——"

"Now, then, what are you staring up at the sky for, as if you read there a new epigram with which to make the king laugh, and the parsons rave?" asked a voice near him; and a hand was laid heavily on his shoulder.

John Heywood did not look round at all; he remained in the same attitude, gazing up steadily at the sky. He had very readily recognized the voice of him who had addressed him; he knew very well that he who stood near him was no other than the bold sorcerer whom he was just then cursing at the bottom of his heart; no other than Thomas Seymour, Earl of Sudley.

"Say, John, is it really an epigram?" asked Thomas Seymour again. "An epigram on the hypocritical, lustful, and sanctimonious priestly rabble, that with blasphemous hypocrisy fawn about the king, and are ever watchful how they can set a trap for one of us honorable and brave men? Is that what Heaven is now revealing to you?"

"No, my lord, I am only looking at a hawk which hovers about there in the clouds. I saw him mount, earl, and only think of the wonder—he had in each talon a dove! Two doves for one hawk. Is not that too much—wholly contrary to law and nature?"

The earl cast on him a penetrating and distrustful look. But John Heywood, remaining perfectly calm and unembarrassed, continued looking at the clouds.

"How stupid such a brute is, and how much to his disadvantage will his very greediness be! For since he holds a dove in each claw, he will not be able to enjoy either of them; because he has no claw at liberty with which to tear them. Soon as he wishes to enjoy the one, the other will escape; when he grabs after that, the other flies away; and so at last he will have nothing at all, because he was too rapacious and wanted more than he could use."

"And you are looking after this hawk in the skies? But you are perhaps mistaken, and he whom you seek is not above there at all, but here below, and perchance quite close to you?" asked Thomas Seymour significantly.

But John Heywood would not understand him.

"Nay," said he, "he still flies, but it will not last long. For verily I saw the owner of the dovecot from which the hawk has stolen the two doves. He had a weapon; and he, be ye sure of it—he will kill this hawk, because he has robbed him of his pet doves."

"Enough, enough!" cried the earl, impatiently. "You would give me a lesson, but you must know I take no counsel from a fool, even were he the wisest."

"In that you are right, my lord, for only fools are so foolish as to hearken to the voice of wisdom. Besides, each man forges his own fortune. And now, wise sir, I will give you a key, which you yourself have forged, and behind which lies your fortune. There, take this key; and if you at midnight slip through the garden to the tower over yonder, this key will open to you the door of the same, and you can then without hesitation mount the spiral staircase and open the door which is opposite the staircase. Behind that you will find the fortune which you have forged for yourself, sir blacksmith, and which will bid you welcome with warm lips and soft arms. And so commending you to God, I must hasten home to think over the comedy which the king has commanded me to write."

"But you do not so much as tell me from whom this message comes?" said Earl Sudley, retaining him. "You invite me to a meeting and give me a key, and I know not who will await me there in that tower."

"Oh, you do not know? There is then more than one who *might* await you there? Well, then, it is the youngest and smallest of the two doves who sends you the key."

"Princess Elizabeth?"

"You have named her, not I!" said John Heywood, as he disengaged himself from the earl's grasp and hurried across the courtyard to betake himself to his lodgings.

Thomas Seymour watched him with a scowl, and then slowly directed his eyes to the key that Heywood had given him.

"The princess then awaits me," whispered he, softly. "Ah, who can read it in the stars? who can know whither the crown will roll when it tumbles from King Henry's head? I love Catharine, but I love ambition still more; and if it is demanded, to ambition must I sacrifice my heart."

CHAPTER XVII.

GAMMER GURTON'S NEEDLE.

SLOWLY and lost in gloomy thought, John Heywood walked toward his lodgings. These lodgings were situated in the second or inner court of the vast palace of Whitehall, in that wing of the castle which contained the apartments of all the higher officers of the royal household, and so those of the court-jesters also; for the king's fool was at that period a very important and respectable personage, who occupied a rank equal to that of a gentleman of the royal bed-chamber.

John Heywood had just crossed this second courtyard, when all at once loud, wrangling voices, and the clear, peculiar ring of a box on the ear, startled him out of his meditations.

He stopped and listened.

His face, before so serious, had now reassumed its usual merry and shrewd expression; his large eyes again glittered with humor and mischief.

"There again verily is my sweet, charming housekeeper, Gammer Gurton," said John Heywood, laughing; "and she no doubt is quarrelling again with my excellent servant, that poor, long-legged, blear-eyed Hodge. Ah! ha! Yesterday I surprised her as she applied a kiss to him, at which he made as doleful a face as if a bee had stung him. To-day I hear how she is boxing his ears. He is perhaps now laughing at it, and thinks it is a rose-leaf which cools his cheek. That Hodge is such a queer bird! But we will at once see what there is to-day, and what farce is being performed now."

He crept softly up-stairs, and, opening the door of his room, closed it again behind him quickly and gently.

Gammer Gurton, who was in the room adjoining, had heard nothing, seen nothing; and had the heavens come tumbling down at that moment, she would have scarcely noticed it; for she had eyes and sense only for this long, lank lackey who stood before her shaking with fear, and staring at her out of his great bluish-white eyes. Her whole soul lay in her tongue; and her tongue ran as fast as a will-wheel, and with the force of thunder.

How, then, could Gammer Gurton well have time and ears to hear her master, who had softly entered his chamber and slyly crept to the door, only half closed, which separated his room from that of the housekeeper?

"How!" screamed Gammer Gurton, "you silly ragamuffin, you wish to make me believe that it was the cat that ran away with my sewing-needle, as if my sewing-needle were a mouse and smelt of bacon, you stupid, bleareyed fool!"

"Ah, you call me a fool," cried Hodge, with a laugh, which caused his mouth to describe a graceful line across his face from ear to ear; "you call me a fool, and that is a great honor for me, for then I am a servant worthy of my master. And as to being blear-eyed, that must be caused by the simple fact that I have nothing all day long before my eyes but you, Gammer Gurton—you, with your face like a full moon—you, sailing through the room like a frigate, and with your grappling-irons, your hands, smashing to pieces everything except your own looking-glass."

"You shall pay me for that, you double-faced, threadbare lout!" screamed Gammer Gurton, as she rushed on Hodge with clenched fist.

But John Heywood's cunning servant had anticipated this; he had already slipped under the large table which stood in the middle of the room. As the housekeeper now made a plunge to drag him out of his extemporary fortress, he gave her such a hearty pinch on the leg, that she sprang back with a scream, and sank, wholly overcome by the pain, into the huge, leather-covered elbow-chair which was near her workstand at the window.

"You are a monster, Hodge," groaned she, exhausted —"a heartless, horrible monster. You have stolen my sewing-needle—you only. For you knew very well that it was my last one, and that, if I have not that, I must go at once to the shopkeeper to buy some needles. And that is just what you want, you weathercock, you. You only want me to go out, that you may have an opportunity to play with Tib."

"Tib? Who is Tib?" asked Hodge as he stretched out his long neck from under the table, and stared at Gammer Gurton with well-assumed astonishment.

"Now this otter wants me yet to tell him who Tib is!" screamed the exasperated dame. "Well, then, I will tell you. Tib is the cook for the major-domo over there—a black-eyed, false, coquettish little devil, who is bad and mean enough to troll away the lover of an honest and virtuous woman, as I am; a lover who is such a pitiful little thing that one would think no one but myself could find him out and see him; nor could I have done it had I not for forty years trained my eyes to the search, and for forty years looked around for the man who was at length to marry me, and make me a respectable mistress. Since my eyes then were at last steadily fixed on this phantom of man, and I found nothing there, I finally discovered you, you cobweb of a man!"

"What! you call me a cobweb?" screamed Hodge, as he crept from under the table, and, drawing himself up to his full height, placed himself threateningly in front of Gammer Gurton's elbow-chair. "You call me a cobweb? Now, I swear to you that you shall henceforth never more be the spider that dwells in that web! For you are a garden-spider, an abominable, dumpy, old garden-spider, for whom a web, such as Hodge is, is much too fine and much too elegant. Be quiet, therefore, old spider, and spin your net elsewhere! You shall not live in my net, but Tib—for, yes, I do know Tib. She is a lovely, charming child of fourteen, as quick and nimble as a kid, with lips red as the coral which you wear on your fat pudding of a neck, with eyes which shine yet brighter than your nose, and with a figure so slender and graceful that she might have been carved out of one of your fingers. Yes, yes, I know Tib. She is an affectionate, good child, who would never be so hard-hearted as to abuse the man she loves, and could not be so mean and pitiful, even in thought, as to wish to marry the man she did not love, just because he is a man. Yes, I know Tib, and now I will go straight to her and ask her if she will marry a good, honest lad, who, to be sure, is somewhat lean, but who doubtless will become fatter if he has any other fare than the meagre, abominable stuff on which Gammer Gurton feeds him; a lad who, to be sure, is blear-eyed, but will soon get over that disease when he no more sees Gammer Gurton, who acts on his eyes like a stinking onion, and makes them always red and running water. Good-by, old onion! I am going to Tib."

But Gammer Gurton whirled up out of her elbow-chair like a top, and was upon Hodge, whom she held by the coat-tail, and brought him to a stand.

"You dare go to Tib again! You dare pass that door and you shall see that the gentle, peaceable, and patient Gammer Gurton is changed into a lioness, when any one tries to tear from her that most sacred and dearest of treasures, her husband. For you are my husband, inasmuch as I have your word that you will marry me."

"But I have not told you when and where I will do it, Gammer Gurton; and so you can wait to all eternity, for only in heaven will I be your husband."

"That is an abominable, malicious lie!" screamed Gammer Gurton. "A good-for-nothing lie, say I! For did you not long ago snivel and beg till I was forced to promise you to make a will, and in it declare Hodge, my beloved husband, sole heir of all my goods and chattels, and bequeath to him everything I have scraped together in my virtuous and industrious life?"

"But you did not make it—the will. You broke your word; and, therefore, I will do the same."

"Yes, I have made it, you greyhound. I have made it; and this very day I was going with you to a justice of the peace and have it signed, and then to-morrow we would have got married."

"You have made the will, you round world of love?"

said Hodge tenderly, as with his long, withered, spindling arms he tried to clasp the gigantic waist of his beloved. "You have made the will and declared me your heir? Come, then, Gammer Gurton, come, let us go to the justice of the peace!"

"But do you not see, then," said Gammer Gurton, with a tender, cat-like purr, "do you not see, then, that you rumple my frill when you hug me so? Let me go, then, and help me find my needle quickly, for without the needle we cannot go to the justice of the peace."

"What, without the needle not go to the justice of the peace?"

"No; for only see this hole which Gib, the cat, tore in my prettiest cap awhile ago, as I took the cap out of the box and laid it on the table. Indeed I cannot go to the justice of the peace with such a hole in my cap! Search then, Hodge, search, so that I can mend my cap, and go with you to the justice of the peace!"

"Lord God, where in the world can it be, the unlucky needle? I must have it, I must find it, so that Gammer Gurton may take her will to the justice of the peace!"

And in frantic desperation, Hodge searched all about on the floor for the lost needle, and Gammer Gurton stuck her large spectacles on her flaming red nose and peered about on the table. So eager was she in the search, that she even let her tongue rest a little, and deep silence reigned in the room.

Suddenly this silence was broken by a voice, which seemed to come from the courtyard. It was a soft, sweet voice that cried: "Hodge, dear Hodge, are you there? Come to me in the court, only for a few minutes! I want to have a bit of a laugh with you!"

It was as though an electric shock had passed through the room with that voice, and struck at the same time both Gammer Gurton and Hodge.

Both startled, and discontinuing the search, stood there wholly immovable, as if petrified.

Hodge especially, poor Hodge, was as if struck by lightning. His great bluish-white eyes appeared to be coming out of their sockets; his long arms hung down, flapping and dangling about like a flail; his knees, half bent, seemed already to be giving way in expectation of the approaching storm.

This storm did not in fact make him wait long.

"That is Tib!" screamed Gammer Gurton, springing like a lioness upon Hodge and seizing him by the shoulders with both her hands. "That is Tib, you thread-like, pitiful greyhound! Well, was I not right, now, when I called you a faithless, good-for-nothing scamp, that spares not innocence, and breaks the hearts of the women as he would a cracker, which he swallows at his pleasure? Was I not right, in saying that you were only watching for me to go out in order to go and sport with Tib?"

"Hodge, my dear, darling Hodge," cried the voice beneath there, and this time louder and more tender than before, "Hodge, oh come, do now, come with me in the court, as you promised me; come and get the kiss for which you begged me this morning!"

"I will be a damned otter, if I begged her for it, and if I understand a single word of what she says!" said Hodge, wholly dumfounded and quaking all over.

"Ah, you understand not a word of what she says?" screamed Gammer Gurton. "Well, but *I* understand it. I understand that everything between us is past and done with, and that I have nothing more to do with you, you Moloch, you! I understand that I shall not go and make my will, to become your wife and fret myself to death over this skeleton of a husband, that I may leave you to chuckle as my heir. No, no, it is past. I am not going to the justice of the peace, and I will tear up my will!"

"Oh, she is going to tear up her will!" howled Hodge; "and then I have tormented myself in vain; in vain have endured the horrible luck of being loved by this old owl!

Oh, oh, she will not make her will, and Hodge will remain the same miserable dog he always was!"

Gammer Gurton laughed scornfully. "Ah, you are aware at last what a pitiable wretch you are, and how much a noble and handsome person, as I am, lowered herself when she made up her mind to pick up such a weed and make him her husband."

"Yes, yes, I know it!" whined Hodge; "and I pray you pick me up and take me, and above all things make your will!"

"No, I will not take you, and I shall not make my will! It is all over with, I tell you; and now you can go as soon as you please to Tib, who has called you so lovingly. But first give me back my sewing-needle, you magpie, you! Give me here my sewing-needle, which you have stolen. It is of no use to you now, for it is not necessary for me to go out in order that you may go and see Tib. We have nothing more to do with each other, and you can go where you wish. My sewing-needle, say I—my needle, or I will hang you as a scarecrow in my pea-patch, to frighten the sparrows out of it. My sewing-needle, or——"

She shook her clenched fist threateningly at Hodge, fully convinced that now, as always before, Hodge would retreat before this menacing weapon of his jealous and irritable lady-love, and seek safety under the bed or the table.

This time, however, she was mistaken. Hodge, who saw that all was lost, felt that his patience was at length exhausted; and his timidity was now changed to the madness of despair. The lamb was transformed into a tiger, and with a tiger's rage he pounced upon Gammer Gurton, and, throwing aside her fist, he dealt her a good sound blow on the cheek.

The signal was given, and the battle began. It was waged by both sides with equal animosity and equal vigor; only Hodge's bony hand made by far the most telling blows on Gammer Gurton's mass of flesh, and was always certain, wherever he struck, to hit some spot of this huge mass; while Gammer Gurton's soft hand seldom touched that thin, threadlike figure, which dexterously parried every blow.

"Stop, you fools!" suddenly shouted a stentorian voice. "See you not, you goblins, that your lord and master is here? Peace, peace then, you devils, and do not be hammering away at one another, but love each other."

"It is the master!" exclaimed Gammer Gurton, lowering her fist in the utmost contrition.

"Do not turn me away, sir!" moaned Hodge; "do not dismiss me from your service because at last I have for once given the old hag a good bruising. She has deserved it a long time, and an angel himself must at last lose patience with her."

"I turn you out of my service!" exclaimed John Heywood, as he wiped his eyes, wet with laughing. "No, Hodge, you are a real jewel, a mine of fun and merriment; and you two have, without knowing it, furnished me with the choicest materials for a piece which, by the king's order, I have to write within six days. I owe you, then, many thanks, and will show my gratitude forthwith. Listen well to me, my amorous and tender pair of turtle-doves, and mark what I have to say to you. One cannot always tell the wolf by his hide, for he sometimes put on a sheep's skin; and so, too, a man cannot always be recognized by his voice, for he sometimes borrows that of his neighbor. Thus, for example, I know a certain John Heywood, who can mimic exactly the voice of a certain little miss named Tib, and wno knows how to warble as she herself: 'Hodge, my dear Hodge!'"

And he repeated to them exactly, and with the same tone and expression, the words that the voice had previously cried.

"Ah, it was you, sir?" cried Hodge, with a broad grin —"that Tib in the court there, that Tib about whom we have been pummelling each other?"

"I was Tib, Hodge—I who was present during the whole of your quarrel, and found it hugely comical to send Tib's voice thundering into the midst of our lovers' quarrel, like a cannon-stroke! Ah, ha! Hodge, that was a fine bomb-shell, was it not? And as I said 'Hodge, my dear Hodge,' you tumbled about like a kernel of corn which a dung-beetle blows with his breath. No, no, my worthy and virtuous Gammer Gurton, it was not Tib who called the handsome Hodge, and more than that, I saw Tib, as your contest began, go out at the courtyard gate."

"It was not Tib!" exclaimed Gammer Gurton, much moved, and happy as love could make her. "It was not Tib, and she was not in the court at all, and Hodge could not then go down to her, while I went to the shopkeeper's to buy needles. Oh, Hodge, Hodge, will you forgive me for this; will you forget the hard words which I spoke in the fury of my anguish, and can you love me again?"

"I will try," said Hodge, gravely; "and without doubt I shall succeed, provided you go to-day forthwith to the justice, and make your will."

"I will make my will, and to-morrow we will go to the priest; shall it not be so, my angel?"

"Yes, we go to the priest to-morrow!" growled Hodge, as with a frightful grimace he scratched himself behind the ears.

"And now come, my angel, and give me a kiss of reconciliation!"

She spread her arms out, and when Hodge did not come to her, but remained immovable, and steadfast in his position, she went to Hodge and pressed him tenderly to her heart.

Suddenly she uttered a shriek, and let go of Hodge. She had felt a terrible pain in her breast. It seemed as though a small dagger had pierced her bosom.

And there it was, the lost needle, and Hodge then was innocent and pure as the early dawn.

He had not mischievously purloined the needle, so that

Gammer Gurton would be compelled to leave her house in order to fetch some new needles from the shopkeeper's; he had not intended to go to Tib, for Tib was not in the court, but had gone out.

"Oh Hodge, Hodge, good Hodge, you innocent dove, will you forgive me?"

"Come to the justice of the peace, Gammer Gurton, and I forgive you!"

They sank tenderly into each other's arms, wholly forgetful of their master, who still stood near them, and looked on, laughing and nodding his head.

"Now, then, I have found the finest and most splendid materials for my piece," said John Heywood, as he left the loving pair and betook himself to his own room. "Gammer Gurton has saved me, and King Henry will not have the satisfaction of seeing me whipped by those most virtuous and most lovely ladies of his court. To work, then, straightway to work!"

He seated himself at his writing-desk, and seized pen and paper.

"But how!" asked he, suddenly pausing. "That is certainly a rich subject for a composition; but I can never in the world get an interlude out of it! What shall I do with it? Abandon this subject altogether, and again jeer at the monks and ridicule the nuns? That is antiquated and worn out! I will write something new, something wholly new, and something which will make the king so merry, that he will not sign a death-warrant for a whole day. Yes, yes, a merry play shall it be, and then I will call it boldly and fearlessly a comedy!"

He seized his pen and wrote: "*Gammer Gurton's Needle, a right pithy, pleasant, and merry comedy.*"

And thus originated the first English comedy, by John Heywood, fool to King Henry the Eighth.*

* This comedy was first printed in the year 1661, but it was represented at Christ College fully a hundred years previously. Who was the author of it is not known with certainty; but it is possible that

CHAPTER XVIII.

LADY JANE.

ALL was quiet in the palace of Whitehall. Even the servants on guard in the vestibule of the king's bed-chamber had been a long time slumbering, for the king had been snoring for several hours; and this majestical sound was, to the dwellers in the palace, the joyful announcement that for one fine night they were exempt from service, and might be free men.

The queen also had long since retired to her apartments, and dismissed her ladies at an unusually early hour. She felt, she said, wearied by the chase, and much needed rest. No one, therefore, was to disturb her, unless the king should order it.

But the king, as we have said, slept, and the queen had no reason to fear that her night's rest would be disturbed.

Deep silence reigned in the palace. The corridors were empty and deserted, the apartments all silent.

Suddenly a figure tripped along softly and cautiously through the long feebly lighted corridor. She was wrapped in a black mantle; a veil concealed her face.

Scarcely touching the floor with her feet, she floated away, and glided down a little staircase. Now she stops and listens. There is nothing to hear; all is noiseless and still.

Then, on again. Now she wings her steps. For here she is sure of not being heard. It is the unoccupied wing of the castle of Whitehall. Nobody watches her here.

On, then, on, adown that corridor, descending those stairs. There she stops before a door leading into the

the writer of it was John Heywood, the epigrammatist and court-jester.—See Dramaturgie oder Theorie und Geschichte der dramatischen Kunst, von Theodore Mundt, vol. i, p. 309. Flogel's Geschichte der Hofnarren, p. 399.

summer-house. She puts her ear to the door, and listens. Then she claps her hands three times.

The sound is reëchoed from the other side.

"Oh, he is there, he is there!" Forgotten now are her cares, forgotten her pains and tears. He is there. She has him again.

She throws open the door. It is dark indeed in the chamber, but *she* sees him, for the eye of love pierces the night; and if she sees him not, yet she feels his presence.

She rests on his heart; he presses her closely to his breast. Leaning on each other, they grope cautiously along through the dark, desolate chamber to the divan at the upper end, and there, both locked in a happy embrace, they sink upon the cushion.

"At last I have you again! and my arms again clasp this divine form, and again my lips press this crimson mouth! Oh, my beloved, what an eternity has this separation been! Six days! Six long nights of agony! Have you not felt how my soul cried out for you, and was filled with trepidation; how I stretched my arms out into the night, and let them fall again disconsolate and trembling with anguish, because they clasped nothing—naught but the cold, vacant night breeze! Did you not hear, my beloved, how I cried to you with sighs and tears, how in glowing dithyrambics I poured forth to you my longing, my love, my rapture? But you, cruel you, remained ever cold, ever smiling. Your eyes were ever flashing in all the pride and grandeur of a Juno. The roses on your cheeks were not one whit the paler. No, no, you have not longed for me; your heart has not felt this painful, blissful anguish. You are first and above all things the proud, cold queen, and next, next the loving woman."

"How unjust and hard you are, my Henry!" whispered she softly. "I have indeed suffered; and perhaps my pains have been more cruel and bitter than yours, for I —I had to let them consume me within. You could pour them forth, you could stretch out your arms after me, you could utter lamentations and sighs. You were not, like me, condemned to laugh, and to jest, and to listen with apparently attentive ear to all those often heard and constantly repeated phrases of praise and adoration from those about me. You were at least free to suffer. I was not. It is true I smiled, but amidst the pains of death. It is true my cheeks did not blanch, but rouge was the veil with which I covered their paleness; and then, Henry, in the midst of my pains and longings, I had, too, a sweet consolation—your letters, your poems, which fell like the dew of heaven upon my sick soul, and restored it to health, for new torments and new hopes. Oh, how I love them—those poems, in whose noble and enchanting language your love and our sufferings are reëchoed! How my whole soul flew forth to meet them when I received them, and how pressed I my lips thousands and thousands of times on the paper which seemed to me redolent with your breath and your sighs! How I love that good, faithful Jane, the silent messenger of our love! When I behold her entering my chamber, with the unsullied paper in hand, she is to me the dove with the olive-leaf, that brings me peace and happiness, and I rush to her, and press her to my bosom; and give her all the kisses I would give you, and feel how poor and powerless I am, because I cannot repay her all the happiness that she brings me. Ah, Henry, how many thanks do we owe to poor Jane!"

"Why do you call her poor, when she can be near you, always behold you, always hear you?"

"I call her poor, because she is unhappy. For she loves, Henry—she loves to desperation, to madness, and she is not loved. She is pining away with grief and pain, and wrings her hands in boundless woe. Have you not noticed how pale she is, and how her eyes become daily more dim?"

"No, I have not seen it, for I see naught but you, and Lady Jane is to me a lifeless image, as are all other women. But what! You tremble; and your whole frame writhes in my arms, as if in a convulsion! And what is that? Are you weeping?"

"Oh, I weep, because I am so happy. I weep, because I was thinking how fearful the suffering must be, to give the whole heart away, and receive nothing in return, naught but death! Poor Jane!"

"What is she to us? We, we love each other. Come, dear one, let me kiss the tears from your eyes; let me drink this nectar, that it may inspire me, and transfigure me to a god! Weep no more—no, weep not; or, if you will do so, be it only in the excess of rapture, and because word and heart are too poor to hold all this bliss!"

"Yes, yes, let us shout for joy; let us be lost in blessedness!" exclaimed she passionately, as with frantic violence she threw herself on his bosom.

Both were now silent, mutely resting on each other's heart.

Oh, how sweet this silence; how entrancing this noiseless, sacred night! How the trees without there murmur and rustle, as if they were singing a heavenly lullaby to the lovers! how inquisitively the pale crescent moon peeps through the window, as though she were seeking the twain whose blessed confidante she is!

But happiness is so swift-winged, and time flies so fast, when love is their companion!

Even now they must part again—now they must again say farewell.

"Not yet, beloved, stay yet! See, the night is still dark; and hark, the castle clock is just striking two. No, go not yet."

"I must, Henry, I must; the hours are past in which I can be happy."

"Oh, you cold, proud soul! Does the head already long again for the crown; and can you wait no longer for the purple to again cover your shoulders? Come, let me kiss your shoulder; and think now, dear, that my crimson lips are also a purple robe."

"And a purple robe for which I would gladly give my crown and my life!" cried she, with the utmost enthusiasm, as she folded him in her arms.

"Do you love me, then? Do you really love me?"

"Yes, I love you!"

"Can you swear to me that you love no one except me?"

"I can swear it, as true as there is a God above us, who hears my oath."

"Bless you for it, you dear, you only one—oh, how shall I call you?—you whose name I may not utter! Oh, do you know that it is cruel never to name the name of the loved one? Withdraw that prohibition; grudge me not the painfully sweet pleasure of being able at least to call you by your name!"

"No," said she, with a shudder; "for know you not that the sleep-walkers awake out of their dreams when they are called by name? I am a somnambulist, who, with smiling courage, moves along a dizzy height; call me by name, and I shall awake, and, shuddering, plunge into the abyss beneath. Ah, Henry, I hate my name, for it is pronounced by other lips than yours. For you I will not be named as other men call me. Baptize me, my Henry; give me another name—a name which is our secret, and which no one knows besides us."

"I name you *Geraldine;* and as Geraldine I will praise and laud you before all the world. I will, in spite of all these spies and listeners, repeat again and again that I love you, and no one, not the king himself, shall be able to forbid me."

"Hush!" said she, with a shudder, "speak not of him! Oh, I conjure you, my Henry, be cautious; think that you have sworn to me ever to think of the danger that threatens us, and will, without doubt, dash us in pieces if you, by only a sound, a look, or a smile, betray the sweet secret that unites us two. Are you still aware what you have sworn to me?"

"I am aware of it! But it is an unnatural Draconian law. What! even when I am alone with you, shall I never be allowed to address you otherwise than with that reverence and restrain which is due the queen? Even when no one can hear us, may I, by no syllable, by none, not the slightest intimation, remind you of our love?"

"No, no, do it not; for this castle has everywhere eyes and ears, and everywhere are spies and listeners behind the tapestry; behind the curtains; everywhere are they concealed and lurking, watching every feature, every smile, every word, whether it may not afford ground for suspicion. No, no, Henry; swear to me by our love that you will never, unless here in this room, address me otherwise than your queen. Swear to me that, beyond these walls, you will be to me only the respectful servant of your queen, and at the same time the proud earl and lord, of whom it is said that never has a woman been able to touch his heart. Swear to me that you will not, by a look, by a smile, by even the gentlest pressure of the hand, betray what beyond this room is a crime for both of us. Let this room be the temple of our love; but when we once pass its threshold, we will not profane the sweet mysteries of our happiness, by allowing unholy eyes to behold even a single ray of it. Shall it be so, my Henry?"

"Yes, it shall be so!" said he, with a troubled voice; "although I must confess that this dreadful illusion often tortures me almost to death. Oh, Geraldine, when I meet you elsewhere, when I observe the eye so icy and immovable, with which you meet my look, I feel as it were my heart convulsed; and I say to myself: 'This is not she, whom I love—not the tender, passionate woman, whom in the darkness of the night I sometimes lock in my arms. This is Catharine, the queen, but not my loved one. A woman cannot so disguise herself; art goes not so far as to falsify the entire nature, the innermost being and life of a person.' Oh, there have been hours, awful, horrible hours, when it seemed to me as though all this were a delusion, a mystification—as though in some way an evil demon assumed the queen's form by night to mock me, poor frenzied visionary, with a happiness that has no existence, but lives only in my imagination. When such thoughts come to me, I feel a frenzied fury, a crushing despair, and I could, regardless of my oath and even the danger that threatens you, rush to you, and, before all the courtly rabble and the king himself, ask: 'Are you really what you seem? Are you, Catharine Parr, King Henry's wife—nothing more, nothing else than that? Or are you, my beloved, the woman who is mine in her every thought, her every breath; who has vowed to me eternal love and unchanging truth; and whom I, in spite of the whole world, and the king, press to my heart as my own?'"

"Unhappy man, if you ever venture that, you doom us both to death!"

"Be it so, then! In death you will at least be mine, and no one would longer dare separate us, and your eyes would no longer look so cold and strangely upon me, as they often now do. Oh, I conjure you, gaze not upon me at all, if you cannot do it otherwise than with those cold, proud looks, that benumb my heart. Turn away your eyes, and speak to me with averted face."

"Then, men will say that I hate you, Henry."

"It is more agreeable to me for them to say you abhor me than for them to see that I am wholly indifferent to you; that I am to you nothing more than the Earl of Surrey, your lord chamberlain."

"No, no, Henry. They shall see that you are more to me than merely that. Before the whole assembled court I will give you a token of my love. Will you then believe, you dear, foolish enthusiast, that I love you, and that it is no demon that rests here in your arms and swears that she loves nothing but you? Say, will you then believe me?"

"I will believe you! But no, there is no need of any sign, or any assurance. Nay, I know it; I feel indeed the sweet reality that cuddles to my side, warm, and filling me with happiness; and it is only the excess of happiness that makes me incredulous."

"I will convince you thoroughly; and you shall doubt no more, not even in the intoxication of happiness. Listen, then. The king, as you know, is about to hold a great tournament and festival of the poets, and it will take place in a few days. Now, then, at this fête I will publicly, in the presence of the king and his court, give you a rosette that I wear on my shoulder, and in the silver fringe of which you will find a note from me. Will that satisfy you, my Henry?"

"And do you still question it, my dear? Do you question it, when you will make me proud and happy above all others of your court?"

He pressed her closely to his heart and kissed her. But suddenly she writhed in his arms, and started up in wild alarm.

"Day is breaking, day is breaking! See there! a red streak is spreading over the clouds. The sun is coming; day is coming, and already begins to dawn."

He endeavored to detain her still; but she tore herself passionately away, and again enveloped her head in her veil.

"Yes," said he, "day is breaking and it is growing light! Let me then, for a moment at least, see your face. My soul thirsts for it as the parched earth for the dew. Come, it is light here at the window. Let me see your eyes."

She tore herself vehemently away. "No, no, you must begone! Hark, it is already three o'clock. Soon everything will be astir in the castle. Did it not seem as if some person passed by the door here? Haste, haste, if you do not wish me to die of dread!" She threw his cloak over him; she drew his hat over his brow; then once more she threw her arms around his neck and pressed on his lips a burning kiss.

"Farewell, my beloved! farewell, Henry Howard! When we see each other again to-day, you are the Earl of Surrey, and I, the queen—not your loved one—not the woman who loves you! Happiness is past, and suffering awakes anew. Farewell."

She herself opened the glass door, and pushed her lover out.

"Farewell, Geraldine; good-night, my dear! Day comes, and I again greet you as my queen, and I shall have to endure again the torture of your cold looks and your haughty smiles."

CHAPTER XIX.

LOYOLA'S GENERAL.

SHE rushed to the window and gazed after him till he had disappeared, then she uttered a deep cry of anguish, and, wholly overcome by her agony, she sank down on her knees weeping and wailing, wringing her hands, and raising them to God.

But just before so happy and joyful, she was now full of woe and anguish; and bitter sighs of complaint came trembling from her lips.

"Oh, oh," moaned she, with sobs; "what terrible agonies are these, and how full of despair the anguish that lacerates my breast! I have lain in his arms; I have received his vows of love and accepted his kisses; and these vows are not mine, and these kisses he gave not to me. He kissed me, and he loves in me only *her* whom I hate. He lays his hands in mine and utters vows of love which he dedicates to her. He thinks and feels for her only—her alone. What a terrible torture this is! To be loved under her name; under her name to receive the vows of love that yet belong to me only—to me alone! For he loves me, me exclusively. They are my lips that he kisses, my form that he embraces; to me are addressed his words and his letters; and it is I that reply to them. He loves me, me only, and yet he puts no faith in me. I am nothing to him, naught but a lifeless image, like other women. This he has told me; and I did not become frenzied; and I had the cruel energy to pass off the tears wrung from me by despair, for tears of rapture. Oh, detestable, horrible mockery of fate—to be what I am not, and not to be what I am!"

And with a shrill cry of agony she tore her hair, and with her fist smote upon her breast, and wept and moaned aloud.

She heard naught; she saw naught; she felt naught but her inexpressible and despairing anguish.

She did not once tremble for herself; she thought not at all of this—that she would be lost if she were found in this place.

And yet at the other side of the room a door had opened, softly and noiselessly, and a man had entered.

He shut the door behind him and walked up to Lady Jane, who still lay on the floor. He stood behind her while she uttered her despairing lamentation. He heard every word of her quivering lips; her whole heart painfully convulsed and torn with grief lay unveiled before him; and she knew it not.

Now he bent over her; and with his hand he lightly touched her shoulder. At this touch she gave a convulsive start, as if hit by the stroke of a sword, and her sobbing was immediately silenced.

An awful pause ensued. The woman lay on the floor motionless, breathless, and near her, tall and cold as a figure of bronze, stood the man.

"Lady Jane Douglas," said he then, sternly and solemnly, "stand up. It becomes not your father's daughter to be upon her knees, when it is not God to whom she kneels. But you are not kneeling to God, but to an idol, which you yourself have made, and to which you have erected a temple in your heart. This idol is called '*Your own personal misfortune.*' But it is written, 'Thou shalt have no other Gods but me.' Therefore I say to you once more, Lady Jane Douglas, rise from your knees, for it is not your God to whom you kneel."

And as though these words exercised a magnetic power over her, she raised herself up slowly from the floor, and now stood there before her father, stern and cold as a statue of marble.

"Cast from you the sorrows of this world, which burden you, and hinder you in the sacred work which God has imposed on you!" continued Earl Douglas in his metallic, solemn voice. "It is written, 'Come unto Me, all ye that labor and are heavy laden, and I will give you rest,' saith our God. But you, Jane, you are to throw down your trouble at the foot of the throne; and your burden will become a crown that will glorify your head."

He laid his hand on her head, but she wildly shook it off.

"No," cried she, with heavy, faltering tongue, as if confused in a dream. "Away with this crown! I wish no crown upon which devils have laid a spell. I wish no royal robe that has been dyed crimson with the blood of my beloved."

"She is still in the delirium of her anguish," muttered the earl, as he contemplated the pale, trembling woman who had now sunk again to her knees, and was staring straight before her with eyes bewildered and stretched wide open. But the looks of the earl remained cold and unmoved, and not the least compassion was aroused in him for his poor daughter, now penetrated with anguish.

"Arise," said he, in a hard, steelly voice. "The Church, by my mouth, commands you to serve her as you have vowed to do; that is to say, with glad heart and a sense of your reliance on God; that is to say, with smiling lips and a serene, beaming eye, as becomes a disciple inspired by faith, and as you have sworn to do in the hands of our lord and master, Ignatius Loyola."

"I cannot! I cannot!" moaned she, in a low tone. "I cannot be glad at heart when despair, like a wild boar, is rending my heart; I cannot command my eye to shine when my eyes are dimmed with tears of anguish. Oh, have pity, have compassion! Remember that you are my father; that I am your daughter—the daughter of a wife whom you loved, and who would find in the grave no rest if she knew how you are racking and torturing me. My mother, my mother, if thy spirit is near me, come and protect me. Let thy mild looks overshadow my head, and breathe a breath of thy love into the heart of this cruel father, who is ready to sacrifice his child on the altar of his God."

"God has called me," said the earl, "and, like Abraham, I too will learn to obey. But I will not adorn my victim with flowers, but with a royal crown. I will not plunge a knife into her breast, but will put a golden sceptre into her hand and say: Thou art a queen before men, but before God be thou a faithful and obedient servant. Thou hast all to command. But the holy Church, to whose service thou hast consecrated thyself, and who will bless thee if thou art faithful, who will dash thee in pieces with her curse if thou darest deal treacherously, she commands thee. No, you are not my daughter, but the priestess of the Church, consecrated to her holy service. No, I have no sympathy with your tears and this anguish, for I see the end of these sorrows, and I know that these tears will be as a diadem of pearls about your temples. Lady Jane Douglas, it is the saintly Loyola who sends you his commands by my mouth. Obey them, not because I am your father, but because I am the general to whom you have sworn obedience and fidelity unto your life's end."

"Then kill me, my father!" said she, feebly. "Let this life end, which is but a torture, a protracted martyrdom. Punish me for my disobedience by plunging your dagger deep into my breast. Punish me, and grudge me not the repose of the grave."

"Poor enthusiast!" said the father; "suppose you, we would be foolish enough to subject you to so light a punishment! No, no, if you dare, in insolent disobedience, rebel against my commands, your penance shall be a terrible one, and your punishment without end. I will not kill *you*, but *him* whom you love; it will be his head that falls; and you will be his murderess. He shall die on the scaffold and you—you shall live in disgrace."

"Oh, horrible!" groaned Jane, as she buried her face in her hands.

Her father continued: "Silly, short-sighted child, who thought she could play with the sword, and did not see that she herself might feel the stroke of this double-edged blade! You wanted to be the servant of the Church, that you might thereby become mistress of the world. You would acquire glory, but this glory must not singe your head with its fiery rays. Silly child! he who plays with fire will be consumed. But we penetrated your thoughts and the wish of which you yourself were unconscious. We looked into the depths of your being, and when we found love there, we made use of love for our own purposes and your salvation. What do you bewail, then, and why do you weep? Have we not allowed you to love? Have we not authorized you to give yourself entirely up to this love? Do you not call yourself Earl Surrey's wife, though you cannot name to me the priest that married you? Lady Jane, obey, and we envy you not the happiness of your love; dare to rebel against us, and disgrace and shame overtake you, and you shall stand before all the world disowned and scoffed at; you the strumpet, that——"

"Stop, my father!" cried Jane, as she sprang vehemently from the floor. "Desist from your terrible words if you do not wish me to die of shame. Nay, I submit, I obey! You are right, I cannot draw back."

"And why would you either? Is it not a life pleasant

and full of enjoyment? Is it not rare good fortune to see our sins transfigured to virtue; to be able to account earthly enjoyment the service of Heaven? And what do you bewail then? That he does not love you? Nay, he does love you; his vows of love still echo in your ears; your heart still trembles with the fruition of happiness. What matters it if the Earl of Surrey with his inward eyes sees the woman he folds in his arms to be another than you? Yet in reality he loves but you alone. Whether you are for him *named* Catharine Parr or Jane Douglas, it is all the same if you only *are* his love."

"But a day will come when he will discover his mistake, and when he will curse me."

"That day will never come. The holy Church will find a way to avert that, if you bow to her will and are obedient to her."

"I do bow to it!" sighed Jane. "I will obey; only promise me, my father, that no harm shall happen to *him;* that I shall not be his murderess."

"No, you shall become his savior and deliverer. Only you must fulfil punctually the work I commit to you. First of all, then, tell me the result of your meeting to-day. He does not doubt that you are the queen?"

"No, he believes it so firmly that he would take the sacrament on it. That is to say, he believes it now because I have promised him to give him publicly a sign by which he may recognize that it is the queen that loves him."

"And this sign?" inquired her father, with a look beaming with joy.

"I have promised him that at the great tournament, the queen will give him a rosette, and that in that rosette he will find a note from the queen."

"Ah, the idea is an admirable one!" exclaimed Lord Douglas, "and only a woman who wishes to avenge herself could conceive it. So, then, the queen will become her own accuser, and herself give into our hands a proof of her guilt. The only difficulty in the way is to bring the queen, without arousing her suspicion, to wear this rosette, and to give it to Surrey."

"She will do it if I beg her to do so, for she loves me; and I shall so represent it to her that she will do it as an act of kindness to me. Catharine is good-natured and agreeable, and cannot refuse a request."

"And I will apprise the king of it. That is to say, I shall take good care not to do this myself, for it is always dangerous to approach a hungry tiger in his cage and carry him his food, because he might in his voracity very readily devour our own hand together with the proffered meat."

"But how?" asked she with an expression of alarm. "Will he content himself with punishing Catharine alone; will he not also crush him—him whom he must look upon as her lover?"

"He will do so. But you yourself shall save him and set him free. You shall open his prison and give him freedom, and he will love you—you, the savior of his life."

"Father, father, it is a hazardous game that you are playing; and it may happen that you will become thereby your daughter's murderer. For, listen well to what I tell you; if *his* head falls, I die by my own hands; if you make me his murderess, you become thereby mine; and I will curse you and execrate you in hell! What to me is a royal crown if it is stained with Henry Howard's blood? What care I for renown and honor, if he is not there to see my greatness, and if his beaming eyes do not reflect back to me the light of my crown? Protect him, therefore; guard his life as the apple of your eye, if you wish me to accept the royal crown that you offer me, so that the King of England may become again a vassal of the Church!"

"And that the whole of devout Christendom may praise Jane Douglas, the pious queen who has succeeded in the holy work of bringing the rebellious and recreant son of the Church, Henry the Eighth, back to the Holy

Father in Rome, to the only consecrated lord of the Church, truly penitent. On, on, my daughter; do not despond. A high aim beckons you, and a brilliant fortune awaits you! Our holy mother, the Church, will bless and praise you, and Henry the Eighth will declare you his queen."

CHAPTER XX.

THE PRISONER.

STILL all was calm and quiet in the palace of Whitehall. Nothing was stirring, and nobody had heard how Lady Jane Douglas left her chamber and glided down the corridor.

No one has heard it, and no eye is awake, and none sees what is now taking place in the queen's room.

She is alone—all alone. The servants are all asleep in their chambers. The queen herself has bolted the doors of the anteroom on the inside, and no other door leads into her boudoir and bedroom, except through this anteroom. She is therefore perfectly secluded, perfectly secure.

Speedily and in haste she envelops herself in a long black mantle, the hood of which she draws well over her head and brow, and which completely covers and conceals her form.

And now she presses on a spring inserted in the frame of a picture. The picture flies back and shows an opening, through which a person can quite conveniently pass out.

Catharine does so. Then she carefully pushes the picture back to its place from the outside, and for a long time walks on in the passage hollowed out of the solid wall, till groping along she at last lays hold again of a knob in the wall. She presses on it; and now at her feet opens a trap-door, through which a feeble light forces its way and renders visible a small narrow staircase there situated. Catharine enters and descends the steps with winged feet. Now at the foot of the staircase she again presses on a secret spring; and again a door opens, through which the queen passes into a large hall.

"Oh," whispered she, fetching a long breath, "the green summer house at last."

She quickly traversed it and opened the next door.

"John Heywood?"

"I am here, queen!"

"Hush, hush! gently as possible, that the watch, who walks up and down just behind the door, may not hear us. Come, we still have a long walk—let us make haste."

Again she pressed on a spring inserted in the wall; and again a door opens. But before Catharine bolts this door, she takes the lamp burning on the table there, which is to lighten the dark and difficult path through which they are now to wend their way.

Now she bolts the door behind them; and they enter a long, dark corridor, at the end of which is found still another staircase, and down which they both go. Numberless steps conduct them below; gradually the air becomes dense, the steps moist. The stillness of the grave is around them. No sound of life, not the least noise, is now perceptible.

They are in a subterranean passage, which stretches out in length before them farther than the eye can reach.

Catharine turns to John Heywood; the lamp lights up her face, which is pale, but exhibits an expression firm and resolute.

"John Heywood, reflect once more! I ask not whether you have courage, for I know that. I only wish to know whether you will employ this courage for your queen?"

"No, not for the queen, but for the noble woman who has saved my son."

"You must then be my protector to-day if we meet

with dangers. But if it be God's will, we shall encounter no dangers. Let us go."

They go vigorously forward, silent all the way.

At length they come to a place where the passage grows broader, and spreads out into a little open chamber, on the side walls of which a few seats are placed.

"We have now accomplished half of the journey," said Catharine; "and here we will rest a little."

She placed the lamp on the small marble table in the middle of the passage, and sat down, pointing to John Heywood to take a seat near her.

"I am not the queen, here," said she; "and you are not the king's fool; but I am a poor weak woman, and you are my protector. You may, therefore, well have the right to sit by me."

But John shook his head with a smile, and sat down at her feet. "St. Catharine, savior of my son, I lie at thy feet, and devoutly return thanks to thee."

"John, are you acquainted with this subterranean passage?" asked the queen.

John gave a sad smile. "I am acquainted with it, queen."

"Ah, you know it? I supposed it was a secret of the king and queen."

"Then you will readily conceive that the fool knows it. For the King of England and the fool are twin brothers. Yes, queen, I know this passage; and I once wended it in anguish and tears."

"What! You yourself, John Heywood?"

"Yes, queen. And now I ask you, do you know the history of this underground passage? You are silent. Now, well for you that you do not know it. It is a long and bloody history, and if I should narrate to you the whole of it, the night would be too short for it. When this passage was built, Henry was still young, and possessed yet a heart. At that time, he loved not merely his wives, but his friends and servants also—specially Cromwell, the all-powerful minister. He then resided at Whitehall, and Henry in the royal apartments of the Tower. But Henry was always longing for his favorite; and so Cromwell one day surprised him with this subterranean passage, the construction of which had occupied a hundred men a whole year. Ah, ah, the king was then very much moved, and thanked his powerful minister for this surprise with tears and hugs. There passed scarcely a day that Henry did not go to Cromwell through this passage. So he saw each day how the palace of Whitehall became more and more splendid and glorious; and when he returned to the Tower, he discovered that this residence was altogether unworthy of a king; but that his minister lived by far more magnificently than the King of England. That, queen, was the cause of Cromwell's fall! The king wanted Whitehall. The sly Cromwell noticed it, and made him a present of his gem, the palace on whose construction and decoration he had labored ten years. Henry accepted the present; but now Cromwell's fall was irrevocable. The king could not, of course, forgive Cromwell for having dared to offer him a present so valuable, that Henry could not or would not repay it. He remained, therefore, Cromwell's debtor; and since this tormented and vexed him, he swore Cromwell's ruin. When Henry moved into Whitehall, it was concluded that Cromwell must ascend the scaffold. Ah, the king is such an economical builder! A palace costs him nothing but the head of a subject. With Cromwell's head he paid for Whitehall; and Wolsey died for Hampton Court."

"Not on the scaffold, though, John."

"Oh, no; Henry preferred merely to break his heart, and not his head. First, he had that wonderful pleasure-villa, Hampton Court, with all its treasures, presented him by Wolsey; then he removed him from all his offices, and deprived him of all his honors. Finally, he was to go to the Tower as a prisoner; but he died on his way thither. No, you are right! Wolsey did not die on the scaffold, he

was put to death much more slowly and more cruelly. He was not killed with the sword, but pricked to death with pins!"

"Did you not say, John, that you had travelled this way once before?"

"Yes, queen, and I did it to bid farewell to the noblest of men, and the truest of friends, Thomas More! I begged and besought Cromwell so long that he had compassion on my anguish, and allowed me to go through this passage to Thomas More, that I might at least receive the blessing and last kiss of affection of this saint. Ah, queen, speak no more of it to me! From that day I became a fool; for I saw it was not worth the trouble to be an honest man, when such men as More are executed as criminals. Come, queen, let us go on!"

"Yes, on, John!" said she, rising. "But do you know then whither we are going?"

"Ah, queen, do I not then know you? and did I not tell you that Anne Askew is to be stretched upon the rack to-morrow, unless she recant?"

"I see that you have understood me," said she, giving him a friendly nod. "Yes, I am going to Anne Askew."

"But how will you, without being seen and discovered, find out her cell?"

"John, even the unhappy have friends. Yes, the queen herself has a few; and so chance, or it may be even God's will, has so arranged matters, that Anne Askew is occupying, just at this time, that small room in which the secret passage terminates."

"Is she alone in that room?"

"Yes, all alone. The guard stands without before the door."

"And should they hear you, and open the door?"

"Then without doubt I am lost, unless God supports me."

They walked on in silence, both too much occupied

with their own thoughts to interrupt them by conversation.

But this long, extended walk at length wearied Catharine. She leaned exhausted against the wall.

"Will you do me a favor, queen?" asked John Heywood. "Permit me to carry you. Your little feet can bear you no farther; make me your feet, your majesty!"

She refused with a friendly smile. "No, John, these are the passion-stations of a saint; and you know one must make the round of them in the sweat of his face, and on his knees."

"Oh, queen, how noble and how courageous you are!" exclaimed John Heywood. "You do good without display, and you shun no danger, if it avails toward the accomplishment of noble work."

"Yet, John," said she, with a bewitching smile, "I dread danger; and just on that account I begged you to accompany me. I shudder at the long, desolate way, at the darkness and grave-like stillness of this passage. Ah, John, I thought to myself, if I came here alone, the shades of Anne Boleyn and Catharine would be roused from their sleep by me who wear their crown; they would hover about me, and seize me by the hand and lead me to their graves, to show me that there is yet room there for me likewise. You see, then, that I am not at all courageous, but a cowardly and trembling woman."

"And nevertheless, you came, queen."

"I reckoned on you, John Heywood. It was my duty to risk this passage, to save, perchance, the life of the poor enthusiastic girl. For it shall not be said that Catharine deserts her friends in misfortune, and that she shrinks back at danger. I am but a poor, weak woman, John, who cannot defend her friends with weapons, and, therefore, I must resort to other means. But see, John, here the path forks! Ah, my God! I know it only from the description that was given me, but no one said anything of this to me. John, which way must we now turn?"

"This way, queen; and here we are at the end of our journey. That path there leads to the torture-chamber, that is to say, to a small grated window, through which one can overlook that room. When King Henry was in special good-humor, he would resort with his friend to this grating to divert himself a little with the tortures of the damned and blasphemers. For you well know, queen, only such as have blasphemed God, or have not recognized King Henry as the pope of their Church, have the honor of the rack as their due. But hush! here we are at the door, and here is the spring that opens it."

Catharine set her lamp on the ground and pressed the spring.

The door turned slowly and noiselessly on its hinges, and softly, like shades, the two entered.

They now found themselves in a small, circular apartment, which seemed to have been originally a niche formed in the wall of the Tower, rather than a room. Through a narrow grated opening in the wall only a little air and light penetrated into this dungeon, the bald, bare walls of which showed the stones of the masonry. There was no chair, no table in the whole space; only yonder in that corner on the earth they had heaped up some straw. On this straw lay a pale, tender creature; the sunken, thin cheeks, transparently white as alabaster; the brow so pure and clear; the entire countenance so peaceful; the bare, meagre arms thrown back over the head; the hands folded over the forehead; the head bent to one side in quiet, peaceful slumber; the delicate, tender form wrapped in a long black dress, gently stretched out, and on her lips a smile, such as only the happy know.

That was Anne Askew, the criminal, the condemned— Anne Askew, who was an atheist only for this, because she did not believe in the king's vast elevation and godlikeness, and would not subject her own free soul to that of the king.

"She sleeps," whispered Catharine, deeply moved.

Wholly involuntarily she folded her hands as she stepped to the couch of the sufferer, and a low prayer trembled on her lips.

"So sleep the just!" said Heywood. "Angels comfort them in their slumbers; and the breath of God refreshes them. Poor girl; how soon, and they will wrench these noble, fair limbs, and torture thee for the honor of God, and open to tones of distress that mouth which now smiles so peacefully!"

"No, no," said the queen, hastily. "I have come to save her, and God will assist me to do it. I cannot spare her slumbers any longer. I must wake her."

She bent down and pressed a kiss on the young girl's forehead. "Anne, awake; I am here! I will save you and set you free. Anne, Anne, awake!"

She slowly raised her large, brilliant eyes, and nodded a salutation to Catharine.

"Catharine Parr!" said she, with a smile. "I expected only a letter from you; and have you come yourself?"

"The guards have been dismissed, and the turnkeys changed, Anne; for our correspondence had been discovered."

"Ah, you will write to me no more in future! And yet your letters were my only comfort," sighed Anne Askew. "But that also is well; and perhaps it will only make the path that I have to tread still easier. The heart must set itself free from all earthly bonds, that the soul may move its pinions freely and easily, and return to God."

"Hear me, Anne, hear," said Catharine in a low and hurried voice. "A terrible danger threatens you! The king has given orders to move you, by means of the rack, to recant."

"Well, and what more?" asked Anne, with smiling face.

"Unfortunate, you know not what you are saying! You know not what fearful agonies await you! You know not the power of pains, which are perhaps still mightier than the spirit, and may overcome it."

"And if I did know them now, what would it avail me?" asked Anne Askew. "You say they will put me to the rack. Well, then, I shall have to bear it, for I have no power to change their will."

"Yet, Anne, yet you have the power! Retract what you have said, Anne! Declare that you repent, and that you perceive that you have been deluded! Say that you will recognize the king as lord of the Church; that you will swear to the six articles, and never believe in the Pope of Rome. Ah, Anne, God sees your heart and knows your thoughts. You have no need to make them known by your lips. He has given you life, and you have no right to throw it away; you must seek to keep it so long as you can. Recant, then! It is perfectly allowable to deceive those who would murder us. Recant, then, Anne, recant! When they in their haughty arrogance demand of you to say what they say, consider them as lunatics, to whom you make apparent concessions only to keep them from raving. Of what consequence is it whether you do or do not say that the king is the head of the Church? From His heavens above, God looks down and smiles at this petty earthly strife which concerns not Him, but men only. Let scholars and theologians wrangle; we women have nothing to do with it. If we only believe in God, and bear Him to our hearts, the form in which we do it is a matter of indifference. But in this case the question is not about God, but merely about external dogmas. Why should you trouble yourself with these? What have you to do with the controversies of the priests? Recant, then, poor enthusiastic child, recant!"

While Catharine, in a low tone and with fluttering breath, thus spoke, Anne Askew had slowly arisen from her couch, and now stood, like a lily, so slender and delicate, confronting the queen.

Her noble countenance expressed deep indignation.

Her eyes shot lightning, and a contemptuous smile was on her lips.

"What! Can you thus advise me?" said she. "Can you wish me to deny my faith, and abjure my God, only to escape earthly pain? And your tongue does not refuse to utter this, and your heart does not shrink with shame while you do it? Look at these arms; what are they worth that I should not sacrifice them to God? See these feeble limbs! Are they so precious that I, like a disgusting niggard, should spare them? No, no, God is my highest good—not this feeble, decaying body! For God I sacrifice it. I should recant? Never! Faith is not enveloped in this or that garb; it must be naked and open. So may mine be. And if I then am chosen to be an example of pure faith, that denies not, and makes profession—well, then, envy me not this preëminence. 'Many are called, but few are chosen.' If I am one of the chosen, I thank God for it, and bless the erring mortals who wish to make me such by means of the torture of the rack. Ah, believe me, Catharine, I rejoice to die, for it is such a sad, desolate, and desperate thing to live. Let me die, Catharine—die, to enter into blessedness!"

"But, poor, pitiable child! this is more than death; it is the torture of earth that threatens you. Oh, bethink you, Anne, that you are only a feeble woman. Who knows whether the rack may not yet conquer your spirit, and whether you, with your mangled limbs, may not by the fury of the pain yet be brought to that point that you will recant and abjure your faith?"

"If I could do that," cried Anne Askew, with flashing eyes, "believe me, queen, as soon as I came to my senses I would lay violent hands on myself, in order to give myself over to eternal damnation, as the punishment of my recantation! God has ordered that I shall be a sign of the true faith. Be His command fulfilled!"

"Well, then, so be it," said Catharine resolutely. "Do not recant, but save yourself from your executioners! I,

Anne, I, will save you! I cannot bear—I cannot think of it—that this dear noble form should be sacrificed to a vile delusion of man; that they will torture to the honor of God a noble likeness of the same God! Oh, come, come, I will save you! I, the queen! Give me your hand. Follow me out of this dungeon. I know a path that leads out of this place; and I will conceal you so long in my own apartments that you can continue your flight without danger."

"No, no, queen, you shall not conceal her with you!" said John Heywood. "You have been graciously pleased to allow me to be your confidant; envy me not, then, a share in your noble work also. Not with you shall Anne Askew find refuge, but with me. Oh, come, Anne, follow your friends. It is life that calls you, that opens the doors to you, and desires to call you by a thousand names to itself! Do you not hear them, all those sweet and alluring voices; do you not see them, all those noble and smiling faces, how they greet you and beckon to you? Anne Askew, it is the noble husband that calls you! You know him not as yet, but he is waiting for you there in the world without. Anne Askew, there are your children, who are stretching their tender arms out to you. You have not yet borne them; but love holds them in her arms, and will bring them to meet you. It is the wife and the mother that the world yet demands of you, Anne. You ought not to shun the holy calling which God has given you. Come, then, and follow us—follow your queen, who has the right to order her subject. Follow the friend, who has sworn that he will watch over you and protect you as a father!"

"Father in heaven, protect me!" exclaimed Anne Askew, falling on her knees and stretching her hands upward. "Father in heaven! they would tear away Thy child, and alienate my heart from Thee! They are leading me into temptation and alluring me with their words. Protect me, my Father; make my ear deaf, that I may not hear them! Give me a sign that I am Thine; that no one has any longer power over me, save Thou alone! A sign, that Thou, Father, callest me!"

And as if God had really heard her prayer, a loud knocking was now perceived at the outer door, and a voice cried: "Anne Askew, awake! and hold yourself ready! The high chancellor and the Bishop of Winchester come to fetch you away!"

"Ah, the rack!" groaned Catharine, as with a shudder she buried her face in her hands.

"Yes, the rack!" said Anne, with a blissful smile. "God calls me!"

John Heywood had approached the queen and impetuously seized her hand. "You see it is in vain," said he, urgently. "Make haste then to save yourself! Hasten to leave this prison before the door there opens."

"No," said Catharine, firmly and resolutely. "No, I stay. She shall not surpass me in courage and greatness of soul! She will not deny her God; well, then, I also will be a witness of my God. I will not in shame cast my eyes to the ground before this young girl; like her, I will frankly and openly profess my faith; like her I will say: 'God alone is Lord of his Church,' God——"

There was a movement without; a key was heard to turn in the lock.

"Queen, I conjure you," besought John Heywood, "by all that is holy to you, by your love, come, come!"

"No, no!" cried she, vehemently.

But now Anne seized her hand, and stretching the other arm toward heaven, she said in a loud, commanding voice: "In the name of God, I order you to leave me!"

While Catharine drew back wholly involuntarily, John Heywood pushed her to the secret door, and urging her out almost with violence, he drew the door to behind them both.

Just as the secret door had closed, the other on the opposite side opened.

"With whom were you speaking?" asked Gardiner, peering around the room with a sharp look.

"With the tempter, that wished to alienate me from God," said she—"with the tempter, who at the approach of your footsteps wanted to fool my heart with fear, and persuade me to recant!"

"You are, then, firmly resolved? you do not retract?" asked Gardiner; and a savage joy shone in his pale, hard countenance.

"No, I do not recant!" said she, with a face beaming with smiles.

"Then, in the name of God and of the king, I take you into the torture-chamber!" cried Chancellor Wriothesley, as he advanced and laid his heavy hand on Anne's shoulder. "You would not hear the voice of love warning you and calling you, so we will now try to arouse you from your madness by the voice of wrath and damnation."

He beckoned to the attendants on the rack, who stood behind him in the open door, and ordered them to seize her and carry her to the torture-chamber.

Anne, smiling, turned them back. "Nay, not so!" said she. "The Saviour went on foot, and bore His cross to the place of execution. I will tread His path. Show me the way, I follow you. But let no one dare touch me. I will show you that not by constraint, but gladly and freely, I tread the path of suffering, which I shall endure for the sake of my God. Rejoice, oh my soul!—sing, my lips! for the bridegroom is near, and the feast is about to begin."

And in exultant tones Anne Askew began to sing a hymn, that had not died away when she entered the torture-chamber.

CHAPTER XXI.

PRINCESS ELIZABETH.

The king sleeps. Let him sleep! He is old and infirm, and God has severely punished the restless tyrant with a vacillating, ever-disquieted, never-satisfied spirit, while He bound his body and made the spirit prisoner of the body; while He made the ambitious king, struggling for the infinite, a slave to his own flesh. How high soever his thoughts soar, still the king remains a clumsy, confined, powerless child of humanity; how much soever his conscience harasses him with disquiet and dread, yet he must be calm and endure it. He cannot run away from his conscience; God has fettered him by the flesh.

The king is sleeping! But the queen is not; and Jane Douglas is not; neither is the Princess Elizabeth.

She has watched with heart beating high. She is restless, and, pacing her room up and down in strange confusion, waited for the hour that she had appointed for the meeting. Now the hour had arrived. A glowing crimson overspread the face of the young princess; and her hand trembled as she took the light and opened the secret door to the corridor. She stood still for a moment, hesitating; then, ashamed of her irresolution, she crossed the corridor and ascended the small staircase which led to the tower-chamber. With a hasty movement she pushed open the door and entered the room. She was at the end of her journey, and Thomas Seymour was already there.

As she saw him, an involuntary trepidation came over her, and for the first time she now became conscious of her hazardous step.

As Seymour, the ardent young man, approached her with a passionate salutation, she stepped shyly back and pushed away his hand.

"How! you will not allow me to kiss your hand?" asked he, and she thought she observed on his face a slight, scornful smile. "You make me the happiest of mortals by inviting me to this interview, and now you stand before me rigid and cold, and I am not once permitted to clasp you in my arms, Elizabeth!"

Elizabeth! He had called her by her first name without her having given him permission to do so. That offended her. In the midst of her confusion, that aroused the pride of the princess, and made her aware how much she must have forgotten her own dignity, when another could be so forgetful of it.

She wished to regain it. At this moment she would have given a year of her life if she had not taken this step—if she had not invited the earl to this meeting.

She wanted to try and regain in his eyes her lost position, and again to become to him the princess.

Pride in her was still mightier than love. She meant her lover should at the same time bow before her as her favored servant.

Therefore she gravely said: "Earl Thomas Seymour, you have often begged us for a private conversation; we now grant it to you. Speak, then! what matter of importance have you to bring before us?"

And with an air of gravity she stepped to an easy-chair, on which she seated herself slowly and solemnly like a queen, who gives audience to her vassals.

Poor, innocent child, that in her unconscious trepidation wished to intrench herself behind her grandeur, as behind a shield, which might conceal her maidenly fear and girlish anxiety!

Thomas Seymour, however, divined her thoughts; and his proud and cold heart revolted against this child's attempt to defy him.

He wanted to humble her; he wished to compel her to bow before him, and implore his love as a gracious gift.

He therefore bowed low to the princess, and respectfully said: "Your highness, it is true I have often besought you for an audience; but you have so long refused me, that at last I could no longer summon up courage to solicit it; and I let my wish be silent and my heart dumb. Therefore seek not now, when these pains have been subdued, to excite them again. My heart should remain dead, my lips mute. You have so willed; and I have submitted to your will. Farewell, then, princess, and may your days be happier and more serene than those of poor Thomas Seymour!"

He bowed low before her, and then went slowly to the door. He had already opened it and was about to step out, when a hand was suddenly laid on his shoulder and drew him with vehement impetuosity back into the room.

"Do you want to go?" asked Elizabeth, with fluttering breath and trembling voice. "You want to leave me, and, flouting me, you want now, it may be, to go to the Duchess of Richmond, your mistress, and relate to her with a sneer that the Princess Elizabeth granted you an interview, and that you have flouted her?"

"The Duchess of Richmond is not my mistress," said the earl, earnestly.

"No, not your mistress; but she will very soon be your wife!"

"She will never be my wife!"

"And why not?"

"Because I do not love her, princess."

A beam of delight passed over Elizabeth's pale, agitated face. "Why do you call me princess?" asked she.

"Because you have come as a princess to favor your poor servant with an audience. But, ah, it would be greatly abusing your princely grace did I want to protract this audience still further. I therefore retire, princess."

And again he approached the door. But Elizabeth rushed after him, and, laying hold of his arms with both her hands, she wildly pushed him back.

Her eyes shot lightning; her lips trembled; a passionate warmth was manifested in her whole being. Now she was the true daughter of her father, inconsiderate and passionate in her wrath, destroying in her ferocity.

"You shall not go," muttered she, with her teeth firmly set. "I will not let you go! I will not let you confront me any longer with that cold, smiling face. Scold me; cast on me the bitterest reproaches, because I have dared to brave you so long; curse me, if you can! Anything but this smiling calmness. It kills me; it pierces my heart like a dagger. For you see well enough that I have no longer the power to withstand you; you see well enough that I love you. Yes, I love you to ecstasy and to desperation; with desire and dread. I love you as my demon and my angel. I am angry, because you have so entirely crushed the pride of my heart. I curse you, because you have made me so entirely your slave; and the next moment I fall on my knees and beseech God to forgive me this crime against you. I love you, I say—not as these soft, gentle-hearted women love, with a smile on the lip; but with madness and desperation, with jealousy and wrath. I love you as my father loved Anne Boleyn, whom, in the hatred of his love and the cruel wrath of his jealousy, he made to mount the scaffold, because he had been told that she was untrue to him. Ah, had I the power, I would do as my father did; I would murder you, if you should dare ever to cease to love me. And now, Thomas Seymour, now say whether you have the courage to desire to leave me?"

She looked bewitching in the flaming might of her passion; she was so young, so ardent; and Thomas Seymour was so ambitious! In his eyes Elizabeth was not merely the beautiful, charming maiden, who loved him; she was more than that: she was the daughter of Henry the Eighth, the Princess of England, perchance some day the heiress of the throne. It is true, her father had disinherited her, and by act of Parliament declared her unworthy of succeeding to the throne.* But Henry's vacil-

* Burnet, vol. i, p. 138.

lating mind might change, and the disowned princess might one day become queen.

The earl thought of this as he gazed on Elizabeth—as he saw her before him, so charming, so young, and so glowing with passion. He thought of it as he now clasped her in his arms, and pressed on her lips a burning kiss.

"No, I will not go," whispered he. "I will never more depart from your side, if you do not wish me to go. I am yours!—your slave, your vassal; and I will never be anything else but this alone. They may betray me; your father may punish me for high treason; yet will I exult in my good fortune, for Elizabeth loves me, and it will be for Elizabeth that I die!"

"You shall not die!" cried she, clinging fast to him. "You shall live, live at my side, proud, great, and happy! You shall be my lord and my master; and if I am ever queen, and I feel here in my heart that I must become so, then will Thomas Seymour be King of England."

"That is to say, in the quiet and secrecy of your chamber I should perhaps be so!" said he with a sigh. "But there without, before the world, I shall still be ever only a servant; and at the best, I shall be called the favorite."

"Never, never, that I swear to you! Said I not that I loved you?"

"But the love of a woman is so changeable! Who knows how long it will be before you will tread under your feet poor Thomas Seymour, when once the crown has adorned your brow."

She looked at him well-nigh horrified. "Can this be, then? Is it possible that one can forget and forsake what he once loved?"

"Do you ask, Elizabeth? Has not your father already his sixth wife?"

"It is true," said she, as mournfully she dropped her head upon her breast. "But I," said she, after a pause; "I shall not be like my father in that. I shall love you eternally! And that you may have a guaranty of my faithfulness, I offer myself to you as your wife."

Astonished, he looked inquiringly into her excited, glowing face! He did not understand her.

But she continued, passionately: " Yes, you shall be my lord and my husband! Come, my beloved, come! I have not called you to take upon yourself the disgraceful *rôle* of the secret lover of a princess—I have called you to be my husband. I wish a bond to unite us two, that is so indissoluble that not even the wrath and will of my father, but only death itself, can sever it. I will give you proof of my love and my devotion; and you shall be forced to acknowledge that I truly love you. Come, my beloved, that I may soon hail you as my husband! "

He looked at her as though petrified. " Whither will you lead me? "

" To the private chapel," said she, innocently. " I have written Cranmer to await me there at daybreak. Let us hasten, then! "

" Cranmer! You have written to the archbishop? " cried Seymour, amazed. " How! what say you? Cranmer awaits us in the private chapel? "

" Without doubt he is waiting for us, as I have written him to do so."

" And what is he to do? What do you want of him? "

She looked at him in astonishment. " What do I want of him? Why, that he may marry us! "

The earl staggered back as if stunned. " And have you written him that also? "

" Nay, indeed," said she, with a charming, childlike smile. " I know very well that it is dangerous to trust such secrets to paper. I have only written him to come in his official robes, because I have an important secret to confess to him."

" Oh, God be praised! We are not lost," sighed Seymour.

" But how, I do not understand you? " asked she.

"You do not extend me your hand! You do not hasten to conduct me to the chapel!"

"Tell me, I conjure you, tell me only this one thing: have you ever spoken to the archbishop of your—no—of our love? Have you ever betrayed to him so much as a syllable of that which stirs our hearts?"

She blushed deeply beneath the steady gaze which he fixed on her. "Upbraid me, Seymour," whispered she. "But my heart was weak and timorous; and as often as I tried to fulfil the holy duty, and confess everything honestly and frankly to the archbishop, I could not do it! The word died on my lips; and it was as though an invisible power paralyzed my tongue."

"So, then, Cranmer knows nothing?"

"No, Seymour, he knows nothing as yet. But now he shall learn all; now we will go before him and tell him that we love each other, and constrain him, by our prayers, to bless our union, and join our hands."

"Impossible!" cried Seymour. "That can never be!"

"How! What do you say?" asked she in astonishment.

"I say that Cranmer will never be so insane, nay, so criminal, as to fulfil your wish. I say that you can never be my wife."

She looked him full and square in the face. "Have you not then told me that you loved me?" asked she. "Have I not sworn to you that I loved you in return? Must we then not be married, in order to sanctify the union of our hearts?"

Seymour sank his eyes to the ground before her pure innocent look, and blushed for shame. She did not understand this blush; because he was silent, she deemed him convinced.

"Come," said she, "come; Cranmer is waiting for us!"

He again raised his eyes and looked at her in amazement. "Do you not see, then, this is all only a dream that can never become reality? Do you not feel that this precious fantasy of your great and noble heart will never be realized? How! are you then so little acquainted with your father as not to know that he would destroy us both if we should dare to set at naught his paternal and his royal authority? Your birth would not secure you from his destroying fury, for you well know he is unyielding and reckless in his wrath; and the voice of consanguinity sounds not so loud in him that it would not be drowned by the thunder of his wrath. Poor child, you have learned that already! Remember with what cruelty he has already revenged himself on you for the pretended fault of your mother; how he transferred to you his wrath against her. Remember that he refused your hand to the Dauphin of France, not for the sake of your happiness, but because he said you were not worthy of so exalted a position. Anne Boleyn's bastard could never become Queen of France. And after such a proof of his cruel wrath against you, will you dare cast in his face this terrible insult?—compel him to recognize a subject, a servant, as his son?"

" Oh, this servant is, however, the brother of a Queen of England!" said she, shyly. " My father loved Jane Seymour too warmly not to forgive her brother."

" Ah, ah, you do not know your father! He has no heart for the past; or, if he has, it is only to take vengeance for an injury or a fault, but not to reward love. King Henry would be capable of sentencing Anne Boleyn's daughter to death, and of sending to the block and rack Catharine Howard's brothers, because these two queens once grieved him and wounded his heart; but he would not forgive me the least offence on account of my being the brother of a queen who loved him faithfully and tenderly till her death. But I speak not of myself. I am a warrior, and have too often looked death in the face to fear him now. I speak only of you, Elizabeth. You have no right to perish thus. This noble head must not be laid upon the block. It is destined to wear a royal crown.

A fortune still higher than love awaits you—fame and power! I must not draw you away from this proud future. The Princess Elizabeth, though abused and disowned, may yet one day mount the throne of England. The Countess Seymour never! she disinherits herself! Follow, then, your high destiny. Earl Seymour retires before a throne."

"That is to say, you disdained me?" asked she, angrily stamping the floor with her foot. "That is to say, the proud Earl Seymour holds the bastard too base for his coronet! That is to say, you love me not!"

"No, it means that I love you more than myself—better and more purely than any other man can love you; for this love is so great that it makes my selfishness and my ambition silent, and allows me to think only of you and your future."

"Ah," sighed she, mournfully, "if you really loved me, you would not consider—you would not see the danger, nor fear death. You would think of nothing, and know nothing, save love."

"Because I think of love, I think of you," said Seymour. "I think that you are to move along over the world, great, powerful, and glorious, and that I will lend you my arm for this. I think of this, that my queen of the future needs a general who will win victories for her, and that I will be that general. But when this goal is reached—when you are queen—then you have the power from one of your subjects to make a husband; then it rests with your own will to elevate me to be the proudest, the happiest, and the most enviable of all men. Extend me your hand, then, and I will thank and praise God that he is so gracious to me; and my whole existence will be spent in the effort to give you the happiness that you are so well entitled to demand."

"And until then?" asked she, mournfully.

"Until then, we will be constant, and love each other!" cried he, as he gently pressed her in his arms.

She gently repelled him. "Will you also be true to me till then?"

"True till death!"

"They have told me that you would marry the Duchess of Richmond, in order thereby to at length put an end to the ancient hatred between the Howards and Seymours."

Thomas Seymour frowned, and his countenance grew dark. "Believe me, this hatred is invincible," said he; "and no matrimonial alliance could wash it away. It is an inheritance from many years in our families; and I am firmly resolved not to renounce my inheritance. I shall just as little marry the Duchess of Richmond, as Henry Howard will my sister, the Countess of Shrewsbury."

"Swear that to me! Swear to me, that you say the truth, and that this haughty and coquettish duchess shall never be your wife. Swear it to me, by all that is sacred to you!"

"I swear it by my love!" exclaimed Thomas Seymour, solemnly.

"I shall then at least have one sorrow the less," sighed Elizabeth. "I shall have no occasion to be jealous. And is it not true," she then said, "is it not true we shall often see each other? We will both keep this secret of this tower faithfully and sacredly; and after days full of privation and disappointment, we will here keep festival the nights full of blissful pleasure and sweet transport. But why do you smile, Seymour?"

"I smile, because you are pure and innocent as an angel," said he, as he reverently kissed her hand. "I smile, because you are an exalted, godlike child, whom one ought to adore upon his knees, and to whom one ought to pray, as to the chaste goddess Vesta! Yes, my dear, beloved child, here we will, as you say, pass nights full of blissful pleasure; and may I be reprobate and damned, if I should ever be capable of betraying this sweet, guileless confidence with which you favor me, and sully your angel purity!"

"Ah, we will be very happy, Seymour!" said she, smiling. "I lack only one thing—a friend, to whom I can tell my happiness, to whom I can speak of you. Oh, it often seems to me as if this love, which must always be concealed, always shut up, must at last burst my breast; as if this secret must with violence break a passage, and roar like a tempest over the whole world. Seymour, I want a confidante of my happiness and my love."

"Guard yourself well against desiring to seek such a one!" exclaimed Seymour, anxiously. "A secret that three know, is a secret no more; and one day your confidante will betray us."

"Not so; I know a woman who would be incapable of that—a woman who loves me well enough to keep my secret as faithfully as I myself; a woman who could be more than merely a confidante, who could be the protectress of our love. Oh, believe me, if we could gain her to our side, then our future would be a happy and a blessed one, and we might easily succeed in obtaining the king's consent to our marriage."

"And who is this woman?"

"It is the queen."

"The queen!" cried Thomas Seymour, with such an expression of horror that Elizabeth trembled; "the queen your confidante? But that is impossible! That would be plunging us both inevitably into ruin. Unhappy child, be very careful not to mention even a single word, a syllable of your relation to me. Be very careful not to betray to her, even by the slightest intimation, that Thomas Seymour is not indifferent to you! Ah, her wrath would dash to pieces you and me!"

"And why do you believe that?" asked Elizabeth, gloomily. "Why do you suppose that Catharine would fly into a passion because Earl Seymour loves me? Or how? —it is she, perhaps, that you love, and you dare not therefore let her know that you have sworn your love to me also? Ah, I now see through it all; I understand it all! You love the queen—her only. For that reason you will not go to the chapel with me; for that reason you swore that you would not marry the Duchess of Richmond; and therefore—oh, my presentiment did not deceive me— therefore that furious ride in Epping Forest to-day. Ah, the queen's horse must of course become raving, and run away, that his lordship, the master of horse, might follow his lady, and with her get lost in the thicket of the woods! —And now," said she, her eyes flashing with anger, and raising her hand to heaven as if taking an oath, " now I say to you: Take heed to yourself! Take heed to yourself, Seymour, that you do not, even by a single word or a single syllable, betray your secret, for that word would crush you! Yes, I feel it, that I am no bastard, that I am my father's own daughter; I feel it in this wrath and this jealousy that rages within me! Take heed to yourself, Seymour, for I will go hence and accuse you to the king, and the traitor's head will fall upon the scaffold!"

She was beside herself. With clenched fists and a threatening air she paced the room up and down. Tears gushed from her eyes; but she shook them out of her eyelashes, so that they fell scattering about her like pearls. Her father's impetuous and untractable nature stirred within her, and his blood seethed in her veins.

But Thomas Seymour had already regained his self-command and composure. He approached the princess and despite her struggles clasped her in his arms.

" Little fool!" said he, between his kisses. " Sweet, dear fool, how beautiful you are in your anger, and how I love you for it! Jealousy is becoming to love; and I do not complain, though you are unjust and cruel toward me. The queen has much too cold and proud a heart ever to be loved by any man. Ah, only to think this is already treason to her virtue and modesty; and surely she has not deserved this from us two, that we should disdain and insult her. She is the first that has always been just to you; and to me she has ever been only a gracious mistress!"

"It is true," murmured Elizabeth, completely ashamed; "she is a true friend and mother; and I have her to thank for my present position at this court."

Then, after a pause, she said, smiling, and extending her hand to the earl: "You are right. It would be a crime to suspect her; and I am a fool. Forgive me, Seymour, forgive my absurd and childish anger; and I promise you in return to betray our secret to no one, not even to the queen."

"Do you swear that to me?"

"I swear it to you! and I swear to you more than that: I will never again be jealous of her."

"Then you do but simple justice to yourself and to the queen also," said the earl, with a smile, as he drew her again to his arms.

But she pushed him gently back. "I must now away. The morning dawns, and the archbishop awaits me in the royal chapel."

"And what will you say to him, beloved?"

"I will make my confession to him."

"How! so you will then betray our love to him?"

"Oh," said she, with a bewitching smile, "that is a secret between us and God; and only to Him alone can we confess it; because He alone can absolve us from it. Farewell, then, Seymour, farewell, and think of me till we see each other again! But when—say, when shall we meet again?"

"When there is a night like this one, beloved, when the moon is not in the heavens."

"Oh, then I could wish there were a change of the moon every week," said she, with the charming innocence of a child. "Farewell, Seymour, farewell; we must part."

She clung to his tall, sturdy form as the ivy twines around the trunk of an oak. Then they parted. The princess slipped again softly and unseen into her apartments, and thence into the royal chapel; the earl descended again the spiral staircase which led to the secret door of the garden.

Unobserved and unseen he returned to his palace; even his valet, who slept in the anteroom, did not see him, as the earl crept past him lightly on his toes, and betook himself to his sleeping-room.

But no sleep came to his eyes that night, and his soul was restless and full of fierce torment. He was angry with himself, and accused himself of treachery and perfidy; and then again, full of proud haughtiness, he still tried to excuse himself and to silence his conscience, which was sitting in judgment on him.

"I love her—her only!" said he to himself. "Catharine possesses my heart, my soul; I am ready to devote my whole life to her. Yes, I love her! I have this day so sworn to her; and she is mine for all eternity!"

"And Elizabeth?" asked his conscience. "Have you not sworn truth and love to her also?"

"No!" said he. "I have only received her oath; I have not given her mine in return. And when I vowed never to marry the Duchess of Richmond; when I swore this 'by my love,' then I thought only of Catharine—of that proud, beautiful, charming woman, at once maidenly and voluptuous; but not of this young, inexperienced, wild child—of this unattractive little princess!"

"But the princess may one day become a queen," whispered his ambition.

"That, however, is very doubtful," replied he to himself. "But it is certain that Catharine will one day be the regent, and if I am at that time her husband, then I am Regent of England."

This was the secret of his duplicity and his double treachery. Thomas Seymour loved nothing but himself, nothing but his ambition. He was capable of risking his life for a woman; but for renown and greatness he would have gladly sacrificed this woman.

For him there was only one aim, one struggle: to become great and powerful above all the nobles of the kingdom—to be the first man in England. And to reach this aim, he would be afraid of no means; he would shrink from no treachery and no sin.

Like the disciples of Loyola, he said, in justification of himself, " the end sanctifies the means."

And thus for him every means was right which conducted him to the end; that is to say, to greatness and glory.

He was firmly convinced that he loved the queen ardently; and in his nobler hours he did really love her. Depending on the moment, a son of the hour, in him feeling and will varied with the rapidity of lightning, and he ever was wholly and completely that with which the moment inflamed him.

When, therefore, he stood before the queen, he did not lie when he swore that he loved her passionately. He really loved her, with double warmth, since she had to his mind in some sort identified herself with his ambition. He adored her, because she was the means that might conduct him to his end; because she might some day hold in her hands the sceptre of England. And on the day when this came to pass, he wished to be her lover and her lord. She had accepted him as her lord, and he was entirely certain of his future sway.

Consequently he loved the queen, but his proud and ambitious heart could never be so completely animated by one love as that there should not be room in it for a second, provided this second love presented him a favorable chance for the attainment of the aim of his life.

Princess Elizabeth had this chance. And if the queen would certainly become one day Regent of England, yet Elizabeth might some day perchance become queen thereof. Of course, it was as yet only a perhaps, but one might manage out of this perhaps to make a reality. Besides, this young, passionate child loved him, and Thomas Seymour was himself too young and too easily excitable to be able to despise a love that presented him with such enticing promises and bright dreams of the future.

"It does not become a man to live for love alone," said he to himself as he now thought over the events of the night. "He must struggle for the highest and wish to reach the greatest, and no means of attaining this end ough he to leave unemployed. Besides, my heart is large enough to satisfy a twofold love. I love them both—both of these fair women who fetch me a crown. Let fate decide to which of the two I shall one day belong!"

CHAPTER XXII.

HENRY HOWARD, EARL OF SURREY.

THE great court festival, so long expected, was at last to take place to-day. Knights and lords were preparing for the tournament; poets and scholars for the feast of the poets. For the witty and brave king wished to unite the two in this festival to-day, in order to give the world a rare and great example of a king who could claim all virtue and wisdom as his own; who could be equally great as a hero and as a divine; equally great as a poet and as a philosopher and a scholar.

The knights were to fight for the honor of their ladies; the poets were to sing their songs, and John Heywood to bring out his merry farces. Ay, even the great scholars were to have a part in this festival; for the king had specially, for this, summoned to London from Cambridge, where he was then professor in the university, his former teacher in the Greek language, the great scholar Croke, to whom belonged the merit of having first made the learned world of Germany, as well as of England, again acquainted with the poets of Greece.* He wished to recite with Croke some scenes from Sophocles to his wondering court; and though, to be sure, there was no one there who understood the Greek tongue, yet all, without doubt, must be enraptured with the wonderful music of the Greek and the amazing erudition of the king.

Preparations were going on everywhere; arrangements were being made; every one was making his toilet, whether it were the toilet of the mind or of the body.

Henry Howard, Earl of Surrey, made his also; that is to say, he had retired to his cabinet, and was busy filing away at the sonnets which he expected to recite to-day, and in which he lauded the beauty and the grace of the fair Geraldine.

He had the paper in his hand, and was lying on the velvet ottoman which stood before his writing-table.

Had Lady Jane Douglas seen him now, she would have been filled with painful rapture to observe how, with head leaned back on the cushion, his large blue eyes raised dreamily to heaven, he smiled and whispered gentle words.

He was wholly absorbed in sweet reminiscences; he was thinking of those rapturous, blessed hours which he a few days before had spent with his Geraldine; and as he thought of them he adored her, and repeated to her anew in his mind his oath of eternal love and inviolable truth.

His enthusiastic spirit was completely filled with a sweet melancholy; and he felt perfectly intoxicated by the magical happiness afforded him by his Geraldine.

She was his—his at last! After struggles so long and painful, after such bitter renunciation, and such mournful resignation, happiness had at last arisen for him; the never expected had at last become indeed a reality. Catharine loved him. With a sacred oath she had sworn to

* Tytler, p. 207.

him that she would one day become his wife; that she would become his wife before God and man.

But when is the day to come on which he may show her to the world as his consort? When will she be at length relieved from the burden of her royal crown? When at length will fall from her those golden chains that bind her to a tyrannical and bloodthirsty husband— to the cruel and arrogant king? When will Catharine at length cease to be queen, in order to become Lady Surrey?

Strange! As he asked himself this, there ran over him a shudder, and an unaccountable dread fell upon his soul.

It seemed to him as if a voice whispered to him: "Thou wilt never live to see that day! The king, old as he is, will nevertheless live longer than thou! Prepare thyself to die, for death is already at thy door!"

And it was not the first time that he had heard that voice. Often before it had spoken to him, and always with the same words, the same warning. Often it seemed to him in his dreams as if he felt a cutting pain about the neck; and he had seen a scaffold, from which his own head was rolling down.

Henry Howard was superstitious; for he was a poet, and to poets it is given to perceive the mysterious connection between the visible and the invisible world; to believe that supernatural powers and invisible forms surround man, and either protect him or else curse him.

There were hours in which he believed in the reality of his dreams—in which he did not doubt of that melancholy and horrible fate which they foretold.

Formerly he had given himself up to it with smiling resignation; but now—since he loved Catharine, since she belonged to him—now he would not die. Now, when life held out to him its most enchanting enjoyments, its intoxicating delights—now he would not leave them—now he dreaded to die. He was therefore cautious and prudent; and, knowing the king's malicious, savage, and jealous character, he had always been extremely careful to avoid everything that might excite him, that might arouse the royal hyena from his slumbers.

But it seemed to him as though the king bore him and his family a special spite; as though he could never forgive them that the consort whom he most loved, and who had the most bitterly wronged him, had sprung from their stock. In the king's every word and every look, Henry Howard felt and was sensible of this secret resentment of the king; he suspected that Henry was only watching for the favorable moment when he could seize and strangle him.

He was therefore on his guard. For now, when Geraldine loved him, his life belonged no longer to himself alone; she loved him; she had a claim on him; his days were, therefore, hallowed in his own eyes.

So he had kept silence under the petty annoyances and vexations of the king. He had taken it even without murmuring, and without demanding satisfaction, when the king had suddenly recalled him from the army that was fighting against France, and of which he was commander-in-chief, and in his stead had sent Lord Hertford, Earl of Sudley, to the army which was encamped before Boulogne and Montreuil. He had quietly and without resentment returned to his palace; and since he could no longer be a general and warrior, he became again a scholar and poet. His palace was now again the resort of the scholars and writers of England; and he was always ready, with true princely munificence, to assist oppressed and despised talent; to afford the persecuted scholar an asylum in his palace. He it was who saved the learned Fox from starvation, and took him into his house, where Horatius Junius and the poet Churchyard, afterward so celebrated, had both found a home—the former as his physician and the latter as his page.*

Love, the arts, and the sciences, caused the wounds

* Nott's Life of the Earl of Surrey.

that the king had given his ambition, to heal over; and he now felt no more rancor; now he almost thanked the king. For to his recall only did he owe his good fortune; and Henry, who had wished to injure him, had given him his sweetest pleasure.

He now smiled as he thought how Henry, who had taken from him the *bâton*, had, without knowing it, given him in return his own queen, and had exalted him when he wished to humble him.

He smiled, and again took in hand the poem in which he wished to celebrate in song, at the court festival that day, the honor and praise of his lady-love, whom no one knew, or even suspected—the fair Geraldine.

"The verses are stiff," muttered he; "this language is so poor! It has not the power of expressing all that fulness of adoration and ecstasy which I feel. Petrarch was more fortunate in this respect. His beautiful, flexible language sounds like music, and it is, even just by itself, the harmonious accompaniment of his love. Ah, Petrarch, I envy thee, and yet would not be like thee. For thine was a mournful and bitter-sweet lot. Laura never loved thee; and she was the mother of twelve children, not a single one of whom belonged to thee."

He laughed with a sense of his own proud success in love, and seized Petrarch's sonnets, which lay near him on the table, to compare his own new sonnet with a similar one of Petrarch's.

He was so absorbed in these meditations, that he had not at all observed that the hanging which concealed the door behind him was pushed aside, and a marvellous young woman, resplendent with diamonds and sparkling with jewelry, entered his cabinet.

For an instant she stood still upon the threshold, and with a smile observed the earl, who was more and more absorbed in his reading.

She was of imposing beauty; her large eyes blazed and glowed like a volcano; her lofty brow seemed in all respects designed to wear a crown. And, indeed, it was a ducal coronet that sparkled on her black hair, which in long ringlets curled down to her full, voluptuous shoulders. Her tall and majestic form was clad in a white satin dress, richly trimmed with ermine and pearls; two clasps of costly brilliants held fast to her shoulders the small mantilla of crimson velvet, faced with ermine, which covered her back and fell down to her waist.

Thus appeared the Duchess of Richmond, the widow of King Henry's natural son, Henry Richmond; the sister of Lord Henry Howard, Earl of Surrey; and the daughter of the noble Duke of Norfolk.

Since her husband had died and left her a widow at twenty, she resided in her brother's palace, and had placed herself under his protection, and in the world they were known as "the affectionate brother and sister."

Ah, how little knew the world, which is ever wont to judge from appearances, of the hatred and the love of these two; how little suspicion had it of the real sentiments of this brother and sister!

Henry Howard had offered his sister his palace as her residence, because he hoped by his presence to lay on her impulsive and voluptuous disposition a restraint which should compel her not to overstep the bounds of custom and decency. Lady Richmond had accepted this offer of his palace because she was obliged to; inasmuch as the avaracious and parsimonious king gave his son's widow only a meagre income, and her own means she had squandered and lavishly thrown away upon her lovers.

Henry Howard had thus acted for the honor of his name; but he loved not his sister; nay, he despised her. But the Duchess of Richmond hated her brother, because her proud heart felt humbled by him, and under obligations of gratitude.

But their hatred and their contempt were a secret that they both preserved in the depths of the heart, and which they scarcely dared confess to themselves. Both had veiled this their inmost feeling with a show of affection, and only once in a while was one betrayed to the other by some lightly dropped word or unregarded look.

CHAPTER XXIII.

BROTHER AND SISTER.

LIGHTLY on the tips of her toes the duchess stole toward her brother, who did not yet observe her. The thick Turkish carpet made her steps inaudible. She already stood behind the earl, and he had not yet noticed her.

Now she bent over his shoulder, and fastened her sparkling eyes on the paper in her brother's hand.

Then she read in a loud, sonorous voice the title of it: "Complaint, because Geraldine never shows herself to her lover unless covered by her veil." * "Ah," said the duchess, laughing, "now, then, I have spied out your secret, and you must surrender to me at discretion. So you are in love; and Geraldine is the name of the chosen one to whom you address your poems! I swear to you, my brother, you will repay me dear for this secret."

"It is no secret at all, sister," said the earl, with a quiet smile, as he rose from the divan and saluted the duchess. "It is so little a secret, that I shall recite this sonnet at the court festival this very evening. I shall not, therefore, need your secrecy, Rosabella."

"So the fair Geraldine never shows herself to you unless in a dark veil, black as the night," said the duchess, musingly. "But tell me, brother, who then is the fair Geraldine? Of the ladies at court, I know not a single one who bears that name."

* Sonnet by Surrey.—See Nott's Life and Works of Surrey.

"So you see from that, the whole is only a fiction—a creation of my fancy."

"No, indeed," said she, smiling; "one does not write with such warmth and enthusiasm unless he is really in love. You sing your lady-love, and you give her another name. That is very plain. Do not deny it, Henry, for I know indeed that you have a lady-love. It may be read in your eyes. And look you! it is on account of this dear one that I have come to you. It pains me, Henry, that you have no confidence in me, and allow me no share in your joys and sorrows. Do you not know, then, how tenderly I love you, my dear, noble brother?"

She put her arm tenderly round his neck, and wanted to kiss him. He bent his head back, and laying his hand on her rosy, round chin, he looked inquiringly and smilingly into her eyes.

"You want something of me, Rosabella!" said he. "I have never yet enjoyed your tenderness and sisterly affection, except when you needed my services."

"How suspicious you are!" cried she, with a charming pout, as she shook his hand away from her face. "I have come from wholly disinterested sympathy; partly to warn you, partly to find out whether your love is perchance fixed upon a lady that would render my warning useless."

"Well, so you see, Rosabella, that I was right, and that your tenderness was not aimless. Now, then, you want to warn me? I have yet to learn that I need any warning."

"Nay, brother! For it would certainly be very dangerous and mischievous for you, if your love should chance not to be in accordance with the command of the king."

A momentary flush spread over Henry Howard's face, and his brow darkened.

"With the king's command?" asked he, in astonishment. "I did not know that Henry the Eighth could control my heart. And, at any rate, I would never concede him that right. Say quickly, then, sister, what is it?

"What means this about the king's command, and what matrimonial scheme have you women been again contriving? For I well know that you and my mother have no rest with the thought of seeing me still unmarried. You want to bestow on me, whether or no, the happiness of marriage; yet, nevertheless, it appears to me that you both have sufficiently learned from experience that this happiness is only imaginary, and that marriage in reality is, at the very least, the vestibule of hell."

"It is true," laughed the duchess; "the only happy moment of my married life was when my husband died. For in that I am more fortunate than my mother, who has her tyrant still living about her. Ah, how I pity my mother!"

"Dare not to revile our noble father!" cried the earl, almost threateningly. "God alone knows how much he has suffered from our mother, and how much he still suffers. He is not to blame for this unhappy marriage. But you have not come to talk over these sad and disgraceful family matters, sister! You wish to warn me, did you say?"

"Yes, warn you!" said the duchess, tenderly, as she took her brother's hand and led him to the ottoman. "Come, let us sit down here, Henry, and let us for once chat confidentially and cordially, as becomes brother and sister. Tell me, who is Geraldine?"

"A phantom, an ideal! I have told you that already."

"You really love, then, no lady at this court?"

"No, none! There is among all these ladies, with whom the queen has surrounded herself, not one whom I am able to love."

"Ah, your heart then is free, Henry; and you will be so much more easily inclined to comply with the king's wish."

"What does the king wish?"

She laid her head on her brother's shoulder, and said in a low whisper: "That the Howard and Seymour families be at last reconciled; that at last they may reconcile the hatred, which has for centuries separated them, by means of a firm and sincere bond of love."

"Ah, the king wants that!" cried the earl, scornfully. "Forsooth, now, he has made a good beginning toward bringing about this reconciliation. He has insulted me before all Europe, by removing me from my command, and investing a Seymour with my rank and dignity; and he requires that I in return shall love this arrogant earl, who has robbed me of what is my due; who has long intrigued and besieged the king's ears with lies and calumnies, till he has gained his end and supplanted me."

"It is true the king recalled you from the army; but this was done in order to give you the first place at his court—to appoint you lord chamberlain to the queen."

Henry Howard trembled and was silent. "It is true," he then muttered; "I am obliged to the king for this place."

"And then," continued the duchess, with an innocent air, "then I do not believe either that Lord Hertford is to blame for your recall. To prove this to you, he has made a proposal to the king, and to me also, which is to testify to you and to all the world how great an honor Lord Hertford esteems it to be allied to the Howards, and above all things to you, by the most sacred bonds."

"Ah, that noble, magnanimous lord!" cried Henry Howard, with a bitter laugh. "As matters do not advance well with laurels, he tries the myrtles; since he can win no battles, he wants to make marriages. Now, sister, let me hear what he has to propose."

"A double marriage, Henry. He asks my hand for his brother Thomas Seymour, provided you choose his sister, Lady Margaret, for your wife."

"Never!" cried the earl. "Never will Henry Howard present his hand to a daughter of that house; never condescend so far as to elevate a Seymour to be his wife. That is well enough for a king—not for a Howard!"

"Brother, you insult the king!"

"Well, I insult him, then! He has insulted me, too, in arranging this base scheme."

"Brother, reflect; the Seymours are powerful, and stand high in the king's favor."

"Yes, in the king's favor they stand high! But the people know their proud, cruel, and arrogant disposition; and the people and nobility despise them. The Seymours have the voice of the king in their favor; the Howards the voice of the whole country, and that is of more consequence. The king can exalt the Seymours, for they stand far beneath him. He cannot exalt the Howards, for they are his equals. Nor can he degrade them. Catharine died on the scaffold—the king became thereby only a hangman—our escutcheon was not sullied by that act!"

"These are very proud words, Henry!"

"They become a son of the Norfolks, Rosabella! Ah, see that petty Lord Hertford, Earl Seymour. He covets a ducal coronet for his sister. He wants to give her to me to wife; for as soon as our poor father dies, I wear his coronet! The arrogant upstarts! For the sister's escutcheon, *my* coronet; for the brother's, *your* coronet. Never, say I, shall that be!"

The duchess had become pale, and a tremor ran through her proud form. Her eyes flashed, and an angry word was already suspended on her lips; but she still held it back. She violently forced herself to calmness and self-possession.

"Consider once more, Henry," said she, "do not decide at once. You speak of our *greatness;* but you do not bear in mind the *power* of the Seymours. I tell you they are powerful enough to tread us in the dust, despite all our greatness. And they are not only powerful at the present; they will be so in the future also; for it is well known in what disposition and what way of thinking the Prince of Wales is trained up. The king is old, weak, and failing; death lurks behind his throne, and will soon enough press him in his arms. Then Edward is king. With him, the heresy of Protestantism triumphs; and however great and numerous our party may be, yet we shall be powerless and subdued. Yes, we shall be the oppressed and persecuted."

"We shall then know how to fight, and if it must be so, to die also!" cried her brother. "It is more honorable to die on the battle-field than to purchase life and humiliation."

"Yes, it is honorable to die on the field of battle; but, Henry, it is a disgrace to come to an end upon the scaffold. And that, my brother, may be your fate, if you do not this time bend your pride; if you do not grasp the hand that Lord Hertford extends to you in reconciliation, but mortally offend him. He will take bloody vengeance, when once he comes into power."

"Let him do it, if he can; my life is in God's hand! My head belongs to the king, but my heart to myself; and that I will never degrade to merchandise, which I may barter for a little security and royal favor."

"Brother, I conjure you, consider it!" cried the duchess, no longer able to restrain her passionate disposition, and all ablaze in her savage wrath. "Dare not in proud arrogance to destroy *my* future also! You may die on the scaffold, if you choose; but I—I will be happy; I will at last, after so many years of sorrow and disgrace, have my share of life's joys also. It is my due, and I will not relinquish it; and you shall not be allowed to tear it from me. Know, then, my brother, I love Thomas Seymour; all my desire, all my hope is fixed on him; and I will not tear this love out of my heart; I will not give him up."

"Well, if you love him, marry him, then!" exclaimed her brother. "Become the wife of this Thomas Seymour! Ask the duke, our father, for his consent to this marriage, and I am certain he will not refuse you, for he is prudent and cautious, and will, better than I, calculate the advantages which a connection with the Seymours may yield our family. Do that, sister, and marry your dearly beloved. I do not hinder you."

"Yes, you do hinder me—you alone!" cried his sister, flaming with wrath. "You will refuse Margaret's hand; you will give the Seymours mortal offence. You thereby make my union with Thomas Seymour impossible! In the proud selfishness of your haughtiness, you see not that you are dashing to atoms my happiness, while you are thinking only of your desire to offend the Seymours. But I tell you, I love Thomas Seymour—nay, I adore him. He is my happiness, my future, my eternal bliss. Therefore have pity on me, Henry! Grant me this happiness, which I implore you for as Heaven's blessing. Prove to me that you love me, and are willing to make this sacrifice for me. Henry, on my knees, I conjure you! Give me the man I love; bend your proud head; become Margaret Seymour's husband, that Thomas Seymour may become mine."

She had actually sunk upon her knees; and her face deluged with tears, bewitchingly beautiful in her passionate emotion, she looked up imploringly to her brother.

But the earl did not lift her up; on the contrary, with a smile, he fell back a step. "How long is it now, duchess," asked he, mockingly, "since you swore that your secretary, Mr. Wilford, was the man whom you loved? Positively, I believed you—I believed it till I one day found you in the arms of your page. On that day, I swore to myself never to believe you again, though you vowed to me, with an oath ever so sacred, that you loved a man. Well, now, you love a man; but what one, is a matter of indifference. To-day his name is Thomas, to-morrow Archibald, or Edward as you please!"

For the first time the earl drew the veil away from his heart, and let his sister see all the contempt and anger that he felt toward her.

The duchess also felt wounded by his words, as by a red-hot iron.

She sprang from her knees; and with flurried breath,

with looks flashing with rage, every muscle of her countenance convulsed and trembling, there she stood before her brother. She was a woman no more; she was a lioness, that, without compassion or pity, will devour him who has dared irritate her.

"Earl of Surrey, you are a shameless wretch!" said she, with compressed, quivering lips. "Were I a man, I would slap you in the face, and call you a scoundrel. But, by the eternal God, you shall not say that you have done this with impunity! Once more, and for the last time, I now ask you, will you comply with Lord Hertford's wish? Will you marry Lady Margaret, and accompany me with Thomas Seymour to the altar?"

"No, I will not, and I will never do it!" exclaimed her brother, solemnly. "The Howards bow not before the Seymours; and never will Henry Howard marry a wife that he does not love!"

"Ah, you love her not!" said she, breathless, gnashing her teeth. "You do not love Lady Margaret; and for this reason must your sister renounce her love, and give up this man whom she adores. Ah, you love not this sister of Thomas Seymour? She is not the Geraldine whom you adore—to whom you dedicate your verses! Well, now, I will find her out—your Geraldine. I will discover her; and then, woe to you and to her! You refuse me your hand to lead me to the altar with Thomas Seymour; well, now, I will one day extend you my hand to conduct you and your Geraldine to the scaffold!"

And as she saw how the earl startled and turned pale, she continued with a scornful laugh: "Ah, you shrink, and horror creeps over you! Does your conscience admonish you that the hero, rigid in virtue, may yet sometimes make a false step? You thought to hide your secret, if you enveloped it in the veil of night, like your Geraldine, who, as you wailingly complain in that poem there, never shows herself to you without a veil as black as night. Just wait, wait! I will strike a light for you, before which all your night-like veils shall be torn in shreds; I will light up the night of your secret with a torch which will be large enough to set on fire the fagot piles about the stake to which you and your Geraldine are to go!"

"Ah, now you let me see for the first time your real countenance," said Henry Howard, shrugging his shoulders. "The angel's mask falls from your face; and I behold the fury that was hidden beneath it. Now you are your mother's own daughter; and at this moment I comprehend for the first time what my father has suffered, and why he shunned not even the disgrace of a divorce, just to be delivered from such a Megæra."

"Oh, I thank you, thank you!" cried she, with a savage laugh. "You are filling up the measure of your iniquity. It is not enough that you drive your sister to despair; you revile your mother also! You say that we are furies; well, indeed, for we shall one day be such to you, and we will show you our Medusa-face, before which you will be stiffened to stone. Henry Howard, Earl of Surrey, from this hour out, I am your implacable enemy; look out for the head on your shoulders, for my hand is raised against it, and in my hand is a sword! Guard well the secret that sleeps in your breast; for you have transformed me to a vampire that will suck your heart's blood. You have reviled my mother, and I will go hence and tell her of it. She will believe me; for she well knows that you hate her, and that you are a genuine son of your father; that is to say, a canting hypocrite, a miserable fellow, who carries virtue on the lips and crime in the heart."

"Cease, I say, cease," cried the earl, "if you do not want me to forget that you are a woman and my sister!"

"Forget it by all means," said she, scornfully. "I have forgotten long since that you are my brother, as you have long since forgotten that you are the son of your mother. Farewell, Earl of Surrey; I leave you and your palace, and will from this hour out abide with my mother, the divorced wife of the Duke of Norfolk. But mark you this: we two are separated from you in our love—but not in our hate! Our hatred to you remains eternal and unchangeable; and one day it will crush you! Farewell, Earl of Surrey; we meet again in the king's presence!"

She rushed to the door. Henry Howard did not hold her back. He looked after her with a smile as she left the cabinet, and murmured, almost compassionately: "Poor woman! I have, perhaps, cheated her out of a lover, and she will never forgive me that. Well, let it be so! Let her, as much as she pleases, be my enemy, and torment me with petty pin-prickings, if she be but unable to harm *her*. I hope, though, that I have guarded well my secret, and she could not suspect the real cause of my refusal. Ah, I was obliged to wrap myself in that foolish family pride, and make haughtiness a cloak for my love. Oh, Geraldine, *thee* would I choose, wert thou the daughter of a peasant; and I would not hold my escutcheon tarnished, if for thy sake I must draw a pale athwart it.—But hark! It is striking four! My service begins! Farewell, Geraldine, I must to the queen!"

And while he betook himself to his dressing-room, to put on his state robes for the great court feast, the Duchess of Richmond returned to her own apartments, trembling and quivering with rage. She traversed these with precipitate haste, and entered her boudoir, where Earl Douglas was waiting for her.

"Well," said he, stepping toward her with his soft, lurking smile, "has he consented?"

"No," said she, gnashing her teeth. "He swore he would never enter into an alliance with the Seymours."

"I well knew that," muttered the earl. "And what do you decide upon now, my lady?"

"I will have revenge! He wants to hinder me from being happy; I will for that make him unhappy!"

"You will do well in that, my lady; for he is an apostate and perjurer; an unfaithful son of the Church. He inclines to the heretical sect, and has forgotten the faith of his fathers."

"I know it!" said she, breathlessly.

Earl Douglas looked at her in astonishment, and continued: "But he is not merely an atheist, he is a traitor also; and more than once he has reviled his king, to whom he, in his pride of heart, believes himself far superior."

"I know it!" repeated she.

"So proud is he," continued the earl, "so full of blasphemous haughtiness, that he might lay his hands upon the crown of England."

"I know it!" said the duchess again. But as she saw the earl's astonished and doubting looks, she added, with an inhuman smile: "I know everything that you want that I should know! Only impute crimes to him; only accuse him; I will substantiate everything, testify to everything that will bring him to ruin. My mother is our ally; she hates the father as hotly as I the son. Bring your accusation, then, Earl Douglas; we are your witnesses!"

"Nay, indeed, my lady," said he, with a gentle, insinuating smile. "I know nothing at all; I have heard nothing; how, then, can I bring an accusation? You know all; to you he has spoken. You must be his accuser!"

"Well, then, conduct me to the king!" said she.

"Will you allow me to give you some more advice first?"

"Do so, Earl Douglas."

"Be very cautious in the choice of your means. Do not waste them all at once, so that if your first thrust does not hit, you may not be afterward without weapons. It is better, and far less dangerous, to surely kill the enemy that you hate with a slow, creeping poison, gradually and day by day, than to murder him at once with a dagger, which may, however, break on a rib and become ineffective. Tell, then, what you know, not at once, but little by little. Administer your drug which is to make the king furious, gradually; and if you do not hit your enemy to-day, think that you will do it so much the more surely to-morrow. Nor do you forget that we have to punish, not merely the heretic Henry Howard, but above all things the heretical queen, whose unbelief will call down the wrath of the Most High upon this land."

"Come to the king," said she, hastily. "On the way you can tell me what I ought to make known and what conceal. I will do implicitly what you say. Now, Henry Howard," said she softly to herself, "hold yourself ready; the contest begins! In your pride and selfishness you have destroyed the happiness of my life—my eternal felicity. I loved Thomas Seymour; I hoped by his side to find the happiness that I have so long and so vainly sought in the crooked paths of life. By this love my soul would have been saved and restored to virtue. My brother has willed otherwise. He has, therefore, condemned me to be a demon, instead of an angel. I will fulfil my destiny. I will be an evil spirit to him." *

CHAPTER XXIV.

THE QUEEN'S TOILET.

THE festivities of the day are concluded, and the gallant knights and champions, who have to-day broken a lance for the honor of their ladies, may rest from their vic-

* The Earl of Surrey, by his refusal to marry Margaret Seymour, gave occasion to the rupture of the proposed alliance between Thomas Seymour and the Duchess of Richmond, his sister. After that the duchess mortally hated him and combined with his enemies against him. The Duchess of Richmond is designated by all the historians of her time as "the most beautiful woman of her century, but also a shameless Messalina."—See Tytler, p. 390. Also Burnet, vol. i, p. 134; Leti, vol. i, p. 83; and Nott's Life of Henry Howard.

tories upon their laurels. The tournament of arms was over, and the tournament of mind was about to begin. The knights, therefore, retired to exchange the coat-of-mail for gold-embroidered velvet apparel; the ladies to put on their lighter evening dresses; and the queen, likewise with this design, had withdrawn to her dressing-room, while the ladies and lords of her court were in attendance in the large anteroom to escort her to the throne.

Without, it was beginning to grow dusky, and the twilight cast its long shadows across this hall, in which the cavaliers of the court were walking up and down with the ladies, and discussing the particularly important events of the day's tourney.

The Earl of Sudley, Thomas Seymour, had borne off the prize of the day, and conquered his opponent, Henry Howard. The king had been in raptures on this account. For Thomas Seymour had been for some time his favorite; perhaps because he was the declared enemy of the Howards. He had, therefore, added to the golden laurel crown which the queen had presented to the earl as the award, a diamond pin, and commanded the queen to fasten it in the earl's ruff with her own hand. Catharine had done so with sullen countenance and averted looks; and even Thomas Seymour had shown himself only a very little delighted with the proud honor with which the queen, at her husband's command, was to grace him.

The rigid popish party at court formed new hopes from this, and dreamed of the queen's conversion and return to the true, pure faith; while the Protestant, " the heretical " party, looked to the future with gloomy despondency, and were afraid of being robbed of their most powerful support and their most influential patronage.

Nobody had seen that, as the queen arose to crown the victor, Thomas Seymour, her handkerchief, embroidered with gold, fell from her hands, and that the earl, after he had taken it up and presented it to the queen, had thrust his hand for a moment, with a motion wholly accidental and undesigned, into his ruff, which was just as white as the small neatly-folded paper which he concealed in it, and which he had found in the queen's handkerchief.

One person had seen it. This little *ruse* of the queen had not escaped John Heywood, who had immediately, by some cutting witticism, set the king to laughing, and tried to draw the attention of the courtiers from the queen and her lover.

He was now standing crowded into the embrasure of a window, and entirely concealed behind the silk curtain; and so, without being seen, he let his falcon eyes roam over the whole room.

He saw everything; he heard everything; and, noticed by none, he observed all.

He saw how Earl Douglas now made a sign to Bishop Gardiner, and how he quickly answered it.

As if by accident, both now left the groups with whom they had just been chatting, and drew near each other, looking about for some place where, unobserved and separated from the rest, they might converse together. In all the windows were standing groups, chatting and laughing; only that window behind the curtain of which John Heywood was concealed, was unoccupied.

So Earl Douglas and the bishop turned thither.

"Shall we attain our end to-day?" asked Gardiner, in a low voice.

"With God's gracious assistance, we shall annihilate all our enemies to-day. The sword already hangs over their heads, and soon it will fall and deliver us from them," said Earl Douglas, solemnly.

"Are you, then, certain of it?" asked Gardiner, and an expression of cruel delight flitted across his malicious, ashy face. "But tell me, how comes it that Archbishop Cranmer is not here?"

"He is sick, and so had to remain at Lambeth."

"May this sickness be the forerunner of his death!" muttered the bishop, devoutly folding his hands.

"It will be so, your highness; God will destroy His enemies and bless us. Cranmer is accused, and the king will judge him without mercy."

"And the queen?"

Earl Douglas was a moment silent, and then said, in a low whisper: "Wait but a few hours more, and she will be queen no longer. Instead of returning from the throne-room to her apartments, we shall accompany her to the Tower."

John Heywood, completely enveloped in the folds of the curtain, held his breath and listened.

"And you are, then, perfectly sure of our victory?" asked Gardiner. "Can no accident, no unforeseen circumstance, snatch it from us?"

"If the queen gives him the rosette—no! For then the king will find Geraldine's love-letter in the silver knot, and she is condemned. So all depends on the queen's wearing the rosette, and not discovering its contents. But see, your highness, there is the Duchess of Richmond approaching us. She makes a sign to me. Now pray for us, your highness, for I am going with her to the king, and she will accuse this hated Catharine Parr! I tell you, bishop, it is an accusation involving life and death; and if Catharine escape one danger, she will run into another. Wait here for me, your highness; I will return soon and tell you the result of our scheme. Lady Jane, also, will soon bring us news here."

He left the window and followed the duchess, who crossed the hall, and with her disappeared through the door that led to the king's apartments.

The ladies and lords of the court laughed and chatted away.

John Heywood stood, with throbbing heart and in breathless anxiety, behind the curtain, close by Gardiner, who had folded his hands and was praying.

While Gardiner prayed, and Douglas accused and calumniated, the queen, suspecting nothing of these plots they were framing against her, was in her toilet-room and being adorned by her women.

She was to-day very beautiful, very magnificent to look upon; at once a woman and queen; at the same time resplendent and modest, with a bewitching smile on her rosy lips; and yet commanding respect in her proud and glorious beauty. None of Henry's queens had so well understood the art of appearing in public, and none remained so much the woman while doing so.

As she now stood before the large mirror, which the Republic of Venice had sent the king as a wedding-gift, and which reflected the figure of the queen sparkling with diamonds, she smiled, for she was obliged to confess to herself that she was very beautiful to-day; and she thought that to-day Thomas Seymour would look upon his love with pride.

As she thought of him, a deep crimson overspread her face, and a thrill flew through her frame. How handsome he had been at the tournament that day; how splendidly he leaped over the barriers; how his eye flashed; how contemptuous had been his smile! And then, that look which he directed over to her at the moment when he had conquered his antagonist, Henry Howard, and hurled the lance from his hand! Oh, her heart was then ready to burst with delight and rapture!

Wholly given up to her reverie, she sank in her gilded arm-chair and cast her eyes to the ground, dreaming and smiling.

Behind her stood her women in respectful silence, waiting for a sign from their mistress. But the queen no longer thought at all of them; she imagined herself alone; she saw nobody but that handsome, manly face for which she had reserved a place in her heart.

Now the door opened, and Lady Jane Douglas entered. She, too, was magnificently dressed, and sparkling with diamonds; she, too, was beautiful, but it was the pallid, dreadful beauty of a demon; and he who looked upon her just then, as she entered the room, would have trembled, and his heart would have been seized with an undefined fear.

She threw a quick glance on her mistress lost in revery; and as she saw that her toilet was finished, she made a sign to the women, who silently obeyed and left the room.

Still Catharine noticed nothing. Lady Jane stood behind her and observed her in the mirror. As she saw the queen smile, her brow darkened and fierce fire flashed in her eyes.

"She shall smile no more," said she to herself. "I suffer thus terribly by her; well, now, she shall suffer too."

Softly and noiselessly she slipped into the next room, the door of which stood ajar, and opened with hurried hand a *carton* filled with ribbons and bows. Then she drew from the velvet pocket, wrought with pearls, which hung at her side, suspended by a gold chain, a dark-red rosette, and threw it into the box. That was all.

Lady Jane now returned to the adjoining room; and her countenance, which had been previously gloomy and threatening, was now proud and joyful.

With a bright smile she walked up to the queen, and kneeling down at her side, she pressed a fervent kiss on the hand that was hanging down.

"What is my queen musing over?" asked she, as she laid her head on Catharine's knee and tenderly looked up at her.

The queen gave a slight start, and raised her head. She saw Lady Jane's tender smile, and her yet searching looks.

Because she felt conscious of guilt, at least of guilty thoughts, she was on her guard, and remembered John Heywood's warning.

"She is observing me," she said to herself; "she seems affectionate; so she is brooding over some wicked plot."

"Ah, it is well you have come, Jane," said she aloud. "You can help me; for, to tell you the truth, I am in great perplexity. I am in want of a rhyme, and I am thinking in vain how I shall find it."

"Ah, are you composing poetry, queen?"

"Why, Jane, does that surprise you? Shall I, the queen, be able, then, to bear off no prize? I would give my precious jewels, if I could succeed in composing a poem to which the king was obliged to award the prize. But I am wanting in a musical ear; I cannot find the rhyme, and so shall be obliged at last to give up the idea of winning laurels also. How the king would enjoy it, though! For, to confess the truth to you, I believe he is a little afraid that Henry Howard will bear off the prize, and he would be very thankful to me if I could contest it with him. You well know the king has no love for the Howards."

"And you, queen?" asked Jane; and she turned so pale, that the queen herself noticed it.

"You are unwell, Jane," said she, sympathizingly. "Really, Jane, you seem to be suffering. You need recreation; you should rest a little."

But Jane had already regained her calm and earnest air, and she succeeded in smiling.

"No, indeed!" said she. "I am well, and satisfied to be permitted to be near you. But will you allow me, queen, to make a request of you?"

"Ask, Jane, ask, and it is granted beforehand; for I know that Jane will request nothing that her friend cannot grant."

Lady Jane was silent, and looked thoughtfully upon the ground. With firm resolution she struggled with herself. Her proud heart reared fiercely up at the thought of bowing before this woman, whom she hated, and of being obliged to approach her with a fawning prayer. She felt such raging hate against the queen, that in that hour she would willingly have given her own life, if she could have first seen her enemy at her feet, wailing and crushed.

Henry Howard loved the queen; so Catharine had robbed her of the heart of him whom she adored. Catharine had condemned her to the eternal torment of renouncing him—to the rack of enjoying a happiness and a rapture that was not hers—to warm herself at a fire which she like a thief had stolen from the altar of another's god.

Catharine was condemned and doomed. Jane had no more compassion. She must crush her.

"Well," asked the queen, "you are silent? You do not tell me what I am to grant you?"

Lady Jane raised her eyes, and her look was serene and peaceful. "Queen," said she, "I encountered in the anteroom one who is unhappy, deeply bowed down. In your hand alone is the power to raise him up again. Will you do it?"

"Will I do it!" exclaimed Catharine, quickly. "Oh, Jane, you well know how much my heart longs to help and be serviceable to the unfortunate! Ah, so many wounds are inflicted at this court, and the queen is so poor in balm to heal them! Allow me this pleasure then, Jane, and I shall be thankful to you, not you to me! Speak then, Jane, speak quickly; who is it that needs my help?"

"Not your help, queen, but your compassion and your grace. Earl Sudley has conquered poor Earl Surrey in the tournament to-day, and you comprehend that your lord chamberlain feels himself deeply bowed and humbled."

"Can I alter that, Jane? Why did the visionary earl, the enthusiastic poet, allow himself a contest with a hero who already knows what he wants, and ever accomplishes what he wills? Oh, it was wonderful to look upon, with what lightning speed Thomas Seymour lifted him out of the saddle! And the proud Earl Surrey, the wise and learned man, the powerful party leader, was forced to bow before the hero, who like an angel Michael had thrown him in the dust."

The queen laughed.

That laugh went through Jane's heart like a cutting sword.

"She shall pay me for that!" said she softly to herself.

"Queen," said she aloud, "you are perfectly right; he has deserved this humiliation; but now, after he is punished, you should lift him up. Nay, do not shake your beautiful head. Do it for your own sake, queen; do it from prudence. Earl Surrey, with his father, is the head of a powerful party, whom this humiliation of the Howards fills with a still more burning hate against the Seymours, and who will, in time to come, take a bloody revenge for it."

"Ah, you frighten me!" said the queen, who had now become serious.

Lady Jane continued: "I saw how the Duke of Norfolk bit his lips, as his son had to yield to Seymour; I heard how one, here and there, muttered low curses and vows of vengeance against the Seymours."

"Who did that? Who dared to do it?" exclaimed Catharine, springing up impetuously from her arm-chair. "Who at this court is so audacious as to wish to injure those whom the queen loves? Name him to me, Jane; I will know his name! I will know it, that I may accuse him to the king. For the king does not want that these noble Seymours should give way to the Howards; he does not want that the nobler, the better, and more glorious, should bow before these quarrelsome, domineering papists. The king loves the noble Seymours, and his powerful arm will protect them against all their enemies."

"And, without doubt, your majesty will assist him in it?" said Jane, smiling.

This smile brought the queen back to her senses again.

She perceived that she had gone too far; that she had betrayed too much of her secret. She must, therefore, repair the damage, and allow her excitement to be forgotten.

Therefore she said, calmly: "Certainly, Jane; I will assist the king to be just. But never will I be unjust, not even against these papists. If I cannot love them, nevertheless no one shall say that I hate them. And besides, it becomes a queen to rise above parties. Say, then, Jane, what can I do for poor Surrey? With what shall we bind up these wounds that the brave Seymour has inflicted on him?"

"You have publicly given the victor in the tournament a token of your great favor—you have crowned him."

"It was the king's order," exclaimed Catharine, warmly.

"Well! He will not, however, command you to reward the Earl of Surrey also, if he likewise should gain the victory this evening. Do it, therefore, of your own accord, queen. Give him openly, before your whole court, a token of your favor! It is so easy for princes to make men happy, to comfort the unfortunate! A smile, a friendly word, a pressure of the hand is sufficient for it. A ribbon that you wear on your dress makes him to whom you present it, proud and happy, and raises him high above all others. Ponder it well, queen; I speak not for Earl Surrey's sake; I am thinking more of yourself. If you have the courage, publicly and in spite of the disgrace with which King Henry threatens the Howards, to be nevertheless just to them, and to recognize *their* merits as well as that of others—believe me, if you do that, the whole of this powerful party, which is now hostile to you, will fall at your feet overcome and conquered. You will at last become the all-powerful and universally loved Queen of England; and, like the heretics, the papists also will call you their mistress and protectress. Consider no longer! Let your noble and generous heart prevail! Spiteful fortune has prostrated Henry Howard in the dust. Extend him your hand, queen, that he may rise again, and again stand there at your court, proud and radiant as he always was. Henry Howard well deserves that you should be gracious to him. Great and beaming like a star, he shines on high above all men; and there is no one who can say that he himself is more prudent or braver, wiser or more learned, noble or greater, than the noble, the exalted Surrey. All England resounds with his fame. The women repeat with enthusiasm his beautiful sonnets and lovesongs; the learned are proud to call him their equal, and the warriors speak with admiration of his feats of arms. Be just, then, queen! You have so highly honored the merit of valor; now, honor the merit of mind also! You have, in Seymour, honored the warrior; now, in Howard, honor the poet and the man!"

"I will do it," said Catharine, as with a charming smile she looked into Jane's glowing and enthusiastic countenance. "I will do it, Jane, but upon one condition!"

"And this condition is——"

Catharine put her arm around Jane's neck, and drew her close to her heart. "That you confess to me, that you love Henry Howard, whom you know how to defend so enthusiastically and warmly."

Lady Jane gave a start, and for a moment leaned her head on the queen's shoulder, exhausted.

"Well," asked she, "do you confess it? Will you acknowledge that your proud, cold heart is obliged to declare itself overcome and conquered?"

"Yes, I confess it," cried Lady Jane, as with passionate vehemence she threw herself at Catharine's feet. "Yes, I love him—I adore him. I know it is a disdained and unhappy love; but what would you have? My heart is mightier than everything else. I love him; he is my god and my lord; I adore him as my savior and lord. Queen, you know all my secret; betray me if you will! Tell it to my father, if you wish him to curse me. Tell it to Henry Howard, if it pleases you to hear how he scoffs at me. For he, queen—he loves me not!"

"Poor unfortunate Jane!" exclaimed the queen, compassionately.

Jane uttered a low cry, and rose from her knees. That was too much. Her enemy commiserated her. She, who was to blame for her sorrow—she bemoaned her fate.

Ah, she could have strangled the queen; she could have plunged a dagger into her heart, because she dared to commiserate her.

"I have complied with your condition, queen," said she, breathing hurriedly. "Will you now comply with my request?"

"And will you really be an advocate for this unthankful, cruel man, who does not love you? Proudly and coldly he passes your beauty by, and you—you intercede for him!"

"Queen, true love thinks not of itself! It sacrifices itself. It makes no question of the reward it receives, but only of the happiness which it bestows. I saw in his pale, sorrowful face, how much he suffered; ought I not to think of comforting him? I approached him, I addressed him; I heard his despairing lamentation over that misfortune, which, however, was not the fault of his activity and courage, but, as all the world saw, the fault of his horse, which was shy and stumbled. And as he, in all the bitterness of his pain, was lamenting that you, queen, would despise and scorn him, I, with full trust in your noble and magnanimous heart, promised him that you would, at my request, yet give him to-day, before your whole court, a token of your favor. Catharine, did I do wrong?"

"No, Jane, no! You did right; and your words shall be made good. But how shall I begin? What shall I do?"

"The earl this evening, after the king has read the Greek scene with Croke, will recite some new sonnets which he has composed. When he has done so, give him some kind of a present—be it what it may, no matter—as a token of your favor."

"But how, Jane, if his sonnets deserve no praise and no acknowledgment?"

"You may be sure that they do deserve it. For Henry Howard is a noble and true poet, and his verses are full of heavenly melody and exalted thoughts."

The queen smiled. "Yes," said she, "you love him ardently; for you have no doubt as to him. We will, therefore, recognize him as a great poet. But with what shall I reward him?"

"Give him a rose that you wear in your bosom—a rosette that is fastened to your dress and shows your colors."

"But alas, Jane, to-day I wear neither a rose nor a rosette."

"Yet you can wear one, queen. A rosette is, indeed, wanting here on your shoulder. Your purple mantle is too negligently fastened. We must put some trimming here."

She went hastily into the next room and returned with the box in which were kept the queen's ribbons embroidered with gold, and bows adorned with jewels.

Lady Jane searched and selected, here and there, a long time. Then she took the crimson velvet rosette, which she herself had previously thrown into the box, and showed it to the queen.

"See, it is at the same time tasteful and rich, for a diamond clasp confines it in the middle. Will you allow me to fasten this rosette on your shoulder, and will you give it to the Earl of Surrey?"

"Yes, Jane, I will give it to him, because you wish it. But, poor Jane, what do you gain by my doing it?"

"At any rate, a friendly smile, queen."

"And is that enough for you? Do you love him so much, then?"

"Yes, I love him!" said Jane Douglas, with a sigh of pain, as she fastened the rosette on the queen's shoulder.

"And now, Jane, go and announce to the master of ceremonies that I am ready, as soon as the king wishes it, to resort to the gallery."

Lady Jane turned to leave the chamber. But, already upon the threshold, she returned once more.

Forgive me, queen, for venturing to make one more request of you. You have, however, just shown yourself too much the noble and true friend of earlier days for me not to venture one more request."

" Now, what is it, poor Jane? "

" I have intrusted my secret not to the queen, but to Catharine Parr, the friend of my youth. Will she keep it, and betray to none my disgrace and humiliation? "

" My word for that, Jane. Nobody but God and ourselves shall ever know what we have spoken."

Lady Jane humbly kissed her hand and murmured a few words of thanks; then she left the queen's room to go in quest of the master of ceremonies.

In the queen's anteroom she stopped a moment, and leaned against the wall, exhausted, and as it were crushed. Nobody was here who could observe and listen to her. She had no need to smile, no need to conceal, beneath a calm and equable appearance, all those tempestuous and despairing feelings which were working within. She could allow her hatred and her resentment, her rage and her despair, to pour forth in words and gestures, in tears and imprecations, in sobs and sighs. She could fall on her knees and beseech God for grace and mercy, and call on the devil for revenge and destruction.

When she had so done, she arose, and her demeanor resumed its wonted cold and calm expression. Only her cheeks were still paler; only a still gloomier fire darted from her eyes, and a scornful smile played about her thin, compressed lips.

She traversed the rooms and corridors, and now she entered the king's anteroom. As she observed Gardiner, who was standing alone and separated from the rest in the embrasure of the window, she went up to him; and John Heywood, who was still hidden behind the curtain, shuddered at the frightful and scornful expression of her features.

She offered the bishop her hand, and tried to smile. "It is done," said she, almost inaudibly.

"What! The queen wears the rosette?" asked Gardiner vivaciously.

"She wears the rosette, and will give it to him."

"And the note is in it?"

"It is concealed under the diamond clasp."

"Oh, then she is lost!" muttered Gardiner. "If the king finds this paper, Catharine's death-warrant is signed."

"Hush!" said Lady Jane. "See! Lord Hertford is coming toward us. Let us go to meet him."

They both left the window and walked out into the hall.

John Heywood immediately slipped from behind the curtain, and, softly gliding along by the wall, left the hall perceived by no one.

Outside, he stopped and reflected.

"I must see this conspiracy to the bottom," said he to himself. "I must find out through whom and by what they wish to destroy her; and I must have sure and undeniable proof in my hands, in order to be able to convict them, and successfully accuse them to the king. Therefore it is necessary to be cautious and prudent. So let us consider what to do. The simplest thing would be to beg the queen not to wear the rosette. But that is only to demolish the web for this time, without, however, being able to kill the spider that wove it. So she must wear the rosette; for besides, without that I should never be able either to find out to whom she is to give it. But the paper that is concealed in the rosette—that I must have—that must not be in it. 'If the king finds this paper, Catharine's death-warrant is signed.' Now, my reverend priest of the devil, the king will not find that paper, for John Heywood will not have it so. But how shall I begin? Shall I tell the queen what I heard? No! She would lose her cheerful spirit and become embarrassed, and the embarrassment would be in the king's eyes the most convincing proof of her guilt. No, I must take this paper out of the rosette without the queen's being aware of it. Boldly to work, then! I must have this paper, and tweak these hypocrites by the nose. How it can be done, it is not clear to me yet; but I will do it—that is enough. Halloo, forward to the queen!"

With precipitant haste he ran through the halls and corridors, while with a smile he muttered away to himself: "Thank God, I enjoy the honor of being the fool; for only the king and the fool have the privilege of being able to enter unannounced every room, even the queen's."

Catharine was alone in her boudoir, when the small door, through which the king was accustomed to resort to her, was softly opened.

"Oh, the king is coming!" said she, walking to the door to greet her husband.

"Yes, the king is coming, for the fool is already here," said John Heywood, who entered through the private door. "Are we alone, queen? Does nobody overhear us?"

"No, John Heywood, we are all alone. What do you bring me?"

"A letter, queen."

"From whom?" asked she, and a glowing crimson flitted over her cheek.

"From whom?" repeated John Heywood, with a waggish smile. "I do not know, queen; but at any rate it is a begging letter; and without doubt you would do well not to read it at all; for I bet you, the shameless writer of this letter demands of you some impossibility—it may be a smile, or a pressure of the hand, a lock of your hair, or perchance even a kiss. So, queen, do not read the begging letter at all."

"John," said she, smiling, and yet trembling with impatience, "John, give me the letter."

"I will sell it to you, queen. I have learned *that* from

the king, who likewise gives nothing away generously, without taking in return more than he gives. So let us trade. I give you the letter; you give me the rosette which you wear on your shoulder there."

"Nay, indeed, John; choose something else—I cannot give you the rosette."

"And by the gods be it sworn!" exclaimed John, with comic pathos, "I give you not the letter, if you do not give me the rosette."

"Silly loon," said the queen, "I tell you I cannot! Choose something else, John; and I conjure you, dear John, give me the letter."

"Then only, when you give me the rosette. I have sworn it by the gods, and what I vow to them, that I stick to! No, no, queen—not those sullen airs, not that angry frown. For if I cannot in earnest receive the rosette as a present, then let us do like the Jesuits and papists, who even trade with the dear God, and snap their fingers at Him. I must keep my oath! I give you the letter, and you give me the rosette; but listen—you only lend it to me; and when I have it in my hand a moment, I am generous and bountiful, like the king, and I make you a present of your own property."

With a quick motion the queen tore the rosette from her shoulder, and handed it to John Heywood.

"Now give me the letter, John."

"Here it is," said John Heywood as he received the rosette. "Take it; and you will see that Thomas Seymour is my brother."

"Your brother?" asked Catharine with a smile, as with trembling hand she broke the seal.

"Yes, my brother, for he is a fool! Ah, I have a great many brothers. The family of fools is so very large!"

The queen no longer heard. She was reading the letter of her lover. She had eyes only for those lines, that told her that Thomas Seymour loved her, adored her, and was pining away with longing after her.

She did not see how John Heywood, with nimble hand, unfastened the diamond clasp from the rosette, and took out of it the little paper that was concealed in the folds of the ribbon.

"She is saved!" murmured he, while he thrust the fatal paper into his doublet, and fastened the clasp again with the pin. "She is saved, and the king will not sign her death-warrant this time."

Catharine had read the letter to the end, and hid it in her bosom.

"Queen, you have sworn to burn up every letter that I bring you from *him;* for, forbidden love-letters are dangerous things. One day they may find a tongue and testify against you! Queen, I will not bring you again another letter, if you do not first burn that one."

"John, I will burn it up when once I have really read it. Just now I read it only with my heart, not with my eyes. Allow me, then, to wear it on my heart a few hours more."

"Do you swear to me that you will burn it up this very day?"

"I swear it."

"Then I will be satisfied this time. Here is your rosette; and like the famous fox in the fable, that pronounced the grapes sour because he could not get them, I say, take your rosette back; I will have none of it."

He handed the queen the rosette, and she smilingly fastened it on her shoulder again.

"John," said she, with a bewitching smile, extending her hand to him, "John, when will you at length permit me to thank you otherwise than with words? When will you at length allow your queen to reward you, for all this service of love, otherwise than with words?"

John Heywood kissed her hand, and said mournfully: "I will demand a reward of you on the day when my tears and my prayers succeed in persuading you to renounce this wretched and dangerous love. On that day I shall have really deserved a reward, and I will accept it from you with a proud heart."

"Poor John! So, then, you will never receive your reward; for that day will never come!"

"So, then, I shall probably receive my reward, but from the king; and it will be a reward whereby one loses hearing and sight, and head to boot. Well, we shall see! Till then, farewell, queen! I must to the king; for somebody might surprise me here, and come to the shrewd conclusion that John Heywood is not always a fool, but sometimes also the messenger of love! I kiss the hem of your garment; farewell, queen!"

He glided again through the private door.

"Now we will at once examine this paper," said he, as he reached the corridor and was sure of being seen by no one.

He drew the paper out of his doublet and opened it. "I do not know the handwriting," muttered her, "but it was a woman that wrote it."

"The letter read: "Do you believe me now, my beloved? I swore to deliver to you to-day, in the presence of the king and all of my court, this rosette; and I have done so. For you I gladly risk my life, for you are my life; and still more beautiful were it to die with you, than to live without you. I live only when I rest in your arms; and those dark nights, when you can be with me, are the light and sunshine of my days. Let us pray Heaven a dark night may soon come; for such a night restores to me the loved one, and to you, your happy wife, Geraldine."

"Geraldine! who is Geraldine?" muttered John Heywood, slipping the paper into his doublet again. "I must disentangle this web of lying and deceit. I must know what all this means. For this is more than a conspiracy— a false accusation. It concerns, as it seems, a reality. This letter the queen is to give to a man; and in it, sweet recollections, happy nights, are spoken of. So he who receives this letter is in league with them against Catharine, and I dare say her worst enemy, for he makes use of love against her. Some treachery or knavery is concealed behind this. Either the man to whom this letter is addressed is deceived—and he is unintentionally a tool in the hands of the papists—or he is in league with them, and has given himself up to the villainy of playing the part of a lover to the queen. But who can he be? Perchance, Thomas Seymour. It were possible; for he has a cold and deceitful heart, and he would be capable of such treachery. But woe be to him if it is he! Then it will be *I* who accuses him to the king; and, by God! his head shall fall! Now away to the king!"

Just as he entered the king's anteroom, the door of the cabinet opened, and the Duchess of Richmond, accompanied by Earl Douglas, walked out.

Lady Jane and Gardiner were standing, as if by accident, near the door.

"Well, have we attained our end there also?" asked Gardiner.

"We have attained it," said Earl Douglas. "The duchess has accused her brother of a *liaison* with the queen. She has deposed that he sometimes leaves the palace by night, and does not return to it before morning. She has declared that for four nights she herself dogged her brother and saw him as he entered the wing of the castle occupied by the queen; and one of the queen's maids has communicated to the duchess that the queen was not in her room on that night."

"And the king listened to the accusation, and did not throttle you in his wrath!"

"He is just in that dull state of rage in which the lava that the crater will afterward pour forth, is just prepared. As yet all is quiet, but be sure there will be an eruption, and the stream of red-hot lava will busy those who have dared excite the god Vulcan."

"And does he know about the rosette?" asked Lady Jane.

"He knows everything. And until that moment he will allow no one to suspect his wrath and fury. He says he will make the queen perfectly secure, in order to get into his hands thereby sure proof of her guilt. Well, we will furnish him this evidence; and hence it follows that the queen is inevitably lost."

"But hark! The doors are opened, and the master of ceremonies comes to summon us to the golden gallery."

"Just walk in," muttered John Heywood, gliding along behind them. "I am still here; and I will be the mouse that gnaws the net in which you want to catch my noble-minded lioness."

CHAPTER XXV.

THE QUEEN'S ROSETTE.

THE golden gallery, in which the tourney of the poets was to take place, presented to-day a truly enchanting and fairy-like aspect. Mirrors of gigantic size, set in broad gilt frames, ornamented with the most perfect carved work, covered the walls, and threw back, a thousand times reflected, the enormous chandeliers which, with their hundreds and hundreds of candles, shed the light of day in the vast hall. Here and there were seen, arranged in front of the mirrors, clusters of the rarest and choicest flowers, which poured through the hall their fragrance, stupefying and yet so enchanting, and outshone in brilliancy of colors even the Turkish carpet, which stretched through the whole room and changed the floor into one immense flower-bed. Between the clumps of flowers were seen tables with golden vases, in which were refreshing beverages; while at the other end of the enormous gallery stood a gigantic sideboard, which contained the choicest and rarest dishes. At present the doors of the sideboard, which, when open, formed a room of itself, were closed.

They had not yet come to the material enjoyments; they were still occupied in absorbing the spiritual. The brilliant and select company that filled the hall was still for some time condemned to be silent, and to shut up within them their laughter and gossip, their backbiting and slander, their flattery and hypocrisy.

Just now a pause ensued. The king, with Croke, had recited to his court a scene from "Antigone"; and they were just taking breath from the wonderful and exalted enjoyment of having just heard a language of which they understood not a word, but which they found to be very beautiful, since the king admired it.

Henry the Eighth had again leaned back on his golden throne, and, panting, rested from his prodigious exertion; and while he rested and dreamed, an invisible band played a piece of music composed by the king himself, and which, with its serious and solemn movement, strangely contrasted with this room so brilliant and cheerful—with this splendid, laughing and jesting assembly.

For the king had bidden them amuse themselves and be gay; to give themselves up to unrestrained chit-chat. It was, therefore, natural for them to laugh, and to appear not to notice the king's exhaustion and repose.

Besides, they had not for a long time seen Henry so cheerful, so full of youthful life, so sparkling with wit and humor, as on this evening. His mouth was overflowing with jests that made the gentlemen laugh, and the beautiful, brilliant women blush, and, above all, the young queen, who sat by him on the rich and splendid throne, and now and then threw stolen and longing glances at her lover, for whom she would willingly and gladly have given her royal crown and her throne.

When the king saw how Catharine blushed, he turned to her, and in his tenderest tone begged her pardon for his jest, which, however, in its sauciness, served only to make his queen still more beautiful, still more bewitching. His words were then so tender and heartfelt, his looks so full of love and admiration, that nobody could doubt but that the queen was in highest favor with her husband, and that he loved her most tenderly.

Only the few who knew the secret of this tenderness of the king, so open and so unreservedly displayed, comprehended fully the danger which threatened the queen; for the king was never more to be dreaded than when he flattered; and on no one did his wrath fall more crushingly than on him whom he had just kissed and assured of his favor.

This was what Earl Douglas said to himself, when he saw with what a cordial look Henry the Eighth chatted with his consort.

Behind the throne of the royal pair was seen John Heywood, in his fantastic and dressy costume, with his face at once noble and cunning; and the king just then broke out into loud, resounding laughter at his sarcastic and satirical observations.

"King, your laugh does not please me to-day," said John Heywood, earnestly. "It smacks of gall. Do you not find it so, queen?"

The queen was startled from her sweet reveries, and that was what John Heywood had wished. He, therefore, repeated his question.

"No, indeed," said she; "I find the king to-day quite like the sun. He is radiant and bright, like it."

"Queen, you do not mean the sun, but the full moon," said John Heywood. "But only see, Henry, how cheerfully Earl Archibald Douglas over there is chatting with the Duchess of Richmond! I love that good earl. He always appears like a blind-worm, which is just in the notion of stinging some one on the heel, and hence it comes that, when near the earl, I always transform myself into a crane. I stand on one leg; because I am then sure to have the other at least safe from the earl's sting. King, were I like you, I would not have those killed that the blind-worm has stung; but I would root out the blind-worms, that the feet of honorable men might be secure from them."

The king cast at him a quick, searching look, which John Heywood answered with a smile.

"Kill the blind-worms, King Henry," said he; "and when you are once at work destroying vermin, it will do no harm if you once more give these priests also a good kick. It is now a long time since we burnt any of them, and they are again becoming arrogant and malicious, as they always were and always will be. I see even the pious and meek bishop of Winchester, the noble Gardiner, who is entertaining himself with Lady Jane over there, smiling very cheerfully, and that is a bad sign; for Gardiner smiles only when he has again caught a poor soul, and prepared it as a breakfast for his lord. I do not mean you, king, but his lord—the devil. For the devil is always hungry for noble human souls; and to him who catches one for him he gives indulgence for his sins for an hour. Therefore Gardiner catches so many souls; for since he sins every hour, every hour he needs indulgence."

"You are very spiteful to-day, John Heywood," said the queen, smiling, while the king fixed his eyes on the ground, thoughtful and musing.

John Heywood's words had touched the sore place of his heart, and, in spite of himself, filled his suspicious soul with new doubts.

He mistrusted not merely the accused, but the accusers also; and if he punished the one as criminals, he would have willingly punished the others as informants.

He asked himself: "What aim had Earl Douglas and Gardiner in accusing the queen; and why had they startled him out of his quiet and confidence?" At that moment, when he looked on his beautiful wife, who sat by him in such serene tranquillity, unembarrassed and smiling, he felt a deep anger fill his heart, not against Catharine, but against Jane, who accused her.

She was so lovely and beautiful! Why did they envy him her? Why did they not leave him in his sweet delusion? But perhaps she was not guilty. No, she was not. The eye of a culprit is not thus bright and clear. The air of infidelity is not thus unembarrassed—of such maidenly delicacy.

Moreover, the king was exhausted and disgusted. One can become satiated even with cruelty; and, at this hour, Henry felt completely surfeited with bloodshed.

His heart—for, in such moments of mental relaxation and bodily enfeeblement, the king even had a heart—his heart was already in the mood of pronouncing the word pardon, when his eye fell on Henry Howard, who, with his father, the Duke of Norfolk, and surrounded by a circle of brilliant and noble lords, was standing not far from the royal throne.

The king felt a deadly stab in his breast, and his eyes darted lightning over toward that group.

How proud and imposing the figure of the noble earl looked; how high he overtopped all others; how noble and handsome his countenance; how kingly was his bearing and whole appearance!

Henry must admit all this; and because he must do so, he hated him.

Nay! no mercy for Catharine! If what her accusers had told him were true—if they could give him the proofs of the queen's guilt, then she was doomed. And how could he doubt it? Had they not told him that in the rosette, which the queen would give Earl Surrey, was contained a love-letter from Catharine, which he would find? Had not Earl Surrey, in a confidential hour, yesterday imparted this to his sister, the Duchess of Richmond, when he wished to bribe her to be the messenger of love between the queen and himself? Had she not accused the queen of having meetings by night with the earl in the deserted tower?

Nay, no compassion for his fair queen, if Henry Howard was her lover.

He must again look over at his hated enemy. There he still stood by his father, the Duke of Norfolk. How sprightly and gracefully the old duke moved; how slim his form; and how lofty and imposing his bearing! The king was younger than the duke; and yet he was fettered to his truckle-chair; yet he sat on his throne like an immovable colossus, while *he* moved freely and lightly, and obeyed his own will, not necessity. Henry could have crushed him— this proud, arrogant earl, who was a free man, whilst his king was nothing but a prisoner to his own flesh, a slave of his unwieldy body.

"I will exterminate it—this proud, arrogant race of Howards!" muttered the king, as he turned with a friendly smile to the Earl of Surrey.

"You have promised us some of your poems, cousin!" said he. "So let us now enjoy them; for you see, indeed, how impatiently all the beautiful women look on England's noblest and greatest poet, and how very angry with me they would be if I still longer withhold this enjoyment from them! Even my fair queen is full of longing after your songs, so rich in fancy; for you well know, Howard, she loves poetry, and, above all things, yours."

Catharine had scarcely heard what the king said. Her looks had encountered Seymour's, and their eyes were fixed on each other's. But she had then cast down to the floor her eyes, still completely filled with the sight of her lover, in order to think of him, since she no longer dared gaze at him.

When the king called her name, she started up and looked at him inquiringly. She had not heard what he had said to her.

"Not even for a moment does she look toward me!" said Henry Howard to himself. "Oh, she loves me not! or at least her understanding is mightier than her love. Oh, Catharine, Catharine, fearest thou death so much that thou canst on that account deny thy love?"

With desperate haste he drew out his portfolio. "I

will compel her to look at me, to think of me, to remember
her oath," thought he. " Woe to her, if she does not fulfil it—if she gives me not the rosette, which she promised
me with so solemn a vow! If she does it not, then I will
break this dreadful silence, and before her king, and before her court, accuse her of treachery to her love. Then,
at least, she will not be able to cast me off; for we shall
mount the scaffold together."

"Does my exalted queen allow me to begin?" asked
he aloud, wholly forgetting that the king had already
given him the order to do so, and that it was *he* only who
could grant such a permission.

Catharine looked at him in astonishment. Then her
glance fell on Lady Jane Douglas, who was gazing over at
her with an imploring expression. The queen smiled; for
she now remembered that it was Jane's beloved who had
spoken to her, and that she had promised the poor young
girl to raise again the dejected Earl of Surrey and to be
gracious to him.

"Jane is right," thought she; "he appears to be deeply depressed and suffering. Ah, it must be very painful
to see those whom one loves suffering. I will, therefore,
comply with Jane's request, for she says this might revive
the earl."

With a smile she bowed to Howard. "I beg you," said
she, " to lend our festival its fairest ornament—to adorn
it with the fragrant flowers of your poesy. You see we are
all burning with desire to hear your verses."

The king shook with rage, and a crushing word was already poised upon his lip. But he restrained himself. He
wanted to have proofs first; he wanted to see them not
merely accused, but doomed also; and for that he needed
proofs of their guilt.

Henry Howard now approached the throne of the royal
pair, and with beaming looks, with animated countenance,
with a voice trembling with emotion, he read his love-song
to the fair Geraldine.

A murmur of applause arose when he had read his first sonnet. The king only looked gloomily, with fixed eyes; the queen alone remained uninterested and cold.

"She is a complete actress," thought Henry Howard, in the madness of his pain. "Not a muscle of her face stirs; and yet this sonnet must remind her of the fairest and most sacred moment of our love."

The queen remained unmoved and cold. But had Henry Howard looked at Lady Jane Douglas, he would have seen how she turned pale and blushed; how she smiled with rapture, and how, nevertheless, her eyes filled with tears.

Earl Surrey, however, saw nothing but the queen; and the sight of her made him tremble with rage and pain. His eyes darted lightning; his countenance glowed with passion; his whole being was in desperate, enthusiastic excitement. At that moment he would have gladly breathed out his life at Geraldine's feet, if she would only recognize him—if she would only have the courage to call him her beloved.

But her smiling calmness, her friendly coolness, brought him to despair.

He crumpled the paper in his hand; the letters danced before his eyes; he could read no more.

But he would not remain mute, either. Like the dying swan, he would breathe out his pain in a last song, and give sound and words to his despair and his agony. He could no longer read; but he improvised.

Like a glowing stream of lava, the words flowed from his lips; in fiery dithyrambic, in impassioned hymns, he poured forth his love and pain. The genius of poesy hovered over him and lighted up his noble and thoughtful brow.

He was radiantly beautiful in his enthusiasm; and even the queen felt herself carried away by his words.

His plaints of love, his longing pains, his rapture and his sad fancies, found an echo in her heart.

She understood him; for she felt the same joy, the same sorrow and the same rapture; only she did not feel all this for him.

But, as we have said, he enchanted her; the current of his passion carried her away. She wept at his laments; she smiled at his hymns of joy.

When Henry Howard at length ceased, profound silence reigned in the vast and brilliant hall.

All faces betrayed deep emotion; and this universal silence was the poet's fairest triumph; for it showed that envy and jealousy were dumb, and that scorn itself could find no words.

A momentary pause ensued; it resembled that sultry, ominous stillness which is wont to precede the bursting of a tempest; when Nature stops a moment in breathless stillness, to gather strength for the uproar of the storm.

It was a significant, an awful pause; but only a few understood its meaning.

Lady Jane leaned against the wall, completely shattered and breathless. She felt that the sword was hanging over their heads, and that it would destroy *her* if it struck her beloved.

Earl Douglas and the Bishop of Winchester had involuntarily drawn near each other, and stood there hand in hand, united for this unholy struggle; while John Heywood had crept behind the king's throne, and in his sarcastic manner whispered in his ear some epigrams, that made the king smile in spite of himself.

But now the queen arose from her seat, and beckoned Henry Howard nearer to her.

"My lord," said she, almost with solemnity, "as a queen and as a woman I thank you for the noble and sublime lyrics which you have composed in honor of a woman! And for that the grace of my king has exalted me to be the first woman in England, it becomes me, in the name of all women, to return to you my thanks. To the poet is due a reward other than that of the warrior. To the victor on the battle-field is awarded a laurel crown. But you have gained a victory not less glorious, for you have conquered hearts! We acknowledge ourselves vanquished, and in the name of all these noble women, I proclaim you their knight! In token of which, accept this rosette, my lord. It entitles you to wear the queen's colors; it lays you under obligation to be the knight of all women!"

She loosened the rosette from her shoulder, and handed it to the earl.

He had sunk on one knee before her, and already extended his hand to receive this precious and coveted pledge.

But at this moment the king arose, and, with an imperious gesture, held back the queen's hand.

"Allow me, my lady," said he, in a voice quivering with rage—"allow me first to examine this rosette, and convince myself that it is worth enough to be presented to the noble earl as his sole reward. Let me see this rosette."

Catharine looked with astonishment into that face convulsed with passion and fury, but without hesitation she handed him the rosette.

"We are lost!" murmured Earl Surrey, while Earl Douglas and Gardiner exchanged with each other looks of triumph; and Jane Douglas murmured in her trembling heart prayers of anxiety and dread, scarcely hearing the malicious and exultant words which the Duchess of Richmond was whispering in her ear.

The king held the rosette in his hand and examined it. But his hands trembled so much that he was unable to unfasten the clasp which held it together.

He, therefore, handed it to John Heywood. "These diamonds are poor," said he, in a curt, dry tone. "Unfasten the clasp, fool; we will replace it with this pin here. Then will the present gain for the earl a double value; for it will come at the same time from me and from the queen."

"How gracious you are to-day!" said John Heywood, smiling—"as gracious as the cat, that plays a little longer with the mouse before she devours it."

"Unfasten the clasp!" exclaimed the king, in a thundering voice, no longer able to conceal his rage. Slowly John Heywood unfastened the clasp from the ribbon. He did it with intentional slowness and deliberation; he let the king see all his movements, every turn of his fingers; and it delighted him to hold those who had woven this plot in dreadful suspense and expectation.

Whilst he appeared perfectly innocent and unembarrassed, his keen, piercing glance ran over the whole assembly, and he noticed well the trembling impatience of Gardiner and Earl Douglas; and it did not escape him how pale Lady Jane was, and how full of expectation were the intent features of the Duchess of Richmond.

"They are the ones with whom this conspiracy originated," said John Heywood to himself. "But I will keep silence till I can one day convict them."

"There, here is the clasp!" said he then aloud to the king. "It stuck as tightly in the ribbon as malice in the hearts of priests and courtiers!"

The king snatched the ribbon out of his hand, and examined it by drawing it through his fingers.

"Nothing! nothing at all!" said he, gnashing his teeth; and now, deceived in his expectations and suppositions, he could no longer muster strength to withstand that roaring torrent of wrath which overflowed his heart. The tiger was again aroused in him; he had calmly waited for the moment when the promised prey would be brought to him; now, when it seemed to be escaping him, his savage and cruel disposition started up within him. The tiger panted and thirsted for blood; and that he was not to get it, made him raging with fury.

With a wild movement he threw the rosette on the ground, and raised his arm menacingly toward Henry Howard.

"Dare not to touch that rosette," cried he, in a voice of thunder, "before you have exculpated yourself from the guilt of which you are accused."

Earl Surrey looked him steadily and boldly in the eye. "Have I been accused, then?" asked he. "Then I demand, first of all, that I be confronted with my accusers, and that my fault be named!"

"Ha, traitor! Do you dare to brave me?" yelled the king, stamping furiously with his foot. "Well, now, I will be your accuser and I will be your judge!"

"And surely, my king and husband, you will be a righteous judge," said Catharine, as she inclined imploringly toward the king and grasped his hand. "You will not condemn the noble Earl Surrey without having heard him; and if you find him guiltless, you will punish his accusers?"

But this intercession of the queen made the king raging. He threw her hand from him, and gazed at her with looks of such flaming wrath, that she involuntarily trembled.

"Traitoress yourself!" yelled he, wildly. "Speak not of innocence—you who are yourself guilty; and before you dare defend the earl, defend yourself!"

Catharine rose from her seat and looked with flashing eyes into the king's face blazing with wrath. "King Henry of England," said she, solemnly, "you have openly, before your whole court, accused your queen of a crime. I now demand that you name it!"

She was of wondrous beauty in her proud, bold bearing —in her imposing, majestic tranquillity.

The decisive moment had come, and she was conscious that her life and her future were struggling with death for the victory.

She looked over to Thomas Seymour, and their eyes met. She saw how he laid his hand on his sword, and nodded to her a smiling greeting.

"He will defend me; and before he will suffer me to

be dragged to the Tower, he himself will plunge his sword into my breast," thought she, and a joyous, triumphant assurance filled her whole heart.

She saw nothing but him, who had sworn to die with her when the decisive moment came. She looked with a smile on the blade which he had already half drawn from its scabbard; and she hailed it as a dear, long-yearned-for friend.

She saw not that Henry Howard also had lain his hand on his sword; that he, too, was ready for her defence, firmly resolved to slay the king himself, before his mouth uttered the sentence of death over the queen.

But Lady Jane Douglas saw it. She understood how to read the earl's countenance; she felt that he was ready to go to death for his beloved; and it filled her heart at once with woe and rapture.

She, too, was now firmly resolved to follow her heart and her love; and, forgetting all else besides these, she hastened forward, and was now standing by Henry Howard.

"Be prudent, Earl Surrey," said she, in a low whisper. "Take your hand from your sword. The queen, by my mouth, commands you to do so!"

Henry Howard looked at her astonished and surprised; but he let his hand slip from the hilt of his sword, and again looked toward the queen.

She had repeated her demand; she had once more demanded of the king—who, speechless and completely overcome with anger, had fallen back into his seat—to name the crime of which she was accused.

"Now, then, my queen, you demand it, and you shall hear it," cried he. "You want to know the crime of which you are accused? Answer me then, my lady! They accuse you of not always staying at night in your sleeping-room. It is alleged that you sometimes leave it for many hours; and that none of your women accompanied you when you glided through the corridors and up the secret stairs to the lonely tower, in which was waiting for you your lover, who at the same time entered the tower through the small street door."

"He knows all!" muttered Henry Howard; and again he laid his hand on his sword, and was about to approach the queen.

Lady Jane held him back. "Wait for the issue," said she. "There is still time to die!"

"He knows all!" thought the queen also; and now she felt within herself the daring courage to risk all, that at least she might not stand there a traitoress in the eyes of her lover.

"He shall not believe that I have been untrue to him," thought she. "I will tell all—confess all, that *he* may know why I went and whither."

"Now answer, my Lady Catharine!" thundered the king. "Answer, and tell me whether you have been falsely accused. Is it true that you, eight days ago, in the night between Monday and Tuesday, left your sleeping-room at the hour of midnight, and went secretly to the lonely tower? Is it true that you received there a man who is your lover?"

The queen looked at him in angry pride. "Henry, Henry, woe to you, that you dare thus insult your own wife!" cried she.

"Answer me! You were not on that night in your sleeping-room?"

"No," said Catharine, with dignified composure, "I was not there."

The king sank back in his seat, and a real roar of fury sounded from his lips. It made the women turn pale, and even the men felt themselves tremble.

Catharine alone had not heeded it at all; she alone had heard nothing save that cry of amazement which Thomas Seymour uttered; and she saw only the angry and upbraiding looks which he threw across at her.

She answered these looks with a friendly and confident

smile, and pressed both her hands to her heart, as she looked at him.

"I will justify myself before him at least," thought she.

The king had recovered from his first shock. He again raised himself up, and his countenance now exhibited a fearful, threatening coolness.

"You confess, then," asked he, "that you were not in your sleeping-room on that night?"

"I have already said so," exclaimed Catharine, impatiently.

The king compressed his lips so violently, that they bled. "And a man was with you?" asked he—"a man with whom you made an assignation, and whom you received in the lonely tower?"

"A man was with me. But I did not receive him in the lonely tower; and it was no assignation."

"Who was that man?" yelled the king. "Answer me! Tell me his name, if you do not want me to strangle you myself!"

"King Henry, I fear death no longer!" said Catharine, with a contemptuous smile.

"Who was that man? Tell me his name!" yelled the king once more.

The queen raised herself more proudly, and her defiant look ran over the whole assembly.

"The man," said she, solemnly, "who was with me on that night—he is named——"

"He is named John Heywood!" said this individual, as he seriously and proudly walked forward from behind the king's throne. "Yes, Henry, your brother, the fool John Heywood, had on that night the proud honor of accompanying your consort on her holy errand; but, I assure you, that he was less like the king, than the king is just now like the fool."

A murmur of surprise ran through the assembly. The king leaned back in his royal seat speechless.

"And now, King Henry," said Catharine, calmly—"now I will tell you whither I went with John Heywood on that night."

She was silent, and for a moment leaned back on her seat. She felt that the looks of all were directed to her; she heard the king's wrathful groan; she felt her lover's flashing, reproachful glances; she saw the derisive smile of those haughty ladies, who had never forgiven her—that she, from a simple baroness, had become queen. But all this made her only still bolder and more courageous.

She had arrived at the turning-point of her life, where she must risk everything to avoid sinking into the abyss.

But Lady Jane also had arrived at such a decisive moment of her existence. She, too, said to herself: "I must at this hour risk all, if I do not want to lose all." She saw Henry Howard's pale, expectant face. She knew, if the queen now spoke, the whole web of their conspiracy would be revealed to him.

She must, therefore, anticipate the queen. She must warn Henry Howard.

"Fear nothing!" whispered she to him. "We were prepared for that. I have put into her hands the means of escape!"

"Will you now at last speak?" exclaimed the king, quivering with impatience and rage. "Will you at last tell us where you were on that night?"

"I will tell!" exclaimed Catharine, rising up again boldly and resolutely. "But woe be to those who drive me to this! For I tell you beforehand, from the accused I will become an accuser who demands justice, if not before the throne of the King of England, yet before the throne of the Lord of all kings! King Henry of England, do you ask me whither I went on that night with John Heywood? I might, perhaps, as your queen and consort, demand that you put this question to me not before so many witnesses, but in the quiet of our chamber; but you seek publicity, and I do not shun it. Well, hear the truth, then, all of you! On that night, between Monday and Tuesday, I was not in my sleeping-apartment, because I had a grave and sacred duty to perform; because a dying woman called on me for help and pity! Would you know, my lord and husband, who this dying woman was? It was Anne Askew!"

"Anne Askew!" exclaimed the king in astonishment; and his countenance exhibited a less wrathful expression.

"Anne Askew!" muttered the others; and John Heywood very well saw how Bishop Gardiner's brow darkened, and how Chancellor Wriothesley turned pale and cast down his eyes.

"Yes, I was with Anne Askew!" continued the queen—"with Anne Askew, whom those pious and wise lords yonder had condemned, not so much on account of her faith, but because they knew that I loved her. Anne Askew was to die, because Catharine Parr loved her! She was to go to the stake, that my heart also might burn with fiery pains! And because it was so, I was obliged to risk everything in order to save her. Oh, my king, say yourself, did I not owe it to this poor girl to try everything in order to save her? On my account she was to suffer these tortures. For they had shamefully stolen from me a letter which Anne Askew, in the distress of her heart, had addressed to me; and they showed this letter to you in order to cast suspicion on me and accuse me to you. But your noble heart repelled the suspicion; and now their wrath fell again on Anne Askew, and she must suffer, because they did not find me punishable. She must atone for having dared to write to me. They worked matters with you so that she was put to the rack. But when my husband gave way to their urging, yet the noble king remained still awake in him. 'Go,' said he, 'rack her and kill her; but see first whether she will not recant.'"

Henry looked astonished into her noble and defiant face. "Do you know that?" asked he. "And yet we were alone, and no human being present. Who could tell you that?"

"When man is no longer able to help, then God undertakes!" said Catharine solemnly. "It was God who commanded me to go to Anne Askew, and try whether I could save her. And I went. But though the wife of a noble and great king, I am still but a weak and timid woman. I was afraid to tread this gloomy and dangerous path alone; I needed a strong manly arm to lean upon; and so John Heywood lent me his."

"And you were really with Anne Askew," interposed the king, thoughtfully—"with that hardened sinner, who despised mercy, and in the stubbornness of her soul would not be a partaker of the pardon that I offered her?"

"My lord and husband," said the queen, with tears in her eyes, "she whom you have just accused stands even now before the throne of the Lord, and has received from her God the forgiveness of her sins! Therefore, do you likewise pardon her; and may the flames of the stake, to which yesterday the noble virgin body of this girl was bound, have consumed also the wrath and hatred which had been kindled in your heart against her! Anne Askew passed away like a saint; for she forgave all her enemies and blessed her tormentors."

"Anne Askew was a damnable sinner, who dared resist the command of her lord and king!" interrupted Bishop Gardiner, looking daggers at her.

"And dare you maintain, my lord, that you at that time fulfilled the commands of your royal master simply and exactly?" asked Catharine. "Did you keep within them with respect to Anne Askew? No! I say; for the king had not ordered you to torture her; he had not bidden you to lacerate in blasphemous wrath a noble human form, and distort that likeness of God into a horrible caricature. And that, my lord, you did! Before God and your king, I accuse you of it—I, the queen! For you know, my lord and husband, I was there when Anne

Askew was racked. I saw her agony; and John Heywood saw it with me."

The eyes of all were now directed inquiringly to the king, of whose ferocity and choler every one expected a violent outbreak.

But this time they were mistaken. The king was so well satisfied to find his consort clear of the crime laid to her charge, that he willingly forgave her for having committed a crime of less weighty character. Besides, it filled him with respect to see his consort confronting her accusers so boldly and proudly; and he felt toward them just as burning wrath and hatred as he had before harbored against the queen. He was pleased that the malignant and persistent persecutors of his fair and proud wife should now be humbled by her before the eyes of all his court.

Therefore he looked at her with an imperceptible smile, and said with deep interest: "But how could this happen, my lady? By what path did you get thither?"

"That is an inquiry which any one except the king is authorized to make. King Henry alone knows the way that I went!" said Catharine, with a slight smile.

John Heywood, who was still standing behind the king's throne, now bent down close to Henry's ear, and spoke with him a long time in a quick, low tone.

The king listened to him attentively; then he murmured so loud that the bystanders could very well understand him: "By God, she is a spirited and brave woman; and we should be obliged to confess that, even were she not our queen!"

"Continue, my lady!" said he then aloud, turning to the queen with a gracious look. "Relate to me, Catharine, what saw you then in the torture-chamber?"

"Oh, my king and lord, it horrifies me only to think of it," cried she, shuddering and turning pale. "I saw a poor young woman who writhed in fearful agony, and whose staring eyes were raised in mute supplication to

Heaven. She did not beg her tormentors for mercy; she wanted from them no compassion and no pity; she did not scream and whine from the pain, though her limbs cracked and her flesh snapped apart like glass; she raised her clasped hands to God, and her lips murmured low prayers, which, perhaps, made the angels of heaven weep, but were not able to touch the hearts of her tormentors. You had ordered her to be racked, if she would not retract. They did not ask her whether she would do this—they racked her. But her soul was strong and full of courage; and, under the tortures of the executioner, her lips remained mute. Let theologians say and determine whether Anne Askew's faith was a false one; but this they will not dare deny: that in the noble enthusiasm of this faith, she was a heroine who at least did not deny her God. At length, worn out with so much useless exertion, the assistant executioners discontinued their bloody work, to rest from the tortures which they had prepared for Anne Askew. The lieutenant of the Tower declared the work of the rack ended. The highest degrees had been applied, and they had proved powerless; cruelty was obliged to acknowledge itself conquered. But the priests of the Church, with savage vehemence, demanded that she should be racked once more. Dare deny that, ye lords, whom I behold standing there opposite with faces pale as death! Yes, my king, the servants of the rack refused to obey the servants of God; for in the hearts of the hangman's drudges there was more pity than in the hearts of the priests! And when they refused to proceed in their bloody work, and when the lieutenant of the Tower, in virtue of the existing law, declared the racking at an end, then I saw one of the first ministers of our Church throw aside his sacred garments; then the priest of God transformed himself into a hangman's drudge, who, with bloodthirsty delight, lacerated anew the noble mangled body of the young girl, and more cruel than the attendants of the rack, unsparingly they broke and dislocated the limbs, which *they* had only squeezed in their screws.* Excuse me, my king, from sketching this scene of horror still further! Horrified and trembling, I fled from that frightful place, and returned to my room, shattered and sad at heart."

Catharine ceased, exhausted, and sank back into her seat.

A breathless stillness reigned around. All faces were pale and colorless. Gardiner and Wriothesley stood with their eyes fixed, gloomy and defiant, expecting that the king's wrath would crush and destroy them.

But the king scarcely thought of them; he thought only of his fair young queen, whose boldness inspired him with respect, and whose innocence and purity filled him with a proud and blissful joy.

He was, therefore, very much inclined to forgive those who in reality had committed no offence further than this, that they had carried out a little too literally and strictly the orders of their master.

A long pause had ensued—a pause full of expectation and anxiety for all who were assembled in the hall. Only Catharine reclined calmly in her chair, and with beaming eyes looked across to Thomas Seymour, whose handsome countenance betrayed to her the gratification and satisfaction which he felt at this clearing up of her mysterious night-wandering.

At last the king arose, and, bowing low before his consort, said in a loud, full-toned voice: "I have deeply and bitterly injured you, my noble wife; and as I publicly accused you, I will also publicly ask your forgiveness! You have a right to be angry with me; for it behooved me, above all, to believe with unshaken firmness in the truth and honor of my wife. My lady, you have made a brilliant vindication of yourself; and I, the king, first of all bow before you, and beg that you may forgive me and impose some penance."

"Leave it to me, queen, to impose a penance on this

* Burnet's "History of the Reformation," vol. i, p. 132.

repentant sinner!" cried John Heywood, gayly. "Your majesty is much too magnanimous, much too timid, to treat him as roughly as my brother King Henry deserves. Leave it to me, then, to punish him; for only the fool is wise enough to punish the king after his deserts."

Catharine nodded to him with a grateful smile. She comprehended perfectly John Heywood's delicacy and nice tact; she apprehended that he wanted by a joke to relieve her from her painful situation, and put an end to the king's public acknowledgment, which at the same time must turn to her bitter reproach—bitter, though it were only self-reproach.

"Well," said she, smiling, "what punishment, then, will you impose upon the king?"

"The punishment of recognizing the fool as his equal!"

"God is my witness that I do so!" cried the king, almost solemnly. "Fools we are, one and all, and we fall short of the renown which we have before men."

"But my sentence is not yet complete, brother!" continued John Heywood. "I furthermore give sentence, that you also forthwith allow me to recite my poem to you, and that you open your ears in order to hear what John Heywood, the wise, has indited!"

"You have, then, fulfilled my command, and composed a new interlude?" cried the king, vivaciously.

"No interlude, but a wholly novel, comical affair—a play full of lampoons and jokes, at which your eyes are to overflow, yet not with weeping, but with laughter. To the right noble Earl of Surrey belongs the proud honor of having presented to our happy England her first sonnets. Well, now, I also will give her something new. I present her the first comedy; and as he sings the beauty of his Geraldine, so I celebrate the fame of Gammer Gurton's sewing-needle—Gammer Gurton's needle—so my piece is called; and you, King Henry, shall listen to it as a punishment for your sins!"

"I will do so," cried the king, cheerfully, "provided you permit it, Kate! But before I do so, I make also one more condition—a condition for you, queen! Kate, you have disdained to impose a penance on me, but grant me at least the pleasure of being allowed to fulfil some wish of yours! Make me a request, that I may grant it you!"

"Well, then, my lord and king," said Catharine with a charming smile, "I beg you to think no more of the incidents of this day, and to forgive those whom I accused, only because their accusation was my vindication. They who brought charges against me have in this hour felt contrition for their own fault. Let that suffice, king, and forgive them, as I do!"

"You are a noble and great woman, Kate!" cried the king; and, as his glance swept over toward Gardiner with an almost contemptuous expression, he continued: "Your request is granted. But woe to them who shall dare accuse you again! And have you nothing further to demand, Kate?"

"Nay, one thing more, my lord and husband!" She leaned nearer to the king's ear, and whispered: "They have also accused your noblest and most faithful servant; they have accused Cranmer. Condemn him not, king, without having heard him; and if I may beg a favor of you, it is this: talk with Cranmer yourself. Tell him of what they have charged him, and hear his vindication."

"It shall be so, Kate," said the king, "and you shall be present! But let this be a secret between us, Kate, and we will carry it out in perfect silence. And now, then, John Heywood, let us hear your composition; and woe to you, if it does not accomplish what you promised—if it does not make us laugh! For you well know that you are then inevitably exposed to the rods of our injured ladies."

"They shall have leave to whip me to death, if I do not make you laugh!" cried John Heywood, gayly, as he drew out his manuscript.

Soon the hall rang again with loud laughter; and in

the universal merriment no one observed that Bishop Gardiner and Earl Douglas slipped quietly away.

In the anteroom without, they stopped and looked at each other long and silently; their countenances expressed the wrath and bitterness which filled them; and they understood this mute language of their features.

"She must die!" said Gardiner in a short and quick tone. "She has for once escaped from our snares; we will tie them all the tighter next time!"

"And I already hold in my hand the threads out of which we will form these snares," said Earl Douglas. "We have to-day falsely accused her of a love-affair. When we do it again, we shall speak the truth. Did you see the looks that Catharine exchanged with the heretical Earl Sudley, Thomas Seymour?"

"I saw them, earl!"

"For these looks she will die, my lord. The queen loves Thomas Seymour, and this love will be her death."

"Amen!" said Bishop Gardiner, solemnly, as he raised his eyes devoutly to heaven. "Amen! The queen has grievously and bitterly injured us to-day; she has insulted and abused us before all the court. We will requite her for it some day! The torture-chamber, which she has depicted in such lively colors, may yet one day open for her, too—not that she may behold another's agonies, but that she may suffer agonies herself. We shall one day avenge ourselves!"

CHAPTER XXVI.

REVENGE.

MISS HOLLAND, the beautiful and much-admired mistress of the Duke of Norfolk, was alone in her magnificently adorned boudoir. It was the hour when ordinarily the duke was wont to be with her; for this reason she was charmingly attired, and had wrapped herself in that light and voluptuous *negligée* which the duke so much liked, because it set off to so much advantage the splendid form of his friend.

But to-day the expected one did not make his appearance: in his stead his valet had just come and brought the fair miss a note from his master. This note she was holding in her hand, while with passionate violence she now walked up and down her boudoir. A glowing crimson blazed upon her cheeks, and her large, haughty eyes darted wild flashes of wrath.

She was disdained—she, Lady Holland, was forced to endure the disgrace of being dismissed by her lover.

There, there, in that letter which she held in her hand, and which burned her fingers like red-hot iron—there it stood in black and white, that he would see her no more; that he renounced her love; that he released her.

Her whole frame shook as she thought of this. It was not the anguish of a loving heart which made her tremble; it was the wounded pride of the woman.

He had abandoned her. Her beauty, her youth no longer had the power to enchain him—the man with white hairs and withered features.

He had written her that he was satiated and weary, not of her, but only of love in general; that his heart had become old and withered like his face; and that there was still in his breast no more room for love, but only for ambition.

Was not that a revolting, an unheard-of outrage—to abandon the finest woman in England for the sake of empty, cold, stern ambition?

She opened the letter once more. Once more she read that place. Then grinding her teeth with tears of anger in her eyes: "He shall pay me for this! I will take vengeance for this insult!"

She thrust the letter into her bosom, and touched the silver bell.

"Have my carriage brought round!" was her order to the servant who entered; and he withdrew in silence.

"I will avenge myself!" muttered she, as with trembling hands she wrapped herself in her large Turkish shawl. "I will avenge myself; and, by the Eternal! it shall be a bloody and swift vengeance! I will show him that I, too, am ambitious, and that my pride is not to be humbled. He says he will forget me. Oh, I will compel him to think of me, even though it be only to curse me!"

With hasty step she sped through the glittering apartments, which the liberality of her lover had furnished so magnificently, and descended to the carriage standing ready for her.

"To the Duchess of Norfolk's!" said she to the footman standing at the door of the carriage, as she entered it.

The servant looked at her in astonishment and inquiringly.

"To the *Duke* of Norfolk; is it not, my lady?"

"No, indeed, to the duchess!" cried she with a frown, as she leaned back on the cushion.

After a short time, the carriage drew up before the palace of the duchess, and with haughty tread and commanding air she passed through the porch.

"Announce me to the duchess immediately," was her order to the lackey who was hurrying to meet her.

"Your name, my lady?"

"Miss Arabella Holland."

The servant stepped back, and stared at her in surprise. "Miss Arabella Holland! and you order me to announce you to the duchess?"

A contemptuous smile played a moment about the thin lips of the beautiful miss. "I see you know me," said she, "and you wonder a little to see me here. Wonder as much as you please, good friend; only conduct me immediately to the duchess."

"I doubt whether her ladyship receives calls to-day," stammered the servant, hesitatingly.

"Then go and ask; and, that I may learn her answer as soon as possible, I will accompany you."

With a commanding air, she motioned to the servant to go before her; and he could not summon up courage to gainsay this proud beauty.

In silence they traversed the suite of stately apartments, and at length stood before a door hung with tapestry.

"I must beg you to wait here a moment, my lady, so that I can announce you to the duchess, who is there in her boudoir."

"No, indeed; I will assume that office myself," said Miss Holland, as with strong hand she pushed back the servant and opened the door.

The duchess was sitting at her writing-table, her back turned to the door through which Arabella had entered. She did not turn round; perhaps she had not heard the door open. She continued quietly writing.

Miss Arabella Holland with stately step crossed the room, and now stood close to the chair of the duchess.

"Duchess, I would like to speak with you," said she, coolly and calmly.

The duchess uttered a cry and looked up. "Miss Holland!" cried she amazed, and hastily rising. "Miss Holland! you here with me, in my house! What do you want here? How dare you cross my threshold?"

"I see you still hate me, my lady," said Arabella, smiling. "You have not yet forgiven me that the duke, your husband, found more delight in my young, handsome face, than in yours, now growing old—that my sprightly, wanton disposition pleased him better than your cold, stately air."

The duchess turned pale with rage, and her eyes darted lightning. "Silence, you shameless creature! silence, or I will call my servants to rid me of you!"

"You will not call them; for I have come to be reconciled with you, and to offer you peace."

"Peace with you!" sneered the duchess—"peace with that shameless woman who stole from me my husband, the father of my children?—who loaded me with the disgrace of standing before the whole world as a repudiated and despised wife, and of suffering myself to be compared with you, that the world might decide which of us two was worthier of his love? Peace with you, Miss Holland?—with the impudent strumpet who squanders my husband's means in lavish luxury, and, with scoffing boldness, robs my children of their lawful property?"

"It is true, the duke is very generous," said Miss Holland, composedly. "He loaded me with diamonds and gold."

"And meanwhile I was doomed almost to suffer want," said the duchess, grinding her teeth.

"Want of love, it may be, my lady, but not want of money; for you are very magnificently fitted up; and every one knows that the Duchess of Norfolk is rich enough to be able to spare the trifles that her husband laid at my feet. By Heaven! my lady, I would not have deemed it worth the trouble to stoop for them, if I had not seen among these trifles his heart. The heart of a man is well worth a woman's stooping for! You have neglected that, my lady, and therefore you lost your husband's heart. I picked it up. That is all. Why will you make a crime of that?"

"That is enough!" cried the duchess. "It does not become me to dispute with you; I desire only to know what gave you the courage to come to me?"

"My lady, do you hate me only? Or do you also hate the duke your husband?"

"She asks me whether I hate him!" cried the duchess, with a wild, scornful laugh. "Yes, Miss Holland, yes! I hate him as ardently as I despise you. I hate him so much that I would give my whole estate—ay, years of my life—if I could punish him for the disgrace he has put upon me."

"Then, my lady, we shall soon understand each other; for I too hate him," said Miss Holland, quietly seating herself on the velvet divan, and smiling as she observed the speechless astonishment of the duchess.

"Yes, my lady, I hate him; and without doubt still more ardently, still more intensely than you yourself; for I am young and fiery; you are old, and have always managed to preserve a cool heart."

The duchess was convulsed with rage; but silently, and with an effort, she gulped down the drop of wormwood which her wicked rival mingled in the cup of joy which she presented to her.

"You do hate him, Miss Holland?" asked she, joyfully.

"I hate him, and I have come to league myself with you against him. He is a traitor, a perfidious wretch, a perjurer. I will take vengeance for my disgrace!"

"Ah, has he then deserted you also?"

"He has deserted me also."

"Well, then, God be praised!" cried the duchess, and her face beamed with joy. "God is great and just; and He has punished you with the same weapons with which you sinned! For your sake, he deserted me; and for the sake of another woman, he forsakes you."

"Not so, my lady!" said Miss Holland, proudly. "A woman like me is not forsaken on account of a woman; and he who loves me will love no other after me. There, read his letter!"

She handed the duchess her husband's letter.

"And what do you want to do now?" asked the duchess, after she had read it.

"I will have revenge, my lady! He says he no longer has a heart to love; well, now, we will so manage, that he may no longer have a head to think. Will you be my ally, my lady?"

"I will."

"And I also will be," said the Duchess of Richmond, who just then opened the door and came out of the adjoining room.

Not a word of this entire conversation had escaped her, and she very well understood that the question was not about some petty vengeance, but her father's head. She knew that Miss Holland was not a woman that, when irritated, pricked with a pin; but one that grasped the dagger to strike her enemy a mortal blow.

"Yes, I too will be your ally," cried the Duchess of Richmond; "we have all three been outraged by the same man. Let, then, our revenge be a common one. The father has insulted you; the son, me. Well, then, I will help you to strike the father, if you in return will assist me to destroy the son."

"I will assist you," said Arabella, smiling; "for I also hate the haughty Earl of Surrey, who prides himself on his virtue, as if it were a golden fleece which God himself had stuck on his breast. I hate him; for he never meets me but with proud disregard; and he alone is to blame for his father's faithlessness."

"I was present when with tears he besought the duke, our father, to free himself from your fetters, and give up this shameful and disgraceful connection with you," said the young duchess.

Arabella answered nothing. But she pressed her hands firmly together, and a slight pallor overspread her cheeks.

"And why are you angry with your brother?" asked the old duchess, thoughtfully.

"Why am I angry with him, do you ask, my mother? I am not angry with him; but I execrate him, and I have sworn to myself never to rest till I have avenged myself. My happiness, my heart, and my future, lay in his hands; and he has remorselessly trodden under his haughty feet these—his sister's precious treasures. It lay with him to make me the wife of the man I love; and he has not done it, though I lay at his feet weeping and wringing my hands."

"But it was a great sacrifice that you demanded," said her mother. "He had to give his hand to a woman he did not love, so that you might be Thomas Seymour's wife."

"Mother, you defend him; and yet he it is that blames you daily; and but yesterday it seemed to him perfectly right and natural that the duke had forsaken you, our mother."

"Did he do that?" inquired the duchess, vehemently. "Well, now, as he has forgotten that I am his mother, so will I forget that he is my son. I am your ally! Revenge for our injured hearts! Vengeance on father and son!"

She held out both hands, and the two young women laid their hands in hers.

"Vengeance on father and son!" repeated they both; and their eyes flashed, and crimson now mantled their cheeks.

"I am tired of living like a hermit in my palace, and of being banished from court by the fear that I may encounter my husband there."

"You shall encounter him there no more," said her daughter, laconically.

"They shall not laugh and jeer at me," cried Arabella. "And when they learn that he has forsaken me, they shall also know how I have avenged myself for it."

"Thomas Seymour can never become my husband so long as Henry Howard lives; for he has mortally offended him, as Henry has rejected the hand of his sister. Perhaps I may become his wife, if Henry Howard is no more," said the young duchess. "So let us consider. How shall we begin, so as to strike them surely and certainly?"

"When three women are agreed, they may well be certain of their success," said Arabella, shrugging her shoulders. "We live—God be praised for it—under a noble and high-minded king, who beholds the blood of his subjects with as much pleasure as he does the crimson of his royal mantle, and who has never yet shrunk back when a death-warrant was to be signed."

"But this time he will shrink back," said the old duchess. "He will not dare to rob the noblest and most powerful family of his kingdom of its head."

"That very risk will stimulate him," said the Duchess of Richmond, laughing; "and the more difficult it is to bring down these heads, so much the more impatiently will he hanker after it. The king hates them both, and he will thank us, if we change his hatred into retributive justice."

"Then let us accuse both of high treason!" cried Arabella. "The duke is a traitor; for I will and can swear that he has often enough called the king a bloodthirsty tiger, a relentless tyrant, a man without truth and without faith, although he coquettishly pretends to be the fountain and rock of all faith."

"If he has said that, and you have heard him, you are in duty bound to communicate it to the king, if you do not want to be a traitoress yourself," exclaimed the young duchess, solemnly.

"And have you not noticed that the duke has for some time borne the same coat-of-arms as the king?" asked the Duchess of Norfolk. "It is not enough for his haughty and ambitious spirit to be the first servant of this land; he strives to be lord and king of it."

"Tell that to the king, and by to-morrow the head of the traitor falls. For the king is as jealous of his kingdom as ever a woman was of her lover. Tell him that the duke bears his coat-of-arms, and his destruction is certain."

"I will tell him so, daughter."

"We are sure of the father, but what have we for the son?"

"A sure and infallible means, that will as certainly dispatch him into eternity as the hunter's tiny bullet slays the proudest stag. Henry loves the queen; and I will furnish the king proof of that," said the young duchess.

"Then let us go to the king!" cried Arabella, impetuously.

"No, indeed! That would make a sensation, and might easily frustrate our whole plan," said the Duchess of Richmond. "Let us first talk with Earl Douglas, and hear his advice. Come; every minute is precious! We owe it to our womanly honor to avenge ourselves. We cannot and will not leave unpunished those who have despised our love, wounded our honor, and trodden under foot the holiest ties of nature!"

CHAPTER XXVII.

THE ACKNOWLEDGMENT.

THE Princess Elizabeth was sitting in her room, melancholy and absorbed in thought. Her eyes were red with weeping; and she pressed her hand on her heart, as if she would repress its cry of anguish.

With a disconsolate, perplexed look she gazed around her chamber, and its solitude was doubly painful to her to-day, for it testified to her forsaken condition, to the disgrace that still rested on her. For were it not so, to-day would have been to the whole court a day of rejoicing, of congratulations.

To-day was Elizabeth's birthday; fourteen years ago to-day, Anne Boleyn's daughter had seen the light of this world.

"Anne Boleyn's daughter!" That was the secret of her seclusion. That was why none of the ladies and lords of the court had remembered her birthday; for that would have been at the same time a remembrance of Anne

Boleyn, of Elizabeth's beautiful and unfortunate mother, who had been made to atone for her grandeur and prosperity by her death.

Moreover, the king had called his daughter Elizabeth a bastard, and solemnly declared her unworthy of succeeding to the throne.

Her birthday, therefore, was to Elizabeth only a day of humiliation and pain. Reclining on her divan, she thought of her despised and joyless past, of her desolate and inglorious future.

She was a princess, and yet possessed not the rights of her birth; she was a young maiden, and yet doomed, in sad resignation, to renounce all the delights and enjoyments of youth, and to condemn her passionate and ardent heart to the eternal sleep of death. For when the Infante of Spain sued for her hand, Henry the Eighth had declared that the bastard Elizabeth was unworthy of a princely husband. But in order to intimidate other suitors also, he had loudly and openly declared that no subject should dare be so presumptuous as to offer his hand to one of his royal daughters, and he who dared to solicit them in marriage should be punished as a traitor.

So Elizabeth was condemned to remain unmarried; and nevertheless she loved; nevertheless she harbored only this one wish, to be the wife of her beloved, and to be able to exchange the proud title of princess for the name of Countess Seymour.

Since she loved him, a new world, a new sun had arisen on her; and before the sweet and enchanting whispers of her love, even the proud and alluring voices of her ambition had to be silent. She no longer thought of it, that she would never be a queen; she was only troubled that she could not be Seymour's wife.

She no longer wanted to rule, but she wanted to be happy. But her happiness reposed on him alone—on Thomas Seymour.

Such were her thoughts, as she was in her chamber

on the morning of her birthday, alone and lonely; and her eyes reddened by tears, her painfully convulsed lips, betrayed how much she had wept to-day; how much this young girl of fourteen years had already suffered.

But she would think no more about it; she would not allow the lurking, everywhere-prying, malicious, and wicked courtiers the triumph of seeing the traces of her tears, and rejoicing at her pains and her humiliation. She was a proud and resolute soul; she would rather have died than to have accepted the sympathy and pity of the courtiers.

"I will work," said she. "Work is the best balm for all pains."

And she took up the elaborate silk embroidery which she had begun for her poor, unfortunate friend, Anne of Cleves, Henry's divorced wife. But the work occupied only her fingers, not her thoughts.

She threw it aside and seized her books. She took Petrarch's Sonnets; and his love plaints and griefs enchained and stirred her own love-sick heart.

With streaming tears, and yet smiling and full of sweet melancholy, Elizabeth read these noble and tender poems. It appeared to her as if Petrarch had only said what she herself so warmly felt. There were her thoughts, her griefs. He had said them in his language; she must now repeat them in her own. She seated herself, and with hands trembling with enthusiasm, fluttering breath, perfectly excited and glowing, in glad haste she began a translation of Petrarch's first sonnet.*

* Elizabeth, who even as a girl of twelve years old spoke four languages, was very fond of composing verses, and of translating the poems of foreign authors. But she kept her skill in this respect very secret, and was always very angry if any one by chance saw one of her poems. After her death there were found among her papers many translations, especially of Petrarch's Sonnets, which were the work of her earliest youth.—Leti, vol. i, p. 150.

A loud knock interrupted her; and in the hastily opened door now appeared the lovely form of the queen.

"The queen!" exclaimed Elizabeth with delight. "Have you come to me at such an early morning hour?"

"And should I wait till evening to wish my Elizabeth happiness on her festival? Should I first let the sun go down on this day, which gave to England so noble and so fair a princess?" asked Catharine. "Or you thought, perhaps, I did not know that this was your birthday, and that to-day my Elizabeth advances from the years of childhood, as a proud maiden full of hope?"

"Full of hope?" said Elizabeth, sadly. "Anne Boleyn's daughter has no hopes; and when you speak of my birthday, you remind me at the same time of my despised birth!"

"It shall be despised no longer!" said Catharine, and, as she put her arm tenderly around Elizabeth's neck, she handed her a roll of parchment.

"Take that, Elizabeth; and may this paper be to you the promise of a joyful and brilliant future! At my request, the king has made this law, and he therefore granted me the pleasure of bringing it to you."

Elizabeth opened the parchment and read, and a radiant expression overspread her countenance.

"Acknowledged! I am acknowledged!" cried she. "The disgrace of my birth is taken away! Elizabeth is no more a bastard—she is a royal princess!"

"And she may some day be a queen!" said Catharine, smiling.

"Oh," cried Elizabeth, "it is not that which stirs me with such joy. But the disgrace of my birth is taken away; and I may freely hold up my head and name my mother's name! Now thou mayst sleep calmly in thy grave, for it is no longer dishonored! Anne Boleyn was no strumpet; she was King Henry's lawful wife, and Elizabeth is the king's legitimate daughter! I thank Thee, my God—I thank Thee!"

And the young, passionate girl threw herself on her knees, and raised her hands and her eyes to heaven.

"Spirit of my glorified mother," said she, solemnly, "I call thee! Come to me! Overshadow me with thy smile, and bless me with thy breath! Queen Anne of England, thy daughter is no longer a bastard, and no one dares venture more to insult her. Thou wert with me when I wept and suffered, my mother; and often in my disgrace and humiliation, it was as if I heard thy voice, which whispered comfort to me; as if I saw thy heavenly eyes, which poured peace and love into my breast! Oh, abide with me now also, my mother—now, when my disgrace is taken away, abide with me in my prosperity; and guard my heart, that it may be kept pure from arrogance and pride, and remain humble in its joy! Anne Boleyn, they laid thy beautiful, innocent head upon the block; but this parchment sets upon it again the royal crown; and woe, woe to those who will now still dare insult thy memory!"

She sprang from her knees and rushed to the wall opposite, on which was a large oil painting, which represented Elizabeth herself as a child playing with a dog.

"Oh, mother, mother!" said she, "this picture was the last earthly thing on which thy looks rested; and to these painted lips of thy child thou gavest thy last kiss, which thy cruel hangman would not allow to thy living child. Oh, let me sip up this last kiss from that spot; let me touch with my mouth the spot that thy lips have consecrated!"

She bent down and kissed the picture.

"And now come forth out of thy grave, my mother," said she, solemnly. "I have been obliged so long to hide, so long to veil thee! Now thou belongest to the world and to the light! The king has acknowledged me as his lawful daughter; he cannot refuse me to have a likeness of my mother in my room."

As she thus spoke, she pressed on a spring set in the broad gilt frame of the picture; and suddenly the painting was seen to move and slowly open like a door, so as to render visible another picture concealed beneath it, which represented the unfortunate Anne Boleyn in bridal attire, in the full splendor of her beauty, as Holbein had painted her, at the desire of her husband the king.

"How beautiful and angelic that countenance is!" said Catharine, stepping nearer. "How innocent and pure those features! Poor queen! Yet thine enemies succeeded in casting suspicion on thee and bringing thee to the scaffold. Oh, when I behold thee, I shudder; and my own future rises up before me like a threatening spectre! Who can believe herself safe and secure, when Anne Boleyn was not secure; when even she had to die a dishonorable death? Ah, do but believe me, Elizabeth, it is a melancholy lot to be Queen of England; and often indeed have I asked the morning whether I, as still Queen of England, shall greet the evening. But no—we will not talk of myself in this hour, but only of you, Elizabeth—of your future and of your fortune. May this document be acceptable to you, and realize all the wishes that slumber in your bosom!"

"One great wish of mine it has fulfilled already," said Elizabeth, still occupied with the picture. "It allows me to show my mother's likeness unveiled! That I could one day do so was her last prayer and last wish, which she intrusted to John Heywood for me. To him she committed this picture. He alone knew the secret of it, and he has faithfully preserved it."

"Oh, John Heywood is a trusty and true friend," said Catharine, heartily; "and it was he who assisted me in inclining the king to our plan and in persuading him to acknowledge you."

With an unutterable expression Elizabeth presented both hands to her. "I thank you for my honor, and the honor of my mother," said she: "I will love you for it as a daughter; and never shall your enemies find with me an open ear and a willing heart. Let us two conclude with each other a league offensive and defensive! Let us keep true to each other; and the enemies of the one shall be the enemies of the other also. And where we see danger we will combat it in common; and we will watch over each other with a true sisterly eye, and warn one another whenever a chance flash brings to light an enemy who is stealing along in the darkness, and wants with his dagger to assassinate us from behind."

"So be it!" said Catharine, solemnly. "We will remain inseparable, and true to one another, and love each other as sisters!"

And as she imprinted a warm kiss on Elizabeth's lips, she continued: "But now, princess, direct your looks once more to that document, of which at first you read only the beginning. Do but believe me, it is important enough for you to read it quite to the end; for it contains various arrangements for your future, and settles on you a suite and a yearly allowance, as is suitable for a royal princess."

"Oh, what care I for these things?" cried Elizabeth, merrily. "That is my major-domo's concern, and he may attend to it."

"But there is yet another paragraph that will interest you more," said Catharine, with a slight smile; "for it is a full and complete reparation to my proud and ambitious Elizabeth. You recollect the answer which your father gave to the King of France when he solicited your hand for the dauphin?"

"Do I recollect it!" cried Elizabeth, her features quickly becoming gloomy. "King Henry said: 'Anne Boleyn's daughter is not worthy to accept the hand of a royal prince.'"

"Well, then, Elizabeth, that the reparation made to you may be complete, the king, while he grants you your lawful title and honor, has decreed that you are permitted to marry only a husband of equal birth; to give your hand only to a royal prince, if you would preserve your right of succeeding to the throne. Oh, certainly, there could

be no more complete recantation of the affront once put
upon you. And that he consented to do this, you owe to
the eloquent intercession of a true and trusty friend; you
have John Heywood to thank for it."

"John Heywood!" cried Elizabeth, in a bitter tone.
"Oh, I thank you, queen, that it was not you who determined my father to this decision. John Heywood did it,
and you call him my friend? You say that he is a true
and devoted servant to us both? Beware of his fidelity,
queen, and build not on his devotedness; for I tell you his
soul is full of falsehood; and while he appears to bow before you in humbleness, his eyes are only searching for the
place on your heel where he can strike you most surely
and most mortally. Oh, he is a serpent, a venomous serpent; and he has just wounded me mortally and incurably.
But no," continued she, energetically, "I will not submit
to this fraud; I will not be the slave of this injurious law!
I will be free to love and to hate as my heart demands; I
will not be shackled, nor be compelled to renounce this
man, whom I perhaps love, and to marry that one, whom I
perhaps abhor."

With an expression of firm, energetic resolve, she took
the roll of parchment and handed it back to Catharine.

"Queen, take this parchment back again; return it to
my father, and tell him that I thank him for his provident
goodness, but will decline the brilliant lot which this act
offers me. I love freedom so much, that even a royal
crown cannot allure me when I am to receive it with my
hands bound and my heart not free."

"Poor child!" sighed Catharine, "you know not,
then, that the royal crown always binds us in fetters and
compresses our heart in iron clamps? Ah, you want to
be free, and yet a queen! Oh, believe me, Elizabeth, none
are less free than sovereigns! No one has less the right
and the power to live according to the dictates of his heart
than a prince."

"Then," exclaimed Elizabeth, with flashing eyes,

"then I renounce the melancholy fortune of being, perchance, one day queen. Then I do not subscribe to this law, which wants to guide my heart and limit my will. What! shall the daughter of King Henry of England allow her ways to be traced out by a miserable strip of parchment? and shall a sheet of paper be able to intrude itself between me and my heart? I am a royal princess; and why will they compel me to give my hand only to a king's son? Ay, you are right; it is not my father that has made this law, for my father's proud soul has never been willing to submit to any such constraint of miserable etiquette. He has loved where he pleased; and no Parliament—no law—has been able to hinder him in this respect. I will be my father's own daughter. I will not submit to this law!"

"Poor child!" said Catharine, "nevertheless you will be obliged to learn well how to submit; for one is not a princess without paying for it. No one asks whether our heart bleeds. They throw a purple robe over it, and though it be reddened with our heart's blood, who then sees and suspects it? You are yet so young, Elizabeth; you yet hope so much!"

"I hope so much, because I have already suffered so much—my eyes have been already made to shed so many tears. I have already in my childhood had to take beforehand my share of the pain and sorrow of life; now I will demand my share of life's pleasure and enjoyment also."

"And who tells you that you shall not have it? This love forces on you no particular husband; it but gives you the proud right, once disputed, of seeking your husband among the princes of royal blood."

"Oh," cried Elizabeth, with flashing eyes, "if I should ever really be a queen, I should be prouder to choose a husband whom I might make a king, than such a one as would make me a queen.* Oh, say yourself, Catharine, must it not be a high and noble pleasure to confer glory and greatness on one we love, to raise him in the omnipo-

---

* Elizabeth's own words.—Leti, vol. ii, p. 62.

tence of our love high above all other men, and to lay our own greatness, our own glory, humbly at his feet, that he may be adorned therewith and make his own possession what is ours?"

"By Heaven, you are as proud and ambitious as a man!" said Catharine, smiling. "Your father's own daughter! So thought Henry when he gave his hand to Anne Boleyn; so thought he when he exalted me to be his queen. But it behooves him thus to think and act, for he is a man."

"He thought thus, because he loved—not because he was a man."

"And you, too, Elizabeth—do you, too, think thus because you love?"

"Yes, I love!" exclaimed Elizabeth, as with an impulsive movement she threw herself into Catharine's arms, and hid her blushing face in the queen's bosom. "Yes, I love! I love like my father—regardless of my rank, of my birth; but feeling only that my lover is of equally high birth in the nobility of his sentiment, in his genius and noble mind; that he is my superior in all the great and fine qualities which should adorn a man, and yet are conferred on so few. Judge now, queen, whether that law there can make me happy. He whom I love is no prince—no son of a king."

"Poor Elizabeth!" said Catharine, clasping the young girl fervently in her arms.

"And why do you bewail my fate, when it is in your power to make me happy?" asked Elizabeth, urgently. "It was you who prevailed on the king to relieve me of the disgrace that rested on me; you will also have power over him to set aside this clause which contains my heart's sentence of condemnation."

Catharine shook her head with a sigh. "My power does not reach so far," said she, sadly. "Ah, Elizabeth, why did you not put confidence in me? Why did you not let me know sooner that your heart cherished a love which is in opposition to this law? Why did you not tell your friend your dangerous secret?"

"Just because it is dangerous I concealed it from you; and just on that account I do not even now mention the name of the loved one. Queen, you shall not through me become a guilty traitoress against your husband; for you well know that he punishes every secret concealed from him as an act of high treason. No, queen; if I am a criminal, you shall not be my accomplice. Ah, it is always dangerous to be the confidant of such a secret. You see that in John Heywood. He alone was my confidant, and he betrayed me. I myself put the weapons into his hands, and he turned them against me."

"No, no," said Catharine, thoughtfully; "John Heywood is true and trusty, and incapable of treachery."

"He has betrayed me!" exclaimed Elizabeth, impetuously. "He knew—he only—that I love, and that my beloved, though of noble, still is not of princely birth. Yet it was he, as you said yourself, who moved the king to introduce this paragraph into the act of succession."

"Then, without doubt, he has wished to save you from an error of your heart."

"No, he has been afraid of the danger of being privy to this secret, and at the cost of my heart and my happiness he wanted to escape this danger. But oh, Catharine, you are a noble, great and strong woman; you are incapable of such petty fear—such low calculation; therefore, stand by me; be my savior and protectress! By virtue of that oath which we have just now mutually taken—by virtue of that mutual clasp of the hands just given—I call you to my help and my assistance. Oh, Catharine, allow me this high pleasure, so full of blessing, of being at some time, perhaps, able to make him whom I love great and powerful by my will. Allow me this intoxicating delight of being able with my hand to offer to his ambition at once power and glory—it may be even a crown. Oh, Catharine, on my knees I conjure you—assist me to repeal this hated law, which wants to bind my heart and my hand!"

In passionate excitement she had fallen before the queen, and was holding up her hands imploringly to her.

Catharine, smiling, bent down and raised her up in her arms. "Enthusiast," said she, "poor young enthusiast! Who knows whether you will thank me for it one day, if I accede to your wish; and whether you will not some time curse this hour which has brought you, perhaps, instead of the hoped-for pleasure, only a knowledge of your delusion and misery?"

"And were it even so," cried Elizabeth, energetically, "still it is better to endure a wretchedness we ourselves have chosen, than to be forced to a happy lot. Say, Catharine—say, will you lend me your assistance? Will you induce the king to withdraw this hated clause? If you do it not, queen, I swear to you, by the soul of my mother, that I will not submit to this law; that I will solemnly, before all the world, renounce the privilege that is offered me; that I——"

"You are a dear, foolish child," interrupted Catharine—"a child, that in youthful presumption might dare wish to fetch the lightnings down from heaven, and borrow from Jupiter his thunderbolt. Oh, you are still too young and inexperienced to know that fate regards not our murmurs and our sighs, and, despite our reluctance and our refusal, still leads us in its own ways, not our own. You will have to learn that yet, poor child!"

"But I will not!" cried Elizabeth, stamping on the floor with all the pettishness of a child. "I will not ever and eternally be the victim of another's will; and fate itself shall not have power to make me its slave!"

"Well, we will see now," said Catharine, smiling. "We will try this time, at least, to contend against fate; and I will assist you if I can."

"And I will love you for it as my mother and my sister at once," cried Elizabeth, as with ardor she threw herself into Catharine's arms. "Yes, I will love you for it; and I will pray God that He may one day give me the opportunity to show my gratitude, and to reward you for your magnanimity and goodness."

CHAPTER XXVIII.

INTRIGUES.

For a few days past the king's gout had grown worse, and, to his wrath and grief, it confined him as a prisoner to his rolling chair.

The king was, therefore, very naturally gloomy and dejected, and hurled the lightnings of his wrath on all those who enjoyed the melancholy prerogative of being in his presence. His pains, instead of softening his disposition, seemed only to heighten still more his natural ferocity; and often might be heard through the palace of Whitehall the king's angry growl, and his loud, thundering invectives, which no longer spared any one, nor showed respect for any rank or dignity.

Earl Douglas, Gardiner, and Wriothesley very well knew how to take advantage of this wrathful humor of the king for their purposes, and to afford the cruel monarch, tortured with pain, one satisfaction at least—the satisfaction of making others suffer also.

Never had there been seen in England so many burnt at the stake as in those days of the king's sickness; never had the prisons been so crowded; never had so much blood flowed as King Henry now caused to be shed.*

* During the king's reign, and at the instigation of the clergy, twenty-eight hundred persons were burnt and executed, because they would not recognize the religious institutions established by the king as the only right and true ones.—Leti, vol. i, p. 84.

But all this did not yet suffice to appease the blood-thirstiness of the king, and his friends and counsellors, and his priests.

Still there remained untouched two mighty pillars of Protestantism that Gardiner and Wriothesley had to overthrow. These were the queen and Archbishop Cranmer.

Still there were two powerful and hated enemies whom the Seymours had to overcome; these were the Duke of Norfolk and his son, the Earl of Surrey.

But the various parties that in turn besieged the king's ear and controlled it, were in singular and unheard-of opposition, and at the same time inflamed with bitterest enmity, and they strove to supplant each other in the favor of the king.

To the popish party of Gardiner and Earl Douglas, everything depended on dispossessing the Seymours of the king's favor; and they, on the other hand, wanted above all things to continue in power the young queen, already inclined to them, and to destroy for the papists one of their most powerful leaders, the Duke of Norfolk.

The one party controlled the king's ear through the queen; the other, through his favorite, Earl Douglas.

Never had the king been more gracious and affable to his consort—never had he required more Earl Douglas's presence than in those days of his sickness and bodily anguish.

But there was yet a third party that occupied an important place in the king's favor—a power which every one feared, and which seemed to keep itself perfectly independent and free from all foreign influences. This power was John Heywood, the king's fool, the epigrammatist, who was dreaded by the whole court.

Only *one* person had influence with him. John Heywood was the friend of the queen. For the moment, then, it appeared as if the "heretical party," of which the queen was regarded as the head, was the most powerful at court.

It was therefore very natural for the popish party to

cherish an ardent hatred against the queen; very natural for them to be contriving new plots and machinations to ruin her and hurl her from the throne.

But Catharine knew very well the danger that threatened her, and she was on her guard. She watched her every look, her every word; and Gardiner and Douglas could not examine the queen's manner of life each day and hour more suspiciously than she herself did.

She saw the sword that hung daily over her head; and, thanks to her prudence and presence of mind, thanks to the ever-thoughtful watchfulness and cunning of her friend Heywood! she had still known how to avoid the falling of that sword.

Since that fatal ride in the wood of Epping Forest, she had not again spoken to Thomas Seymour alone; for Catharine very well knew that everywhere, whithersoever she turned her steps, some spying eye might follow her, some listener's ear might be concealed, which might hear her words, however softly whispered, and repeat them where they might be interpreted into a sentence of death against her.

She had, therefore, renounced the pleasure of speaking to her lover otherwise than before witnesses, and of seeing him otherwise than in the presence of her whole court.

What need had she either for secret meetings? What mattered it to her pure and innocent heart that she was not permitted to be alone with him? Still she might see him, and drink courage and delight from the sight of his haughty and handsome face; still she might be near him, and could listen to the music of his voice, and intoxicate her heart with his fine, euphonious and vigorous discourse.

Catharine, the woman of eight-and-twenty, had preserved the enthusiasm and innocence of a young girl of fourteen. Thomas Seymour was her first love; and she loved him with that purity and guileless warmth which is indeed peculiar to the first love only.

It sufficed her, therefore, to see him; to be near him;

to know that he loved her; that he was true to her; that all his thoughts and wishes belonged to her, as hers to him.

And that she knew. For there ever remained to her the sweet enjoyment of his letters—of those passionately written avowals of his love. If she was not permitted to say also to him how warmly and ardently she returned this love, yet she could write it to him.

It was John Heywood, the true and discreet friend, that brought her these letters, and bore her answers to him, stipulating, as a reward for this dangerous commission, that they both should regard him as the sole confidant of their love; that both should burn up the letters which he brought them. He had not been able to hinder Catharine from this unhappy passion, but wanted at least to preserve her from the fatal consequences of it. Since he knew that this love needed a confidant, he assumed this rôle, that Catharine, in the vehemence of her passion and in the simplicity of her innocent heart, might not make others sharers of her dangerous secret.

John Heywood therefore watched over Catharine's safety and happiness, as she watched over Thomas Seymour and her friends. He protected and guarded her with the king, as she guarded Cranmer, and protected him from the constantly renewed assaults of his enemies.

This it was that they could never forgive the queen—that she had delivered Cranmer, the noble and liberal-minded Archbishop of Canterbury, from their snares. More than once Catharine had succeeded in destroying their intriguing schemes, and in rending the nets that Gardiner and Earl Douglas, with so sly and skilful a hand, had spread for Cranmer.

If, therefore, they would overthrow Cranmer, they must first overthrow the queen. For this there was a real means—a means of destroying at once the queen and the hated Seymours, who stood in the way of the papists.

If they could prove to the king that Catharine entertained criminal intercourse with Thomas Seymour, then were they both lost; then were the power and glory of the papists secured.

But whence to fetch the proofs of this dangerous secret, which the crafty Douglas had read only in Catharine's eyes, and for which he had no other support than his bare conviction? How should they begin to influence the queen to some inconsiderate step, to a speaking witness of her love?

Time hung so heavily on the king's hands! It would have been so easy to persuade him to some cruel deed—to a hasty sentence of death!

But it was not the blood of the Seymours for which the king thirsted. Earl Douglas very well knew that. He who observed the king day and night—he who examined and sounded his every sigh, each of his softly murmured words, every twitch of his mouth, every wrinkle of his brow—he well knew what dark and bloody thoughts stirred the king's soul, and whose blood it was for which he thirsted.

The royal tiger would drink the blood of the Howards; and that they still lived in health, and abundance, and glory, while he, their king and master, lonely and sad, was tossing on his couch in pain and agony—that was the worm which gnawed at the king's heart, which made his pains yet more painful, his tortures yet keener.

The king was jealous—jealous of the power and greatness of the Howards. It filled him with gloomy hatred to think that the Duke of Norfolk, when he rode through the streets of London, was everywhere received with the acclamations and rejoicing of the people, while he, the king, was a prisoner in his palace. It was a gnawing pain for him to know that Henry Howard, Earl of Surrey, was praised as the handsomest and greatest man of England; that he was called the noblest poet; the greatest scholar; while yet he, the king, had also composed his poems and written his learned treatises, aye, even a particular devout book, which he had printed for his people, and ordered them to read instead of the Bible.*

It was the Howards who everywhere disputed his fame. The Howards supplanted him in the favor of his people, and usurped the love and admiration which were due to the king alone, and which should be directed toward no one but him. He lay on his bed of pain, and without doubt the people would have forgotten him, if he had not by the block, the stake, and the scaffold, daily reminded them of himself. He lay on his bed of pain, while the duke, splendid and magnificent, exhibited himself to the people and transported them with enthusiasm by the lavish and kingly generosity with which he scattered his money among the populace.

Yes, the Duke of Norfolk was the king's dangerous rival. The crown was not secure upon his head so long as the Howards lived. And who could conjecture whether in time to come, when Henry closed his eyes, the exultant love of the people might not call to the throne the Duke of Norfolk, or his noble son, the Earl of Surrey, instead of the rightful heir—instead of the little boy Edward, Henry's only son?

When the king thought of that, he had a feeling as though a stream of fire were whirling up to his brain; and he convulsively clenched his hands, and screamed and roared that he would take vengeance—vengeance on those hated Howards, who wanted to snatch the crown from his son.

Edward, the little boy of tender age—he alone was the divinely consecrated, legitimate heir to the king's crown. It had cost his father so great a sacrifice to give his people this son and successor! In order to do it, he had sacrificed Jane Seymour, his own beloved wife; he had let the mother be put to death, in order to preserve the son, the heir of his crown.

And the people did not once thank the king for this sacrifice that Jane Seymour's husband had made for them.

* Burnet, vol. i, p. 95.

The people received with shouts the Duke of Norfolk, the father of that adulterous queen whom Henry loved so much that her infidelity had struck him like the stab of a poisoned dagger.

These were the thoughts that occupied the king on his bed of pain, and upon which he dwelt with all the wilfulness and moodiness of a sick man.

"We shall have to sacrifice these Howards to him!" said Earl Douglas to Gardiner, as they had just again listened to a burst of rage from their royal master. "If we would at last succeed in ruining the queen, we must first destroy the Howards."

The pious bishop looked at him inquiringly, and in astonishment.

Earl Douglas smiled. "Your highness is too exalted and noble to be always able to comprehend the things of this world. Your look, which seeks only God and heaven, does not always see the petty and pitiful things that happen here on the earth below."

"Oh, but," said Gardiner, with a cruel smile, "I see them, and it charms my eye when I see how God's vengeance punishes the enemies of the Church here on earth. Set up then, by all means, a stake or a scaffold for these Howards, if their death can be to us a means to our pious and godly end. You are certain of my blessing and my assistance. Only I do not quite comprehend how the Howards can stand in the way of our plots which are formed against the queen, inasmuch as they are numbered among the queen's enemies, and profess themselves of the Church in which alone is salvation."

"The Earl of Surrey is an apostate, who has opened his ear and heart to the doctrines of Calvin!"

"Then let his head fall, for he is a criminal before God, and no one ought to have compassion on him! And what is there that we lay to the charge of the father?"

"The Duke of Norfolk is well-nigh yet more dangerous than his son; for although a Catholic, he has not nevertheless the right faith; and his soul is full of unholy sympathy and injurious mildness. He bewails those whose blood is shed because they were devoted to the false doctrine of the priests of Baal; and he calls us both the king's blood-hounds."

"Well, then, cried Gardiner with an uneasy, dismal smile, " we will show him that he has called us by the right name; we will rend him in pieces!"

"Besides, as we have said, the Howards stand in the way of our schemes in relation to the queen," said Earl Douglas, earnestly. " The king's mind is so completely filled with this one hatred and this one jealousy, that there is no room in it for any other feeling, for any other hate. It is true he signs often enough these death-warrants which we lay before him; but he does it, as the lion, with utter carelessness and without anger, crushes the little mouse that is by chance under his paws. But if the lion is to rend in pieces his equal, he must beforehand be put into a rage. When he is raging, then you must let him have his prey. The Howards shall be his first prey. But, then, we must exert ourselves, that when the lion again shakes his mane his wrath may fall upon Catharine Parr and the Seymours."

" The Lord our God will be with us, and enlighten us, that we may find the right means to strike His enemies a sure blow!" exclaimed Gardiner, devoutly folding his hands.

" I believe the right means are already found," said Earl Douglas, with a smile; " and even before this day descends to its close, the gates of the Tower will open to receive this haughty and soft-hearted Duke of Norfolk and this apostate Earl Surrey. Perchance we may even succeed in striking at one blow the queen together with the Howards. See! an equipage stops before the grand entrance, and I see the Duchess of Norfolk and her daughter, the Duchess of Richmond, getting out of the carriage. Only see! they are making signs to us. I have promised to conduct these two noble and pious ladies to the king, and I shall do so. Whilst we are there, pray for us, your highness, that our words, like well-aimed arrows, may strike the king's heart, and then rebound upon the queen and the Seymours!"

CHAPTER XXIX.

THE ACCUSATION.

In vain had the king hoped to master his pains, or at least to forget them, while he tried to sleep. Sleep had fled from the king's couch; and as he now sat in his rolling-chair, sad, weary, and harassed with pain, he thought, with gloomy spite, that the Duke of Norfolk told him but yesterday that sleep was a thing under his control, and he could summon it to him whenever it seemed good to him.

This thought made him raving with anger; and grinding his teeth, he muttered: "He can sleep; and I, his lord and king—I am a beggar that in vain whines to God above for a little sleep, a little forgetfulness of his pains! But it is this traitorous Norfolk that prevents me from sleeping. Thoughts of him keep me awake and restless. And I cannot crush this traitor with these hands of mine; I am a king, and yet so powerless and weak, that I can find no means of accusing this traitor, and convicting him of his sinful and blasphemous deeds. Oh, where may I find him —that true friend, that devoted servant, who ventures to understand my unuttered thoughts, and fulfil the wishes to which I dare not give a name?"

Just as he was thus thinking, the door behind him opened and in walked Earl Douglas. His countenance was proud and triumphant, and so wild a joy gleamed from his eyes that even the king was surprised at it.

"Oh," said he, peevishly, "you call yourself my friend;

and you are cheerful, Douglas, while your king is a poor prisoner whom the gout has chained with brazen bands to this chair."

"You will recover, my king, and go forth from this imprisonment as the conqueror, dazzling and bright, that by his appearance under God's blessing treads all his enemies in the dust—that triumphs over all those who are against him, and would betray their king!"

"Are there, then, any such traitors, who threaten their king?" asked Henry, with a dark frown.

"Ay, there are such traitors!"

"Name them to me!" said the king, trembling with passionate impatience. "Name them to me, that my arm may crush them and my avenging justice overtake the heads of the guilty."

"It is superfluous to mention them, for you, King Henry, the wise and all-knowing—you know their names."

And bending down closer to the king's ear, Earl Douglas continued: "King Henry, I certainly have a right to call myself your most faithful and devoted servant, for I have read your thoughts. I have understood the noble grief that disturbs your heart, and banishes sleep from your eyes and peace from your soul. You saw the foe that was creeping in the dark; you heard the low hiss of the serpent that was darting his venomous sting at your heel. But you were so much the noble and intrepid king, that you would not yourself become the accuser—nay, you would not once draw back the foot menaced by the serpent. Great and merciful, like God Himself, you smiled upon him whom you knew to be your enemy. But I, my king—I have other duties. I am like the faithful dog, that has eyes only for the safety of his master, and falls upon every one that comes to menace him. I have seen the serpent that would kill you, and I will bruise his head!"

"And what is the name of this serpent of which you speak?" asked the king; and his heart beat so boisterously that he felt it on his trembling lips.

"It is called," said Earl Douglas, earnestly and solemnly—"it is called Howard!"

The king uttered a cry, and, forgetting his gout and his pains, arose from his chair.

"Howard!" said he, with a cruel smile. "Say you that a Howard threatens our life? Which one is it? Name me the traitor!"

"I name them both—father and son! I name the Duke of Norfolk and the Earl of Surrey! I say that they both are traitors, who threaten the life and honor of my king, and with blasphemous arrogance dare stretch out their hands even to the crown!"

"Ah, I knew it, I knew it!" screamed the king. "And it was this that made me sleepless, and ate into my body like red-hot iron."

And as he fastened on Douglas his eyes flashing with rage, he asked, with a grim smile: "Can you prove that these Howards are traitors? Can you prove that they aim at my crown?"

"I hope to be able to do so," said Douglas. "To be sure, there are no great convincing facts——"

"Oh," said the king, interrupting him with a savage laugh, "there is no need of great facts. Give into my hand but a little thread, and I will make out of it a cord strong enough to haul the father and son up to the gallows at one time."

"Oh, for the son there is proof enough," said the earl, with a smile; "and as regards the father, I will produce your majesty some accusers against him, who will be important enough to bring the duke also to the block. Will you allow me to bring them to you immediately?"

"Yes, bring them, bring them!" cried the king. "Every minute is precious that may lead these traitors sooner to their punishment."

Earl Douglas stepped to the door and opened it. Three veiled female figures entered and bowed reverentially.

"Ah," whispered the king, with a cruel smile, as he sank back again into his chair, "they are the three Fates that spin the Howards' thread of life, and will now, it is to be hoped, break it off. I will furnish them with the scissors for it; and if they are not sharp enough, I will, with my own royal hands, help them to break the thread."

"Sire," said Earl Douglas, as, at a sign from him, the three women unveiled themselves—"sire, the wife, the daughter, and the mistress of the Duke of Norfolk have come to accuse him of high treason. The mother and the sister of the Earl of Surrey are here to charge him with a crime equally worthy of death."

"Now verily," exclaimed the king, "it must be a grievous and blasphemous sin which so much exasperates the temper of these noble women, and makes them deaf to the voice of nature!"

"It is indeed such a sin," said the Duchess of Norfolk, in a solemn tone; and, approaching a few paces nearer to the king, she continued: "Sire, I accuse the duke, my divorced husband, of high treason and disloyalty to his king. He has been so bold as to appropriate your own royal coat-of-arms; and on his seal and equipage, and over the entrance of his palace, are displayed the arms of the kings of England."

"That is true," said the king, who, now that he was certain of the destruction of the Howards, had regained his calmness and self-possession, and perfectly reassumed the air of a strict, impartial judge. "Yes, he bears the royal arms on his shield, but yet, if we remember rightly, the crown and paraph of our ancestor Edward the Third are wanting."

"He has now added this crown and this paraph to his coat-of-arms," said Miss Holland. "He says he is entitled to them; for that, like the king, he also is descended in direct line from Edward the Third; and, therefore, the royal arms belong likewise to him."

"If he says that, he is a traitor who presumes to call

his king and master his equal," cried the king, coloring up with a grim joy at now at length having his enemy in his power.

"He is indeed a traitor," continued Miss Holland. "Often have I heard him say he had the same right to the throne of England as Henry the Eighth; and that a day might come when he would contend with Henry's son for that crown."

"Ah," cried the king, and his eyes darted flashes so fierce that even Earl Douglas shrank before them, "ah, he will contend with my son for the crown of England! It is well, now; for now it is my sacred duty, as a king and as a father, to crush this serpent that wants to bite me on the heel; and no compassion and no pity ought now to restrain me longer. And were there no other proofs of his guilt and his crime than these words that he has spoken to you, yet are they sufficient, and will rise up against him, like the hangman's aids who are to conduct him to the block."

"But there are yet other proofs," said Miss Holland, laconically.

The king was obliged to unbutton his doublet. It seemed as though joy would suffocate him.

"Name them!" commanded he.

"He dares deny the king's supremacy; he calls the Bishop of Rome the sole head and holy Father of the Church."

"Ah, does he so?" exclaimed the king, laughing. "Well, we shall see now whether this holy Father will save this faithful son from the scaffold which we will erect for him. Yes, yes, we must give the world a new example of our incorruptible justice, which overtakes every one, however high and mighty he may be, and however near our throne he may stand. Really, really, it grieves our heart to lay low this oak which we had planted so near our throne, that we might lean upon it and support ourselves by it; but justice demands this sacrifice, and we will make it—not in wrath and spite, but only to meet the sacred and painful duty of our royalty. We have greatly loved this duke, and it grieves us to tear this love from our heart."

And with his hand, glittering with jewels, the king wiped from his eyes the tears which were not there.

"But how?" asked the king, then, after a pause, "will you have the courage to repeat your accusation publicly before Parliament? Will you, his wife, and you, his mistress, publicly swear with a sacred oath to the truth of your declaration?"

"I will do so," said the duchess, solemnly, "for he is no longer my husband, no longer the father of my children, but simply the enemy of my king; and to serve *him* is my most sacred duty."

"I will do so," cried Miss Holland, with a bewitching smile; "for he is no longer my lover, but only a traitor, an atheist, who is audacious enough to recognize as the holy head of Christendom that man at Rome who has dared to hurl his curse against the sublime head of our king. It is this, indeed, that has torn my heart from the duke, and that has made me now hate him as ardently as I once loved him."

With a gracious smile, the king presented both his hands to the two women. "You have done me a great service to-day, my ladies," said he, "and I will find a way to reward you for it. I will give you, duchess, the half of his estate, as though you were his rightful heir and lawful widow. And you, Miss Holland, I will leave in undisputed possession of all the goods and treasures that the enamored duke has given you."

The two ladies broke out into loud expressions of thanks and into enthusiastic rapture over the liberal and generous king, who was so gracious as to give them what they already had, and to bestow on them what was already their own property.

"Well, and are you wholly mute, my little duchess," asked the king after a pause, turning to the Duchess of

Richmond, who had withdrawn to the embrasure of a window.

"Sire," said the duchess, smiling, "I was only waiting for my cue."

"And this cue is——"

"Henry Howard, Earl of Surrey! As your majesty knows, I am a merry and harmless woman; and I understand better how to laugh and joke than to talk much seriously. The two noble and fair ladies have accused the duke, my father; and they have done so in a very dignified and solemn manner. I wish to accuse my brother, Henry Howard; but you must exercise forbearance, if my words sound less solemn and elevated. They have told you, sire, that the Duke of Norfolk is a traitor and a criminal who denominates the Pope of Rome, and not you, my exalted king, the head of the Church. Now, the Earl of Surrey is neither a traitor nor a papist; and he has neither devised criminal plots against the throne of England, nor has he denied the supremacy of the king. No, sire, the Earl of Surrey is no traitor and no papist!"

The duchess paused, and looked with a malicious and droll smile into the astonished faces of those present.

A dark frown gathered on the king's brow, and his eyes, which just before had looked so cheerful, were now fixed with an angry expression on the young duchess.

"Why, then, my lady, have you made your appearance here?" asked he. "Why have you come here, if you have nothing further to say than what I already know—that the Earl of Surrey is a very loyal subject, and a man without any ambition, who neither courts the favor of my people nor thinks of laying his traitorous hands on my crown?"

The young duchess shook her head with a smile. "I know not whether he does all that," said she. "I have indeed heard that he said, with bitter scorn, that you, my king, wanted to be the protector of religion, yet you yourself were entirely without religion and without belief. Also, he of late broke out into bitter curses against you, because you had robbed him of his field-marshal's staff, and given it to Earl Hertford, that noble Seymour. Also, he meant to see whether the throne of England were so firm and steady that it had no need of his hand and his arm to prop it. All that I have of course heard from him; but you are right, sire, it is unimportant—it is not worth mentioning, and therefore I do not even make it as an accusation against him."

"Ah, you are always a mad little witch, Rosabella!" cried the king, who had regained his cheerfulness. "You say you will not accuse him, and yet you make his head a plaything that you poise upon your crimson lips. But take care, my little duchess—take care, that this head does not fall from your lips with your laughing, and roll down to the ground; for I will not stop it—this head of the Earl of Surrey, of whom you say that he is no traitor."

"But is it not monotonous and tiresome, if we accuse the father and son of the same crime?" asked the duchess, laughing. "Let us have a little variation. Let the duke be a traitor; the son, my king, is by far a worse criminal!"

"Is there, then, a still worse and more execrable crime than to be a traitor to his king and master, and to speak of the anointed of the Lord without reverence and love?"

"Yes, your majesty, there is a still worse crime; and of that I accuse the Earl of Surrey. He is an adulterer!"

"An adulterer!" repeated the king, with an expression of abhorrence. "Yes, my lady, you are right; that is a more execrable and unnatural crime, and we shall judge it strictly. For it shall not be said that modesty and virtue found no protector in the king of this land, and that he will not as a judge punish and crush all those who dare sin against decency and morals. Oh, the Earl of Surrey is an adulterer, is he?"

"That is to say, sire, he dares with his sinful love to pursue a virtuous and chaste wife. He dares to raise his wicked looks to a woman who stands as high above him as the sun above mortals, and who, at least by the greatness and high position of her husband, should be secure from all impure desires and lustful wishes."

"Ah," cried the king, indignantly, "I see already whither that tends. It is always the same accusation; and now I say, as you did just now, let us have a little variation! The accusation I have already often heard; but the proofs are always wanting."

"Sire, this time, it may be, we can give the proofs," said the duchess, earnestly. "Would you know, my noble king, who the Geraldine is to whom Henry Howard addresses his love-songs? Shall I tell you the real name of this woman to whom, in the presence of your sacred person and of your whole court, he uttered his passionate protestations of love and his oath of eternal faithfulness? Well, now, this Geraldine—so adored, so deified—is the queen!"

"That is not true!" cried the king, crimson with anger; and he clenched his hands so firmly about the arms of his chair that it cracked. "That is not true, my lady!"

"It is true!" said the duchess, haughtily and saucily. "It is true, sire, for the Earl of Surrey has confessed to me myself that it is the queen whom he loves, and that Geraldine is only a melodious appellation for Catharine."

"He has confessed it to you yourself?" inquired the king, with gasping breath. "Ah, he dares love his king's wife? Woe to him, woe!"

He raised his clenched fist threateningly to heaven, and his eyes darted lightning. "But how!" said he, after a pause—"has he not recently read before us a poem to his Geraldine, in which he thanks her for her love, and acknowledges himself eternally her debtor for the kiss she gave him?"

"He has read before your majesty such a poem to Geraldine."

The king uttered a low cry, and raised himself in his seat. "Proofs," said he, in a hoarse, hollow voice—"proofs—or, I tell you, your own head shall atone for this accusation!"

"This proof, your majesty, *I* will give you!" said Earl Douglas, solemnly. "It pleases your majesty, in the fulness of your gentleness and mercy, to want to doubt the accusation of the noble duchess. Well, now, I will furnish you infallible proof that Henry Howard, Earl of Surrey, really loves the queen, and that he really dares to extol and adore the king's wife as *his* Geraldine. You shall with your own ears, sire, hear how Earl Surrey swears his love to the queen."

The scream which the king now uttered was so frightful, and gave evidence of so much inward agony and rage, that it struck the earl dumb, and made the cheeks of the ladies turn pale.

"Douglas, Douglas, beware how you rouse the lion!" gasped the king. "The lion might rend you yourself in pieces!"

"This very night I will give you the proof that you demand, sire. This very night you shall hear how Earl Surrey, sitting at the feet of his Geraldine, swears to her his love."

"It is well!" said the king. "This night, then! Woe to you, Douglas, if you cannot redeem your word!"

"I will do so, your majesty. For this, it is only necessary that you will be graciously pleased to swear to me that you will not, by a sigh or a breath, betray yourself. The earl is suspicious; and the fear of an evil conscience has sharpened his ear. He would recognize you by your sigh, and his lips would not speak those words and avowals which you desire to hear."

"I swear to you that I will not by any sigh or breath betray my presence!" said the king, solemnly. "I swear this to you by the holy mother of God! But now let that suffice. Air—air—I suffocate! Everything swims before my eyes. Open the window, that a little air may flow in! Ah! that is good! This air at least is pure, and not infected with sin and slander!"

And the king had Earl Douglas roll him to the opened

window, and inspired in long draughts that pure fresh air. Then he turned to the ladies with an agreeable smile.

"My ladies," said he, "I thank you! You have to-day shown yourselves my true and devoted friends! I shall ever remember it, and I beg of you, if at any time you need a friend and protector, to apply to us with all confidence. We shall never forget what great service you have to-day rendered us."

He nodded to them in a friendly manner, whilst, with a majestic wave of the hand, he dismissed them, and concluded the audience.

"And now, Douglas," exclaimed the king, vehemently, as soon as the ladies had retired—"now I have had enough of this dreadful torture! Oh, you say I am to punish the traitors—these Surreys—and you inflict on me the most frightful pains of the rack!"

"Sire, there was no other means of delivering up this Surrey to you. You were wishing that he were a criminal; and I shall prove to you that he is so."

"Oh, I shall then be able at least to tread his hated head under my feet" said the king, grinding his teeth. "I shall no more tremble before this malicious enemy, who goes about among my people with his hypocritical tongue, while I, tortured with pain, sit in the dungeon of my sickroom. Yes, yes, I thank you, Douglas, that you will hand him over to my arm of vengeance; and my soul is full of joy and serenity at it. Ah, why were you obliged to cloud this fair, this sublime hour? Why was it necessary to weave the queen into this gloomy web of guilt and crime? Her cheerful smile and her radiant looks have ever been an enjoyment so dear to my eyes."

"Sire, I do not by any means say that the queen is guilty. Only there was no other means to prove to you Earl Surrey's guilt than that you should hear for yourself his confession of love to the queen."

"And I will hear it!" cried the king, who had now already overcome the sentimental emotion of his heart.

"Yes, I will have full conviction of Surrey's guilt; and woe to the queen, should I find her also guilty! This night, then, earl! But till then, silence and secrecy! We will have father and son seized and imprisoned at the same hour; for otherwise the imprisonment of the one might easily serve as a warning to the other, and he might escape my just wrath. Ah, they are so sly—these Howards—and their hearts are so full of cunning and malice! But now they shall escape me no more; now they are ours! How it does me good to think that! And how briskly and lightly my heart leaps! It is as though a stream of new life were rushing through my veins, and a new power were infused into my blood. Oh, it was these Howards that made me sick. I shall be well again when I know that they are in the Tower. Yes, yes, my heart leaps with joy, and this is to be a happy and blessed day. Call the queen hither to me, that I may once more enjoy her rosy face before I make it turn pale with terror. Yes, let the queen come, and let her adorn herself; I want to see her once more in the full splendor of her youth and her royalty, before her star goes out in darkness. I will once more delight myself with her before I make her weep. Ah, know you, Douglas, that there is no enjoyment keener, more devilish, and more heavenly, than to see such a person who smiles and suspects nothing, while she is already condemned; who still adorns her head with roses, while the executioner is already sharpening the axe that is to lay that head low; who still has hopes of the future, and of joy and happiness, while her hour of life has already run out; while I have already bidden her stop and descend into the grave! So, call the queen to me; and tell her that we are in a merry mood, and want to jest and laugh with her! Call all the ladies and lords of our court; and have the royal saloons opened: and let them be radiant with the brilliancy of the lights; and let us have music—loud, crashing music—for we want at least to make this a merry day for us since it seems as though we should have a sad and unhappy night. Yes, yes, a merry day we will have; and after that, let come what come may! The saloons shall resound with laughter and joyfulness; and naught but rejoicing and fun shall be heard in the great royal saloons. And invite also the Duke of Norfolk, my noble cousin, who shares with me my royal coat-of-arms. Yes, invite him, that I may enjoy once more his haughty and imposing beauty and grandeur before this august sun is extinguished and leaves us again in night and darkness. Then invite also Wriothesley, the high chancellor, and let him bring with him a few gallant and brave soldiers of our body-guard. They are to be the noble duke's suite, when he wishes to leave our feast and go homeward—homeward —if not to his palace, yet to the Tower, and to the grave. Go, go, Douglas, and attend to all this for me! And send me here directly my merry fool, John Heywood. He must pass away the time for me till the feast begins. He must make me laugh and be gay."

"I will go and fulfil your orders, sire," said Earl Douglas. "I will order the feast, and impart your commands to the queen and your court. And first of all, I will send John Heywood to you. But pardon me, your majesty, if I venture to remind you that you have given me your royal word not to betray our secret by a single syllable, or even by a sigh."

"I gave my word, and I will keep it!" said the king. "Go now, Earl Douglas, and do what I have bidden you!"

Wholly exhausted by this paroxysm of cruel delight, the king sank back in his seat, and moaning and groaning he rubbed his leg, the piercing pains of which he had for a moment forgotten, but which now reminded him of their presence with so much the more cruel fury.

"Ah, ah!" moaned the king. "He boasts of being able to sleep when he pleases. Well, this time we will be the one to lull this haughty earl to sleep. But it will be a sleep out of which he is never to awake again!"

While the king thus wailed and suffered, Earl Douglas hastened with quick, firm step through the suite of royal apartments. A proud, triumphant smile played about his lips, and a joyful expression of victory flashed from his eyes.

"Triumph! triumph! we shall conquer!" said he, as he now entered his daughter's chamber and extended his hand to Lady Jane. "Jane, we have at last reached the goal, and you will soon be King Henry's seventh wife!"

A rosy shimmer flitted for a moment over Lady Jane's pale, colorless cheeks, and a smile played about her lips—a smile, however, which was more sad than loud sobs could have been."

"Ah," said she in a low tone, "I fear only that my poor head will be too weak to wear a royal crown."

"Courage, courage, Jane, lift up your head, and be again my strong, proud daughter!"

"But, I suffer so much, my father," sighed she. "It is hell that burns within me!"

"But soon, Jane, soon you shall feel again the bliss of heaven! I had forbidden you to grant Henry Howard a meeting, because it might bring us danger. Well, then, now your tender heart shall be satisfied. To-night you shall embrace your lover again!"

"Oh," murmured she, "he will again call me his Geraldine, and it will not be I, but the queen, that he kisses in my arms!"

"Yes, to-day, it will still be so, Jane; but I swear to you that to-day is the last time that you are obliged to receive him thus."

"The last time that I see him?" asked Jane, with an expression of alarm.

"No, Jane, only the last time that Henry Howard loves in you the queen, and not you yourself."

"Oh, he will never love me!" murmured she, sadly.

"He will love you, for you it will be that will save his life. Hasten, then, Jane, haste! Write him quickly one of those tender notes that you indite with so masterly a hand. Invite him to a meeting to-night at the usual time and place."

"Oh, I shall at last have him again!" whispered Lady Jane; and she stepped to the writing-table and with trembling hand began to write.

But suddenly she stopped, and looked at her father sharply and suspiciously.

"You swear to me, my father, that no danger threatens him if he comes?"

"I swear to you, Jane, that you shall be the one to save his life! I swear to you, Jane, that you shall take vengeance on the queen—vengeance for all the agony, the humiliation and despair that you have suffered by her. To-day she is yet Queen of England! To-morrow she will be nothing more than a criminal, who sighs in the confinement of the Tower for the hour of her execution. And you will be Henry's seventh queen. Write, then, my daughter, write! And may love dictate to you the proper words!"

CHAPTER XXX.

THE FEAST OF DEATH.

For a long time the king had not appeared in such good spirits as on this festive evening. For a long time he had not been so completely the tender husband, the good-natured companion, the cheerful *bon-vivant*.

The pains of his leg seemed to have disappeared, and even the weight of his body seemed to be less burdensome than usual, for more than once he rose from his chair, and walked a few steps through the brilliantly lighted saloon, in which the ladies and lords of his court, in festive attire, were moving gently to and fro; in which music and laughter resounded.

How tender he showed himself toward the queen to-day; with what extraordinary kindness he met the Duke of Norfolk; with what smiling attention he listened to the Earl of Surrey, as he, at the king's desire, recited some new sonnets to Geraldine!

This marked preference for the noble Howards enraptured the Roman Catholic party at court, and filled it with new hopes and new confidence.

But one there was who did not allow himself to be deceived by this mask which King Henry had to-day put on over his wrathful face.

John Heywood had faith neither in the king's cheerfulness nor in his tenderness. He knew the king; he was aware that those to whom he was most friendly often had the most to fear from him. Therefore, he watched him; and he saw, beneath this mask of friendliness, the king's real angry countenance sometimes flash out in a quick, hasty look.

The resounding music and the mad rejoicing no more deceived John Heywood. He beheld Death standing behind this dazzling life; he smelt the reek of corruption concealed beneath the perfume of these brilliant flowers.

John Heywood no longer laughed and no longer chatted. He watched.

For the first time in a long while the king did not need to-day the exciting jest and the stinging wit of his fool in order to be cheerful and in good humor.

So the fool had time and leisure to be a reasonable and observant man; and he improved the time.

He saw the looks of mutual understanding and secure triumph that Earl Douglas exchanged with Gardiner, and it made him mistrustful to notice that these favorites of the king, at other times so jealous, did not seem to be at all disturbed by the extraordinary marks of favor which the Howards were enjoying this evening.

Once he heard how Gardiner asked Wriothesley, as he passed by, "And the soldiers of the Tower?" and how he replied just as laconically, "They stand near the coach, and wait."

It was, therefore, perfectly clear that somebody would be committed to prison this very day. There was, therefore, among the laughing, richly-attired, and jesting guests of this court, one who this very night, when he left these halls radiant with splendor and pleasure, was to behold the dark and gloomy chambers of the Tower.

The only question was, who that one was for whom the brilliant comedy of this evening was to be changed to so sad a drama.

John Heywood felt his heart oppressed with an unaccountable apprehension, and the king's extraordinary tenderness toward the queen terrified him.

As now he smiled on Catharine, as he now stroked her cheeks, so had the king smiled on Anne Boleyn in the same hour that he ordered her arrest; so had he stroked Buckingham's cheek on the same day that he signed his death-warrant.

The fool was alarmed at this brilliant feast, resounding music, and the mad merriment of the king. He was horrified at the laughing faces and frivolous jests, which came streaming from all those mirthful lips.

O Heaven! they laughed, and death was in the midst of them; they laughed, and the gates of the Tower were already opened to admit one of those merry guests of the king into that house which no one in those days of Henry the Eighth left again, save to go to the stake or to ascend the scaffold!

Who was the condemned? For whom were the soldiers below at the carriage waiting? John Heywood in vain racked his brain with this question.

Nowhere could he spy a trace that might lead him on the right track; nowhere a clew that might conduct him through this labyrinth of horrors.

"When you are afraid of the devil, you do well to put yourself under his immediate protection," muttered John

Heywood; and sad and despondent at heart, he crept behind the king's throne and crouched down by it on the ground.

John Heywood had such a little, diminutive form, and the king's throne was so large and broad, that it altogether concealed the little crouching fool.

No one had noticed that John Heywood was concealed there behind the king. Nobody saw his large, keen eyes peeping out from behind the throne and surveying and watching the whole hall.

John Heywood could see everything and hear everything going on in the vicinity of the king. He could observe every one who approached the queen.

He saw Lady Jane likewise, who was standing by the queen's seat. He saw how Earl Douglas drew near his daughter, and how she turned deadly pale as he stepped up to her.

John Heywood held his breath and listened.

Earl Douglas stood near his daughter, and nodded to her with a peculiar smile. " Go, now, Jane, go and change your dress. It is time. Only see how impatiently and longingly Henry Howard is already looking this way, and with what languishing and enamored glances he seems to give a hint to the queen. Go then, Jane, and think of your promise."

" And will you, my father, also think of your promise?" inquired Lady Jane, with trembling lips. " Will no danger threaten him?"

" I will, Jane. But now make haste, my daughter, and be prudent and adroit."

Lady Jane bowed, and murmured a few unintelligible words. Then she approached the queen, and begged permission to retire from the feast, because a severe indisposition had suddenly overtaken her.

Lady Jane's countenance was so pale and deathlike, that the queen might well believe in the indisposition of her first maid of honor, and she allowed her to retire.

Lady Jane left the hall. The queen continued the conversation with Lord Hertford, who was standing by her.

It was a very lively and warm conversation, and the queen therefore did not heed what was passing around her; and she heard nothing of the conversation between the king and Earl Douglas.

John Heywood, still crouching behind the king's throne, observed everything and heard every word of this softly whispered conversation.

"Sire," said Earl Douglas, "it is late and the hour of midnight is drawing nigh. Will your majesty be pleased to conclude the feast? For you well know that at midnight we must be over there in the green summer-house, and it is a long way there."

"Yes, yes, at midnight!" muttered the king. "At midnight the carnival is at an end; and we shall tear off our mask, and show our wrathful countenance to the criminals! At midnight we must be over in the green summer-house. Yes, Douglas, we must make haste; for it would be cruel to let the tender Surrey wait still longer. So we will give his Geraldine liberty to leave the feast; and we ourselves must begin our journey. Ah, Douglas, it is a hard path that we have to tread, and the furies and gods of vengeance bear our torches. To work, then—to work!"

The king arose from his seat, and stepped to the queen, to whom he presented his hand with a tender smile.

"My lady, it is late," said he; "and we, who are king of so many subjects—we are, nevertheless, in turn, the subject of a king. This is the physician, and we must obey him. He has ordered me to seek my couch before midnight, and, as a loyal subject must do, I obey. We wish you, therefore, a good-night, Kate; and may your beautiful eyes on the morrow also shine as starlike as they do to-night."

"They will shine to-morrow as to-night, if my lord and husband is still as gracious to me to-morrow as to-day," said Catharine, with perfect artlessness and without embarrassment, as she gave her hand to the king.

Henry cast on her a suspicious, searching look, and a peculiar, malicious expression was manifested in his face.

"Do you believe then, Kate, that we can ever be ungracious to you?" asked he.

"As to that, I think," said she, with a smile, "that even the sun does not always shine; and that a gloomy night always succeeds his splendor."

The king did not reply. He looked her steadily in the face, and his features suddenly assumed a gentler expression.

Perhaps he had compassion on his young wife. Perhaps he felt pity for her youth and her enchanting smile, which had so often revived and refreshed his heart.

Earl Douglas at least feared so.

"Sire," said he, "it is late. The hour of midnight is drawing nigh."

"Then let us go," exclaimed the king, with a sigh. "Yes once again, good-night, Kate! Nay, do not accompany me! I will leave the hall quite unobserved; and I shall be pleased, if my guests will still prolong the fair feast till morning. All of you remain here! No one but Douglas accompanies me."

"And your brother, the fool!" said John Heywood, who long before had come out of his hiding-place and was now standing by the king. "Yes, come, brother Henry; let us quit this feast. It is not becoming for wise men of our sort to grant our presence still longer to the feast of fools. Come to your couch, king, and I will lull your ear to sleep with the sayings of my wisdom, and enliven your soul with the manna of my learning."

While John Heywood thus spoke, it did not escape him that the features of the earl suddenly clouded and a dark frown settled on his brow.

"Spare your wisdom for to-day, John," said the king; "for you would indeed be preaching only to deaf ears. I am tired, and I require not your erudition, but sleep. Good-night, John."

The king left the hall, leaning on Earl Douglas's arm.

"Earl Douglas does not wish me to accompany the king," whispered John Heywood. "He is afraid the king might blab out to me a little of that diabolical work which they will commence at midnight. Well, I call the devil, as well as the king, my brother, and with his help I too will be in the green-room at midnight. Ah, the queen is retiring; and there is the Duke of Norfolk leaving the hall. I have a slight longing to see whether the duke goes hence luckily and without danger, or if the soldiers who stand near the coach, as Wriothesley says, will perchance be the duke's bodyguard for this night."

Slipping out of the hall with the quickness of a cat, John Heywood passed the duke in the anteroom and hurried on to the outer gateway, before which the carriages were drawn up.

John Heywood leaned against a pillar and watched. A few minutes, and the duke's tall and proud form appeared in the entrance-hall; and the footman, hurrying forward, called his carriage.

The carriage rolled up; the door was opened.

Two men wrapped in black mantles sat by the coachman; two others stood behind as footmen, while a fifth was by the open door of the carriage.

The duke first noticed him as his foot had already touched the step of the carriage.

"This is not my equipage! These are not my people!" said he; and he tried to step back. But the pretended servant forced him violently into the carriage and shut the door.

"Forward!" ordered he. The carriage rolled on. A moment still, John Heywood saw the duke's pale face appear at the open carriage window, and it seemed to him as though he were stretching out his arms, calling for help —then the carriage disappeared in the night.

"Poor duke!" murmured John Heywood. "The gates of the Tower are heavy, and your arm will not be strong enough to open them again, when they have once closed behind you. But it avails nothing to think more about him now. The queen is also in danger. Away, then, to the queen!"

With fleet foot John Heywood hastened back into the castle. Through passages and corridors he slipped hurriedly along.

Now he stood in the corridor which led to the apartments of the queen.

"I will constitute her guard to-night," muttered John Heywood, as he hid himself in one of the niches in the corridor. "The fool by his prayers will keep far from the door of his saint the tricks of the devil, and protect her from the snares which the pious Bishop Gardiner and the crafty courtier Douglas want to lay for her feet. My queen shall not fall and be ruined. The fool yet lives to protect her."

CHAPTER XXXI.

THE QUEEN

FROM the niche in which John Heywood had hid himself he could survey the entire corridor and all the doors opening into it—could see everything and hear everything without being himself seen, for the projecting pilaster completely shaded him.

So John Heywood stood and listened. All was quiet in the corridor. In the distance was now and then heard the deadened sound of the music; and the confused hum of many voices from the festive halls forced its way to the listener's ear.

This was the only thing that John Heywood perceived. All else was still.

But this stillness did not last long. The corridor was lighted up, and the sound of rapidly approaching footsteps was heard.

It was the gold-laced lackeys, who bore the large silver candelabra to light the queen, who, with her train of ladies, was passing through the corridor.

She looked wondrously beautiful. The glare of the candles borne before her illumined her countenance, which beamed with cheerfulness. As she passed the pillar behind which John Heywood was standing, she was talking in unrestrained gayety with her second maid of honor; and a clear and lively laugh rang from her lips, which disclosed both rows of her dazzling white teeth. Her eyes sparkled; her cheeks were flushed with a rich red; bright as stars glittered the diamonds in the diadem that encircled her lofty brow; like liquid gold shone her dress of gold brocade, the long trail of which, trimmed with black ermine, was borne by two lovely pages.

Arrived at the door of her bed-chamber, the queen dismissed her pages and lackeys, and permitted only the maid of honor to cross the threshold of her chamber with her.

In harmless gossip the pages glided down the corridor and the staircase. Then came the lackeys who bore the candelabra. They also left the corridor.

Now all was quiet again. Still John Heywood stood and listened, firmly resolved to speak to the queen yet that night, even should he be obliged to wake her from sleep. Only he wanted to wait till the maid of honor also had left the queen's room.

Now the door opened, and the maid of honor came out. She crossed the corridor to that side where her own apartments were situated. John Heywood heard her open the door and then slide the bolt on the inside.

"Now but a brief time longer, and I will go to the queen," muttered John Heywood.

He was just going to leave his lurking-place, when he

perceived a noise as if a door were slowly and cautiously opened.

John Heywood cowered again close behind the pillar, and held his breath to listen.

A bright light fell over the corridor. A dress came rustling nearer and nearer.

John Heywood gazed astounded and amazed at the figure, which just brushed past without seeing him.

That figure was Lady Jane Douglas—Lady Jane, who, on account of indisposition, had retired from the feast in order to betake herself to rest. Now, when all rested, she watched—when all laid aside their festive garments, she had adorned herself with the same. Like the queen, she wore a dress of gold brocade, trimmed with ermine, and, like her, a diadem of diamonds adorned Lady Jane's brow.

Now she stood before the queen's door and listened. Then a fierce sneer flitted across her deathly pale face, and her dark eyes flashed still more.

"She sleeps," muttered she. "Only sleep, queen—sleep till we shall come to wake you! Sleep, so that I can wake for you."

She raised her arm threateningly toward the door, and wildly shook her head. Her long black ringlets encircled and danced around her sullen brow like the snakes of the furies; and pale and colorless, and with demon-like beauty, she resembled altogether the goddess of vengeance, in scornful triumph preparing to tread her victim beneath her feet.

With a low laugh she now glided adown the corridor, but not to that staircase yonder, but farther down to the end, where on the wall hung a life-size picture of Henry the Sixth. She pressed on a spring: the picture flew open, and through the door concealed behind it Lady Jane left the corridor.

"She is going to the green-room to a meeting with Henry Howard!" whispered John Heywood, who now stepped forth from behind the pillar. "Oh, now I comprehend it all; now the whole of this devilish plot is clear to me; Lady Jane is Earl Surrey's lady-love, and they want to make the king believe that it is the queen. Doubtless this Surrey is with them in the conspiracy, and perhaps he will call Jane Douglas by the name of the queen. They will let the king see her but a moment. She wears a gold brocade dress and a diamond diadem like the queen; and thereby they hope to deceive Henry. She has the queen's form precisely; and everybody knows the astonishing similarity and likeness of Lady Jane's voice to that of the queen. Oh, oh, it is a tolerably cunning plot! But nevertheless you shall not succeed, and you shall not yet gain the victory. Patience, only patience! We likewise will be in the green-room, and face to face with this royal counterfeit we will place the genuine queen!"

With hurried step John Heywood also left the corridor, which was now lonely and still, for the queen had gone to rest.

Yes, the queen slept, and yet over yonder in the green-room everything was prepared for her reception.

It was to be a very brilliant and extraordinary reception; for the king, in his own person, had betaken himself to that wing of the castle, and the chief master of ceremonies, Earl Douglas, had accompanied him.

To the king, this excursion, which he had to make on foot, had been very troublesome; and this inconvenience had made him only still more furious and excited, and the last trace of compassion for his queen had disappeared from the king's breast, for on Catharine's account he had been obliged to make this long journey to the green-room; and with a grim joy Henry thought only how terrible was to be his punishment for Henry Howard and also for Catharine.

Now that Earl Douglas had brought him hither, the king no longer had any doubts at all of the queen's guilt. It was no longer an accusation—it was proof. For never in the world would Earl Douglas have dared to bring him, the king, hither, if he were not certain that he would give him here infallible proofs.

The king, therefore, no longer doubted; at last Henry Howard was in his power, and he could no more escape him. So he was certain of being able to bring these two hated enemies to the block, and of feeling his sleep no longed disturbed by thoughts of his two powerful rivals.

The Duke of Norfolk had already passed the gates of the Tower, and his son must soon follow him thither.

At this thought the king felt an ecstasy so savage and bloodthirsty, that he wholly forgot that the same sword that was to strike Henry Howard's head was drawn on his queen also.

They were now standing in the green-room, and the king leaned panting and moaning on Earl Douglas's arm.

The large wide room, with its antique furniture and its faded glory, was only gloomily and scantily lighted in the middle by the two wax candles of the candelabrum that Earl Douglas had brought with him; while further away it was enveloped in deep gloom, and seemed to the eye through this gloom to stretch out to an interminable length.

"Through the door over there comes the queen," said Douglas; and he himself shrank at the loud sound of his voice, which in the large, desolate room became of awful fulness. "And that, there, is Henry Howard's entrance. Oh, he knows that path very thoroughly; for he has often enough already travelled it in the dark night, and his foot no longer stumbles on any stone of offence!"

"But he will perchance stumble on the headsman's block!" muttered the king, with a cruel laugh.

"I now take the liberty of asking one question more," said Douglas; and the king did not suspect how stormily the earl's heart beat at this question. "Is your majesty satisfied to see the earl and the queen make their appearance at this meeting? Or, do you desire to listen to a little of the earl's tender protestations?"

"I will hear not a little, but all!" said the king. "Ah, let us allow the earl yet to sing his swan-like song before he plunges into the sea of blood!"

"Then," said Earl Douglas, "then we must put out this light, and your majesty must be content merely to hear the guilty ones, and not to see them also. We will then betake ourselves to the boudoir here, which I have opened for this purpose, and in which is an easy-chair for your majesty. We will place this chair near the open door, and then your majesty will be able to hear every word of their tender whisperings."

"But how shall we, if we extinguish this our only light, at last attain to a sight of this dear loving pair, and be able to afford them the dramatic surprise of our presence?"

"Sire, as soon as the Earl of Surrey enters, twenty men of the king's bodyguard will occupy the anteroom through which the earl must pass; and it needs but a call from you to have them enter the hall with their torches. I have taken care also that before the private back-gate of the palace two coaches stand ready, the drivers of which know very well the street that leads to the Tower!"

"*Two* coaches?" said the king, laughing. "Ah, ah, Douglas, how cruel we are to separate the tender, loving pair on this journey which is yet to be their last! Well, perhaps we can compensate them for it, and allow these turtledoves to make the last trip—the trip to the stake—together. No, no, we will not separate them in death. Together they may lay their heads on the block."

The king laughed, quite delighted with his jest, while, leaning on the earl's arm, he crossed to the little boudoir on the other side, and took his place in the armchair set near the door.

"Now we must extinguish the light; and may it please

your majesty to await *in silence* the things that are to come."

The earl extinguished the light, and deep darkness and a grave-like stillness now followed.

But this did not last long. Now was heard quite distinctly the sound of footsteps. They came nearer and nearer—now a door was heard to open and shut again, and it was as though some one were creeping softly along on his toes in the hall.

"Henry Howard!" whispered Douglas.

The king could scarcely restrain the cry of savage, malicious delight that forced its way to his lips.

The hated enemy was then in his power; he was convicted of the crime; he was inevitably lost.

"Geraldine!" whispered a voice, "Geraldine!"

And as if his low call had already been sufficient to draw hither the loved one, the secret door here quite close to the boudoir opened. The rustling of a dress was very distinctly heard, and the sound of footsteps.

"Geraldine!" repeated Earl Surrey.

"Here I am, my Henry!"

With an exclamation of delight, the woman rushed forward toward the sound of the loved voice.

"The queen!" muttered Henry; and in spite of himself he felt his heart seized with bitter grief.

He saw with his inward eye how they held each other in their embrace. He heard their kisses and the low whisper of their tender vows, and all the agonies of jealousy and wrath filled his soul. But yet the king prevailed upon himself to be silent and swallow down his rage. He wanted to hear everything, to know everything.

He clenched his hands convulsively, and pressed his lips firmly together to hold in his panting breath. He wanted to hear.

How happy they both were! Henry had wholly forgotten that he had come to reproach her for her long silence; she did not think about this being the last time she might see her lover.

They were with each other, and this hour was theirs. What did the whole world matter to them? What cared they whether or not mischief and ruin threatened them hereafter?

They sat by each other on the divan, quite near the boudoir. They jested and laughed; and Henry Howard kissed away the tears that the happiness of the present caused his Geraldine to shed.

He swore to her eternal and unchanging love. In blissful silence she drank in the music of his words; and then she reiterated, with jubilant joy, his vows of love.

The king could scarcely restrain his fury.

The heart of Earl Douglas leaped with satisfaction and gratification. "A lucky thing that Jane has no suspicion of our presence," thought he—"otherwise she would have been less unrestrained and ardent, and the king's ear would have imbibed less poison."

Lady Jane thought not at all of her father; she scarcely remembered that this very night would destroy her hated rival the queen.

Henry Howard had called her his Geraldine only. Jane had entirely forgot that it was not she to whom her lover had given this name.

But he himself finally reminded her of it.

"Do you know, Geraldine," said Earl Surrey—and his voice, which had been hitherto so cheerful and sprightly, was now sad—"do you know, Geraldine, that I have had doubts of you? Oh, those were frightful, horrible hours; and in the agony of my heart I came at last to the resolution of going to the king and accusing myself of this love that was consuming my heart. Oh, fear naught! I would not have accused you. I would have even denied that love which you have so often and with such transporting reality sworn to me. I would have done it in order to see whether my Geraldine could at last gain courage and strength to acknowledge her love openly and frankly; whether her heart had the power to burst that iron band which the deceitful rules of the world had placed around it; whether she would acknowledge her lover when he was willing to die for her. Yes, Geraldine, I wanted to do it, that I might finally know which feeling is stronger in you—love or pride—and whether you could then still preserve the mask of indifference, when death was hovering over your lover's head. Oh, Geraldine, I should deem it a fairer fate to die united with you, than to be obliged to still longer endure this life of constraint and hateful etiquette."

"No, no," said she, trembling, "we will not die. My God, life is indeed so beautiful when you are by my side! And who knows whether a felicitous and blissful future may not still await us?"

"Oh, should we die, then should we be certain of this blissful future, my Geraldine. There, above, there is no more separation—no more renunciation for us. There above, you are mine, and the bloody image of your husband no longer stands between us."

"It shall no longer do so, even here on earth," whispered Geraldine. "Come, my beloved; let us fly far, far hence, where no one knows us—where we can cast from us all this hated splendor, to live for each other and for love."

She threw her arms about her lover, and in the ecstasy of her love she had wholly forgotten that she could never indeed think to flee with him, that he belonged to her only so long as he saw her not.

An inexplicable anxiety overpowered her heart; and in this anxiety she forgot everything—even the queen and the vengeance she had vowed.

She now remembered her father's words, and she trembled for her lover's life.

If now her father had not told her the truth—if now he had notwithstanding sacrificed Henry Howard in order to ruin the queen—if she was not able to save him, and through her fault he were to perish on the scaffold——

But still this hour was hers, and she would enjoy it.

She clung fast to his breast; she drew him with irresistible force to her heart, which now trembled no longer for love, but from a nameless anxiety.

"Let us fly! Let us fly!" repeated she, breathlessly. See! This hour is yet ours. Let us avail ourselves of it; for who knows whether the next will still belong to us?"

"No! it is no longer yours," yelled the king, as he sprang like a roused lion from his seat. "Your hours are numbered, and the next already belongs to the hangman!"

A piercing shriek burst from Geraldine's lips. Then was heard a dull fall.

"She has fainted," muttered Earl Douglas.

"Geraldine, Geraldine, my loved one!" cried Henry Howard. "My God, my God! she is dying! You have killed her! Woe to you!"

"Woe to yourself!" said the king, solemnly. "Here with the light! Here, you folks!"

The door of the anteroom opened, and in it appeared four soldiers with torches in their hands.

"Light the candles, and guard the door!" said the king, whose dazzled eyes were not yet able to bear this bright glare of light which now suddenly streamed through the room.

The soldiers obeyed his orders. A pause ensued. The king had put his hand before his eyes, and was struggling for breath and self-control.

When at length he let his hand glide down, his features had assumed a perfectly calm, almost a serene expression.

With a hasty glance he surveyed the room. He saw the queen in her dress glistening with gold; he saw how she lay on the floor, stretched at full length, her face turned to the ground, motionless and rigid.

He saw Henry Howard, who knelt by his beloved and was busy about her with all the anxiety and agony of a lover. He saw how he pressed her hands to his lips; how he put his hand to her head to raise it from the floor.

The king was speechless with rage. He could only lift his arm to beckon the soldiers to approach; to point to Henry Howard, who had not yet succeeded in raising the queen's head from the floor.

"Arrest him!" said Earl Douglas, lending words to the king's mute sign. "In the king's name arrest him, and conduct him to the Tower!"

"Yes, arrest him!" said the king; and, as with youthful speed he walked up to Henry Howard and put his hand heavily on his shoulder, he with terrible calmness continued: "Henry Howard, your wish shall be fulfilled; you shall mount the scaffold for which you have so much longed!"

The earl's noble countenance remained calm and unmoved; his bright beaming eye fearlessly encountered the eye of the king flashing with wrath.

"Sire," said he, "my life is in your hand, and I very well know that you will not spare it. I do not even ask you to do so. But spare this noble and beautiful woman, whose only crime is that she has followed the voice of her heart. Sire, I alone am the guilty one. Punish me, then —torture me, if you like—but be merciful to her."

The king broke out into a loud laugh. "Ah, he begs for her!" said he. "This little Earl Surrey presumes to think that his sentimental love-plaint can exercise an influence on the heart of his judge! No, no, Henry Howard; you know me better. You say, indeed, that I am a cruel man, and that blood cleaves to my crown. Well, now, it is our pleasure to set in our crown a new blood-red ruby; and if we want to take it from Geraldine's heart's blood, your sonnets will not hinder us from doing so, my good little earl. That is all the reply I have to make to you; and I think it will be the last time that we shall meet on earth!"

"There above we shall see each other again, King Henry of England!" said Earl Surrey, solemnly. "There above Henry the Eighth will no more be the judge, but the condemned criminal; and your bloody and accursed deeds will witness against you!"

The king laughed. "You avail yourself of your advantage," said he. "Because you have nothing more to lose and the scaffold is sure of you, you do not stick at heaping up the measure of your sins a little more, and you revile your legitimate, God-appointed king! But you should bear in mind, earl, that before the scaffold there is yet the rack, and that it is very possible indeed that a painful question might there be put to the noble Earl Surrey, to which his agonies might prevent him from returning an answer. Now, away with you! We have nothing more to say to each other on earth!"

He motioned to the soldiers, who approached the Earl of Surrey. As they reached their hands toward him, he turned on them a look so proud and commanding that they involuntarily recoiled a step.

"Follow me!" said Henry Howard, calmly; and, without even deigning the king a single look more, with head proudly erect, he walked to the door.

Geraldine still lay on the ground—her face turned to the floor. She stirred not. She seemed to have fallen into a deep swoon.

Only as the door with a sullen sound closed behind Earl Surrey, a low wail and moan was perceived—such as is wont to struggle forth at the last hour from the breast of the dying.

The king did not heed it. He still gazed, with eyes stern and flashing with anger, toward the door through which Earl Surrey had passed.

"He is unyielding," muttered he. "Not even the rack affrights him; and in his blasphemous haughtiness he moves along in the midst of the soldiers, not as a prisoner, but as a commander. Oh, these Howards are destined to torment me; and even their death will scarcely be a full satisfaction to me."

"Sire," said Earl Douglas, who had observed the king with a keen, penetrating eye, and knew that he had now reached the height of his wrath, at which he shrank from no deed of violence and no cruelty—" sire, you have sent Earl Surrey to the Tower. But what shall be done with the queen, who lies there on the floor in a swoon?"

The king roused himself from his reverie; and his bloodshot eyes were fixed on Geraldine's motionless form with so dark an expression of hate and rage, that Earl Douglas exultingly said to himself: "The queen is lost! He will be inexorable!"

"Ah, the queen!" cried Henry, with a savage laugh. "Yea, verily, I forgot the queen. I did not think of this charming Geraldine! But you are right, Douglas; we must think of her and occupy ourselves a little with her! Did you not say that a second coach was ready? Well, then, we will not hinder Geraldine from accompanying her beloved. She shall be where he is—in the Tower, and on the scaffold! We will therefore wake this sentimental lady and show her the last duty of a cavalier by conducting her to her carriage!"

He was about to approach the figure of the queen lying on the floor. Earl Douglas held him back.

"Sire," said he, "it is my duty—as your faithful subject, who loves you and trembles for your welfare—it is my duty to implore you to spare yourself and preserve your precious and adored person from the venomous sting of anger and grief. I conjure you, therefore, do not deign to look again on this woman, who has so deeply injured you. Give me your orders—what am I to do with her— and allow me first of all to accompany you to your apartments."

"You are right," said the king, "she is not worthy of having my eyes rest on her again; and she is even too contemptible for my anger! We will call the soldiers that they may conduct this traitress and adulteress to the tower, as they have done her paramour."

"Yet for that there is needed still a formality. The queen will not be admitted into the Tower without the king's written and sealed order."

"Then I will draw up that order."

"Sire, in that cabinet yonder may be found the necessary writing-materials, if it please your majesty."

The king leaned in silence on the earl's arm, and allowed himself to be led again into the cabinet.

With officious haste Earl Douglas made the necessary arrangements. He rolled the writing-table up to the king; he placed the large sheet of white paper in order, and slipped the pen into the king's hand.

"What shall I write?" asked the king, who, by the exertion of his night's excursion, and of his anger and vexation, began at length to be exhausted.

"An order for the queen's imprisonment, sire."

The king wrote. Earl Douglas stood behind him, with eager attention, in breathless expectation, his look steadily fixed on the paper over which the king's hand, white, fleshy, and sparkling with diamonds, glided along in hasty characters.

He had at length reached his goal. When at last he should hold in his hand the paper which the king was then writing—when he had induced Henry to return to his apartments before the imprisonment of the queen had taken place—then was he victorious. Not that woman there would he then imprison; but, with the warrant in his hand, he would go to the real queen, and take her to the Tower.

Once in the Tower, the queen could no longer defend herself; for the king would see her no more; and if before the Parliament she protested her innocence in ever so sacred oaths, still the king's testimony must convict her; for he had himself surprised her with her paramour.

No, there was no escape for the queen. She had once succeeded in clearing herself of an accusation, and proving her innocence, by a rebutting *alibi*. But this time she was irretrievably lost, and no *alibi* could deliver her.

The king completed his work and arose, whilst Douglas, at his command, was employed in setting the king's seal to the fatal paper.

From the hall was heard a slight noise, as though some person were cautiously moving about there.

Earl Douglas did not notice it; he was just in the act of pressing the signet hard on the melted sealing-wax.

The king heard it, and supposed that it was Geraldine, and that she was just waking from her swoon and rising.

He stepped to the door of the hall, and looked toward the place where she was lying. But no—she had not yet risen; she still lay stretched at full length on the floor.

"She has come to; but she still pretends to be in a swoon," thought the king; and he turned to Douglas.

"We are done," said he; "the warrant for imprisonment is prepared, and the sentence of the adulterous queen is spoken. We have done with her forever; and never shall she again behold our face, or again hear our voice. She is sentenced and damned, and the royal mercy has nothing more to do with this sinner. A curse on the adulteress! A curse on the shameless woman who deceived her huband, and gave herself up to a traitorous paramour! Woe to her, and may shame and disgrace forever mark her name, which——"

Suddenly the king stopped and listened. The noise that he had heard just before was now repeated louder and quicker; it came nearer and nearer.

And now the door opened and a figure entered—a figure which made the king stare with astonishment and admiration. It came nearer and nearer, light, graceful, and with the freshness of youth; a gold-brocade dress enveloped it; a diadem of diamonds sparkled on the brow; and brighter yet than the diamonds beamed the eyes.

"No, the king was not mistaken. It was the queen.

She was standing before him—and yet she still lay motionless and stiff upon the floor yonder.

The king uttered a cry, and, turning pale, reeled a step backward.

"The queen!" exclaimed Douglas, in terror; and he trembled so violently that the paper in his hand rattled and fluttered.

"Yes, the queen!" said Catharine, with a haughty smile. "The queen, who comes to scold her husband, that, contrary to his physician's orders, he still refrains from his slumbers at so late an hour of the night."

"And the fool!" said John Heywood, as with humorous pathos he stepped forward from behind the queen—"the fool, who comes to ask Earl Douglas how he dared deprive John Heywood of his office, and usurp the place of king's fool to Henry, and deceive his most gracious majesty with all manner of silly pranks and carnival tricks."

"And who"—asked the king, in a voice quivering with rage, fastening his flashing looks on Douglas with an annihilating expression—"who, then, is that woman there? Who has dared with such cursed mummery to deceive the king, and calumniate the queen?"

"Sire," said Earl Douglas, who very well knew that his future and that of his daughter depended on the present moment, and whom this consciousness had speedily restored to his self-possession and calmness—"sire, I beseech your majesty for a moment of private explanation; and I shall be entirely successful in vindicating myself."

"Do not grant it him, brother Henry," said John Heywood; "he is a dangerous juggler; and who knows whether he may not yet, in his private conversation, convince you that he is king, and you nothing more than his lickspittle, fawning, hypocritical servant Earl Archibald Douglas."

"My lord and husband, I beg you to hear the earl's justification," said Catharine, as she extended her hand to the king with a bewitching smile. "It would be cruel to condemn him unheard."

"I will hear him, but it shall be done in your presence, Kate, and you yourself shall decide whether or not his justification is sufficient."

"No indeed, my husband; let me remain an entire stranger to this night's conspiracy, so that spite and anger may not fill my heart and rob me of the supreme confidence which I need, to be able to walk on at your side happy and smiling in the midst of my enemies."

"You are right, Kate," said the king, thoughtfully. "You have many enemies at our court; and we have to accuse ourselves that we have not always succeeded in stopping our ear to their malicious whisperings, and in keeping ourselves pure from the poisonous breath of their calumny. Our heart is still too artless, and we cannot even yet comprehend that men are a disgusting, corrupt race, which one should tread beneath his feet, but never take to his heart. Come, Earl Douglas, I will hear you; but woe to you, if you are unable to justify yourself!"

He retired to the embrasure of the large window of the boudoir. Earl Douglas followed him thither, and let the heavy velvet curtain drop behind them.

"Sire," said he, hardily and resolutely, "the question now is this: Whose head would you rather give over to the executioner, mine or the Earl of Surrey's? You have the choice between the two. You are aware that I have ventured for a moment to deceive you. Well, send me to the Tower then, and set free the noble Henry Howard, that he may henceforth disturb your sleep and poison your days; that he may further court the love of the people, and perhaps some day rob your son of the throne that belongs to him. Here is my head, sire; it is forfeited to the headsman's axe, and Earl Surrey is free!"

"No, he is not free, and never shall be!" said the king, grinding his teeth.

"Then, my king, I am justified; and instead of being angry with me, you will thank me? It is true I have played a hazardous game, but I did so in the service of my king. I did it because I loved him, and because I read on your lofty clouded brow the thoughts that begirt with darkness my master's soul, and disturbed the sleep of his nights. You wanted to have Henry Howard in your power; and this crafty and hypocritical earl knew how to conceal his guilt so securely under the mask of virtue and loftiness of soul! But I knew him, and behind this mask I had seen his face distorted with passion and crime. I wanted to unmask him; but for this, it was necessary that I should deceive first him, and then for the hour even yourself. I knew that he burned with an adulterous love for the queen, and I wanted to avail myself of the madness of this passion, in order to bring him surely and unavoidably to a richly-deserved punishment. But I would not draw the pure and exalted person of the queen into this net with which we wanted to surround Earl Surrey. I was obliged, then, to seek a substitute for her; and I did so. There was at your court a woman whose whole heart belongs, after God, to the king alone; and who so much adores him, that she would be ready at any hour gladly to sacrifice for the king her heart's blood, her whole being—ay, if need be, even her honor itself—a woman, sire, who lives by your smile, and worships you as her redeemer and savior—a woman whom you might, as you pleased, make a saint or a strumpet; and who, to please you, would be a shameless Phyrne or a chaste veiled nun."

"Tell me her name, Douglas," said the king, "tell me it! It is a rare and precious stroke of fortune to be so loved; and it would be a sin not to want to enjoy this good fortune."

"Sire, I will tell you her name when you have first forgiven me," said Douglas, whose heart leaped for joy, and who well understood that the king's anger was already mollified and the danger now almost overcome. "I said to this woman: 'You are to do the king a great service; you are to deliver him from a powerful and dangerous foe! You are to save him from Henry Howard!' 'Tell me what I must do!' cried she, her looks beaming with joy. 'Henry Howard loves the queen. You must be the queen to him. You must receive his letters, and answer them in the queen's name. You must grant him interviews by night, and, favored by the darkness of the night, make him believe that it is the queen whom he holds in his arms. He must be convinced that the queen is his lady-love; and in his thoughts, as in his deeds, he must be placed before the king as a traitor and criminal whose head is forfeited to the headsman's axe. One day we will let the king be a witness of a meeting that Henry Howard believes he has with the queen; it will then be in his power to punish his enemy for his criminal passion, which is worthy of death!' And as I thus spoke to the woman, sire, she said with a sad smile: 'It is a disgraceful and dishonorable part that you assign me; but I undertake it, for you say I may thereby render a service to the king. I shall disgrace myself for him; but he will perhaps bestow upon me in return a gracious smile; and then I shall be abundantly rewarded.'"

"But this woman is an angel!" cried the king, ardently—"an angel whom we should kneel to and adore. Tell me her name, Douglas!"

"Sire, as soon as you have forgiven me! You know now all my guilt and all my crime. For, as I bade that noble woman, so it came to pass, and Henry Howard has gone to the Tower in the firm belief that it was the queen whom he just now held in his arms."

"But why did you leave me in this belief, Douglas? Why did you fill my heart with wrath against the noble and virtuous queen also?"

"Sire, I dared not reveal the deception to you before you had sentenced Surrey, for your noble and just moral sense would have been reluctant to punish him on account of a crime that he had not committed; and in your first wrath you would also have blamed this noble woman who has sacrificed herself for her king."

"It is true," said the king, "I should have misjudged this noble woman, and, instead of thanking her, I should have destroyed her."

"Therefore, my king, I quietly allowed you to make out an order for the queen's incarceration. But you remember well, sire, I begged you to return to your apartments before the queen was arrested. Well, now, *there* I should have disclosed to you the whole secret, which I could not tell you in the presence of that woman. For she would die of shame if she suspected that you knew of her love for the king, so pure and self-sacrificing, and cherished in such heroic silence."

"She shall never know it, Douglas! But now at length satisfy my desire. Tell me her name."

"Sire, you have forgiven me, then? You are no longer angry with me that I dared to deceive you?"

"I am no longer angry with you, Douglas; for you have acted rightly. The plan, which you have contrived and carried out with such happy results, was as crafty as it was daring."

"I thank you, sire; and I will now tell you the name. That woman, sire, who at my wish gave herself up a sacrifice to this adulterous earl, who endured his kisses, his embraces, his vows of love, in order to render a service to her king—that woman was my daughter, Lady Jane Douglas!"

"Lady Jane!" cried the king. "No, no, this is a new deception. That haughty, chaste, and unapproachable Lady Jane—that wonderfully beautiful marble statue really has then a heart in her breast, and that heart belongs to me? Lady Jane, the pure and chaste virgin, has made for me this prodigious sacrifice, of receiving this hated Surrey as her lover, in order, like a second Delilah, to deliver him into my hand? No, Douglas, you are lying to me. Lady Jane has not done that!"

"May it please your majesty to go yourself and take a look at that fainting woman, who was to Henry Howard the queen."

The king did not reply to him; but he drew back the curtain and reëntered the cabinet, in which the queen was waiting with John Heywood.

Henry did not notice them. With youthful precipitation he crossed the cabinet and the hall. Now he stood by the figure of Geraldine still lying on the floor.

She was no longer in a swoon. She had long since regained her consciousness; and terrible were the agonies and tortures that rent her heart. Henry Howard had incurred the penalty of the headsman's axe, and it was she that had betrayed him.

But her father had sworn to her that she should save her lover.

She durst not die then. She must live to deliver Henry Howard.

There were burning, as it were, the fires of hell in her poor heart; but she was not at liberty to heed these pains. She could not think of *herself*—only of *him*—of Henry Howard, whom she must deliver, whom she must save from an ignominious death.

For *him* she sent up her fervent prayers to God; for him her heart trembled with anxiety and agony, as the king now advanced to her, and, bending down, gazed into her eyes with a strange expression, at once scrutinizing and smiling.

"Lady Jane," said he then, as he presented her his hand, "arise from the ground and allow your king to express to you his thanks for your sublime and wonderful sacrifice! Verily, it is a fair lot to be a king; for then one has at least the power of punishing traitors, and of rewarding those that serve us. I have to-day done the one, and I will not neglect to do the other also. Stand up, then, Lady Jane; it does not become you to lie on your knees before me."

"Oh, let me kneel, my king," said she, passionately; "let me beseech you for mercy, for pity! Have compassion, King Henry—compassion on the anxiety and agony which I endure. It is not possible that this is all a reality! that this juggling is to be changed into such terrible earnest! Tell me, King Henry—I conjure you by the agonies which I suffer for your sake—tell me, what will you do with Henry Howard? Why have you sent him to the Tower?"

"To punish the traitor as he deserves," said the king, as he cast a dark and angry look across at Douglas, who had also approached his daughter, and was now standing close by her.

Lady Jane uttered a heartrending cry, and sank down again, senseless and completely exhausted.

The king frowned. "It is possible," said he—"and I almost believe it—that I have been deceived in many ways this evening, and that now again my guilelessness has been played upon in order to impose upon me a charming story. However, I have given my word to pardon; and it shall not be said that Henry the Eighth, who calls himself God's vicegerent, has ever broken his word; nor even that he has punished those whom he has assured of exemption from punishment. My Lord Douglas, I will fulfil my promise. I forgive you."

He extended his hand to Douglas, who kissed it fervently. The king bent down closer to him. "Douglas," whispered he, "you are as cunning as a serpent; and I now see through your artfully-woven web! You wanted to destroy Surrey, but the queen was to sink into the abyss with him. Because I am indebted to you for Surrey, I forgive you what you have done to the queen. But take heed to yourself, take heed that I do not meet you again on the same track; do not ever try again, by a look, a word, ay, even by a smile, to cast suspicion on the queen. The slightest attempt would cost you your life! That I swear to you by the holy mother of God; and you know that I have never yet broken that oath. As regards Lady Jane, we do not want to consider that she has misused the name of our illustrious and virtuous consort in order to draw this lustful and adulterous carl into the net which you had set for him; she obeyed your orders, Douglas; and we will not now decide what other motives besides have urged her to this deed. She may settle that with God and her own conscience, and it does not behoove us to decide about it."

"But it behooves me, perhaps, my husband, to ask by what right Lady Jane has dared to appear here in this attire, and to present to a certain degree a counterfeit of her queen?" asked Catharine in a sharp tone. "I may well be allowed to ask what has made my maid of honor, who left the festive hall sick, now all at once so well that she goes roaming about the castle in the night time, and in a dress which seems likely to be mistaken for mine? Sire, was this dress perchance a craftily-devised stratagem, in order to really confound us with one another? You are silent, my lord and king. It is true, then, they have wanted to carry out a terrible plot against me; and, without the assistance of my faithful and honest friend, John Heywood, who brought me here, I should without doubt be now condemned and lost, as the Earl of Surrey is."

"Ah, John, it was you then that brought a little light into this darkness?" cried the king, with a cheerful laugh, as he laid his hand on Heywood's shoulder. "Now, verily, what the wise and prudent did not see, that the fool has seen through!"

"King Henry of England," said John Heywood, solemnly, "many call themselves wise, and yet they are fools; and many assume the mask of folly, because fools are allowed to be wise."

"Kate," said the king, "you are right; this was a bad night for you, but God and the fool have saved you and me. We will both be thankful for it. But it is well if you do as you before wished, and ask and inquire nothing more concerning the mysteries of this night. It was brave in you to come here, and I will be mindful of it. Come, my little queen, give me your arm and conduct me to my apartments. I tell you, child, it gives me joy to be able to lean on your arm, and see your dear sprightly face blanched by no fear or terrors of conscience. Come, Kate, you alone shall lead me, and to you alone will I trust myself."

"Sire, you are too heavy for the queen," said the fool, as he put his neck under the other arm. "Let me share with her the burden of royalty."

"But before we go," said Catharine, "I have, my husband, one request. Will you grant it?"

"I will grant you everything that you may ask, provided you will not require me to send you to the Tower."

"Sire, I wish to dismiss my maid of honor, Lady Jane Douglas, from my service—that is all," said the queen, as her eyes glanced with an expression of contempt, and yet at the same time of pain, at the form of her friend of other days, prostrate on the floor.

"She is dismissed!" said the king. "You will choose another maid of honor to-morrow. Come, Kate!"

And the king, supported by his consort and John Heywood, left the room with slow and heavy steps.

Earl Douglas watched them with a sullen, hateful expression. As the door closed after them he raised his arm threateningly toward heaven, and his trembling lips uttered a fierce curse and execration.

"Vanquished! vanquished again!" muttered he, gnashing his teeth. "Humbled by this woman whom I hate, and whom I will yet destroy! Yes, she has conquered this time; but we will commence the struggle anew, and our envenomed weapon shall nevertheless strike her at last!"

Suddenly he felt a hand laid heavily on his shoulder, and a pair of glaring, flaming eyes gazed at him.

"Father," said Lady Jane, as she threw her right hand threateningly toward heaven—"father, as true as there is a God above us, I will accuse you yourself to the king as a traitor—I will betray to him all your accursed plots—if you do not help me to deliver Henry Howard!"

Her father looked with an expression almost melancholy in her face, painfully convulsed and pale as marble. " I will help you! " said he. " I will do it, if you will help me also, and further my plans."

" Oh, only save Henry Howard, and I will sign myself away to the devil with my heart's blood! "said Jane Douglas, with a horrible smile. " Save his life, or, if you have not the power to do that, then at least procure me the happiness of being able to die with him."

CHAPTER XXXII.

UNDECEIVED.

PARLIAMENT, which had not for a long time now ventured to offer any further opposition to the king's will— Parliament had acquiesced in his decree. It had accused Earl Surrey of high treason; and, on the sole testimony of his mother and his sister, he had been declared guilty of *lèse majesté* and high treason. A few words of discontent at his removal from office, some complaining remarks about the numerous executions that drenched England's soil with blood—that was all that the Duchess of Richmond had been able to bring against him. That he, like his father, bore the arms of the Kings of England—that was the only evidence of high treason of which his mother the Duchess of Norfolk could charge him.[*]

These accusations were of so trivial a character, that the Parliament well knew they were not the ground of his arrest, but only a pretext for it—only a pretext, by which the king said to his pliant and trembling Parliament: " This man is innocent; but I will that you condemn him, and therefore you will account the accusation sufficient."

[*] Tytler, p. 402. Burnet, vol. i, p. 95.

Parliament had not the courage to oppose the king's will. These members of Parliament were nothing more than a flock of sheep, who, in trembling dread of the sharp teeth of the dog, go straight along the path which the dog shows them.

The king wanted them to condemn the Earl of Surrey, and they condemned him.

They summoned him before their judgment-seat, and it was in vain that he proved his innocence in a speech spirited and glowing with eloquence. These noble members of Parliament would not see that he was innocent.

It is true, indeed, there were a few who were ashamed to bow their heads so unreservedly beneath the king's sceptre, which dripped with blood like a headsman's axe. There were still a few to whom the accusation appeared insufficient; but they were outvoted; and in order to give Parliament a warning example, the king, on the very same day, had these obstinate ones arrested and accused of some pretended crime. For this people, enslaved by the king's cruelty and savage barbarity, were already so degenerate and debased in self-consciousness, that men were always and without trouble found, who, in order to please the king and his bloodthirstiness and sanctimonious hypocrisy, degraded themselves to informers, and accused of crime those whom the king's dark frown had indicated to them as offenders.

So Parliament had doomed the Earl of Surrey to die, and the king had signed his death-warrant.

Early next morning he was to be executed; and in the Tower-yard the workmen were already busy in erecting the scaffold on which the noble earl was to be beheaded.

Henry Howard was alone in his cell. He had done with life and earthly things. He had set his house in order and made his will; he had written to his mother and sister, and forgiven them for their treachery and accusation; he had addressed a letter to his father, in which he exhorted him, in words as noble as they were touching, to steadfastness and calmness, and bade him not to weep for him, for death was his desire, and the grave the only refuge for which he longed.

He had then, as we have said, done with life; and earthly things no longer disturbed him. He felt no regret and no fear. Life had left him nothing more to wish; and he almost thanked the king that he would so soon deliver him from the burden of existence.

The future had nothing more to offer him; why then should he desire it? Why long for a life which could be for him now only an isolated, desolate, and gloomy one? For Geraldine was lost to him! He knew not her fate; and no tidings of her had penetrated to him through the solitary prison walls. Did the queen still live? Or had the king in his wrath murdered her on that very night when Henry was carried to the Tower, and his last look beheld his beloved lying at her husband's feet, swooning and rigid.

What had become of the queen—of Henry Howard's beloved Geraldine? He knew nothing of her. He had hoped in vain for some note, some message from her; but he had not dared to ask any one as to her fate. Perhaps the king desisted from punishing her likewise. Perhaps his murderous inclination had been satisfied by putting Henry Howard to death; and Catharine escaped the scaffold. It might, therefore, have been ruinous to her, had he, the condemned, inquired after her. Or, if she had gone before him, then he was certain of finding her again, and of being united with her forevermore beyond the grave.

He believed in a hereafter, for he loved; and death did not affright him, for after death came the reunion with her, with Geraldine, who either was already waiting for him there above, or would soon follow him.

Life had nothing more to offer him. Death united him to his beloved. He hailed death as his friend and savior, as the priest who was to unite him to his Geraldine.

He heard the great Tower clock of the prison which with threatening stroke made known the hour; and each passing hour he hailed with a joyous throb of the heart. The evening came and deep night descended upon him—the last night that was allotted to him—the last night that separated him from his Geraldine.

The turnkey opened the door to bring the earl a light, and to ask whether he had any orders to give. Heretofore it had been the king's special command not to allow him a light in his cell; and he had spent these six long evenings and nights of his imprisonment in darkness. But to-day they were willing to give him a light; to-day they were willing to allow him everything that he might still desire. The life which he must leave in a few hours was to be once more adorned for him with all charms and enjoyments which he might ask for. Henry Howard had but to wish, and the jailer was ready to furnish him everything.

But Henry Howard wished for nothing; he demanded nothing, save that they would leave him alone—save that they would remove from his prison this light which dazzled him, and which opposed to his enrapturing dreams the disenchanting reality.

The king, who had wanted to impose a special punishment in condemning him to darkness—the king had, contrary to his intention, become thereby his benefactor. For with darkness came dreams and fantasies. With the darkness came Geraldine.

When night and silence were all around him, then there was light within; and an enchanting whisper and a sweet, enticing voice resounded within him. The gates of his prison sprang open, and on the wings of thought Henry Howard soared away from that dismal and desolate place. On the wings of thought he came to *her*—to his Geraldine.

Again she was by him, in the large, silent hall. Again night lay upon them, like a veil concealing, blessing, and enveloping them; and threw its protection over their embraces and their kisses. Solitude allowed him to hear again the dear music of her voice, which sang for him so enchanting a melody of love and ecstasy.

Henry Howard must be alone, so that he can hear his Geraldine. Deep darkness must surround him, so that his Geraldine can come to him.

He demanded, therefore, for his last night, nothing further than to be left alone, and without a light. The jailer extinguished the light and left the cell. But he did not shove the great iron bolt across the door. He did not put the large padlock on it, but he only left the door slightly ajar, and did not lock it at all.

Henry Howard took no notice of this. What cared he, whether this gate was locked or no—he who no longer had a desire for life and freedom!

He leaned back on his seat, and dreamed with eyes open. There below in the yard they were working on the scaffold which Henry Howard was to ascend as soon as day dawned. The dull monotony of the strokes of the hammers fell on his ear. Now and then the torches, which lighted the workmen at their melancholy task, allowed to shine up into his cell a pale glimmer of light, which danced on the walls in ghost-like shapes.

"There are the ghosts of all those that Henry has put to death," thought Henry Howard; "they gather around me; like will-o'-the-wisps, they dance with me the dance of death, and in a few hours I shall be forever theirs."

The dull noise of hammers and saws continued steadily on, and Henry Howard sank deeper and deeper in reverie.

He thought, he felt, and desired nothing but Geraldine. His whole soul was concentrated in that single thought of *her*. It seemed to him he could bid his spirit see her, as though he could command his senses to perceive her. Yes, she was there; he felt—he was conscious of her presence. Again he lay at her feet, and leaned his head on her knee, and listened again to those charming revelations of her love.

Completely borne away from the present, and from

existence, he saw, he felt, only *her*. The mystery of love was perfected, and, under the veil of night, Geraldine had again winged her way to him, and he to her.

A happy smile played about his lips, which faltered forth rapturous words of greeting. Overcome by a wonderful hallucination, he saw his beloved approaching him; he stretched out his arms to clasp her; and it did not arouse him when he felt instead of her only the empty air.

"Why do you float away from me again, Geraldine?" asked he, in a low tone. "Wherefore do you withdraw from my arms, to whirl with the will-o'-the-wisps in the death-dance? Come, Geraldine, come; my soul burns for you. My heart calls you with its last faltering throb. Come, Geraldine, oh, come!"

What was that? It was as though the door were gently opened, and the latch again gently fastened. It was as though a foot were moving softly over the floor—as though the shape of a human form shaded for a moment the flickering light which danced around the walls.

Henry Howard saw it not.

He saw naught but his Geraldine, whom he with so much fervency and longing wished by his side. He spread his arms; he called her with all the ardor, all the enthusiasm of a lover.

Now he uttered a cry of ecstasy. His prayer of love was answered. The dream had become a reality. His arms no longer clasped the empty air; they pressed to his breast the woman whom he loved, and for whom he was to die.

He pressed his lips to her mouth and she returned his kisses. He threw his arms around her form, and she pressed him fast, fast to her bosom.

Was this a reality? Or was it madness that was creeping upon him and seizing upon his brain, and deceiving him with fantasies so enchanting?

Henry Howard shuddered as he thought this, and, falling upon his knees, he cried in a voice trembling with agony and love: "Geraldine, have pity on me! Tell me that this is no dream, that I am not mad—that you are really—you are Geraldine—you—the king's consort, whose knees I now clasp! Speak, oh speak, my Geraldine!"

"I am she!" softly whispered she. "I am Geraldine—am the woman whom you love, and to whom you have sworn eternal truth and eternal love! Henry Howard, my beloved, I now remind you of your oath! Your life belongs to me. This you have vowed, and I now come to demand of you that which is my own!"

"Ay, my life belongs to you, Geraldine! But it is a miserable, melancholy possession, which you will call yours only a few hours longer."

She threw her arms closely around his neck; she raised him to her heart; she kissed his mouth, his eyes. He felt her tears, which trickled like hot fountains over his face; he heard her sighs, which struggled from her breast like death-groans.

"You must not die!" murmured she, amid her tears. "No, Henry, you must live, so that I too can live; so that I shall not become mad from agony and sorrow for you! My God, my God, do you not then feel how I love you? Know you not, then, that your life is my life, and your death my death?"

He leaned his head on her shoulder, and, wholly intoxicated with happiness, he scarcely heard what she was speaking.

She was again there! What cared he for all the rest?

"Geraldine," softly whispered he, "do you recollect still how we first met each other? how our hearts were united in one throb, how our lips clung to each other in one kiss? Geraldine, my life, my loved one, we then swore that naught could separate us, that our love should survive the grave! Geraldine, do you remember that still?"

"I remember it, my Henry! But you shall not die yet; and not in death, but in life, shall your love for me be proved! Ay, we will live, live! And *your* life shall be *my* life, and where *you* are, there will I be also! Henry, do you remember that you vowed this to me with a solemn oath!"

"I remember it, but I cannot keep my word, my Geraldine! Hear you how they are sawing and hammering there below? Know you what that indicates, dearest?"

"I know it, Henry! It is the scaffold that they are building there below. The scaffold for you and me. For I too will die if you will not live; and the axe that seeks your neck shall find mine also, if you wish not that we both live!"

"Do I wish it! But how can we, beloved?"

"We can, Henry, we can! All is ready for the flight! It is all arranged, everything prepared! The king's signet-ring has opened to me the gates of the prison; the omnipotence of gold has won over your jailer. He will not see it, when two persons instead of one leave this dungeon. Unmolested and without hinderance, we will both leave the Tower by ways known only to him, over secret corridors and staircases, and will go aboard a boat which is ready to take us to a ship, which lies in the harbor prepared to sail, and which as soon as we are aboard weighs anchor and puts to sea with us. Come, Henry, come! Lay your arm in mine, and let us leave this prison!"

She threw both her arms around his neck, and drew him forward. He pressed her fast to his heart and whispered: "Yes, come, come, my beloved! Let us fly! To you belongs my life, you alone!"

He raised her up in his arms, and hastened with her to the door. He pushed it hastily open with his foot and hurried forward down the corridor; but having arrived just at the first turn he reeled back in horror.

Before the door were standing soldiers with shouldered arms. There stood also the lieutenant of the Tower, and two servants behind him with lighted candles.

Geraldine gave a scream, and with anxious haste rearranged the thick veil that had slipped from her head.

Henry Howard also had uttered a cry, but not on account of the soldiers and the frustrated flight.

His eyes, stretched wide open, stared at this figure at his side, now so closely veiled.

It seemed to him as though like a spectre a strange face had risen up close by him—as though it were not the beloved head of the queen that rested there on his shoulder. He had seen this face only as a vision, as the fantasy of a dream; but he knew with perfect certainty that it was not *her* countenance, not the countenance of his Geraldine.

The lieutenant of the Tower motioned to his servants, and they carried the lighted candles into the earl's cell.

Then he gave Henry Howard his hand and silently led him back into the prison.

Henry Howard exhibited no reluctance to follow him; but his hand had seized Geraldine's arm, and he drew her along with him; his eye rested on her with a penetrating expression, and seemed to threaten her.

They were now again in the room which they had before left with such blessed hopes.

The lieutenant of the Tower motioned to the servants to retire, then turned with solemn earnestness to Earl Surrey.

"My lord," said he, "it is at the king's command that I bring you these lights. His majesty knows all that has happened here this night. He knew that a plot was formed to rescue you; and while they believed they were deceiving him, the plotters themselves were deceived. They had succeeded under various artful false pretences in influencing the king to give his signet-ring to one of his lords. But his majesty was already warned, and he already knew that it was not a man, as they wanted to make him believe, but a woman, who came, not to take leave of you, but to deliver you from prison.—My lady, the jailer whom you imagined that you had bribed was a faithful servant of the king. He betrayed your plot to me; and it was I who ordered him to make a show of favoring your deed. You will not be able to release Earl Surrey; but if such is your command, I will myself see you to the ship that lies in the harbor for you ready to sail. No one will hinder you, my lady, from embarking on it; Earl Surrey is not permitted to accompany you!—My lord, soon the night is at an end, and you know that it will be your last night. The king has ordered that I am not to prevent this lady, if she wishes to spend this night with you in your room. But she is allowed to do so only on the condition that the lights in your room remain burning. That is the king's express will, and these are his own words: 'Tell Earl Surrey that I allow him to love his Geraldine, but that he is to open his eyes to see her! That he may see, you will give him a light; and I command him not to extinguish it so long as Geraldine is with him. Otherwise he may confound her with another woman; for in the dark one cannot distinguish even a harlequin from a queen!'—You have now to decide, my lord, whether this lady remains with you, or whether she goes, and the light shall be put out!"

"She shall remain with me, and I very much need the light!" said Earl Surrey; and his penetrating look rested steadily on the veiled figure, which shook at his words, as if in an ague.

"Have you any other wish besides this, my lord?"

"None, save that I may be left alone with her."

The lieutenant bowed and left the room.

They were now alone again, and stood confronting each other in silence. Naught was heard but the beating of their hearts, and the sighs of anguish that burst from Geraldine's trembling lips.

It was an awful, a terrible pause. Geraldine would gladly have given her life could she thereby have extinguished the light and veiled herself in impenetrable darkness.

But the earl would see. With an angry, haughty look,

he stepped up to her, and, as with commanding gesture he raised his arm, Geraldine shuddered and submissively bowed her head.

"Unveil your face!" said he, in a tone of command.

She did not stir. She murmured a prayer, then raised her clasped hands to Henry and in a low moan, said: "Mercy! mercy!"

He extended his hand and seized the veil.

"Mercy!" repeated she, in a voice of still deeper supplication—of still greater distress.

But he was inexorable. He tore the veil from her face and stared at her. Then with a wild shriek he reeled back and covered his face with his hands.

Jane Douglas durst not breathe or stir. She was pale as marble; her large, burning eyes were fastened with an unutterable expression of entreaty upon her lover, who stood before her with covered head, and crushed with anguish. She loved him more than her life, more than her eternal salvation; and yet she it was that had brought him to this hour of agony.

At length Earl Surrey let his hands fall from his face, and with a fierce movement dashed the tears from his eyes.

As he looked at her, Jane Douglas wholly involuntarily sank upon her knees, and raised her hands imploringly to him. "Henry Howard," said she, in a low whisper, "I am Geraldine! Me have you loved; my letters have you read with ecstasy, and to me have you often sworn that you loved my mind yet more than my appearance. And often has my heart been filled with rapture, when you told me you would love me however my face might change, however old age or sickness might alter my features. You remember, Henry, how I once asked you whether you would cease to love me, if now God suddenly put a mask before my face, so that you could not recognize my features. You replied to me: 'Nevertheless, I should love and adore you; for what in you ravishes me, is not your face, but you yourself—yourself with your glorious being and nature. It is your soul and your heart which can never change, which lie before me like a holy book, clear and bright!' That was your reply to me then, as you swore to love me eternally. Henry Howard, I now remind you of your oath! I am your Geraldine. It is the same soul, the same heart; only God has put a mask upon my face!"

Earl Surrey had listened to her with eager attention, with increasing amazement.

"It is she! It is really!" cried he, as she ceased. "It is Geraldine!"

And wholly overcome, wholly speechless with anguish, he sank into a seat.

Geraldine flew to him; she crouched at his feet; she seized his drooping hand and covered it with kisses. And amid streaming tears, often interrupted by her sighs and her sobs, she recounted to him the sad and unhappy history of her love; she unveiled before him the whole web of cunning and deceit, that her father had drawn around them both. She laid her whole heart open and unveiled before him. She told him of her love, of her agonies, of her ambition, and her remorse. She accused herself; but she pleaded her love as an excuse, and with streaming tears, clinging to his knees, she implored him for pity, for forgiveness.

He thrust her violently from him, and stood up in order to escape her touch. His noble countenance glowed with anger; his eyes darted lightning; his long flowing hair shaded his lofty brow and his face like a sombre veil. He was beautiful in his wrath, beautiful as the archangel Michael trampling the dragon beneath his feet. And thus he bent down his head toward her; thus he gazed at her with flashing and contemptuous looks.

"I forgive you?" said he. "Never will that be! Ha, shall I forgive you?—you, who have made my entire life a ridiculous lie, and transformed the tragedy of my love into a disgusting farce? Oh, Geraldine, how I have loved you;

and now you have become to me a loathsome spectre, before which my soul shudders, and which I must execrate! You have crushed my life, and even robbed my death of its sanctity; for now it is no longer the martyrdom of my love, but only the savage mockery of my credulous heart. Oh, Geraldine, how beautiful it would have been to die for you!—to go to death with your name upon my lips!—to bless you!—to thank you for my happy lot, as the axe was already uplifted to smite off my head! How beautiful to think that death does not separate us, but is only the way to an eternal union; that we should lose each other but a brief moment here, to find each other again forevermore!"

Geraldine writhed at his feet like a worm trodden upon; and her groans of distress and her smothered moans were the heartrending accompaniment of his melancholy words.

"But that is now all over!" cried Henry Howard; and his face, which was before convulsed with grief and agony, now glowed again with wrath. "You have poisoned my life and my death; and I shall curse you for it, and my last word will be a malediction on the harlequin Geraldine!"

"Have pity!" groaned Jane. "Kill me, Henry; stamp my head beneath your feet; only let this torture end!"

"Nay, no pity!" yelled he, wildly; "no pity for this impostor, who has stolen my heart and crept like a thief into my love! Arise, and leave this room; for you fill me with horror; and when I behold you, I feel only that I must curse you! Ay, a curse on you and shame, Geraldine! Curse on the kisses that I have impressed on your lips—on the tears of rapture that I have wept on your bosom. When I ascend the scaffold, I will curse you, and my last words shall be: 'Woe to Geraldine!—for she is my murderess!'"

He stood there before her with arm raised on high, proud and great in his wrath. She felt the destroying lightning of his eyes, though she durst not look up at him, but lay at his feet moaning and convulsed, and concealing her face in her veil, as she shuddered at her own picture.

"And this be my last word to you Geraldine," said Henry Howard, panting for breath: "Go hence under the burden of my curse, and live—if you can!"

She unveiled her head, and raised her countenance toward him. A contemptuous smile writhed about her deathly pale lips. "Live!" said she. "Have we not sworn to die with each other? Your curse does not release me from my oath, and when you descend into the grave, Jane Douglas will stand upon its brink, to wail and weep until you make a little place for her there below; until she has softened your heart and you take her again, as your Geraldine, into your grave. Oh, Henry! in the grave, I no longer wear the face of Jane Douglas—that hated face, which I would tear with my nails. In the grave, I am Geraldine again. There I may again lie close to your heart, and again you will say to me: 'I love not your face and your external form! I love you yourself; I love your heart and mind; and that can never change; and can never be otherwise!'"

"Silence!" said he, roughly; "silence, if you do not want me to run mad! Cast not my own words in my face. They defile me, for falsehood has desecrated and trodden them in the mire. No! I will not make room for you in my grave. I will not again call you Geraldine. You are Jane Douglas, and I hate you, and I hurl my curse upon your criminal head! I tell you——"

He suddenly paused, and a slight convulsion ran through his whole frame.

Jane Douglas uttered a piercing scream, and sprang from her knees.

Day had broken; and from the prison-tower sounded the dismal, plaintive stroke of the death-bell.

"Do you hear, Jane Douglas?" said Surrey. "That

bell summons me to death. You it is that has poisoned my last hour. I was happy when I loved you. I die in despair, for I despise and hate you."

"No, no, you dare not die!" cried she, clinging to him with passionate anguish. "You dare not go to the grave with that fierce curse upon your lips. I cannot be your murderess. Oh, it is not possible that they will put you to death—you, the beautiful, the noble and the virtuous Earl Surrey. My God, what have you done to excite their wrath? You are innocent; and they know it. They cannot execute you; for it would be murder! You have committed no offence; you have been guilty of nothing; no crime attaches to your noble person. It is indeed no crime to love Jane Douglas, and me have you loved—me alone."

"No, not you," said he proudly; "I have nothing to do with Lady Jane Douglas. I loved the queen, and I believed she returned my love. That is my crime."

The door opened: and in solemn silence the lieutenant of the Tower entered with the priests and his assistants. In the door was seen the bright-red dress of the headsman, who was standing upon the threshold with face calm and unmoved.

"It is time!" solemnly said the lieutenant.

The priest muttered his prayers, and the assistants swung their censers. Without, the death-bell kept up its wail; and from the court was heard the hum of the mob, which, curious and bloodthirsty as it ever is, had streamed hither to behold with laughing mouth the blood of the man who but yesterday was its favorite.

Earl Surrey stood there a moment in silence. His features worked and were convulsed, and a deathlike pallor covered his cheeks.

He trembled, not at death, but at dying. It seemed to him that he already felt on his neck the cold broad-axe which that frightful man there held in his hand. Oh, to die on the battle-field—what a boon it would have been!

To come to an end on the scaffold—what a disgrace was this!

"Henry Howard, my son, are you prepared to die?" asked the priest. "Have you made your peace with God? Do you repent of your sins, and do you acknowledge death as a righteous expiation and punishment? Do you forgive your enemies, and depart hence at peace with yourself and with mankind?"

"I am prepared to die," said Surrey, with a proud smile; "the other questions, my father, I will answer to my God."

"Do you confess that you were a wicked traitor? And do you beg the forgiveness of your noble and righteous, your exalted and good king, for the blasphemous injury to his sacred majesty?"

Earl Surrey looked him steadily in the eye. "Do you know what crime I am accused of?"

The priest cast down his eyes, and muttered a few unintelligible words.

With a haughty movement of the head, Henry Howard turned from the priest to the lieutenant of the Tower.

"Do you know my crime, my lord?" said he.

But the lord lieutenant also dropped his eyes, and remained silent.

Henry Howard smiled. "Well, now, I will tell you. I have, as it becomes me, my father's son, borne the arms of our house on my shield and over the entrance of my palace, and it has been discovered that the king bears the same arms that we do. That is my high treason! I have said that the king is deceived in many of his servants, and often promotes his favorites to high honors which they do not deserve. That is my offence against his majesty; and it is that for which I shall lay my head upon the block.* But

---

* These two insignificant accusations were the only points that could be made out against the Earl of Surrey. Upon these charges, brought by his mother and sister, he was executed.—Tytler, p. 492; Burnet, vol. i, p. 75; Leti, vol. i, p. 108.

make yourself easy; I shall myself add to my crimes one more, so that they may be grievous enough to make the conscience of the righteous and generous king quiet. I have given up my heart to a wretched and criminal love, and the Geraldine whom I have sung in many a poem, and have celebrated even before the king, was nothing but a miserable coquettish strumpet!"

Jane Douglas gave a scream, and sank upon the ground as if struck by lightning.

"Do you repent of this sin, my son?" asked the priest. "Do you turn your heart away from this sinful love, in order to turn it to God?"

"I not only repent of this love, but I execrate it! and now, my father, let us go; for you see, indeed, my lord is becoming impatient. He bears in mind that the king will find no rest until the Howards also have gone to rest. Ah, King Henry! King Henry! Thou callest thyself the mighty king of the world, and yet thou tremblest before the arms of thy subject! My lord, if you go to the king to-day, give him Henry Howard's greeting; and tell him, I wish his bed may be as easy to him as the grave will be to me. Now, come, my lords! It is time."

With head proudly erect and calm step, he turned to the door. But now Jane Douglas sprang from the ground; now she rushed to Henry Howard and clung to him with all the might of her passion and agony. "I leave you not!" cried she, breathless and pale as death. "You dare not repulse me, for you have sworn that we shall live and die together."

He hurled her from him in fierce wrath, and drew himself up before her, lofty and threatening.

"I forbid you to follow me!" cried he, in a tone of command. She reeled back against the wall and looked at him, trembling and breathless.

He was still lord over her soul; she was still subject to him in love and obedience. She could not therefore summon up courage to defy his command.

She beheld him as he left the room and passed down the corridor with his dreadful train; she heard their footsteps gradually die away; and then suddenly in the yard sounded the hollow roll of the drum.

Jane Douglas fell on her knees to pray, but her lips trembled so much that she could find no words for her prayer.

The roll of the drum ceased in the court below, and only the death-bell still continued to wail and wail. She heard a voice speaking loud and powerful words.

It was *his* voice; it was Henry Howard that was speaking. And now again the hollow roll of the drums drowned his voice.

"He dies! He dies, and I am not with him!" cried she, with a shriek; and she gathered herself up, and as if borne by a whirlwind she dashed out of the room, through the corridor, and down the stairs.

There she stood in the court. That dreadful black pile above there, in the midst of this square crowded with men—that was the scaffold. Yonder she beheld *him* prostrate on his knees. She beheld the axe in the headsman's hand; she saw him raise it for the fatal stroke.

She was a woman no longer, but a lioness! Not a drop of blood was in her cheeks. Her nostrils were expanded and her eyes darted lightning.

She drew out a dagger that she had concealed in her bosom, and made a path through the amazed, frightened, yielding crowd.

With one spring she had rushed up the steps of the scaffold. She now stood by him on the top of it—close by that kneeling figure.

There was a flash through the air. She heard a peculiar whiz—then a hollow blow. A red vapor-like streak of blood spurted up, and covered Jane Douglas with its crimson flood.

"I come, Henry, I come!" cried she, with a wild shout. "I shall be with thee in death!"

And again there was a flash through the air. It was the dagger that Jane Douglas plunged into her heart.

She had struck well. No sound—no groan burst from her lips. With a proud smile she sank by her lover's headless corpse, and with a last dying effort she said to the horrified headsman: "Let me share his grave! Henry Howard, in life and in death I am with thee!"

CHAPTER XXXIII.

NEW INTRIGUES.

HENRY HOWARD was dead; and now one would have thought the king might be satisfied and quiet, and that sleep would no longer flee from his eyelids, since Henry Howard, his great rival, had closed his eyes forever; since Henry Howard was no longer there, to steal away his crown, to fill the world with the glory of his deeds, to dim the genius of the king by his own fame as a poet.

But the king was still dissatisfied. Sleep still fled from his couch.

The cause of this was that his work was only just half done. Henry Howard's father, the Duke of Norfolk, still lived. The cause of this was, that the king was always obliged to think of this powerful rival; and these thoughts chased sleep from his eyelids. His soul was sick of the Howards; therefore his body suffered such terrible pains.

If the Duke of Norfolk would close his eyes in death, then would the king also be able to close his again in refreshing sleep! But this court of peers—and only by such a court could the duke be judged—this court of peers was so slow and deliberate! It worked far less rapidly, and was not near so serviceable, as the Parliament which had so quickly condemned Henry Howard. Why must the old Howard bear a ducal title? Why was he not like his son, only an earl, so that the obedient Parliament might condemn him?

That was the king's inextinguishable grief, his gnawing pain, which made him raving with fury and heated his blood, and thereby increased the pains of his body.

He raved and roared with impatience. Through the halls of his palace resounded his savage vituperation. It made every one tremble and quake, for no one was sure that it was not he that was to fall that day a victim to the king's fury. No one could know whether the king's ever-increasing thirst for blood would not that day doom him.

With the most jealous strictness the king, from his sick-couch, watched over his royal dignity; and the least fault against that might arouse his wrath and bloodthirstiness. Woe to those who wanted still to maintain that the pope was the head of the Church! Woe to those who ventured to call God the only Lord of the Church, and honored not the king as the Church's holy protector! The one, like the other, were traitors and sinners, and he had Protestants and Roman Catholics alike executed, however near they stood to his own person, and however closely he was otherwise bound to them.

Whoever, therefore, could avoid it, kept himself far from the dreaded person of the king; and whoever was constrained by duty to be near him, trembled for his life, and commended his soul to God.

There were only four persons who did not fear the king, and who seemed to be safe from his destroying wrath. There was the queen, who nursed him with devoted attention, and John Heywood, who with untiring zeal sustained Catharine in her difficult task, and who still sometimes succeeded in winning a smile from the king. There were, furthermore, Gardiner, bishop of Winchester, and Earl Douglas.

Lady Jane Douglas was dead. The king had therefore forgiven her father, and again shown himself gracious and friendly to the deeply-bowed earl. Besides, it was such an agreeable and refreshing feeling to the suffering king to have some one about him who suffered yet more than he himself! It comforted him to know that there could be agonies yet more horrible than those pains of the body under which he languished. Earl Douglas suffered these agonies; and the king saw with a kind of delight how his hair turned daily more gray, and his features became more relaxed and feeble. Douglas was younger than the king, and yet how old and gray his face was beside the king's well-fed and blooming countenance!

Could the king have seen the bottom of his soul, he would have had less sympathy with Earl Douglas's sorrow.

He considered him only as a tender father mourning the death of his only child. He did not suspect that it was less the father that Jane's painful death had smitten, than the ambitious man, the fanatical Roman Catholic, the enthusiastic disciple of Loyola, who with dismay saw all his plans frustrated, and the moment drawing nigh when he would be divested of that power and consideration which he enjoyed in the secret league of the disciples of Jesus.

With him, therefore, it was less the *daughter*, for whom he mourned, than *the king's seventh wife*. And that Catharine wore the crown, and not his daughter—not Jane Douglas—this it was that he could never forgive the queen.

He wanted to take vengeance on the queen for Jane's death; he wanted to punish Catharine for his frustrated hopes, for his desires that she had trampled upon.

But Earl Douglas durst not himself venture to make another attempt to prejudice the king's mind against his consort. Henry had interdicted him from it under the penalty of his wrath. With words of threatening, he had warned him from such an attempt; and Earl Douglas very well knew that King Henry was inflexible in his determination, when the matter under consideration was the execution of a threatened punishment.

Yet what Douglas durst not venture, that Gardiner could venture—Gardiner, who, thanks to the capriciousness of the sick king, had for the few days past enjoyed again the royal favor so unreservedly that the noble Archbishop Cranmer had received orders to leave the court and retire to his episcopal residence at Lambeth.

Catharine had seen him depart with anxious forebodings; for Cranmer had ever been her friend and her support. His mild and serene countenance had ever been to her like a star of peace in the midst of this tempest-tossed and passion-lashed court life; and his gentle and noble words had always fallen like a soothing balm on her poor trembling heart.

She felt that with his departure she lost her noblest support, her strengthening aid, and that she was now surrounded only by enemies and opponents. True, she still had John Heywood, the faithful friend, the indefatigable servant; but since Gardiner had exercised his sinister influence over the king's mind, John Heywood durst scarcely risk himself in Henry's presence. True, she had also Thomas Seymour, her lover; but she knew and felt that she was everywhere surrounded by spies and eavesdroppers, and that now it required nothing more than an interview with Thomas Seymour—a few tender words —perchance even only a look full of mutual understanding and love, in order to send him and her to the scaffold.

She trembled not for herself, but for her lover. That made her cautious and thoughtful. That gave her courage never to show Thomas Seymour other than a cold, serious face; never to meet him otherwise than in the circle of her court; never to smile on him; never to give him her hand.

She was, however, certain of her future. She knew that a day would come on which the king's death would deliver her from her burdensome grandeur and her painful royal crown; when she should be free—free to give her hand to the man whom alone on earth she loved, and to become his wife.

She waited for that day, as the prisoner does for the hour of his release; but like him she knew that a premature attempt to escape from her dungeon would bring her only ruin and death, and not freedom.

She must be patient and wait. She must give up all personal intercourse with her lover; and even his letters John Heywood could bring her but very seldom, and only with the greatest caution. How often already had not John Heywood conjured her to give up this correspondence also! how often had he not with tears in his eyes besought her to renounce this love, which might one day be her ruin and her death! Catharine laughed at his gloomy forebodings, and opposed to his dark prophecies a bravery reliant on the future, the joyous courage of her love.

She would not die, for happiness and love were awaiting her; she would not renounce happiness and love, for the sake of which she could endure this life in other respects—this life of peril, of resignation, of enmity, and of hatred.

But she wanted to live in order to be happy hereafter. This thought made her brave and resolute; it gave her courage to defy her enemies with serene brow and smiling lip; it enabled her to sit with bright eye and rosy cheeks at the side of her dreaded and severe husband, and, with cheerful wit and inexhaustible good-humor, jest away the frown from his brow, and vexation from his soul.

But just because she could do this, she was a dangerous antagonist to Douglas and Gardiner. Just on that account, it was to be their highest effort to destroy this beautiful young woman, who durst defy them and weaken their influence with the king. If they could but succeed in rendering the king's mind more and more gloomy; if they could but completely fill him again with fanatical religious zeal; then, and then only, could they hope to attain their end; which end was this: to bring back the king as a contrite, penitent, and humble son of the only saving mother Church, and to make him again, from a proud, vain, and imperious prince, an obedient and submissive son of the pope.

The king was to renounce this vain and blasphemous arrogance of wishing to be himself head of his Church. He was to turn away from the spirit of novelty and heresy, and again become a faithful and devout Catholic.

But in order that they might attain this end, Catharine must be removed from him; he must no longer behold her rosy and beautiful face, and no longer allow himself to be diverted by her sensible discourse and her keen wit.

"We shall not be able to overthrow the queen," said Earl Douglas to Gardiner, as the two stood in the king's anteroom, and as Catharine's cheerful chit-chat and the king's merry laugh came pealing to them from the adjoining room. "No, no, Gardiner, she is too powerful and too crafty. The king loves her very much; and she is such an agreeable and refreshing recreation to him."

"Just on that account we must withdraw her from him," said Gardiner, with a dark frown. "He must turn away his heart from this earthly love; and after we shall have mortified this love in him, this savage and arrogant man will return to us and to God, contrite and humble."

But we shall not be able to mortify it, friend. It is so ardent and selfish a love."

So much the greater will be the triumph, if our holy admonitions are successful in touching his heart, Douglas. It is true he will suffer very much if he is obliged to give up this woman. But he needs precisely this suffering in order to become contrite and penitent. His mind must first be entirely darkened, so that we can illuminate it with the light of faith. He must first be rendered perfectly isolated and comfortless in order to bring him back to the holy communion of the Church, and to find him again accessible to the consolations of that faith which alone can save."

"Ah," sighed Douglas, "I fear that this will be a useless struggle. The king is so vain of his self-constituted high-priesthood!"

"But he is such a weak man, and such a great sinner!" said Gardiner, with a cold smile. "He trembles so much at death and God's judgment, and our holy mother the Church can give him absolution, and by her holy sacraments render death easy to him. He is a wicked sinner and has stings of conscience. This it is that will bring him back again to the bosom of the Catholic Church."

"But when will that come to pass? The king is sick, and any day may put an end to his life. Woe to us, if he die before he has given the power into our hands, and nominated us his executors! Woe to us, if the queen is appointed regent, and the king selects the Seymours as her ministers! Oh, my wise and pious father, the work that you wish to do must be done soon, or it must remain forever unaccomplished."

"It shall be done this very day," said Gardiner, solemnly; and bending down closer to the earl's ear, he continued: "we have lulled the queen into assurance and self-confidence, and by this means she shall be ruined this very day. She relies so strongly on her power over the king's disposition, that she often summons up courage even to contradict him, and to set her own will in opposition to his. That shall be her ruin this very day! For mark well, earl; the king is now again like a tiger that has been long fasting. He thirsts for blood! The queen has an aversion to human blood, and she is horrified when she hears of executions. So we must manage that these opposing inclinations may come into contact, and contend with each other."

"Oh, I understand now," whispered Douglas; "and I bow in reverence before the wisdom of your highness. You will let them both contend with their own weapons."

"I will point out a welcome prey to his appetite for blood, and give her silly compassion an opportunity to contend with the king for his prey. Do you not think, earl, that this will be an amusing spectacle, and one refreshing to the heart, to see how the tiger and dove struggle with each other? And I tell you the tiger thirsts so much for blood! Blood is the only balm that he applies to his aching limbs, and by which alone he imagines that he can restore peace and courage to his tortured conscience and his dread of death. Ah, ha! we have told him that, with each new execution of a heretic, one of his great sins would be blotted out, and that the blood of the Calvinists serves to wash out of his account-book some of his evil deeds. He would be so glad to be able to appear pure and guiltless before the tribunal of his God! Therefore he needs very much heretical blood. But hark—the hour strikes which summons me to the royal chamber! There has been enough of the queen's laughing and chit-chat. We will now endeavor to banish the smile forever from her face. She is a heretic; and it is a pious work, well pleasing to God, if we plunge her headlong into ruin!"

"May God be with your highness, and assist you by His grace, that you may accomplish this sublime work!"

"God will be with us, my son, since for Him it is that we labor and harass ourselves. To His honor and praise we bring these misbelieving heretics to the stake, and make the air re-echo with the agonizing shrieks of those who are racked and tortured. That is music well pleasing to God; and the angels in heaven will triumph and be glad when the heretical and infidel Queen Catharine also has to strike up this music of the damned. Now I go to the holy labor of love and godly wrath. Pray for me, my son, that I may succeed. Remain here in the anteroom, and await my call; perhaps we shall need you. Pray for us, and with us. Ah, we still owe this heretical queen a grudge for Anne Askew. To-day we will pay her. Then she accused us, to-day we will accuse her, and God and His host of saints and angels are with us."

And the pious and godly priest crossed himself, and

with head humbly bowed and a soft smile about his thin, bloodless lips, strode through the hall in order to betake himself to the king's chamber.

CHAPTER XXXIV.

THE KING AND THE PRIEST.

"GOD bless and preserve your majesty!" said Gardiner as he entered, to the king, who just then was sitting with the queen at the chess-board. With frowning brow and compressed lips he looked over the game, which stood unfavorable for him, and threatened him with a speedy checkmate.

It was not wise in the queen not to let the king win; for his superstitious and jealous temper looked upon such a won game of chess as withal an assault on his own person. And he who ventured to conquer him at chess was always to Henry a sort of traitor that threatened his kingdom, and was rash enough to attempt to seize the crown.

The queen very well knew that, but—Gardiner was right—she was too self-confident. She trusted a little to her power over the king; she imagined he would make an exception in her favor. And it was so dull to be obliged ever to be the losing and conquered party at this game; to permit the king always to appear as the triumphant victor, and to bestow on his game praise which he did not deserve. Catharine wanted to allow herself for once the triumph of having beaten her husband. She fought him man to man; she irritated him by the ever-approaching danger.

The king, who at the beginning had been cheerful, and laughed when Catharine took up one of his pieces—the king now no longer laughed. It was no more a game. It was a serious struggle; and he contended with his consort for the victory with impassioned eagerness.

Catharine did not even see the clouds which were gathering on the king's brow. Her looks were directed only to the chess-board; and, breathless with expectation and glowing with eagerness, she considered the move she was about to make.

But Gardiner was very well aware of the king's secret anger; and he comprehended that the situation was favorable for him.

With soft, sneaking step he approached the king, and, standing behind him, looked over the game.

"You are checkmated in four moves, my husband!" said the queen with a cheerful laugh, as she made her move.

A still darker frown gathered on the king's brow, and his lips were violently compressed.

"It is true, your majesty," said Gardiner. "You will soon have to succumb. Danger threatens you from the queen."

Henry gave a start, and turned his face to Gardiner with an expression of inquiry. In his exasperated mood against the queen, the crafty priest's ambiguous remark struck him with double keenness.

Gardiner was a very skilful hunter; the very first arrow that he shot had hit. But Catharine, too, had heard it whiz. Gardiner's slow, ambiguous words had startled her from her artless security; and as she now looked into the king's glowing, excited face, she comprehended her want of prudence.

But it was too late to remedy it. The king's checkmate was unavoidable; and Henry himself had already noticed his defeat.

"It is all right!" said the king, impetuously. "You have won, Catharine, and, by the holy mother of God! you can boast of the rare good fortune of having vanquished Henry of England!"

"I will not boast of it, my noble husband!" said she, with a smile. "You have played with me as the lion does with the puppy, which he does not crush only because he has compassion on him, and he pities the poor little creature. Lion, I thank you. You have been magnanimous to-day. You have let me win."

The king's face brightened a little. Gardiner saw it. He must prevent Catharine from following up her advantage further.

"Magnanimity is an exalted, but a very dangerous virtue," said he, gravely; "and kings above all things dare not exercise it; for magnanimity pardons crimes committed, and kings are not here to pardon, but to punish."

"Oh, no, indeed," said Catharine; "to be able to be magnanimous is the noblest prerogative of kings; and since they are God's representatives on earth, they too must exercise pity and mercy, like God himself."

The king's brow again grew dark, and his sullen looks stared at the chess-board.

Gardiner shrugged his shoulders, and made no reply. He drew a roll of papers out of his gown and handed it to the king.

"Sire," said he, "I hope you do not share the queen's views; else it would be bad for the quiet and peace of the country. Mankind cannot be governed by mercy, but only through fear. Your majesty holds the sword in his hands. If you hesitate to let it fall on evil-doers, they will soon wrest it from your hands, and you will be powerless!"

"Those are very cruel words, your highness!" exclaimed Catharine, who allowed herself to be carried away by her magnanimous heart, and suspected that Gardiner had come to move the king to some harsh and bloody decision.

She wanted to anticipate his design; she wanted to move the king to mildness. But the moment was unpropitious for her.

The king, whom she had just before irritated by her victory over him, felt his vexation heightened by the opposition which she offered to the bishop; for this opposition was at the same time directed against himself. The king was not at all inclined to exercise mercy; it was, therefore, a very wicked notion of the queen's to praise mercy as the highest privilege of princes.

With a silent nod of the head, he took the papers from Gardiner's hands, and opened them.

"Ah," said he, running over the pages, "your highness is right; men do not deserve to be treated with mercy, for they are always ready to abuse it. Because we have for a few weeks lighted no fagot-piles and erected no scaffolds, they imagine that we are asleep; and they begin their treasonable and mischievous doings with redoubled violence, and raise their sinful fists against us, in order to mock us. I see here an accusation against one who has presumed to say that there is no king by the grace of God; and that the king is a miserable and sinful mortal, just as well as the lowest beggar. Well, we will concede this man his point—we will not be to him a king by the grace of God, but a king by the wrath of God! We will show him that we are not yet quite like the lowest beggar, for we still possess at least wood enough to build a pile of fagots for him."

And as the king thus spoke, he broke out into a loud laugh, in which Gardiner heartily chimed.

"Here I behold the indictment of two others who deny the king's supremacy," continued Henry, still turning over the leaves of the papers. They revile me as a blasphemer, because I dare call myself God's representative—the visible head of His holy Church; they say that God alone is Lord of His Church, and that Luther and Calvin are more exalted representatives of God than the king himself. Verily we must hold our royalty and our God-granted dignity very cheap, if we should not punish these transgressors, who blaspheme in our sacred person God Himself."

He continued turning over the leaves. Suddenly a deep flush of anger suffused his countenance, and a fierce curse burst from his lips.

He threw the paper on the table, and struck it with his clenched fist. "Are all the devils let loose, then?" yelled he, in wrath. "Does sedition blaze so wildly in my land, that we have no longer the power to subdue it? Here a fanatical heretic on the public street has warned the people not to read that holy book which I myself, like a well-intentioned and provident father and guardian, wrote for my people, and gave it them that they might be edified and exalted thereby. And this book that felon has shown to the people, and said to them: 'You call that the king's book; and you are right; for it is a wicked book, a work of hell, and the devil is the king's sponsor!' Ah, I see well we must again show our earnest and angry face to this miserable, traitorous rabble, that it may again have faith in the king. It is a wretched, disgusting, and contemptible mob—this people! They are obedient and humble only when they tremble and feel the lash. Only when they are trampled in the dust, do they acknowledge that we are their master; and when we have racked them and burnt, they have respect for our excellency. We must, however, brand royalty on their bodies so that they may be sensible of it as a reality. And by the eternal God, we will do that! Give me the pen here that I may sign and ratify these warrants. But dip the pen well, your highness, for there are eight warrants, and I must write my name eight times. Ah, ah, it is a hard and fatiguing occupation to be a king, and no day passes without trouble and toil!"

"The Lord our God will bless this toil to you!" said Gardiner, solemnly, as he handed the king the pen.

Henry was preparing to write, as Catharine laid her hand on his, and checked him.

"Do not sign them, my husband," said she, in a voice of entreaty. "Oh, by all that is sacred to you, I conjure you not to let yourself be carried away by your momentary vexation; let not the injured man be mightier in you than the righteous king. Let the sun set and rise on your wrath; and then, when you are perfectly calm, perfectly composed—then pronounce judgment on these accused. For consider it well, my husband, these are eight death-warrants that you are here about to sign; and with these few strokes of the pen, you will tear eight human beings from life, from family, and from the world; you will take from the mother, her son; from the wife, her husband; and from the infant children, their father. Consider it, Henry; it is so weighty a responsibility that God has placed in your hand, and it is presumptuous not to meet it in holy earnestness and undisturbed tranquillity of mind."

"Now, by the holy mother!" cried the king, striking vehemently upon the table, "I believe, forsooth, you dare excuse traitors and blasphemers of their king! You have not heard then of what they are accused?"

"I have heard it," said Catharine, more and more warmly; "I have heard, and I say, nevertheless, sign not those death-warrants, my husband. It is true these poor creatures have grievously erred, but they erred as human beings. Then let your punishment also be human. It is not wise, O king, to want to avenge so bitterly a trifling injury to your majesty. A king must be exalted above reviling and calumny. Like the sun, he must shine upon the just and the unjust, no one of whom is so mighty that he can cloud his splendor and dim his glory. Punish evil-doers and criminals, but be noble and magnanimous toward those who have injured your person."

"The king is no person that can be injured!" said Gardiner. "The king is a sublime idea, a mighty, world-embracing thought. Whoever injures the king, has not injured a person, but a divinely instituted royalty—the universal thought that holds together the whole world!"

"Whoever injures the king has injured God!" yelled the king; "and whoever seizes our crown and reviles us, shall have his hand struck off, and his tongue torn out, as is done to atheists and patricides!"

"Well, strike off their hand then, mutilate them; but

do not kill them!" cried Catharine, passionately. "Ascertain at least whether their crime is so grievous as they want to make you believe, my husband. Oh, it is so easy now to be accused as a traitor and atheist! All that is needed for it is an inconsiderate word, a doubt, not as to God, but to his priests and this Church which you, my king, have established; and of which the lofty and peculiar structure is to many so new and unusual that they ask themselves in doubt whether that is a Church of God or a palace of the king, and that they lose themselves in its labyrinthine passages, and wander about without being able to find the exit."

"Had they faith," said Gardiner, solemnly, "they would not lose their way; and were God with them, the entrance would not be closed to them."

"Oh, I well know that *you* are always inexorable!" cried Catharine, angrily. "But it is not to you either that I intercede for mercy, but to the king; and I tell you, sir bishop, it would be better for you, and more worthy of a priest of Christian love, if you united your prayers with mine, instead of wanting to dispose the king's noble heart to severity. You are a priest; and you have learned in your own life that there are many paths that lead to God, and that we, one and all, doubt and are perplexed which of them is right."

"How!" screamed the king, as he rose from his seat and gazed at Catharine with angry looks. "You mean, then, that the heretics also may find themselves on a path that leads to God?"

"I mean," cried she, passionately, "that Jesus Christ, too, was called an atheist, and executed. I mean that Stephen was stoned by Paul, and that, nevertheless, both are now honored as saints and prayed to as such. I mean, that Socrates was not damned because he lived before Christ, and so could not be acquainted with his religion; and that Horace and Julius Cæsar, Phidias and Plato, must yet be called great and noble spirits, even though they were heathen. Yes, my lord and husband, I mean that it behooves us well to exercise gentleness in matters of religion, and that faith is not to be obtruded on men by main force as a burden, but is to be bestowed upon them as a benefit through their own conviction."

"So you do not hold these eight accused to be criminals worthy of death?" asked Henry with studied calmness, and a composure maintained with difficulty.

"No, my husband! I hold that they are poor, erring mortals, who seek the right path, and would willingly travel it; and who, therefore, ask in doubt all along, 'Is this the right way?'"

"It is enough!" said the king, as he beckoned Gardiner to him, and, leaning on his arm, took a few steps across the room. "We will speak no more of these matters. They are too grave for us to wish to decide them in the presence of our gay young queen. The heart of woman is always inclined to gentleness and forgiveness. You should have borne that in mind, Gardiner, and not have spoken of these matters in the queen's presence."

"Sire, it was, however, the hour that you appointed for consultation on these matters."

"Was it the hour!" exclaimed the king, quickly. "Well, then we did wrong to devote it to anything else than grave employments; and you will pardon me, queen, if I beg you to leave me alone with the bishop. Affairs of state must not be postponed."

He presented Catharine his hand, and with difficulty, and yet with a smiling countenance, conducted her to the door. As she stopped, and, looking him in the eye with an expression inquiring and anxious, opened her lips to speak to him, he made an impatient gesture with his hand, and a dark frown gathered on his brow.

"It is late," said he, hastily, "and we have business of state."

Catharine did not venture to speak; she bowed in silence and left the room. The king watched her with sullen brow and angry looks. Then he turned round to Gardiner.

"Now," asked he, "what do you think of the queen?"

"I think," said Gardiner, so slowly and so deliberately that each word had time to penetrate the king's sensitive heart like the prick of a needle—"I think that she does not deem them criminals that call the holy book which you have written a work of hell; and that she has a great deal of sympathy for those heretics who will not acknowledge your supremacy."

"By the holy mother, I believe she herself would speak thus, and avow herself among my enemies, if she were not my wife!" cried the king, in whose heart rage began already to seethe like lava in a volcano.

"She does it already, although she is your wife, sire! She imagines her exalted position renders her unamenable, and protects her from your righteous wrath; therefore she does what no one else dares do, and speaks what in the mouth of any other would be the blackest treason."

"What does she? and what says she?" cried the king. "Do not hesitate to tell me, your highness. It behooves me well to know what my wife does and says."

"Sire, she is not merely the secret patroness of heretics and reformers, but she is also a professor of their faith. She listens to their false doctrine with eager mind, and receives the cursed priests of this sect into her apartments, in order to hear their fanatical discourse and hellish inspiration. She speaks of these heretics as true believers and Christians; and denominates Luther the light that God has sent into the world to illuminate the gloom and falsehood of the Church with the splendor of truth and love—that Luther, sire, who dared write you such shameful and insulting letters, and ridiculed in such a brutal manner your royalty and your wisdom."

"She is a heretic; and when you say that, you say everything!" screamed the king. The volcano was ripe for an eruption, and the seething lava must at last have an outlet. "Yes, she is a heretic!" repeated the king; "and yet we have sworn to exterminate these atheists from our land."

"She very well knows that she is secure from your wrath," said Gardiner, with a shrug of his shoulders. "She relies on the fact that she is the queen, and that in the heart of her exalted husband love is mightier than the faith."

"Nobody shall suppose that he is secure from my wrath, and no one shall rely on the security afforded him by my love. She is a proud, arrogant, and audacious woman!" cried the king, whose looks were just then fixed again on the chess-board, and whose spite was heightened by the remembrance of the lost game. "She ventures to brave us, and to have a will other than ours. By the holy mother, we will endeavor to break her stubbornness, and bend her proud neck beneath our will! Yes, I will show the world that Henry of England is still the immovable and incorruptible. I will give the heretics an evidence that I am in reality the defender and protector of the faith and of religion in my land, and that nobody stands too high to be struck by my wrath, and to feel the sword of justice on his neck. She is a heretic; and we have sworn to destroy heretics with fire and sword. We shall keep our oath."

"And God will bless you with His blessing. He will surround your head with a halo of fame; and the Church will praise you as her most glorious pastor, her exalted head."

"Be it so!" said the king, as with youthful alacrity he strode across the room; and, stepping to his writing-table, with a vigorous and fleet hand he wrote down a few lines.

Gardiner stood in the middle of the room with his hands folded; and his lips murmured in an undertone a prayer, while his large flashing eyes were fastened on the king with a curious and penetrating expression.

"Here, your highness," the king then said, "take this

paper—take it and order everything necessary. It is an arrest-warrant; and before the night draws on, the queen shall be in the Tower."

"Verily, the Lord is mighty in you!" cried Gardiner, as he took the paper; "the heavenly hosts sing their hallelujah and look down with rapture on the hero who subdues his own heart to serve God and the Church."

"Take it and speed you!" said the king, hastily. "In a few hours everything must be done. Give Earl Douglas the paper, and bid him go with it to the lord-lieutenant of the Tower, so that he himself may repair hither with the yeomen of the guard. For this woman is yet a queen, and even in the criminal I will still recognize the queen. The lord-lieutenant himself must conduct her to the Tower. Hasten then, say I! But, hark you, keep all this a secret, and let nobody know anything of it till the decisive moment arrives. Otherwise her friends might take a notion to implore my mercy for this sinner; and I abhor this whining and crying. Silence, then, for I am tired and need rest and sleep. I have, as you say, just done a work well pleasing to God; perhaps He may send me, as a reward for it, invigorating and strengthening sleep, which I have now so long desired in vain."

And the king threw back the curtains of his couch, and, supported by Gardiner, laid himself on the downy cushion.

Gardiner drew the curtains again, and thrust the fatal paper into his pocket. Even in his hands it did not seem to him secure enough. What! might not some curious eye fasten on it, and divine its contents? Might not some impertinent and shameless friend of the queen snatch this paper from him, and carry it to her and give her warning? No, no, it was not secure enough in his hands. He must hide it in the pocket of his gown. There, no one could find it, no one discover it.

So there he hid it. In the gown with its large folds it was safe; and, after he had thus concealed the precious paper, he left the room with rapid strides, in order to acquaint Earl Douglas with the glorious result of his plans.

Not a single time did he look back. Had he done so, he would have sprung back into that room as a tiger pounces on his prey. He would have plunged, as the hawk stoops at the dove, at that piece of white paper that lay there on the floor, exactly on the spot where Gardiner was before standing when he placed into his pocket the arrest-warrant written by the king.

Ah, even the gown of a priest is not always close enough to conceal a dangerous secret; and even the pocket of a bishop may sometimes have holes in it.

Gardiner went away with the proud consciousness of having the order of arrest in his pocket; and that fatal paper lay on the floor in the middle of the king's chamber.

Who will come to pick it up? Who will become the sharer of this dangerous secret? To whom will this mute paper proclaim the shocking news that the queen has fallen into disgrace, and is this very day to be dragged to the Tower as a prisoner?

All is still and lonely in the king's apartment. Nothing is stirring, not even the heavy damask curtains of the royal couch.

The king sleeps. Even vexation and anger are a good lullaby; they have so agitated and prostrated the king, that he has actually fallen asleep from weariness.

Ah, the king should have been thankful to his wife for his vexation at the lost game of chess, and his wrath at Catharine's heretical sentiments. These had fatigued him: these had lulled him to sleep.

The warrant of arrest still lay on the floor. Now, quite softly, quite cautiously, the door opens. Who is it that dares venture to enter the king's room unsummoned and unannounced?

There are only three persons who dare venture that:

the queen, Princess Elizabeth, and John Heywood the fool. Which of the three is it?

It is Princess Elizabeth, who comes to salute her royal father. Every forenoon at this hour she had found the king in his room. Where was he then to-day? As she looked around the room with an inquiring and surprised air, her eye fell on that paper which lay there on the floor. She picked it up, and examined it with childish curiosity. What could this paper contain? Surely it was no secret— else, it would not lie here on the floor.

She opened it and read. Her fine countenance expressed horror and amazement; a low exclamation escaped her lips. But Elizabeth had a strong and resolute soul; and the unexpected and the surprising did not dull her clear vision, nor cloud her sharp wit. The queen was in danger. The queen was to be imprisoned. *That,* this dreadful paper shrieked in her ear; but she durst not allow herself to be stunned by it. She must act; she must warn the queen.

She hid the paper in her bosom, and light as a zephyr she floated away again out of the chamber.

With flashing eyes and cheeks reddened by her rapid race Elizabeth entered the queen's chamber; with passionate vehemence she clasped her in her arms and tenderly kissed her.

"Catharine, my queen, and my mother," said she, "we have sworn to stand by and protect each other when danger threatens us. Fate is gracious to me, for it has given into my hand the means of making good my oath this very day. Take that paper and read! It is an order for your imprisonment, made out by the king himself. When you have read it, then let us consider what is to be done, and how we can avert the danger from you."

"An order of imprisonment!" said Catharine, with a shudder, as she read it. "An order of imprisonment— that is to say, a death-warrant! For when once the threshold of that frightful Tower is crossed, it denotes that it is never to be left again; and if a queen is arrested and accused, then is she also already condemned. Oh, my God, princess, do you comprehend that—to have to die while life still throbs so fresh and warm in our veins? To be obliged to go to death, while the future still allures us with a thousand hopes, a thousand wishes? My God, to have to descend into the desolate prison and into the gloomy grave, while the world greets us with alluring voices, and spring-tide has scarcely awoke in our heart!"

Streams of tears burst from her eyes, and she hid her face in her trembling hands.

"Weep not, queen," whispered Elizabeth, herself trembling and pale as death. "Weep not; but consider what is to be done. Each minute, and the danger increases; each minute brings the evil nearer to us."

"You are right," said Catharine, as she again raised her head, and shook the tears from her eyes. "Yes, you are right; it is not time to weep and wail. Death is creeping upon me; but I—I will not die. I live still; and so long as there is a breath in me I will fight against death. God will assist me; God will help me to overcome this danger also, as I have already done so many others."

"But what will you do? where can you begin? You know not the accusation. You know not who accuses you, nor with what you are charged."

"Yet I suspect it!" said the queen, musingly. "When I now recall to mind the king's angry countenance, and the malicious smile of that malignant priest, I believe I know the accusation. Yes—everything is now clear to me. Ah, it is the heretic that they would sentence to death. Well, now, my lord bishop, I still live; and we will see which of us two will gain the victory!"

With proud step and glowing cheeks she hurried to the door. Elizabeth held her back. "Whither are you going?" cried she, in astonishment.

"To the king!" said she, with a proud smile. "He has heard the bishop; now he shall hear me also. The king's disposition is fickle and easily changed. We will now see which cunning is the stronger—the cunning of the priest or the cunning of the woman. Elizabeth, pray for me. I go to the king; and you will either see me free and happy, or never again."

She imprinted a passionate kiss on Elizabeth's lips, and hurriedly left the chamber.

CHAPTER XXXV.

CHESS-PLAY.

It was many days since the king had been as well as he was to-day. For a long time he had not enjoyed such refreshing sleep as on the day when he signed the warrant for the queen's imprisonment. But he thought nothing at all about it. Sleep seemed to have obliterated all recollection of it from his memory. Like an anecdote which you listen to, and smile at for the moment, but soon forget, so had the whole occurrence vanished again from him. It was an anecdote of the moment—a transient interlude—nothing further.

The king had slept well, and he had no care for anything else. He stretched himself, and lay lounging on his couch, thinking with rapture how fine it would be if he could enjoy such sweet and refreshing repose every day, and if no bad dreams and no fear would frighten away sleep from his eyes. He felt very serene and very goodhumored; and had any one now come to beg a favor of the king, he would have granted it in the first joy after such invigorating sleep. But he was alone; no one was with him; he must repress his gracious desires. But no. Was it not as though something were stirring and breathing behind the curtains?

The king threw back the curtains, and a soft smile flitted over his features; for before his bed sat the queen. There she sat with rosy cheeks and sparkling eyes, and greeted him with a roguish smile.

"Ah, Kate, it is you!" cried the king. "Well, now, I understand how it happened that I have had such a sound and refreshing sleep! You stood by as my good angel, and scared the pains and bad dreams away from my couch."

And as he said this, he reached out his hand and tenderly stroked her velvet cheek. He did not at all recollect that he had already, as it were, devoted that charming head to the scaffold, and that in a few hours more those bright eyes were to b.hold naught but the night of the dungeon. Sleep, as we have said, had lulled to rest also the recollection of this; and the evil thoughts had not yet awoke again in him. To sign an order of arrest or a death-warrant was with the king such a usual and every-day matter, that it constituted no epoch in his life, and neither burdened him with troubles of conscience nor made his heart shudder and tremble.

But Catharine thought of it, and as the king's hand stroked her cheek, it was as though death were just then touching her, never again to release her. However, she overcame this momentary horror, and had the courage to preserve her serene and innocent air.

"You call me your good angel, my husband," said she, with a smile; "but yet I am nothing more than your little Puck, who bustles about you, and now and then makes you laugh with his drolleries."

"And a dear little Puck you are, Katie," cried the king, who always gazed upon his wife's rosy and fresh countenance with real satisfaction.

"Then I will prove myself this very day your Puck, and allow you no more repose on your couch," said she, as she made a mock effort to raise him up. "Do you know, my husband, why I came here? A butterfly has tapped at my window. Only think now, a butterfly in winter! That betokens that this time winter is spring; and the clerk of the weather above there has confounded January with March. The butterfly has invited us, king; and only see! the sun is winking into the window to us, and says we have but to come out, as he has already dried the walks in the garden below, and called forth a little grass on the plat. And your rolling chair stands all ready, my lord and husband, and your Puck, as you see, has already put on her furs, and clad herself in armor against the winter, which, however, is not there!"

"Well, then, help me, my dearest Puck, so that I can arise, and obey the command of the butterfly and the sun and my lovely wife," cried the king, as he put his arm around Catharine's neck, and slowly raised himself from the couch.

She busied herself about him with officious haste; she put her arm tenderly on his shoulder and supported him, and properly arranged for him the gold chain, which had slipped out of place on his doublet, and playfully plaited the lace ruff which was about his neck.

"Is it your order, my husband, that your servants come?—the master of ceremonies, who, without doubt, awaits your beck in the anteroom—the lord bishop—who awhile ago made such a black-looking face at me? But how! my husband, your face, too, is now in an eclipse? How? Has your Puck perchance said something to put you out of tune?"

"No, indeed!" said the king, gloomily; but he avoided meeting her smiling glance and looking in her rosy face.

The evil thoughts had again awoke in him; and he now remembered the warrant of arrest that he had given Gardiner. He remembered it, and he regretted it. For she was so fair and lovely—his young queen; she understood so well by her jests to smooth away care from his brow, and affright vexation from his soul—she was such an agreeable and sprightly pastime, such a refreshing means of driving away *ennui*.

Not for her sake did he regret what he had done, but only on his own account. From selfishness alone, he repented having issued that order for the queen's imprisonment. Catharine observed him. Her glance, sharpened by inward fear, read his thoughts on his brow, and understood the sigh which involuntarily arose from his breast. She again seized courage; she might succeed in turning away by a smile the sword that hung over her head.

"Come, my lord and husband," said she, cheerfully, "the sun beckons to us, and the trees shake their heads indignantly because we are not yet there."

"Yes, come, Kate," said the king, rousing himself with an effort from his brown study; "come, we will go down into God's free air. Perhaps He is nearer to us there, and may illuminate us with good thoughts and wholesome resolutions. Come, Kate."

The queen gave him her arm, and, supported on it, the king advanced a few steps. But suddenly Catharine stood still; and as the king fastened on her his inquiring look, she blushed and cast down her eyes.

"Well!" asked the king, "why do you linger?"

"Sire, I was considering your words; and what you say about the sun and wholesome resolutions has touched my heart and startled my conscience. My husband, you are right: God is there without, and I dare not venture to behold the sun, which is God's eye, before I have made my confession and received absolution. Sire, I am a great sinner, and my conscience gives me no rest. Will you be my confessor, and listen to me?"

The king sighed. "Ah," thought he, "she is hurrying to destruction, and by her own confession of guilt she will make it impossible for me to hold her guiltless!"

"Speak!" said he aloud.

"First," said she, with downcast eyes—"first, I must confess to you that I have to-day deceived you, my lord and king. Vanity and sinful pride enticed me to this; and childish anger made me consummate what vanity whispered to me. But I repent, my king; I repent from the bottom of my soul, and I swear to you, my husband— yes, I swear to you by all that is sacred to me, that it is the first and only time that I have deceived you. And never will I venture to do it again, for it is a dismal and awful feeling to stand before you with a guilty conscience."

"And in what have you deceived us, Kate?" asked the king; and his voice trembled.

Catharine drew from her dress a small roll of paper, and, humbly bowing, handed it to the king. "Take and see for yourself, my husband," said she.

With hurried hand the king opened the paper, and then looked in utter astonishment, now at its contents, and now at the blushing face of the queen.

"What!" said he, "you give me a pawn from the chess-board! What does that mean?"

"That means," said she, in a tone of utter contrition— "that means, that I stole it from you, and thereby cheated you out of your victory. Oh, pardon me, my husband! but I could no longer endure to lose always, and I was afraid you would no more allow me the pleasure of playing with you, when you perceived what a weak and contemptible antagonist I am. And behold, this little pawn was my enemy! It stood near my queen and threatened her with check, while it discovered check to my king from your bishop. You were just going to make this move, which was to ruin me, when Bishop Gardiner entered. You turned away your eyes and saluted him. You were not looking on the game. Oh, my lord and husband, the temptation was too alluring and seductive; and I yielded to it. Softly I took the pawn from the board, and slipped it into my pocket. When you looked again at the game, you seemed surprised at first; but your magnanimous and lofty spirit had no suspicion of my base act; so you innocently played on; and so I won the game of chess. Oh, my king, will you pardon me, and not be angry with me?"

The king broke out into a loud laugh, and looked with an expression of tenderness at Catharine, who stood before him with downcast eyes, abashed and blushing. This sight only redoubled his merriment, and made him again and again roar out with laughter.

"And is that all your crime, Kate?" asked he, at length, drying his eyes. "You have stolen a pawn from me—this is your first and only deception?"

"Is it not indeed great enough, sire? Did I not purloin it because I was so high-minded as to want to win a game of chess from you? Is not the whole court even now acquainted with my splendid luck? And does it not know that I have been the victor to-day, whilst yet I was not entitled to be so—whilst I deceived you so shamefully?"

"Now, verily," said the king, solemnly, "happy are the men who are not worse deceived by their wives than you have deceived me to-day; and happy are the women whose confessions are so pure and innocent as yours have been to-day! Do but lift up your eyes again, my Katie; that sin is forgiven you; and by God and by your king it shall be accounted to you as a virtue."

He laid his hand on her head, as if in blessing, and gazed at her long and silently. Then, said he, laughingly: "According to this, then, my Kate, I should have been the victor of to-day, and not have lost that game of chess."

"No," said she, dolefully, "I must have lost it, if I had not stolen the pawn."

Again the king laughed. Catharine said, earnestly: "Do but believe me, my husband, Bishop Gardiner alone is the cause of my fall. Because he was by, I did not want to lose. My pride revolted to think that this haughty and arrogant priest was to be witness of my defeat. In mind, I already saw the cold and contemptuous smile with which he would look down on me, the vanquished; and my heart rose in rebellion at the thought of being humbled before him. And now I have arrived at the second part of my fault which I want to confess to you to-day. Sire, I must acknowledge another great fault to you. I have grievously offended against you to-day, in that I contradicted you, and withstood your wise and pious words. Ah, my husband, it was not done to spite you, but only to vex and annoy the haughty priest. For I must confess to you, my king, I hate this Bishop of Winchester—ay, yet more—I have a dread of him; for my foreboding heart tells me that he is my enemy, that he is watching each of my looks, each of my words, so that he can make from them a noose to strangle me. He is the evil destiny that creeps up behind me and would one day certainly destroy me, if your beneficent hand and your almighty arm did not protect me. Oh, when I behold him, my husband, I would always gladly fly to your heart, and say to you: 'Protect me, my king, and have compassion on me! Have faith in me and love me; for if you do not, I am lost! The evil fiend is there to destroy me.'"

And, as she thus spoke, she clung affectionately to the king's side, and, leaning her head on his breast, looked up to him with a glance of tender entreaty and touching devotion.

The king bent down and kissed her brow. "Oh, *sancta simplicitas*," softly murmured he—"she knows not how nigh she is to the truth, and how much reason she has for her evil forebodings!" Then he asked aloud: "So, Kate, you believe that Gardiner hates you?"

"I do not believe it, I know it!" said she. "He wounds me whenever he can; and though his wounds are made only with pins, that comes only from this, that he is afraid that you might discover it if he drew a dagger on me, whilst you might not notice the pin with which he secretly wounds me. And what was his coming here to-day other than a new assault on me? He knows very well —and I have never made a secret of it—that I am an enemy to this Roman Catholic religion the pope of which has dared to hurl his ban against my lord and husband;

and that I seek with lively interest to be instructed as to the doctrine and religion of the so-called reformers."

"They say that you are a heretic," said the king, gravely.

"Gardiner says that! But if I am so, you are so too, my king; for your belief is mine. If I am so, so too is Cranmer, the noble Archbishop of Canterbury; for he is my spiritual adviser and helper. But Gardiner wishes that I were a heretic, and he wants me likewise to appear so to you. See, my husband, why it was that he laid those eight death-warrants before you awhile ago. There were eight, all heretics, whom you were to condemn—not a single papist among them; and yet I know that the prisons are full of papists, who, in the fanaticism of their persecuted faith, have spoken words just as worthy of punishment as those unfortunate ones whom you were to-day to send from life to death by a stroke of your pen. Sire, I should have prayed you just as fervently, just as suppliantly, had they been papists whom you were to sentence to death! But Gardiner wanted a proof of my heresy; and therefore he selected eight heretics, for whom I was to oppose your hard decree."

"It is true," said the king, thoughtfully; "there was not a single papist among them! But tell me, Kate—are you really a heretic, and an adversary of your king?"

With a sweet smile she looked deep into his eyes, and humbly crossed her arms over her beautiful breast. "Your adversary!" whispered she. "Are you not my husband and my lord? Was not the woman made to be subject to the man? The man was created after the likeness of God, and the woman after the likeness of man. So the woman is only the man's second self; and he must have compassion on her in love; and he must give her of his spirit, and influence her understanding from his understanding. Therefore your duty is to instruct me, my husband; and mine is, to learn of you. And of all the women in the world, to no one is this duty made so easy as to me; for God has been gracious to me and given me as my husband a king whose prudence, wisdom, and learning are the wonder of all the world." *

"What a sweet little flatterer you are, Kate!" said the king, with a smile; "and with what a charming voice you want to conceal the truth from us! The truth is, that you yourself are a very learned little body, who has no need at all to learn anything from others, but who would be well able to instruct others." †

"Oh, if it is so, as you say," cried Catharine, "well, then would I teach the whole world to love my king as I do, and to be subject to him in humility, faithfulness, and obedience, as I am."

And as she thus spoke, she threw both her arms about the king's neck, and leaned her head with a languishing expression upon his breast.

The king kissed her, and pressed her fast to his heart. He thought no longer of the danger that was hovering over Catharine's head; he thought only that he loved her, and that life would be very desolate, very tedious and sad without her.

"And now, my husband," said Catharine, gently disengaging herself from him—"now, since I have confessed to you and received absolution from you—now let us go down into the garden, so that God's bright sun may shine into our hearts fresh and glad. Come, my husband, your chair is ready; and the bees and the butterflies, the gnats and the flies, have already practised a hymn, with which they are going to greet you, my husband."

Laughing and jesting, she drew him along to the adjoining room, where the courtiers and the rolling-chair were standing ready; and the king mounted his triumphal car, and allowed himself to be rolled through the carpeted

---

* The queen's own words, as they have been given by all historical writers. See on this point Burnet, vol. i, p. 84; Tytler, p. 413; Larrey's "Histoire d'Angleterre," vol. ii, p. 201; Leti, vol. i, p. 154.

† Historical. The king's own words.

corridors, and down the staircases, transformed into broad inclined planes of marble, into the garden.

The air had the freshness of winter and the warmth of spring. The grass like a diligent weaver was already beginning to weave a carpet over the black level of the square; and already here and there a tiny blossom, curious and bashful, was peeping out and appeared to be smiling in astonishment at its own premature existence. The sun seemed so warm and bright; the heavens were so blue! At the king's side went Catharine, with such rosy cheeks and sparkling eyes. Those eyes were always directed to her husband; and her charming prattle was to the king like the melodious song of birds, and made his heart leap for pleasure and delight. But how? What noise all at once drowned Catharine's sweet prattle? And what was it that flashed up there at the end of that large alley which the royal pair with their suite had just entered?

It was the noise of soldiers advancing; and shining helmets and coats-of-mail flashed in the sunlight.

One band of soldiers held the outlet from the alley; another advanced up it in close order. At their head were seen striding along Gardiner and Earl Douglas, and at their side the lieutenant of the Tower.

The king's countenance assumed a lowering and angry expression and his cheeks were suffused with crimson. With the quickness of youth he rose from his chair, and, raised to his full height, he looked with flaming eyes at the procession.

The queen seized his hand and pressed it to her breast. "Ah," said she, with a low whisper, "protect me, my husband, for fear already overpowers me again! It is my enemy—it is Gardiner—that comes, and I tremble."

"You shall no longer tremble before him, Kate!" said the king. "Woe to them, that dare make King Henry's consort tremble! I will speak with Gardiner."

And almost roughly pushing aside the queen, the king,

utterly heedless in his violent excitement of the pain of his foot, went in a quick pace to meet the advancing troop.

He ordered them by his gesture to halt, and called Gardiner and Douglas to him. "What want you here? And what means this strange array?" asked he, in a rough tone.

The two courtiers stared at him with looks of amazement, and durst not answer him.

"Well!" asked the king, with ever-rising wrath, "will you at length tell me by what right you intrude into my garden with an armed host—specially at the same hour that I am here with my consort? Verily, there is no sufficient excuse for such a gross violation of the reverence which you owe your king and master; and I marvel, my lord master of ceremonies, that you did not seek to prevent this indecorum!"

Earl Douglas muttered a few words of apology, which the king did not understand, or did not want to understand.

"The duty of a master of ceremonies is to protect his king from every annoyance, and you, Earl Douglas, offer it to me yourself. Perchance you want thereby to show that you are weary of your office. Well, then, my lord, I dismiss you from it, and that your presence may not remind me of this morning's transaction, you will leave the court and London! Farewell, my lord!"

Earl Douglas, turning pale and trembling, staggered a few steps backward, and gazed at the king with astonishment. He wanted to speak, but Henry, with a commanding wave of the hand, bade him be silent.

"And now for you, my lord bishop!" said the king, and his eyes were turned on Gardiner with an expression so wrathful and contemptuous, that he turned pale and looked down to the ground. "What means this strange train with which the priest of God approaches his royal master to-day? And under what impulse of Christian love are you going to hold to-day a heretic hunt in the garden of your king?"

"Sire," said Gardiner, completely beside himself, "your majesty well knows why I come; it was at your majesty's command that I with Earl Douglas and the lieutenant of the Tower came, in order to——"

"Dare not to speak further!" yelled the king, who became still more angry because Gardiner would not understand him and comprehend the altered state of his mind. "How dare you make a pretence of my commands, whilst I, full of just amazement, question you as to the cause of your appearance? That is to say, you want to charge your king with falsehood. You want to excuse yourself by accusing me. Ah, my worthy lord bishop, this time you are thwarted in your plan, and I disavow you and your foolish attempt. No! there is nobody here whom you shall arrest; and, by the holy mother of God, were your eyes not blind, you would have seen that here, where the king is taking an airing with his consort, there could be no one whom these catchpolls had to look for! The presence of the royal majesty is like the presence of God; it dispenses happiness and peace about it; and whoever is touched by his glory, is graced and sanctified thereby."

"But, your majesty," screamed Gardiner, whom anger and disappointed hope had made forgetful of all considerations, "you wanted me to arrest the queen; you yourself gave me the order for it; and now when I come to execute your will—now you repudiate me."

The king uttered a yell of rage, and with lifted arm moved some steps toward Gardiner.

But suddenly he felt his arm held back. It was Catharine, who had hurried up to the king. "Oh, my husband," said she, in a low whisper, "whatever he may have done, spare him! Still he is a priest of the Lord; and so let his sacred robe protect him, though perchance his deeds condemn him!"

"Ah, do you plead for him?" cried the king. "Really, my poor wife, you suspect not how little ground you have to pity him, and to beg my mercy for him.* But you are right. We will respect his cassock, and think no more of what a haughty and intriguing man is wrapped in it.— But beware, priest, that you do not again remind me of that. My wrath would then inevitably strike you; and I should have as little mercy for you as you say I ought to show to other evil-doers. And inasmuch as you are a priest, be penetrated with a sense of the gravity of your office and the sacredness of your calling. Your episcopal see is at Winchester, and I think your duties call you thither. We no longer need you, for the noble Archbishop of Canterbury is coming back to us, and will have to fulfil the duties of his office near us and the queen. Farewell!"

He turned his back on Gardiner, and, supported on Catharine's arm, returned to his rolling-chair.

"Kate," said he, "just now a lowering cloud stood in your sky, but, thanks to your smile and your innocent face, it has passed harmlessly over. Methinks we still owe you special thanks for this; and we would like to show you that by some office of love. Is there nothing that would give you special delight, Kate?"

"Oh, yes," said she, with fervor. "Two great desires burn in my heart."

"Then name them, Kate; and, by the mother of God, if it is in the power of a king to fulfil them, I will do it."

Catharine seized his hand and pressed it to her heart. "Sire," said she, "they wanted to have you sign eight death-warrants to-day. Oh, my husband, make of these eight criminals eight happy, thankful subjects; teach them to love that king whom they have reviled—teach their children, their wives and mothers to pray for you, whilst you restore life and freedom to these fathers, these sons and husbands, and while you, great and merciful, like Deity, pardon them."

"So shall it be!" cried the king, cheerfully. "Our hand shall have to-day no other work than to rest in yours;

* The king's own words.—See Leti, vol. i, p. 132.

and we will spare it from making these eight strokes of the pen. The eight evil-doers are pardoned; and they shall be free this very day."

With an exclamation of rapturous delight Catharine pressed Henry's hand to her lips, and her face shone with pure happiness.

"And your second wish?" asked the king.

"My second wish," said she, with a smile, "pleads for the freedom of a poor prisoner—for the freedom of a human heart, sire."

The king laughed. "A human heart? Does that then run about on the street, so that it can be caught and made a prisoner of?"

"Sire, you have found it, and incarcerated it in your daughter's bosom. You want to put Elizabeth's heart in fetters, and by an unnatural law compel her to renounce her freedom of choice. Only think—to want to bid a woman's heart, before she can love, to inquire first about the genealogical tree, and to look at the coat-of-arms before she notices the man!"

"Oh, women, women, what foolish children you are, though!" cried the king, laughingly. "The question is about thrones, and you think about your hearts! But come, Kate, you shall still further explain that to me; and we will not take back our word, for we have given it you from a free and glad heart."

He took the queen's arm, and, supported on it, walked slowly up the alley with her. The lords and ladies of the court followed them in silence and at a respectful distance; and no one suspected that this woman, who was stepping along so proud and magnificent, had but just now escaped an imminent peril of her life; that this man, who was leaning on her arm with such devoted tenderness, had but a few hours before resolved on her destruction.*

* All this plot instigated by Gardiner against the queen is, in minutest details, historically true, and is found substantially the same in all historical works.

And whilst chatting confidentially together they both wandered through the avenues, two others with drooping head and pale face left the royal castle, which was to be to them henceforth a lost paradise. Sullen spite and raging hate were in their hearts, but yet they were obliged to endure in silence; they were obliged to smile and to seem harmless, in order not to prepare a welcome feast for the malice of the court. They felt the spiteful looks of all these courtiers, although they passed by them with downcast eyes. They imagined they heard their malicious whispers, their derisive laughter; and it pierced their hearts like the stab of a dagger.

At length they had surmounted it—at length the palace lay behind them, and they were at least free to pour out in words the agony that consumed them—free to be able to break out into bitter execrations, into curses and lamentations.

"Lost! all is lost!" said Earl Douglas to himself in a hollow voice. "I am thwarted in all my plans. I have sacrificed to the Church my life, my means, ay, even my daughter, and it has all been in vain. And, like a beggar, I now stand on the street forsaken and without comfort; and our holy mother the Church will no longer heed the son who loved her and sacrificed himself for her, since he was so unfortunate, and his sacrifice unavailing."

"Despair not!" said Gardiner, solemnly. "Clouds gather above us; but they are dispersed again. And after the day of storm, comes again the day of light. Our day also will come, my friend. Now, we go hence, our heads strewn with ashes, and bowed at heart; but, believe me, we shall one day come again with shining face and exultant heart; and the flaming sword of godly wrath will glitter in our hands, and a purple robe will enfold us, dyed in the blood of heretics whom we offer up to the Lord our God as a well-pleasing sacrifice. God spares us for a better time; and our banishment, believe me, friend, is but a refuge that God has prepared for us this evil time which we are approaching."

"You speak of an evil time, and nevertheless you hope, your highness?" asked Douglas, gloomily.

"And nevertheless I hope!" said Gardiner, with a strange and horrible smile, and, bending down closer to Douglas, he whispered: "the king has only a few days more to live. He does not suspect how near he is to his death, and nobody has the courage to tell him. But his physician has confided it to me. His vital forces are consumed, and death stands already before his door to throttle him."

"And when he is dead," said Earl Douglas, shrugging his shoulders, "his son Edward will be king, and those heretical Seymours will control the helm of state! Call you that hope, your highness?"

"I call it so."

"Do you not know that Edward, young as he is, is nevertheless a fanatical adherent of the heretical doctrine, and at the same time a furious opponent of the Church in which alone is salvation?"

"I know it, but I know also that Edward is a feeble boy; and there is current in our Church a holy prophecy which predicts that his reign is only of short duration. God only knows what his death will be, but the Church has often before seen her enemies die a sudden death. Death has been often before this the most effective ally of our holy mother the Church. Believe me, then, my son, and hope, for I tell you Edward's rule will be of short duration. And after him *she* will ascend the throne, the noble and devout Mary, the rigid Catholic, who hates heretics as much as Edward loves them. Oh, friend, when Mary ascends the throne, we shall rise from our humiliation, and the dominion will be ours. Then will all England become, as it were, a single great temple, and the fagot-piles about the stake are the altars on which we will consume the heretics, and their shrieks of agony are the holy psalms which we will make them strike up to the honor of God and His holy Church. Hope for this time, for I tell you it will soon come."

"If *you* say so, your highness, then it will come to pass," said Douglas, significantly. "I will then hope and wait. I will save myself from evil days in Scotland, and wait for the good."

"And I go, as this king by the wrath of God has commanded, to my episcopal seat. The wrath of God will soon call Henry hence. May his dying hour be full of torment, and may the Holy Father's curse be realized and fulfilled in him! Farewell! We go with palms of peace forced on us; but we will return with the flaming sword, and our hands will be dripping with heretic blood."

They once more shook hands and silently departed, and before evening came on they had both left London.*

* Gardiner's prophecy was soon fulfilled. A few days after Gardiner had fallen into disgrace Henry, the Eighth died, and his son Edward, yet a minor, ascended the throne. But his rule was of brief duration. After a reign of scarcely six years, he died a youth of the age of sixteen years, and his sister Mary, called the *Catholic*, ascended the throne. Her first act was to release Gardiner, who under Edward's reign had been confined as a prisoner in the Tower, and to appoint him her minister, and later, to the place of lord chancellor. He was one of the most furious persecutors of the Reformers. Once he said at a council in the presence of the bigoted queen: "These heretics have a soul so black that it can be washed clean only in their own blood." He it was, too, who urged the queen to such severe and odious measures against the Princess Elizabeth, and caused her to be a second time declared a bastard and unworthy of succeeding to the throne. When Mary died, Gardiner performed, in Westminster Abbey, where she was entombed, the service for the dead in the presence of her successor, Queen Elizabeth. Gardiner's discourse was an enthusiastic eulogium of the deceased queen, and he set forth, as her special merit, that she hated the heretics so ardently and had so many of them executed. He closed with an invective against the Protestants, in which he so little spared the young queen, and spoke of her in such injurious terms, that he was that very day committed to prison.—Leti. vol. i, p. 314.

A short time after this eventful walk in the garden of Whitehall, the queen entered the apartments of the Princess Elizabeth, who hastened to meet her with a burst of joy, and clasped her wildly in her arms.

"Saved!" whispered she. "The danger is overcome, and again you are the mighty queen, the adored wife!"

"And I have you to thank that I am so, princess! Without that warrant of arrest which you brought me, I was lost. Oh, Elizabeth, but what a martyrdom it was! To smile and jest, whilst my heart trembled with dread and horror; to appear innocent and unembarrassed, whilst it seemed to me as if I heard already the whiz of the axe that was about to strike my neck! Oh, my God, I passed through the agonies and the dread of a whole lifetime in that one hour! My soul has been harassed till it is wearied to death, and my strength is exhausted. I could weep, weep continually over this wretched, deceitful world, in which to wish right and to do good avail nothing; but in which you must dissemble and lie, deceive and disguise yourself, if you do not want to fall a victim to wickedness and mischief. But ah, Elizabeth, even my tears I dare shed only in secret, for a queen has no right to be melancholy. She must seem ever cheerful, ever happy and contented; and only God and the still, silent night know her sighs and her tears."

"And you may let me also see them, queen," said Elizabeth, heartily; "for you well know you may trust and rely on me."

Catharine kissed her fervently. "You have done me a great service to-day, and I have come," said she, "to thank you, not with sounding words only, but by deeds. Elizabeth, your wish will be fulfilled. The king will repeal the law which was to compel you to give your hand only to a husband of equal birth."

"Oh," cried Elizabeth, with flashing eyes, "then I shall, perhaps, some day be able to make him whom I love a king."

Catharine smiled. "You have a proud and ambitious heart," said she. "God has endowed you with extraordinary ability. Cultivate it and seek to increase it; for my prophetic heart tells me that you are destined to become, one day, Queen of England.* But who knows whether then you will still wish to elevate him whom you now love, to be your husband? A queen, as you will be, sees with other eyes than those of a young, inexperienced maiden. Perchance I may not have done right in moving the king to altar this law; for I am not acquainted with the man that you love; and who knows whether he is worthy that you should bestow on him your heart, so innocent and pure?"

Elizabeth threw both her arms about Catharine's neck, and clung tenderly to her. "Oh," said she, "he would be worthy to be loved even by you, Catharine; for he is the noblest and handsomest cavalier in the whole world; and though he is no king, yet he is a king's brother-in-law, and will some day be a king's uncle."

Catharine felt her heart, as it were, convulsed, and a slight tremor ran through her frame. "And am I not to learn his name?" asked she.

"Yes, I will tell you it now; for now there is no longer danger in knowing it. The name of him whom I love, queen, is Thomas Seymour."

Catharine uttered a scream, and pushed Elizabeth passionately away from her heart. "Thomas Seymour?" cried she, in a menacing tone. "What! do you dare love Thomas Seymour?"

"And why should I not dare?" asked the young girl in astonishment. "Why should I not give him my heart, since, thanks to your intercession, I am no longer bound to choose a husband of equal birth? Is not Thomas Seymour one of the first of this land? Does not all England look on him with pride and tenderness? Does not every woman to whom he deigns a look, feel herself honored? Does

* Catharine's own words.—See Leti, vol. i, p. 172.

not the king himself smile and feel more pleased at heart, when Thomas Seymour, that young, bold, and spirited hero, stands by his side?"

"You are right!" said Catharine, whose heart every one of these enthusiastic words lacerated like the stab of a dagger—"yes, you are right. He is worthy of being loved by you—and you could hit upon no better choice. It was only the first surprise that made me see things otherwise than they are. Thomas Seymour is the brother of a queen: why then should he not also be the husband of a royal princess?"

With a bashful blush, Elizabeth hid her smiling face in Catharine's bosom. She did not see with what an expression of alarm and agony the queen observed her; how her lips were convulsively compressed, and her cheeks covered with a death-like pallor.

"And he?" asked she, in a low tone. "Does Thomas Seymour love you?"

Elizabeth raised her head and looked at the questioner in amazement "How!" said she. "Is it possible, then, to love, if you are not loved?"

"You are right," sighed Catharine. "One must be very humble and silly to be able to do that."

"My God! how pale you are, queen!" cried Elizabeth, who just now noticed Catharine's pale face. "Your features are distorted; your lips tremble. My God! what does this mean?"

"It is nothing!" said Catharine, with a smile full of agony. "The excitement and alarm of to-day have exhausted my strength. That is all. Besides, a new grief threatens us, of which you as yet know nothing. The king is ill. A sudden dizziness seized him, and made him fall almost lifeless at my side. I came to bring you the king's message; now duty calls me to my husband's sickbed. Farewell, Elizabeth."

She waved a good-by to her with her hand, and with hurried step left the room. She summoned up courage to conceal the agonies of her soul, and to pass proud and stately through the halls. To the courtiers bowing before her, she would still be the queen, and no one should suspect what agony was torturing her within like flames of fire. But at last arrived at her boudoir—at last sure of being overheard and observed by no one—she was no longer the queen, but only the agonized, passionate woman.

She sank on her knees, and cried, with a heart-rending wail of anguish: "My God, my God, grant that I may become mad, so that I may no longer know that he has forsaken me!"

CHAPTER XXXVI.

THE CATASTROPHE.

AFTER days of secret torture and hidden tears, after nights of sobbing anguish and wailing sorrow, Catharine had at last attained to inward peace; she had at last taken a firm and decisive resolution.

The king was sick unto death; and however much she had suffered and endured from him, still he was her husband; and she would not stand by his deathbed as a perjured and deceitful woman; she would not be constrained to cast down her eyes before the failing gaze of the dying king. She would renounce her love—that love, which, however, had been as pure and chaste as a maiden's prayer —that love, which was as unapproachably distant as the blush of morn, and yet had stood above her so vast and brilliant, and had irradiated the gloomy pathway of her life with celestial light.

She would make the greatest of sacrifices; she would give her lover to another. Elizabeth loved him. Catharine would not investigate and thoroughly examine the point, whether Thomas Seymour returned her love, and whether the oath he had taken to her, the queen, was really nothing more than a fancy of the brain, or a falsehood. No, she did not believe it; she did not believe that Thomas Seymour was capable of treachery, of double-dealing. But Elizabeth loved him; and she was young and beautiful, and a great future lay before her. Catharine loved Thomas Seymour strongly enough not to want to deprive him of this future, but gladly to present herself a sacrifice to the happiness of her lover. What was she —the woman matured in grief and suffering—in comparison with this youthful and fresh blossom, Elizabeth? What had she to offer her beloved further than a life of retirement, of love, and of quiet happiness? When once the king is dead and sets her free, Edward the Sixth ascends the throne; and Catharine then is nothing more than the forgotten and disregarded widow of a king; while Elizabeth, the king's sister, may perhaps bring a crown as her dower to him whom she loves.

Thomas Seymour was ambitious. Catharine knew that. A day might come when he would repent of having chosen the widow of a king instead of the heiress to a throne.

Catharine would anticipate that day. She would of her own free-will resign her lover to Princess Elizabeth. She had by a struggle brought her mind to this sacrifice; she had pressed her hands firmly on her heart, so as not to hear how it wailed and wept.

She went to Elizabeth, and said to her with a sweet smile: "To-day I will bring your lover to you, princess. The king has fulfilled his promise. He has to-day with his last dying strength signed this act, which gives you liberty to choose your husband, not from the ranks of princes alone, but to follow your own heart in your choice. I will give this act to your lover, and assure him of my assistance and aid. The king is suffering very much to-day, and his consciousness fails more and more. But be certain, if he is in a condition to hear me, I will spend all my powers of persuasion in inclining him to your wish, and in moving him to give his consent to your marriage with Earl Sudley. I now go to receive the earl. So tarry in your room, princess, for Seymour will soon come to bring you the act."

Whilst she thus spoke, it seemed to her as though her heart were pierced by red-hot daggers; as though a two-edged sword were cleaving her breast. But Catharine had a strong and courageous soul. She had sworn to herself to endure this torture to the end; and she endured it. No writhing of her lips, no sigh, no outcry, betrayed the pain that she was suffering. And if, indeed, her cheeks were pale, and her eye dim, they were so because she had spent nights watching by her husband's sick-bed, and because she was mourning for the dying king.

She had the heroism to embrace tenderly this young maiden to whom she was just going to present her love as a sacrifice, and to listen with a smile to the enthusiastic words of gratitude, of rapture and expectant happiness which Elizabeth addressed to her.

With tearless eyes and firm step she returned to her own apartments; and her voice did not at all tremble, as she bade the chamberlain in attendance to summon to her the master of horse, Earl Sudley. Only she had a feeling as though her heart was broken and crushed; and quite softly, quite humbly, she whispered: " I shall die when he is gone. But so long as he is here, I will live; and he shall not have a suspicion of what I suffer! "

And while Catharine suffered so dreadfully, Elizabeth was jubilant with delight and rapture; for at last she stood at the goal of her wishes, and this very day she was to become the betrothed of her lover. Oh, how slow and sluggish crept those minutes along! How many eternities had she still to wait before he would come—he, her lover, and soon her husband! Was he already with the queen? Could she expect him already? She stood as if spellbound at the window, and looked down into the courtyard. Through that great gateway over there he must come; through that door yonder he must go, in order to reach the queen's apartments.

She uttered an exclamation, and a glowing blush flitted across her face. There, there, he was. Yonder drew up his equipage; his gold-laced lackeys opened the door and he alighted. How handsome he was, and how magnificent to look upon! How noble and proud his tall figure! How regularly beautiful his fresh, youthful face! How saucy the haughty smile about his mouth; and how his eyes flamed and flashed and shone in wantonness and youthful happiness. His look glanced for a moment at Elizabeth's window. He saluted her, and then entered the door leading to the wing of the palace of Whitehall occupied by the queen. Elizabeth's heart beat so violently that she felt almost suffocated. Now he must have reached the great staircase—now he was above it—now he was entering the queen's apartments—he traverses the first, the second, the third chamber. In the fourth Catharine was waiting for him.

Elizabeth would have given a year of her life to hear what Catharine would say to him, and what reply he would make to the surprising intelligence—a year of her life to be able to see his rapture, his astonishment, and his delight. He was so handsome when he smiled, so bewitching when his eyes blazed with love and pleasure.

Elizabeth was a young, impulsive child. She had a feeling as if she must suffocate in the agony of expectation; her heart leaped into her mouth; her breath was stifled in her breast, she was so impatient for happiness.

"Oh, if he does not come soon I shall die!" murmured she. "Oh, if I could only at least see him, or only hear him!" All at once she stopped; her eyes flashed up, and a bewitching smile flitted across her features. "Yes," said she, "I will see him, and I will hear him. I can do it, and I will do it. I have the key which the queen gave me, and which opens the door that separates my rooms from hers. With that key I may reach her bed-chamber, and next to the bed-chamber is her boudoir, in which, without doubt, she will receive the earl. I will enter quite softly, and, hiding myself behind the hanging which separates the bed-chamber from the boudoir, I shall be able to see him, and hear everything that he says!"

She laughed out loud and merrily, like a child, and sprang for the key, which lay on her writing-table. Like a trophy of victory she swung it high above her on her hand and cried, "I will see him!" Then light, joyful, and with beaming eye, she left the room.

She had conjectured rightly. Catharine received the earl in her boudoir. She sat on the divan standing opposite the door which led into the reception-room. That door was open, and so Catharine had a perfect view of the whole of that large space. She could see the earl as he traversed it. She could once more enjoy, with a rapture painfully sweet, his proud beauty, and let her looks rest on him with love and adoration. But at length he crossed the threshold of the boudoir; and now there was an end of her happiness, of her sweet dream, and of her hopes and her rapture. She was nothing more than the queen, the wife of a dying king; no longer Earl Seymour's beloved, no longer his future and his happiness.

She had courage to greet him with a smile; and her voice did not tremble when she bade him shut the door leading into the hall, and drop the hanging. He did so, gazing at her with looks of surprise. He did not comprehend that she dared give him an interview; for the king was still alive, and even with his tongue faltering in death he might destroy them both.

Why did she not wait till the morrow? On the morrow the king might be already dead; and then they could see each other without constraint and without danger. Then was she his, and naught could longer stand in the way between them and happiness. Now, when the king was near his death—now he loved her only—he loved but Catharine. His ambition had decided his heart. Death had become the judge over Seymour's double affection and divided heart, and with King Henry's death Elizabeth's star had also paled.

Catharine was the widow of a king; and without doubt this tender husband had appointed his young and adored wife Regent during the minority of the Prince of Wales. Catharine then would have still five years of unlimited sway, of royal authority and sovereign power. If Catharine were his wife, then would he, Thomas Seymour, share this power; and the purple robes of royalty, which rested on her shoulders, would cover him also; and he would help her bear that crown which doubtless might sometimes press heavily on her tender brow. He would, in reality, be the regent, and Catharine would be so only in name. She, the Queen of England, and he, king of this queen. What a proud, intoxicating thought was that! And what plans, what hopes might not be twined with it! Five years of sway—was not that a time long enough to undermine the throne of the royal boy and to sap his authority? Who could conjecture whether the people, once accustomed to the regency of the queen, might not prefer to remain under her sceptre, instead of committing themselves to this feeble youth? The people must be constrained so to think, and to make Catharine, Thomas Seymour's wife, their reigning queen.

The king was sick unto death, and Catharine was, without doubt, the regent—perchance some day the sovereign queen.

Princess Elizabeth was only a poor princess, entirely without a prospect of the throne; for before her came Catharine, came Edward, and finally Mary, Elizabeth's eldest sister. Elizabeth had not the least prospect of the throne, and Catharine the nearest and best founded.

Thomas Seymour pondered this as he traversed the apartments of the queen; and when he entered her presence, he had convinced himself that he loved the queen only, and that it was she alone whom he had always loved.

Elizabeth was forgotten and despised. She had no prospect of the throne—why, then, should he love her?

The queen, as we have said, ordered him to shut the door of the boudoir and to drop the hanging. At the same moment that he did this, the hanging of the opposite door, leading into the sleeping apartment, moved—perhaps only the draught of the closing door had done it. Neither the queen nor Seymour noticed it. They were both too much occupied with themselves. They saw not how the hanging again and again gently shook and trembled. They saw not how it was gently opened a little in the middle; nor did they see the sparkling eyes which suddenly peeped through the opening in the hanging; nor suspected they that it was the Princess Elizabeth who had stepped behind the curtain, the better to see and hear what was taking place in the boudoir.

The queen had arisen and advanced a few steps to meet the earl. As she now stood before him—as their eyes met, she felt her courage sink and her heart fail.

She was compelled to look down at the floor to prevent him from seeing the tears which involuntarily came into her eyes. With a silent salutation she offered him her hand. Thomas Seymour pressed it impulsively to his lips, and looked with passionate tenderness into her face. She struggled to collect all her strength, that her heart might not betray itself. With a hurried movement she withdrew her hand from him, and took from the table a roll of paper containing the new act of succession signed by the king.

"My lord," said she, "I have called you hither, because I would like to intrust a commission to you. I beg you to carry this parchment to the Princess Elizabeth, and be pleased to deliver it to her. But before you do that, I will make you acquainted with its contents. This parchment contains a new law relative to the succession, which has already received the sanction of the king. By virtue of this, the royal princesses are no longer under the necessity of uniting themselves with a husband who is a sovereign prince, if they wish to preserve their hereditary claim on the throne unimpaired. The king gives the princesses the right to follow their own hearts; and their claim to the succession is not to suffer thereby, if the husband chosen is neither a king nor a prince. That, my lord, is the contents of this parchment which you are to carry to the princess, and without doubt you will thank me for making you the messenger of these glad tidings."

"And why," asked he, in astonishment—"why does your majesty believe that this intelligence should fill me with special thankfulness?"

She collected all her powers; she prayed to her own heart for strength and self-control.

"Because the princess has made me the confidante of her love, and because I am consequently aware of the tender tie which binds you to her," said she, gently; and she felt that all the blood had fled from her cheeks.

The earl looked into her face in mute astonishment. Then his inquiring and searching glance swept all around the room.

"We are overheard, then?" asked he, in a low voice. "We are not alone?"

"We are alone," said Catharine, aloud. "Nobody can hear us, and God alone is witness of our conversation."

Elizabeth, who stood behind the hanging, felt her cheeks glow with shame, and she began to repent what she had done. But she was nevertheless, as it were, spellbound to that spot. It was certainly mean and unworthy of a princess to eavesdrop, but she was at that time but a young girl who loved, and who wanted to observe her lover. So she stayed; she laid her hand on her anxiously-throbbing heart, and murmured to herself: "What will he say? What means this anxious dread that comes over me?"

"Well," said Thomas Seymour, in an entirely altered

tone, " if we are alone, then this mask which hides my face
may fall; then the cuirass which binds my heart may be
loosened. Hail, Catharine, my star and my hope! No one,
you say, hears us, save God alone; and God knows our love,
and He knows with what longing, and what ecstasy, I have
sighed for this hour—for this hour, which at length again
unites me to you. My God, it is an eternity since I have
seen you, Catharine; and my heart thirsted for you as a
famishing man for a refreshing draught. Catharine, my
beloved, blessed be you, that you have at last called me to
you!"

He opened his arms for her, but she repulsed him
sharply. "You are mistaken in the name, earl," said she,
bitterly. "You say Catharine, and mean Elizabeth! It
is the princess that you love; to Elizabeth belongs your
heart, and she has devoted her heart to you. Oh, earl, I
will favor this love, and be certain I will not cease from
prayer and supplication till I have inclined the king to
your wishes, till he has given his consent to your marriage
with the Princess Elizabeth."

Thomas Seymour laughed. "This is a masquerade,
Catharine; and you still wear a mask over your beautiful
and charming face. Oh, away with that mask, queen! I
want to behold you as you are. I want to see again your
own beautiful self; I want to see the woman who belongs
to me, and who has sworn to be mine, and who has, with a
thousand sacred oaths, vowed to love me, to be true to me,
and to follow me as her husband and her lord. Or how,
Catharine! Can you have forgotten your oath? Can you
have become untrue to your own heart? Do you want to
cast me away, and throw me, like a ball of which you are
tired, to another?"

"Oh," said she, quite unconsciously, "I—I can never
forget and never be untrue."

"Well, then, my Catharine, the bride and wife of my
future, what then are you speaking to me of Elizabeth?—
of this little princess, who sighs for love as the flower-bud

for the sun, and takes the first man whom she finds in her way for the sun after which she pines? What care we for Elizabeth, my Catharine? And what have we to do with that child in this hour of long-wished-for reunion?"

"Oh, he calls me a child!" murmured Elizabeth. "I am nothing but a child to him!" And she pressed her hands on her mouth in order to repress her cry of anger and anguish, and to prevent them from hearing her teeth, which were chattering as though she were in a chill.

With irresistible force Thomas Seymour drew Catharine into his arms. "Avoid me no longer," said he, in tender entreaty. "The hour has come which is finally to determine our destiny! The king is at the point of death, and my Catharine will at length be free—free to follow her own heart. At this hour I remind you of your oath! Do you remember still that day when you referred me to this hour? Do you still know, Catharine, how you vowed to be my wife and to receive me as the lord of your future? Oh, my beloved, that crown which weighed down your head will soon be taken away. Now I yet stand before you as your subject, but in a few hours it will be your lord and your husband that stands before you; and he will ask: 'Catharine, my wife, have you kept with me the faith you swore to me? Have you been guiltless of perjury in respect of your vows and your love? Have you preserved my honor, which is your honor also, clear from every spot; and can you, free from guilt, look me in the eye?'"

He gazed at her with proud, flashing eyes, and before his commanding look her firmness and her pride melted away like ice before the sunshine. Again he was the master, whose right it was to rule her heart; and she again the lowly handmaid, whose sweetest happiness it was to submit and bow to the will of her lover.

"I can look you frankly in the eye," murmured she, "and no guilt burdens my conscience. I have loved naught but you, and my God only dwells near you in my heart."

Wholly overcome, wholly intoxicated with happiness, she leaned her head upon his shoulder, and as he clasped her in his arms, as he covered with kisses her now unresisting lips, she felt only that she loved him unutterably, and that there was no happiness for her except with him.

It was a sweet dream, a moment of most exquisite ecstasy. But it was only a moment. A hand was laid violently on her shoulder, a hoarse angry voice called her name; and as she looked up, she encountered the wild glance of Elizabeth, who stood before her with deathly pale cheeks, with trembling lips, with expanded nostrils, and eyes darting flashes of wrath and hatred.

"This, then, is the friendly service which you swore to me?" said she, gnashing her teeth. "Did you steal into my confidence, and with scoffing mouth spy out the secrets of my heart, in order to go away and betray them to your paramour? That you might in his arms ridicule this pitiable maiden, who allowed herself for the moment to be betrayed by her heart, and took a felon for an honorable man! Woe, woe to you, Catharine, for I tell you I will have no compassion on the adulteress, who mocks at me, and betrays my father!"

She was raving; completely beside herself with anger, she dashed away the hand which Catharine laid on her shoulder, and sprang back from the touch of her enemy like an irritated lioness.

Her father's blood fumed and raged within her, and, a true daughter of Henry the Eighth, she concealed in her heart only bloodthirsty and revengeful thoughts.

She cast on Thomas Seymour a look of dark wrath, and a contemptuous smile played about her lips. "My lord," said she, " you have called me a child who allows herself to be easily deceived, because she longs so much for the sun and for happiness. You are right: I was a child; and I was foolish enough to take a miserable liar for a nobleman, who was worthy of the proud fortune of being loved by a king's daughter. Yes, you are right; that was a childish dream. Thanks to you, I have now awoke from it; and you have matured the child into a woman, who laughs at the folly of her youth, and despises to-day what she adored yesterday. I have nothing to do with you; and you are even too insignificant and too contemptible for my anger. But I tell you, you have played a hazardous game, and you will lose. You courted a queen and a princess, and you will gain neither of them: not the one, for she despises you; not the other, for she ascends the scaffold!"

With a wild laugh she was hurrying to the door, but Catharine with a strong hand held her back and compelled her to remain. "What are you going to do?" asked she, with perfect calmness and composure.

"What am I going to do?" asked Elizabeth, her eyes flashing like those of a lioness. "You ask me what I will do? I will go to my father, and tell him what I have here witnessed! He will listen to me; and his tongue will still have strength enough to pronounce your sentence of death! Oh, my mother died on the scaffold, and yet she was innocent. We will see, forsooth, whether you will escape the scaffold—you, who are guilty!"

"Well, then, go to your father," said Catharine; "go and accuse me. But first you shall hear me. This man whom I loved, I wanted to renounce, in order to give him to you. By the confession of your love, you had crushed my happiness and my future. But I was not angry with you. I understood you heart, for Thomas Seymour is worthy of being loved. But you are right; for the king's wife it was a sinful love, however innocent and pure I may have been. On that account I wanted to renounce it; on that account I wanted, on the first confession from you, to silently sacrifice myself. You yourself have now made it an impossibility. Go, then, and accuse us to your father, and fear not that I will belie my heart. Now, that the crisis has come, it shall find me prepared; and on the scaffold I will still account myself blest, for Thomas Seymour loves me!"

"Ay, he loves you, Catharine!" cried he, completely overcome and enchanted by her noble, majestic bearing. "He loves you so warmly and ardently, that death with you seems to him an enviable lot; and he would not exchange it for any throne nor for any crown."

And as he thus spoke, he put his arms around Catharine's neck, and impetuously drew her to his heart.

Elizabeth uttered a fierce scream, and sprang to the door. But what noise was that which all at once drew nigh; which suddenly, like a wild billow, came roaring on, and filled the anterooms and the halls? What were these affrighted, shrieking voices calling? What were they screaming to the queen, and the physicians, and the priest?

Elizabeth stopped amazed, and listened. Thomas Seymour and Catharine, arm linked in arm, stood near her. They scarcely heard what was taking place; they looked at each other and smiled, and dreamed of love and death and an eternity of happiness.

Now the door flew open; there was seen John Heywood's pale face; there were the maids of honor and the court officials. And all shrieked and all wailed: "The king is dying! He is struck with apoplexy! The king is at the point of death!"

"The king calls you! The king desires to die in the arms of his wife!" said John Heywood, and, as he quietly pushed Elizabeth aside and away from the door as she was pressing violently forward, he added: "The king will see nobody but his wife and the priest; and he has authorized me to call the queen!"

He opened the door; and through the lines of weeping and wailing court officials and servants, Catharine moved on, to go to the death-bed of her royal husband.

CHAPTER XXXVII.

"LE ROI EST MORT—VIVE LA REINE!"

KING HENRY lay a-dying. That life full of sin, full of blood and crime, full of treachery and cunning, full of hypocrisy and sanctimonious cruelty—that life was at last lived out. That hand, which had signed so many death-warrants, was now clutched in the throes of death. It had stiffened at the very moment when the king was going to sign the Duke of Norfolk's death-warrant.* And the king was dying with the gnawing consciousness that he had no longer the power to throttle that enemy whom he hated. The mighty king was now nothing more than a feeble, dying old man, who was no longer able to hold the pen and sign this death-warrant for which he had so long hankered and hoped. Now it lay before him, and he no longer had the power to use it. God, in His wisdom and His justice, had decreed against him the most grievous and horrible of punishments; He had left him his consciousness; He had not crippled him in mind, but in body only. And that motionless and rigid mass which, growing chill in death, lay there on the couch of purple trimmed with gold—that was the king—a king whom agony of conscience did not permit to die, and who now shuddered and was horrified in view of death, to which he had, with relentless cruelty, hunted so many of his subjects.

Catharine and the Archbishop of Canterbury, the noble Cranmer, stood at his bedside: and whilst in convulsive agony he grasped Catharine's hands, he listened to the devout prayers which Cranmer was saying over him.

Once he asked with mumbling tongue: "My lord, what kind of a world then is that where those who condemn others to die, are condemned to die themselves?" † And as the pious Cranmer, touched by the agonies and tortures of conscience which he read in the king's looks, and

* Historical.   † The king's own words.—Leti, vol. i, p. 16.

full of pity for the dying tyrant, sought to comfort him, and spoke to him of the mercy of God which has compassion on every sinner, the king groaned out: "No, no! No mercy for him who knew no mercy!"

At length this awful struggle of death with life was ended; and death had vanquished life. The king had closed his eyes to earth, to open them again there above, as a guilt-laden sinner in the presence of God.

For three days his death was kept a secret. They wanted first to have everything arranged, and to fill up the void which his death must make. They wanted, when they spoke to the people of the dead king, to show them also at the same time the living king. And since they knew that the people would not weep for the dead, they were to rejoice for the living; since they would sing no funeral psalms, they were to let their hymns of joy resound.

On the third day the gates of Whitehall were thrown open, and a gloomy funeral train moved through the streets of London. In dead silence the populace saw borne past them the coffin of the king, before whom they had trembled so much, and for whom they now had not a word of mourning or of pity—no tears for the dead who for seven-and-thirty years had been their king.

They were bearing the coffin to Westminster Abbey to the splendid monument which Wolsey had built there for his royal master. But the way was long, and the panting horses with black housings, which drew the hearse, had often to stop and rest. And all of a sudden, as the carriage stood still on one of the large open squares, blood was seen to issue from the king's coffin. It streamed down in crimson currents and flowed over the stones of the streets. The people with a shudder stood around and saw the king's blood flowing, and thought how much blood he had spilt on that same spot, for the coffin was standing on the square where the executions were wont to take place, and where the scaffolds were erected and the stakes set.

As the people stood gazing at the blood which flowed from the king's coffin, two dogs sprang forth from the crowd and, with greedy tongue, licked the blood of King Henry the Eighth. But the people, shuddering and horror-stricken, fled in all directions, and talked among themselves of the poor priest who a few weeks before was executed here on this very spot, because he would not recognize the king as the supreme lord of the Church and God's vicegerent; of that unfortunate man who cursed the king, and on the scaffold said: "May the dogs one day drink the blood of this king who has shed so much innocent blood!" And now the curse of the dying man had found its fulfilment, and the dogs had drunk the king's blood.*

When the gloomy funeral train had left the palace of Whitehall, when the king's corpse no longer infected the halls with its awful stench of corruption, and the court was preparing to do homage to the boy Edward as the new king, Thomas Seymour, Earl of Sudley, entered the room of the young royal widow. He came in a magnificent mourning suit, and his elder brother, Edward Seymour, and Cranmer, archbishop of Canterbury, walked by his side.

With a blush and a sweet smile, Catharine bade them welcome.

"Queen," said Thomas Seymour with solemn air, "I come to-day to claim of you the fulfilment of your vow! Oh, do not cast down your eyes, nor blush for shame. The noble archbishop knows your heart, and he knows that it is as pure as the heart of a maiden, and that an unchaste thought has never sullied your pure soul. And my brother would not be here, had he not faith in and respect for a love which has preserved itself so faithful and constant amidst storms and dangers. I have selected these two noble friends as my suitors, and in their presence I will ask you: 'Queen Catharine, the king is dead, and no

* Historical.—See Tytler, p. 481.

fetters longer bind your heart; will you not give it me as my own? Will you accept me as your husband, and sacrifice for me your royal title and your exalted position?'"

With a bewitching smile she gave him her hand. "You well know," whispered she, "that I sacrifice nothing for you, but receive from you all of happiness and love that I hope for."

"Will you then, in the presence of these two friends, accept me as your future husband, and plight me your vow of truth and love?"

Catharine trembled and cast down her eyes with the bashfulness of a young girl. "Alas!" whispered she, "do you not then see my mourning dress? Is it becoming to think of happiness, while the funeral lamentations have scarcely died away?"

"Queen Catharine," said Archbishop Cranmer, "let the dead bury their dead! Life also has its rights; and man should not give up his claim on happiness, for it is a most holy possession. You have endured much and suffered much, queen, but your heart is pure and without guilt; therefore you may now, with a clear conscience, bid welcome to happiness also. Do not delay about it. In God's name I have come to bless your love, and give to your happiness a holy consecration."

"And I," said Edward Seymour, "I have begged of my brother the honor of being allowed to accompany him in order to say to your majesty that I know how to duly appreciate the high honor which you show our family, and that, as your brother-in-law, I shall ever be mindful that you were once my queen and I your subject."

"But I," cried Thomas Seymour, "I would not delay coming to you, in order that I might show you that love only brings me to you, and that no other consideration could induce me. The king's will is not yet opened, and I know not its contents. But however it may determine with respect to all of us, it cannot diminish or increase my happiness in possessing you. Whatever you may be, you will ever be to me only the adored woman, the ardently loved wife; and only to assure you of this, I have come this very day."

Catharine extended her hand to him with a bewitching smile. "I have never doubted of you, Seymour," whispered she, "and never did I love you more ardently than when I wanted to renounce you."

She bowed her head on her lover's shoulder, and tears of purest joy bedewed her cheeks. The Archbishop of Canterbury joined their hands, and blessed them as betrothed lovers; and the elder Seymour, Earl Hertford, bowed and greeted them as a betrothed couple.

On that very same day the king's will was opened. In the large gilded hall, in which King Henry's merry laughter and thundering voice of wrath had so often resounded, were now read his last commands. The whole court was assembled, as it was wont to be for a joyous festival; and Catharine once more sat on the royal throne. But the dreaded tyrant, the bloodthirsty King Henry the Eighth, was no longer at her side; but the poor pale boy, Edward, who had inherited from his father neither energy nor genius, but only his thirst for blood and his canting hypocrisy. At his side stood his sisters, the Princesses Mary and Elizabeth. Both were pale and of a sad countenance; but with both, it was not for their father that they were grieving.

Mary, the bigoted Roman Catholic, saw with horror and bitter anguish the days of adversity which were about to befall her church; for Edward was a fanatical opponent of the Roman Catholic religion, and she knew that he would shed the blood of the papists with relentless cruelty. On this account it was that she mourned.

But Elizabeth, that young girl of ardent heart—she thought neither of her father nor of the dangers threatening the Church; she thought only of her love, she felt only that she had been deprived of a hope, of an illusion—that she had awoke from a sweet and enchanting dream to the rude and barren reality. She had given up her first love, but her heart bled and the wound still smarted.

The will was read. Elizabeth looked toward Thomas Seymour during this solemn and portentous reading. She wanted to read in his countenance the impression made on him by these grave words, so pregnant with the future; she wanted to search the depths of his soul, and to penetrate the secret thoughts of his heart. She saw how he turned pale when, not Queen Catharine, but his brother, Earl Hertford, was appointed regent during Edward's minority; she saw the sinister, almost angry look which he threw at the queen; and with a cruel smile she murmured: "I am revenged! He loves her no longer!"

John Heywood, who was standing behind the queen's throne, had also observed the look of Thomas Seymour, yet not like Elizabeth, with a rejoicing, but with a sorrowful heart, and he dropped his head upon his breast and murmured: "Poor Catharine! He will hate her, and she will be very unhappy."

But she was still happy. Her eye beamed with pure delight when she perceived that her lover was, by the king's will, appointed High Admiral of England and guardian of the young king. She thought not of herself, but only of him, of her lover; and it filled her with the proudest satisfaction to see him invested with places of such high honor and dignity.

Poor Catharine! Her eye did not see the sullen cloud which still rested on the brow of her beloved. She was so happy and so innocent, and so little ambitious! For her this only was happiness, to be her lover's, to be the wife of Thomas Seymour.

And this happiness was to be hers. Thirty days after the death of King Henry the Eighth she became the wife of the high admiral, Thomas Seymour, Earl of Sudley. Archbishop Cranmer solemnized their union in the chapel at Whitehall, and the lord protector, now Duke of Somerset, formerly Earl of Hertford, the brother of Thomas Seymour, was the witness of this marriage, which was, however, still kept a secret, and of which there were to be no other witnesses. When, however, they resorted to the chapel for the marriage, Princess Elizabeth came forward to meet the queen, and offered her hand.

It was the first time they had met since the dreadful day on which they confronted each other as enemies—the first time that they had again seen each other eye to eye.

Elizabeth had wrung this sacrifice from her heart. Her proud soul revolted at the thought that Thomas Seymour might imagine that she was still grieving for him, that she still loved him. She would show him that her heart was entirely recovered from that first dream of her youth—that she had not the least regret or pain.

She accosted him with a haughty, cold smile, and presented Catharine her hand. "Queen," said she, "you have so long been a kind and faithful mother to me, that I may well once more claim the right of being your daughter. Let me, therefore, as your daughter, be present at the solemn transaction in which you are about to engage; and allow me to stand at your side and pray for you, whilst the archbishop performs the sacred service, and transforms the queen into the Countess of Sudley. May God bless you, Catharine, and give you all the happiness that you deserve!"

And Princess Elizabeth knelt at Catharine's side, as the archbishop blest this new marriage tie. And while she prayed her eye again glided over toward Thomas Seymour, who was standing there by his young wife. Catharine's countenance beamed with beauty and happiness, but upon Thomas Seymour's brow still lay the cloud that had settled there on that day when the king's will was opened—that will which did *not* make Queen Catharine regent, and which thereby destroyed Thomas Seymour's proud and ambitious schemes.

And that cloud remained on Thomas Seymour's brow.

It sank down lower and still lower. It soon overshadowed the happiness of Catharine's love, and awakened her from her short dream of bliss.

What she suffered, how much of secret agony and silent woe she endured, who can wish to know or conjecture? Catharine had a proud and a chaste soul. She concealed from the world her pain and her grief, as bashfully as she had once done her love. Nobody suspected what she suffered and how she struggled with her crushed heart.

She never complained; she saw bloom after bloom fall from her life; she saw the smile disappear from her husband's countenance; she heard his voice, at first so tender, gradually harden to harsher tones; she felt his heart growing colder and colder, and his love changing into indifference, perhaps even into hate.

She had devoted her whole heart to love, but she felt day by day, and hour by hour, that her husband's heart was cooling more and more. She felt, with dreadful heartrending certainty, she was his with all her love. But he was no longer hers.

And she tormented her heart to find out why he no longer loved her—what she had been guilty of, that he turned away from her. Seymour had not the delicacy and magnanimity to conceal from her his inward thoughts; and at last she comprehended why he neglected her.

He had hoped that Catharine would be Regent of England, that he then would be consort of *the regent.* Because it had not hapened so, his love had died.

Catharine felt this, and she died of it. But not suddenly, not at once, did death release her from her sorrows and racking tortures. Six months she had to suffer and struggle with them. After six months she died.

Strange rumors were spread at her death; and John Heywood never passed by Earl Seymour without gazing at him with an angry look, and saying: "You have murdered the beautiful queen! Deny it, if you can!"

Thomas Seymour laughed, and did not consider it

worth his while to defend himself against the accusations of the fool. He laughed, notwithstanding he had not yet put off the mourning he wore for Catharine.

In these mourning garments he ventured to approach the Princess Elizabeth, to swear to her his ardent love, and sue for her hand. But Elizabeth repelled him with coldness and haughty contempt; and, like the fool, the princess also said: "You have murdered Catharine! I cannot be the wife of a murderer!"

And God's justice punished the murderer of the innocent and noble Catharine; and scarcely three months after the death of his wife, the high admiral had to ascend the scaffold, and was executed as a traitor.

By Catharine's wish, her books and papers were given to her true friend John Heywood, and he undertook with the greatest care an examination of the same. He found among her papers many leaves written by herself, many verses and poems, which breathed forth the sorrowfulness of her spirit. Catharine herself had collected them into a book, and with her own hand she had given to the book this title: "*Lamentations of a Sinner.*"

Catharine had wept much as she penned these "Lamentations"; for in many places the manuscript was illegible, and her tears had obliterated the characters.

John Heywood kissed the spots where the traces of her tears remained, and whispered: "The sinner has by her suffering been glorified into a saint; and these poems are the cross and the monument which she has prepared for her own grave. I will set up this cross, that the good may take comfort, and the wicked flee from it." And he did so. He had the "Lamentations of a Sinner" printed; and this book was the fairest monument of Catharine.

THE END.

www.ingramcontent.com/pod-product-compliance
Lightning Source LLC
Chambersburg PA
CBHW032141010526
44111CB00035B/717